AN INTRODUCTION TO

METAPHYSICS

AN INTRODUCTION TO

METAPHYSICS

JACK S. CRUMLEY II

broadview press

BROADVIEW PRESS — www.broadviewpress.com
Peterborough, Ontario, Canada

Founded in 1985, Broadview Press remains a wholly independent publishing house. Broadview's focus is on academic publishing; our titles are accessible to university and college students as well as scholars and general readers. With over 800 titles in print, Broadview has become a leading international publisher in the humanities, with world-wide distribution. Broadview is committed to environmentally responsible publishing and fair business practices.

Library and Archives Canada Cataloguing in Publication

Title: An introduction to metaphysics / Jack S. Crumley II.
Names: Crumley, Jack S., II, author.
Description: Includes bibliographical references and index.
Identifiers: Canadiana (print) 20210345896 | Canadiana (ebook) 20210345969 | ISBN 9781554813759
    (softcover) | ISBN 9781770488236 (PDF) | ISBN 9781460407721 (EPUB)
Subjects: LCSH: Metaphysics.
Classification: LCC BD111 .C78 2022 | DDC 110—dc23

Broadview Press handles its own distribution in North America:
PO Box 1243, Peterborough, Ontario K9J 7H5, Canada
555 Riverwalk Parkway, Tonawanda, NY 14150, USA
Tel: (705) 743-8990; Fax: (705) 743-8353
email: customerservice@broadviewpress.com

For all territories outside of North America, distribution is handled by Eurospan Group.

Broadview Press acknowledges the financial support of the Government of Canada for our publishing activities.

Canada

Edited by Robert M. Martin
Book design by Michel Vrana
Illustrations by Gillian Wilson

PRINTED IN CANADA

For Vlada
for a world never imagined

CONTENTS

PREFACE

METAPHYSICS IS A FASCINATING AND CHALLENGING DISCIPLINE. No doubt a good part of the wonder that begins philosophy is to be found in metaphysics. Sooner or later our endeavors seem to run into or brush up against metaphysics. Writing this book, dedicated solely to several of the perennial and central issues in metaphysics, has been similarly both fascinating and challenging. I have been guided by a double aim and a hope. The double aim is that readers of different levels, of different levels of familiarity with philosophy, will be able to follow the pace and development of the text, and that they will come away with a deeper understanding of the motives and arguments that constitute these several perennial central topics in metaphysics. The hope of course is that readers will experience some of the wonder and fascination that animate metaphysical inquiry. That hope is reflected in the chapters (I hope)—that initial accessible material prepares the reader for the more challenging and rigorous arguments and nuanced positions.

Of course the book is principally targeted to upper-division undergraduates. I think others—beginning students in philosophy or interested readers or beginning graduate students—will also gain from reading the book, whether that gain is preparing for further study in philosophy or satisfying some curiosity about metaphysics.

This is a topical introduction to metaphysics that also takes seriously both the history of philosophy and contemporary developments. Metaphysics extends over a much broader range of topics than those covered here. Again, a double aim guides the selection of the topics. The first is the selection of topics, as suggested, that have been both central and perennial in philosophy in general and metaphysics in particular. The second is to also find topics that will engage the reader's interest and aid in thinking more rigorously about metaphysical topics that come up in many areas but do not always receive the thoughtfulness they deserve. Both those aims are reflected in my desire that the book preserve rigor and accessibility, knowing that at times those will pull in different directions.

In almost all the chapters, I want to give the reader a balanced sense of where the issues and arguments came from and where things stand now. And it is my desire that it is not simply a passing nod in either direction, that some genuine development is given to both the history of and the current developments in philosophy. The chapter "Things," for example, develops several historical views, beginning with a detailed account of Aristotle's substance view, and works into more contemporary issues, such as the "special composition question."

The chapters are relatively self-contained, thus allowing readers (and instructors) freedom of choice in the order in which they are approached. Within chapters it is also possible to "pick and choose" which sections to read. There are cross-references from one chapter to another, but where it is important to the present discussion, a "reminder" is included.

A word about the text boxes. It is my intention that they serve different functions. Some are intended as *lagniappe*, a little something extra to round out the text or simply to put it into a broader frame; e.g., the boxes on Heloise and Abelard or the topic of free will appearing in literature. Others are intended to provide philosophical background or elaboration to the text development without interrupting the flow of that development, such as the box on Quine and ontological relativity. Still others are intended to at least introduce a related philosophical issue, which could not be developed further, with the box on fictional objects perhaps being a good example.

First, I wish to thank Broadview for giving me this opportunity. More specifically, I especially want to thank Stephen Latta, my editor, and Don LePan, CEO, for encouraging me to take up this opportunity and, more importantly, for their long-suffering patience while I completed this task. I would have never attempted this project without their support. Second, I hope that four professors from my days in New Orleans—my teachers and colleagues—do not mind my "tying" them to this book. Radu Bogdan, Ronna Burger, Graeme Forbes, and the late Norton Nelkin—I am grateful for their having shown me areas in philosophy that I otherwise would have never appreciated, especially metaphysics, and most certainly grateful for their giving me the tools to set out on such a project. I know I have not measured up to the standards they set, but I am nonetheless grateful for their having shown me how it should be done. And I want to thank my students. Actually I want to thank them for the looks they give me during class, or just the way they contort their faces when they hear something that they don't understand or is so dazzling new to them that they need more information to be able to synthesize what they've heard. These charmingly shy signals so often alerted me that I needed to think again about the best way to present the material, so that they too could both learn metaphysics and be fascinated by it.

Five people read all or several chapters of the text, and I owe them a very real debt of gratitude. I am grateful to the anonymous reader who read several chapters and provided support, advice, and suggestions that led to my reorganizing parts of chapters and my attempting to further clarify parts of the material. Those comments came at a very important point in the writing of the text. In addition, Laura Buzzard of Broadview read several chapters and made many helpful suggestions. I am also grateful to Paige Pinto, formerly of Broadview, who read and offered thoughtful suggestions on several of the more recently written chapters. My editor Stephen Latta was willing to take the time to look closely at the text of several chapters. His suggestions, about both content and presentation, significantly improved the text.

I came to appreciate Bob Martin's dedication, expertise, and generosity with his copy editing of the previous two texts. But I can't thank him enough for his help on this text, especially on some of the more challenging topics. To have someone with his expertise in so many areas of philosophy, his dedication and his patience—which I'm sure I tested...—is a genuine gift to an author. I am very indebted to him and extremely grateful.

The few words of the dedication page are best left to describe the love and support of an incredible woman these past years.

My little Andie. The little guy was with me through the writing of the entire text. Looking over my shoulder to see him sleeping, to feel him underneath the table, to see the love in his little face when he would stretch and put his paws on my lap always reminded me what was really important. I still look for him. Dogs love. I am so specially gifted, little one, that for six and a half wonderful years I was able to witness your joy and love. Thank you, Andie ... I miss you so, little one.

INTRODUCTION

Metaphysics

Plato and Aristotle observed that philosophy begins in wonder. The lore of Western philosophy has it that Thales—its first philosopher—fell into a well while he was walking and "wondering."

A CENTRAL PART OF PHILOSOPHY IS CALLED METAPHYSICS. WHAT ARE we wondering about in metaphysics? No help in answering this question is given by a bit of philosophical lore explaining the origin of this word. One of Aristotle's treatises was (later) titled *Metaphysics* because in one of the first libraries of Aristotle's work, this particular treatise came *after*—in Greek "meta"—a treatise entitled *Physics* (which should not be confused with the physics texts of today).

But Aristotle does go some way in explaining what he is about: he observes he is engaged in the study of being *qua* being. "Qua" is a Latin word, which means "in its character as" or, a bit roughly, "as this kind of thing." Looking at students *qua* students thus is considering them *just as* students, leaving aside issues of their biological makeup or family backgrounds or the movies they like. And to say that we want to study *being qua being* is to say that we want to look at all the things there are just insofar as they *are*. An important subdiscipline of metaphysics is ontology. **Ontology** may be understood as the study of the *kinds* of being(s) that exist—the most basic kinds, that is, not shoes, dogs, ice-cream cones, library books.... And all that *exists* falls into one or another category.

This "all-encompassing" character perhaps leads to a second character-ization of metaphysics as a more general study than our other specific disci-plines, e.g., art, religion, science. Metaphysics attempts to describe and explain the general features of everything. But what are these "general" features? It's sometimes thought that physics tries to reveal the general characteristics of everything, but metaphysics tries to go beyond this. (So the original derivation of the word was perhaps informative after all.)

Metaphysics looks at all the particular disciplines—as well as others—and notices still further general questions. Questions about free will and whether human beings have it, about the conditions under which an object remains the same object (or the same person!), or about whether there are more kinds of things than those that science studies (is everything physical, or are there some nonphysical things?)—all of these are metaphysical questions. **Metaphysics**, then, in its most general form, asks about what kinds of things there are in the world, about their nature, and about the structure or relationship among these things.

What is it to inquire into the *nature* of something? The Greek word *physis* or *phusis* is translated as *nature*. This can be understood as a reference to the natural world. But it can also be understood to refer to the *essence* of something. "Essence" refers to those characteristics or features intrinsic to some "thing" that make it that particular thing or that *kind* of thing. Metaphysics is thus concerned with the essential nature of some thing or property. The first and second chapters, for example, ask about the nature or the essence or nature of *truth*.

There's some overlap between metaphysics and other disciplines. Indeed various natural and social sciences may be seen as inquiring into the nature of something or some feature of our experience, or even—us. It is not always easy to draw the line between science and philosophy, or religion and phi-losophy, or art and philosophy, or logic and philosophy. The psychologist or neuroscientist who claims we have no free will, or the scientist who claims that there is nothing beyond the natural world, or the theologian who insists on the existence of a nonphysical soul, or the poet who claims there is something more to love than chemical or psychological states, has most likely begun raising metaphysical questions. Indeed, in some of the chapters that follow, we will advert to and draw on various scientific theories.

Raising metaphysical or ontological questions is of course to raise philosophical questions. And this perhaps invites the question of how to characterize philosophy.

Unsurprisingly, the English language inherits the term "philosophy" from ancient Greek, *philosophia*. It was Aristotle's teacher Plato who shaped the meaning of the term. Before Plato's writings, a group of people we now call *Sophists* were often known as philosophers. Traveling teachers in Greece, they offered to teach rhetoric—the art of speaking and convincing—to those willing to pay the tuition. Although Greek writing had been around for a few hundred years at the time, it was still very much an oral culture. Speaking ability and the ability to persuade were honored and celebrated. And in the course of teaching the ability to speak persuasively, some of the sophists took positions on the nature of knowledge and reality, and on how to behave or act: what we now call ethics or morals.

We see in Plato's writings, however, a different notion of philosophy. In one of his works—*Republic*—he characterizes the philosopher as someone who loves the truth and the whole of truth. In another—*Symposium*, still one of the most famous works on the *nature* of love—Plato represents the philosopher as the lover of beauty. Not the lover of beautiful bodies or beautiful minds, though the love of beauty and truth, as well as of "good," finds its expression in the love of wisdom. The literal rendering of the Greek word *philosophia* is "love of wisdom." Everyone by nature may desire to know, but the philosopher loves knowing, loves wisdom, and not just some of it, but all of it.

Philosophy includes many areas or disciplines in addition to metaphysics. Other main areas are epistemology, ethics, and logic. And there are many others, including political philosophy, philosophy of mind, philosophy of language, philosophy of science, of mathematics, of religion, of art, of history, of technology. Indeed, name an area of human endeavor or inquiry, and there is likely to be a series of *philosophical* questions worth asking: What's the difference between science and pseudo-science? Is faith rational? What makes something a work of art? Rightly or wrongly, philosophers think there are *basic* or *foundational* issues or questions that go beyond the boundaries of science or art or religion or linguistics, and that these questions are the province of philosophy. Mathematicians may tell us that there are two different ways to represent numbers in set theory. But to ask whether numbers are just handy tools made up by people, or whether they exist "on their own," or why the physical world seems to have mathematical properties—well, those are philosophical questions.

Common Sense and Metaphysics

Contemporary philosophers, when discussing metaphysics, sometimes advert to the "commonsense view" (to criticize or defend it). This might seem a little surprising. After all, metaphysics is a difficult and (apparently) abstruse discipline. How could common sense have a metaphysical view? However, there are aspects or features of the world that are implicit or taken for granted in many of our practical interactions with the world around us and in our discussions or talk about the world.

One of the more obvious is that the world comprises many distinct objects or individuals. They range in size from the very small—"atomically" small—to the very large, such as planets and stars. How many objects are there? Common sense takes a broad view of what is a distinct object or individual. Dinosaurs, mountains, trees, medium size-cities, electrons, self-help books, and stars are all objects. We can get some idea of how many there are of each of these—the "how many?" question makes sense. So we have a rough-and-ready idea about what makes something a particular thing rather than a collection or a part of something. But there's a lot more to say about this general kind of judgment.

Setting aside "how many?" commonsense metaphysics holds that objects have properties and are distinct from or separate from other individuals. Again, the commonsense view takes a broad view of properties, or qualities, or characteristics. Colors or scents, mass or charge, size or velocity: these are but some of the properties different objects may possess. Some properties we detect by means of our senses. We *see* that the book is blue or *taste* that this morsel of food is sweet. Other properties are detected by instruments or are determined by scientific theory.

The *distinctness* or *separateness* of objects is similarly a presumption of or taken for granted by common sense. One way to think of objects as distinct—hence, individual—is that the continued existence of some object apparently does not depend on the existence of other objects. This table will still be here even if the chairs are chopped into firewood and tossed into the furnace. Cut down that cherry tree and the tomato plant will remain.

Of course, this independence of existence of objects is not to deny that objects typically *causally interact* with other objects or are the *cause of the existence* of some other object. The beavers cause a change in the flow of the stream. The presence of the Torrey pine causes the curve in the trunk of the magnolia tree, as it "tries" to escape the shade of the pine and reach the sunlight. The panda Hua Mei came into existence *because of* mother Bai Yun and father Shi Shi. Similarly the cause of your existence, that there is this object that is you, we typically identify as your parents.

Objects thus are *related to* other objects. Neil Armstrong walked on the moon. Mars is between Earth and Jupiter. Karina bops Kelly with a magazine. This sodium ion is related to that chlorine ion, because of a chemical bond. Common sense counts these as *external* relations. That is, the identity of an object or what the object is doesn't change because of some relation to another object. Kelly remains the same, despite having been bopped. No matter the "walking on" relation, there are still two separate objects, Armstrong and the moon. And presumably, were Mars to decompose into billions of pieces that continued to orbit the sun along the Martian path, Earth and Jupiter would still be Earth and Jupiter. (This issue becomes more complex with a consideration of *intrinsic* relations, and whether there are any.)

The preceding merely sketches some features that seem to be part of the common understanding of the metaphysical aspects of the world (at least as that is viewed in the history of Western philosophy). Every one of the metaphysical views of "common sense" may, however, be wrong. Investigation is needed, and that's where philosophical metaphysics comes in.

Some Important Concepts

Like any discipline, philosophy has a set of concepts or terms it employs. Some you have undoubtedly come across, but perhaps with a slightly different sense given to them. Other concepts are more likely unfamiliar. The first concept we'll discuss is that of *concept*.

Concepts refer to or pick out certain properties or objects. For example, my concept of a university refers to some things and not to others. The place where I teach is a university; the restaurant where I occasionally dine is not. We sometimes want to explain or analyze concepts by saying when the concept applies. Analyzing "university" should explain the basis for identifying things that are and those things that aren't universities.

The idea that an analysis of a concept gives us the conditions that pick out all and only things of a certain kind is sometimes characterized as providing **necessary and sufficient conditions** for the application of a concept. Necessary conditions are like minimum requirements. A necessary condition of being President of the United States is being at least thirty-five years of age. Somewhat more technically, A is a necessary condition of B if and only if B cannot occur without the occurrence of A. But sufficient conditions are enough to bring about a particular event or property. That is, it is a sufficient condition of being president-elect of the United States that one gets a majority of the votes cast by the Electoral College. More technically, A is a sufficient condition of B if and only if whenever A occurs, B also occurs, or whenever A is satisfied or met, B will also be satisfied or met. This brings us to *necessary and sufficient conditions*, indicated by the phrase "if and only if." Necessary and sufficient conditions are often important in mathematics, logic, and semantic theory. Conceptual, logical or semantic connections may be necessary and sufficient. For example, a figure is a square if and only if it has four sides, equal in length. Or, being an unmarried male is necessary and sufficient for being a bachelor.

At various times and in various eras, philosophers have attempted to provide the necessary and sufficient conditions of central concepts and metaphysics. For example, attempts at providing the necessary and sufficient conditions for considering something to be a *substance*. Of course, such attempts involve trying to explain why a certain analysis of a concept is the best analysis.

A somewhat related term might be introduced here: "logically possible." Put simply, a sentence (or a **proposition**—what's expressed by a sentence) is **logically possible** if it is not self-contradictory. "Polar bears are white" is logically possible, and so is "Polar bears are green." Neither is self-contradictory, though one is in fact true and the other false. Alternatively, we might say that a proposition is **necessary** if its denial or contradictory is not logically possible. A sentence is not logically possible when it is self-contradictory. For example, "A triangle has four sides" is self-contradictory and therefore not logically possible. Thus, "A triangle has three sides" is necessary. Logical possibility is different from physical possibility, which only asserts that something doesn't contradict physical law. For example, it is not physically possible that my car goes faster than the speed of light, or that I can fly by flapping my arms. Both are, however, logically possible.

These notions of necessary and logically possible propositions turn out to be important for many of the claims philosophers give, as well as many of the arguments they offer.

As we will use the concept, a **belief** is a mental state that has a particular **content**; this content represents some object as having some property or characteristic. Beliefs, then, are **representational states** by virtue of their having certain contents. Typically, the contents of a belief—what the belief is about—is described by means of propositions. Thus, for example, my belief that the coffee is cold represents that the coffee is cold. By virtue of their propositional content, beliefs can be either true or false. That is, they can represent things either correctly or incorrectly. If Andie believes that the ball is in the backyard, then his belief is either true or false, depending on whether the ball is actually in the backyard. If Sally believes that Santa knows if she's been bad or good, her belief is false, but not because Santa actually knows this; rather because (too bad!) there isn't any such person; she's just representing the world a way that it isn't.

Many metaphysical questions and answers can be traced back to Socrates, Plato, and Aristotle, in the fifth and fourth centuries BCE. One metaphysical tradition with ancient roots is **realism**: the idea that some particular kinds of thing exist independently of our beliefs—and are thus *mind-independent*. (What makes a belief true, then, is apparently that it corresponds with this mind-independent reality.) A person might be a realist, for example, about numbers and arithmetic, holding that even if there were no people who thought about it or ever performed division or addition, 2+2 would still equal 4. One can also be a realist about colors, thinking that even if there were no sentient beings to perceive them, objects would still have color.

A more obvious sort of realism is about the external world, the world of common sense. A realist about the external world holds that, independently of whatever we believe, independently of our thoughts about it, stars and starfish, planets and people, rocks and rutabagas, apples and animals exist. The second notion is a realism *about truth*. For a significant range of propositions or statements, the truth (or falsity) of those statements is an objective fact independent of what we think. Anti-realism about truth, by contrast, holds that (at least in some cases) "true" statements are just those that we individually, or as a culture, approve or count as "true." Chapter 3 explores in greater detail the broader issue of realism, including realism about truth.

This brings us to another venerable "fault line" in metaphysics. Some have suggested that the natural or the physical world is all that exists. Such a view naturalism or **physicalism**. Since, in the physicalist view, there is only one kind of thing—physical things—this view is a type of **monism**. ("Monism" comes from the Greek word *monos*, meaning "one"; in this context, it refers to the belief that everything that exists is the same type of thing.) Holding to physicalism is one way of being a monist. Some have thought that, in addition to the physical world, there are also nonphysical objects or kinds or properties. Among the objects typically offered as nonphysical are souls or minds, as well as mental "contents" like ideas or experiences. As hinted above, many take numbers or geometrical objects to be nonphysical. Properties or attributes similarly might be nonphysical. **Dualism** is the view that in addition to our normal physical objects and properties, there also exist nonphysical or immaterial objects; and, most often, the nonphysical objects in question are minds and their properties. In this view then, for example, a belief or a pain or a memory are properties of a mind, and both mind and its "state" are nonphysical. Of course we now know that we have brains and neurons firing, but dualists insist that we also have nonphysical minds and their nonphysical properties.

Argument, Counterexample, and Explanation

A story is told about a "contest" in the emperor's court in ancient China, during the Warring States period (about 470 to 220 BCE): debates between "orthodox" philosophers and the *Logicians* or the *School of Names* (*ming chià*). The impetus for the contest seems to have been that the Logicians frequently offered brief, apparently paradoxical claims to summarize their views about the relation between names and reality, such as "An egg has feathers" and "A white horse is not a horse."[1] The denouement of the story is that one of the orthodox philosophers' representatives concluded the contest by asking the emperor which he'd rather believe: the difficult and the false (the *ming chià's* view) or the "simple and the true." This *argument* apparently had the desired effect; little remains of the School of Names' work.

This historical vignette points to something important about philosophy. Philosophers present their views in different ways, sometimes in long treatises, sometimes "axiomatically," sometimes in paradox or aphorism. Now some philosophers are happy with the notion of a "philosophical method," while others are more suspicious. Still, philosophers with very different philosophical temperaments and intuitions rely on what we might call basic *forms* of presenting

---

1   Fung 1962.

their views, forms that can be found in philosophers' work from China to Greece, from Heraclitus to Heidegger, from Augustine to Wittgenstein. And one standard form is argument.

Deductive arguments are those intended to be "truth preserving." That is, the truth of the premises (the reasons) is intended to guarantee the truth of the conclusion. In *valid* deductive arguments—deductive arguments that are "structured" properly—the truth of the premises in fact guarantee the truth of the conclusion. In other words, valid deductive arguments always satisfy this condition: If the premises are true, then the conclusion *must* be true, e.g.,

> Philosophy professors are snappy dressers.
> Sam is a philosophy professor.
> So, Sam is a snappy dresser.

If these two premises are true, because of the form or pattern of the argument, the conclusion is guaranteed to be true. And if it turns out that the premises are indeed true, then the argument is not only valid, but *sound*. Find yourself a sound argument, and you have found—many would claim—an indisputable conclusion! This little argument above is valid, but almost everyone would dispute its *soundness*. Most introductory logic books present students with ways of identifying valid and invalid arguments. The soundness of an argument is harder to judge, and often requires looking outside of logic (or philosophy)—in other areas, such as history or science, or in observation (e.g., of the clothes of philosophy professors)—in order to assess the truth of the premises.

Philosophers—and introductory logic textbooks—are often interested in *bad* arguments, too. Not that they recommend your using them. Rather, they worry that some *other* philosophical position relies on a bad argument, in particular what is called an *informal fallacy*: a common pattern of bad reasoning that looks persuasive at first glance, but is actually flawed. Introductory logic textbooks typically list, explain, and give examples of at least a couple dozen informal fallacies. Here we note one in particular, that of *begging the question*.[2] Arguments that beg the question are *circular arguments*. They use as a premise or a reason what they are supposed to prove. It should be noted that it is sometimes controversial whether or not a given argument begs the question.

---

2   The mistake of taking "begging the question" to mean *raising the question* has become common. Correcting your friends when they use the term this way may make them respect you more. Or not.

Indeed some famous arguments in philosophy have critics who maintain that they beg the question. This sort of disagreement about the evaluation of an argument is part of the give and take of philosophical analysis.

One way to help understand a philosopher's position—and especially to understand the "strength" of the philosopher's claims—is to identify the premises and conclusion of the argument being made. Yet it is not always an easy task to identify the premises or structure of an argument. As a means of identifying an argument's structure, it is sometimes helpful to see the argument as part of a larger context or in connection with a philosopher's other arguments. This "getting clear" about the structure of an argument is one form of philosophical analysis, or more generally, understanding a text.

In Book I of Plato's *Republic*, Socrates responds to his host's definition of justice, which Socrates characterized as in part "paying what is owed." Socrates argues against this definition of justice as "paying one's debts" by means of a *counterexample*. Socrates points out that if a neighbor left weapons with you, and later returned for them while clearly intoxicated, you should not return the weapons. By means of the counterexample, Socrates thus implies that "paying one's debts" can't be the right definition of justice, because sometimes *not* paying one's debts is the right thing to do.

Arguing by counterexample is a frequent tool of philosophers. Counterexamples highlight *inconsistent* beliefs or statements—two or more statements that cannot all be true at the same time. Socrates suggests that it's *inconsistent* to believe both that justice is paying one's debts and that there are times one should not return what is owed. More generally, if a philosopher's position leads to some claim or statement that is inconsistent with an obviously or apparently true statement, then that is reason enough to wonder about the philosopher's position.

Philosophers also frequently rely on *explanation* as a means of articulating and defending a view. They take a concept or a set of concepts and explain how those concepts are useful for understanding some set of phenomena or some aspect of our lives. For example, the concept of consciousness has figured prominently in the views of philosophers of very different philosophical persuasions. We find philosophers putting forward these different views by providing an explanation of different "types" of consciousness or how they are related to one another.

In a sense this is explaining by a kind of "conceptual configuring" or bringing together a "constellation" of concepts. The relations among (or the "configuration" of) these concepts shows us how to think about a certain area or topic. Jean-Paul Sartre, for example, relies on the notions of consciousness and negation (among others) to explain the nature of human freedom. Ludwig Wittgenstein relies on the concepts of game, of "form of life," and use to explain the nature of linguistic meaning.

This type of explanation is perhaps different from the type of explanation involved in science. Some have thought that scientists explain an event or some phenomenon by citing a hypothesis (or law) and then deducing (providing a deductive argument) for the cause of that event or phenomenon. Whether or not this is the correct understanding of scientific explanation, philosophical explanation should not be restricted to this pattern.

"Philosophical method" is not exhausted by the above. Contemporary interpreters of Plato, for example, have argued that properly understanding Plato requires understanding the dramatic setting of Plato's dialogues.[3] The aphoristic style of a Nietzsche or the numbered propositions with subsequent "explanation" of a Paul Weiss in his *Modes of Being*[4] are other examples of the diverse ways in which philosophers sometimes present their positions, and their arguments. Consequently, philosophers—and philosophy professors, especially—often suggest that the best way to see how philosophers proceed or to see what the philosophical positions are is to ... well ... go take a look.

Key Concepts

- metaphysics
- concepts
- necessary and sufficient conditions
- proposition
- logically possible
- necessary
- belief
- content
- representational states
- realism
- physicalism
- monism
- dualism

---

3   E.g., Strauss 1964; Rosen 2008; Griswold 1988.
4   Weiss 1958.

CHAPTER ONE

TRUTH I

Three Classic Views

DOES *TRUTH* NEED AN ANCHOR?[1] WE USE "TRUE" AND "TRUTH" IN DIF-
ferent ways. At times we think of truth with a Capital T—Truth, as in *The
Truth*. When we think of truth in this way, it seems as though we are thinking
of some one perhaps very abstract thing to which our understanding of the
world is tied. At other times we might say of some object that it is a true home
or a true work of art. On some occasion we might say of someone that he is
a true friend or that she is a true scholar. Here we seem to be thinking of the
"true" as telling us that something is genuine. So here, our use of "true" is tied
to our understanding of what counts as the genuine article.

But these kinds of truth are not the kind we'll be thinking about in this
chapter. Here the subject seems much more simple and down to earth: the
question is merely, What is it that makes a sentence (or belief) true? It seems
as if there's an easy answer here: A sentence is true just when what it says is

---

1   The term "anchor" is adopted from Marian David.

1

the way things are. So "There is fried chicken in the refrigerator" is true just in case there really is fried chicken in the refrigerator. But, as we'll see, that's hardly the end of the story.

Investigating the *nature of truth* generally occurs in tandem with at least implicitly thinking about *reality* or *the way the world is*. A theory of truth—a theory that tells us about the nature or essence of truth—is explicitly or implicitly connected to reality. Seeing truth in this way locates it as part of the field of metaphysics. The principal true "things" of interest here, what it is that philosophers have in mind when they investigate theories of truth, are true beliefs, or opinions, or true sentences or statements. It is this sense of "true" that is the target of theories of truth in this and the next chapter.

You might think initially that what makes a sentence or a belief true is a simple and straightforward matter. That simple answer seems to be something like this: true sentences tell us the way things are. For example, what makes the sentences "Kira is by the pool" or "Andie is sleeping on the couch" true? Well, Kira *really* is by the pool and Andie *really* is sleeping on the couch. The story turns out to be a little more complicated. But roughly, we expect a theory of truth to tell us the "conditions" that make a sentence true.

Thoughts or beliefs, and many of our utterances, *represent*. And the true ones are accurate representations. Here we are inclined in one direction: to think of a reality outside of ourselves and our way of talking. Beliefs, opinions, thoughts, representations are true, it might be held, only if there is something *outside* of our way of talking or the whole collection of our beliefs that anchors truth. Here it is tempting to point to "facts" in particular cases. Reality—the world, as it is in itself, no matter how we think of it—would be an anchor. When I say to Brian, "I was born on Coronado Island," whether my statement is true or not depends on the *facts*.

There is another inclination, however: we want to know how it all hangs together. Our beliefs, our representations should *make sense*, or *fit together*. In order to determine whether to accept a particular claim, we might ask, "Does this fit with what I already believe, or is it contradicted by my prior beliefs?" Is this enough of an anchor? Is this—the fitting together of all our beliefs—enough to tie our beliefs down, to count them as true?

A third inclination also guides our understanding of truth: we think that true beliefs ought to be useful. Go look for anchors if you want, someone might say, but the only anchor that matters is the consequences of our thoughts and beliefs. Tell me what difference it makes in your experience, this someone might say, and that will reveal whether your belief is true.

These three ways of thinking of truth are known as correspondence, coherence and pragmatism. They are the focus of this chapter.

But before we get to them:

Sentences, Statements and Propositions

Throughout the text we will see references to sentences, statements and propositions. In many instances, it won't matter which we talk about. However, in this chapter and the next, there are, in certain contexts, reasons to distinguish them. In different contexts, the same term has a different meaning. For example, many basic logic texts identify *statements* as declarative sentences that are either true or false. In other contexts, the term *statement* is understood as more or less interchangeable with *proposition*. Here the idea is that a statement or proposition is what is expressed by or the meaning of a particular sentence.

Perhaps the clearest of the three is *sentence*. Sentences are, course, strings of words in a particular language that follow the grammatical rules of that language. Sentences fall into different grammatical categories: declarative (e.g., The book is on the table), interrogatory (e.g., What color is Fred's new car?), and imperative or command (e.g., Close the door quietly).

Philosophers have typically been interested in the truth or falsity of sentences, statements, or propositions. Very simply, they are either correct or incorrect in what they tell us about the world. But philosophers differ over which of the three categories are the basic *truth bearers*. That is, they differ over which of these categories is basic with respect to truth and falsity. And this is reflected in the theories of truth, as we will see in this and the next chapter.

One last brief thought. The concept of proposition is one of the more vexed in philosophy. Some hold that propositions are "made up" of concepts, some that they are made up of structures of objects. They are thus abstract objects, like numbers or sets. Others deny that propositions even exist.

These differences reflect the importance of the notion of truth, not only in metaphysics, but in philosophies of mind, language, in logic and epistemology.

Correspondence: Connecting Truth and the World

Correspondence theory roughly coincides with the seemingly straightforward thought that sentences or beliefs are true to the extent that they "match up" with or reflect some part of the world. Aphrodite's assertion that there is fried chicken

in the refrigerator is true if and only if it matches the world. Some care must be taken here, however. But connection to the world isn't sufficient. Truth is reflecting (via beliefs, sentences, propositions) the world *accurately*.[2] However, if we want a *theory of truth*, or an analysis of truth, we need to go deeper than this.

Something seems right about this idea of matching or reflection. Some philosophers and perhaps our ordinary views typically understand our cognitive aim as "mirroring" the world.[3] Philosophers have thus been led to the thought that truth is best understood as *correspondence with the facts*. This is the **correspondence theory of truth**, a theory about the truth of sentences: A sentence is true if and only if it corresponds to the facts. Correspondence is thus a relation between sentences and some features of the world.

Some explanations of the correspondence view rely, not on sentences, but on statements. But both sentences and statements are representations (but for the moment, just for simplicity, we'll talk just about sentences). What do they represent? Most simply they represent, according to theorists, some aspect of the world or a way that the world is. Suppose Aphrodite says "There is fried chicken in the refrigerator." Her sentence is about some aspect of the world: the refrigerator and what's inside it. Her sentence *represents*. Different theorists characterize differently what is represented: things or events or facts or **states of affairs** (ways that things are or might be). We might *represent* some thing as having a particular property, e.g., The Mill Pond is frozen over. Or we might represent two objects as having some relation, e.g., Francisca danced with Fabio.

An important alternative to representation of a *thing* or *things* is representation of a *state of affairs*. States of affairs are, for example, that the Mill Pond is frozen over, or that Francisca danced with Fabio. Or we might represent some event as occurring or beginning or ending or having occurred, etc.; e.g., the Mill Pond freezing over (or having frozen over), or Francisca starting to dance with Fabio.

For some advocates, a state of affairs is something like *Sam eating cake* or *Caesar being murdered by Cassius and Brutus*. Perhaps the best way to bring out the difference is that the *fact that* Caesar was murdered by Cassius and Brutus includes (at least) three objects. But the state of affairs is a single whole, without parts. As a rough analogy, think of the *graduation ceremony* and the fact that Francisca and Felicia graduated along with 47 other students.

---

2   See Aristotle 1941d, *Metaphysics* 1011b25, where he defines "truth" much like this.

3   E.g., Richard Rorty 1976. See also *For Further Reading*.

The latter fact has many component parts. Yet the graduation ceremony is a single event or whole—a happening, as it were.

On the surface, it may not seem that much turns on these differences, but correspondence theorists may adopt one way rather than another because they think it makes the theory more perspicuous or makes it easier to defend the theory against some objection. Thus, some critics object that "facts" are not part of the things in the world, that it's a mistake to treat facts as part of our ontology. Does the world contain not only fried chicken and refrigerators and relations (such as *x being in y*) but also *facts* about fried chicken?

The correspondence view has been widely held throughout the history of philosophy. Many consider Aristotle to have first articulated it, but versions of it can be found in Plato's dialogues.[4] Philosophers such as Thomas Aquinas, René Descartes, David Hume, Bertrand Russell, and Ludwig Wittgenstein (in his early work[5]) were committed to a correspondence notion of truth. Russell in 1912 may have been the first to use the idea of truth as correspondence with the facts: "Thus a belief is true when there is a corresponding fact and is false when there is no corresponding fact."[6]

As noted at the beginning of the chapter, correspondence views are substantial views of the nature of truth. Like other substantialists, correspondence theorists hold that a theory of truth reveals some significant property that all true representations have. Their "definition" of truth reveals its nature.

Correspondence theory is thus the project of identifying the nature of truth in virtue of having identified the nature of the relation or correlation between true representations and something about the world. The task of the correspondence theorist is then clear: specify (1) the nature of the relation of correspondence and (2) the *type* of "thing" correlated with true representations.

Russell and Wittgenstein: An Ideal Language

In the first part of the twentieth century, both Bertrand Russell and Ludwig Wittgenstein defended a version of the correspondence-to-the-facts theory of truth.[7] (The views of both changed over the years, but we'll look here only at their earlier views.)

---

4   But see Donald Davidson 1996.
5   Wittgenstein 2007[/1922].
6   Russell 1959, Chap. XII.
7   Wittgenstein, *op. cit.*, and Russell 1918–19/1955; also Russell 1949, esp. Chaps. 10–16 and 21.

Common to both Wittgenstein and Russell is the idea that a fact is some part or aspect of the world. Francisca waits at a stop light, while cars pass through the intersection, pedestrians walk in crosswalks, a car turns into the gas station. She says 'The light is red'. Her statement is true only if the light is in fact red. (Don't forget that a theory of truth is supposed to explain true belief as well. Thus the correspondence theory similarly holds that Francisca's belief that the light is red is true only if the light is in fact red. But for brevity, we'll talk for a while only about sentences.)

Correspondence, in their view, consists in the *structural* similarity between the proposition expressed by a sentence and the correlative fact. The term "proposition" is common to both Wittgenstein and Russell, although Russell's view of what was true—belief or proposition—varied at times.

What is a proposition? Here's one way of thinking about it. When Francisca utters the sentence 'The light is red', the word 'light' corresponds to—refers to—the traffic light: a real object, external to Francisca; and the word 'red' corresponds to—refers to—the *redness*. But the proposition her sentence expresses does more than refer to an object and a characteristic. It has a structure that includes the two, such that the characteristic is attributed to the object. The sentence is true if that proposition—that *structured* set of references—corresponds to the object with that *structure* in the world.

Basic propositions display a relationship between a property and an object. Perhaps you have seen the notational symbolism from predicate logic. The corresponding logic proposition Ra (where a names the referent of "this" and R is the predicate, or the name of the property *red*) reveals the logical structure of the content of Francisca's belief. The now-revealed logical structure of a proposition—*by analogy*—reveals the *metaphysical* structure of the fact or the relevant part of the world. Correspondence then is a kind of "bearing a structural analogy." The structure of the proposition is analogous to the structure of the fact. So, truth is correspondence with the facts.

There are, however, problems with this view. If it is to be a general theory of truth, it must serve ordinary observational truths, but also theoretical truths, including science, logic, and mathematics. For example, when someone says "The solution to the quadratic equation $x^2 + 1 = 0$ is, $\sqrt{-1}$" to what in the world does that true statement correspond? Ideally whether talking about chicken quarters, quarks, or numbers, there is, we suppose, a uniform notion of correspondence. (We will see that there are other types of truths that correspondence theory must explain.)

While we frequently appeal to the idea of a "fact," the theorist needs a bit more precision. Correspondence theory should offer us a means of identifying and distinguishing facts. Does the world contain not only fried chicken but also *facts* about fried chicken? Is the fact that fried chicken is in the refrigerator a distinct fact from the fact that there are cooked food items from last night's dinner in the big white appliance in the kitchen?

Some have worried about counting *facts* as part of the objective world, along with cats, the planet Mars, fried chicken, gravitational fields, colors, and so on. One aspect of this general worry is simply that it's unclear when we have one fact and when we have more than one. To use a simple, standard example, "the cat is on the mat." How many facts are identified by this proposition? *a being on b* might be understood as a different relation than *b being underneath a*. Does the "cat is on the mat" name both these facts also—*the cat is standing on the mat* and *the cat is sleeping on the mat*?

Another concern arises for correspondence. Ask Aphrodite what there is in the world, and she will give you a list, e.g., cats, the planet Mars, fried chicken, gravitational fields, colors; but she will also confidently tell you, "There are no unicorns." Such sentences are known as *negative existentials*—sentences that deny the existence of certain types of objects. (Another negative existential: There are no hobbits.) If the proposition expressed by her sentence is composed of objects, there is a problem here: no object corresponds to the word "unicorns"; so what proposition is expressed?

We agree with Aphrodite: *it's true* that there are no unicorns. But to which fact does this assertion correspond? Russell at one time seriously entertained the existence of *negative facts*. In his lectures on logical atomism, in response to the question whether negative facts were anything more than a [verbal] definition, Russell says:

> It seems to me the business of metaphysics is to describe the world, and it is in my opinion a real definite question whether in a complete description of the world you would have to mention negative facts or not.[8]

Asked for a definition of negative facts, he notes that if there are such things, no general definition could be given, that its "negativeness is an ultimate."

---

8   Russell 1918–19/1955, p. 215.

Philosophers who incorporate the idea of propositions in their theory of truth often want that idea to serve double duty: to elucidate also the idea of *meaning*. The meaning of Francisca's sentence is given by the proposition it expresses. But "There are no unicorns" and "There are no hobbits" are identical with regard to propositional expression (the things in the world they are about—in both cases, nothing). But they are surely not identical in meaning. Tolkien aficionados "know" that hobbits are very different from unicorns.

There is a sort of parallel concern for universal propositions such as "all whales are mammals" or "all electrons have a negative charge." Wittgenstein treated universal statements as infinite conjunctions. For example, "all giraffes are mammals" is in fact a series of singular statements about each particular giraffe (that it is a mammal) joined together by the conjunction "and"; thus: "Fred (our name for one giraffe) is a mammal; AND Sally (our name for another giraffe) is a mammal; AND Seymour...", But it seems unlikely that neither the utterer of a sentence about all giraffes nor the believer of a proposition about all giraffes had Fred or Sally or Seymour or any other particular giraffe in mind—not to mention these plus all the rest of the giraffes. Are we even capable of having this huge number of beliefs? It is doubtful that these huge conjunctions capture the *content* that is expressed by sentences or beliefs.

Russell, on the other hand, accepted the existence of "universal facts." It's understandable why Russell's theory seems to require universal facts. Universal claims, such as "All elephants are mammals," must correspond to some fact. It is a least problematic, however, that there is some fact "containing" each and every elephant that has existed or currently exists or will exist. Like negative facts, the appeal to universal facts might seem arbitrary.

Austin: Language and States of Affairs

"Correspondence with the facts" received a different treatment from J.L. Austin about three decades after the correspondence accounts of Wittgenstein and Russell.

> When is a statement true? The temptation is to answer ... "When it corresponds to the facts." And as a piece of standard English this can hardly be wrong. Indeed I confess I do not really think it is wrong at all ...[9]

---

9   Austin 1950a/1979, p. 121.

Instead of speaking of propositions and facts, Austin relies on *statements*—using sentences to make particular claims[10]—and states of affairs, a circumstance or situation, either possible or actual (explained further below).[11] Recall that states of affairs are single wholes, as for example the state of affairs of *the cat being on the mat* is a single whole.

Austin explicates the notion of correspondence through an appeal to linguistic conventions that correlate statements with states of affairs. Linguistic conventions govern our use of sentences; that is, they "guide" us as to the appropriate circumstances for using some sentence or other.

We thus *use* sentences to *make* claims. What are these sentences and claims about? They are about *possible* states of affairs, some of which *obtain*.

Note here that when we say "possible" we include the merely possible as well as the actual. Thus Mitt Romney *won the 2012 election* and *Mitt Romney lost the 2012 election* are both possible states of affairs. This technical notion of "obtaining" is still frequent in various areas in philosophy, roughly meaning "occurs" or "happens" (or "obtained," for "has occurred" or "has happened"). So, when Kiersten *claims* "The wine bottle is empty" and that state of affairs obtains, her statement is true.[12] On the other hand, when Fabio introduces Jack to Kiersten and claims "Jack drives a Mercedes," that statement is false because the state of affairs *Jack drives a Mercedes* does not obtain.

Austin's view, then, does not include propositions as links between sentences and the world. Instead the demonstrative conventions of a linguistic community link words with situations in the world.[13] Austin calls these "historic situations," not because they are especially epic or momentous, rather because they are happenings in the world. These conventions are learned when we learn a language and are necessarily shared if we are to communicate with one another about "historic situations." (Perhaps more precisely: we must share an understanding of how instances of each sentence may be used to make statements about some episode or aspect of the world.) Somewhat bluntly, correspondence is but another way of identifying the "language link" that ties speaker, audience and world together. It does not, however, signal some special ontology. Rather, it is, as Austin notes, "... a series of truisms."[14]

---

10   Austin 1950a/1979, p. 120.
11   See also Robert Audi 1995, p. 765.
12   Austin 1950a/1979, p. 123.
13   Austin 1950a/1979, p. 122.
14   *Ibid.*, p. 121.

Unlike the early Wittgenstein, Austin rejects the idea that a statement (or sentence) must picture reality in virtue of its form or structure.[15] Instead of picturing, making a claim is part of the communicative function of language. Kiersten's statement is telling her companion that the bottle is empty; she is letting an audience know something about what she believes is happening in the world.[16] And this communication is effected because competent speakers share an understanding of the linguistic conventions. So just as Austin's view does away with propositions, as what is expressed by utterances and what corresponds to the world, it does away with facts as elements of the external world in addition to objects and events.[17] This mistake arises from thinking that statements *state facts*.[18] Such a view he considers "bogus and unhelpful."[19] Instead, Austin turns to the notion of states of affairs and whether they *obtain*. There is thus a basic metaphysical difference between Austin's and the Russell-Wittgenstein view of truth as correspondence.

"Causal" Correspondence

In the 1970s, a new approach to the correspondence view tied a formal truth theory to a theory of reference. What was needed, according to some philosophers, was a theory of truth that was physicalist in nature and that could provide an understanding of mental content—that is, a theory that would tell us or explain for us the *aboutness* of a thought, what "hooks up" thought and content.[20] When Francisca thinks that Andre baked a coconut meringue pie, in virtue of what is "Andre" connected to that funny fellow over there, and similarly in virtue of what is "coconut meringue pie" referring to or picking out this kind of round, tasty pastry thing and not something else?

Michael Devitt holds a view, intending it to explain this "aboutness" while maintaining **realism**[21]—that is, the view that the objects we talk and think about, their properties and relations, exist and are independent of our representations of them. In the passage below, Devitt provides a succinct account

---

15   Austin 1950a/1979, p. 124.
16   *Ibid.*
17   *Ibid.*, p. 123.
18   Austin 1950b/1979, p. 169.
19   *Ibid.*
20   Field 1972, 1978.
21   See his *Realism and Truth* 1991.

of his correspondence view. What he says will be familiar to you: it's much like what we discussed above. We'll see the important difference in a moment.

> Consider a true sentence with a very simple structure: the predication 'a is F.' This sentence is true in virtue of the fact that there exists an object which 'a' designates and which is among the objects 'F' applies to. So this sentence is true because it has a predicational structure containing words standing in certain referential relations to parts of reality and because of the way reality is. Provided that reality is objective and mind-independent, then the sentence is *correspondence*-true.... The only entities we need are the familiar ones we already have [e.g., chairs, cheetahs, carbon atoms]... and the only relations we need are ones of reference between parts of the sentence and the objects. If we could generalize this approach ... we would be well on the way, at least, to explaining the correspondence notion of truth.[22]

Start with a simple subject—a predicate sentence. The subject term "names" an object, while the predicate term similarly names or picks out some property or relation. For example, "Sam is eating," or "that banana is green." In each sentence, the subject names or designates a particular object, while the predicate names some property—eating or being green. Recall our earlier mention of the notational symbolism from predicate logic: Devitt's 'a is F' is a less formal way of expressing the sentence Fa. Similarly, making appropriate substitutions in the two sentences above, we have Es and Gb. This symbolism will be more important later, but it calls attention to something very important for the causal correspondence theorist.

Beginning with very simple subject—predicate sentences, we have names for objects and properties or relations. Once we understand which objects or properties are named by some sentence, we understand the conditions under which the sentence is true. "Sam" picks out or refers to that blonde-haired gentleman there, sitting at the table. And "is eating" names a certain attribute, let's say, consuming food. So, the sentence "Sam is eating" is true if and only if the particular gentleman named by "Sam" has the attribute referred to by "is eating." Or—as we will see later—"Sam is eating" is true if and only if Sam is eating.

---

22   1991, p. 28.

A pressing question now arises: in virtue of what is "Sam" connected with this particular object, sitting here at this table? Or: why is the term "banana" correlated with this type of slightly curved fruit? That is, why does "banana" correspond to this piece of fruit in the bowl on the table, or on the shelf in the market? Notice that Devitt appeals, for this, to the relation of *reference*, and he gives a causal account of this relation.

The insight of tying reference to a *causal* relation was borrowed from Saul Kripke. "Sam" refers to this person at the table because, at some earlier point, someone initially "baptized" (Kripke's phrase) this object as "Sam." Your later and perhaps distant use of "Sam" also refers to this person because you participate in a causal chain that traces back to that initial "dubbing" (another Kripke phrase). Sam's parents originally assigned the name to this object; subsequently others are introduced: "this is Sam." And this chain of introductions, this causal chain, continues until we hear Sarah say, "Sam is eating." Her sentence *corresponds to Sam* because of the causal reference relation between the name "Sam" and Sam. The name corresponds to the object because of its causal connection to the object.

Now—whenever and wherever it occurred—the English phrase "is eating" is causally connected to a particular activity. We (English speakers) use the phrase to refer to the activity of consuming food. "Eating" (as is a thought about eating) and the activity are causally connected. When Kiersten says Sam is eating, she is talking about the activity because she participates in some (very long) causal chain.

Causal correspondence theory thus provides a way of explaining "corresponds to the facts." Certain words correspond because they refer; that is, they are causally connected to parts of the world. They refer to or correspond to the "facts"—objects in the world and their properties (and in slightly more complicated language, relations between objects). Of course, to have a theory of truth for a language such as English, as Devitt notes, more will need to be done. The basic thought is to build up more complicated sentences from simpler basic sentences. For example, the sentence "Deirdre threw the bouquet over her right shoulder because she wanted Aphrodite to catch it," while structurally complex, in principle can be built up from our understanding of the reference relations for simpler semantic units and their constituent words and phrases.

Proponents of the causal correspondence view of truth note that they can avoid metaphors, such as "picturing" or "mirroring." Nor is there any need for "facts," since our sentences refer only to objects and their properties and relations. And it is, according to these theorists, causal relations that underlie or explain the notion of correspondence. Despite participating in a lengthy causal chain, Andie asserting "Caesar crossed the Rubicon" is true because in 49 BCE, Julius Caesar—the object named by "Caesar"—engaged in an activity designated by "crossed"—leading a legion of his army across—a particular river in northern Italy that is named by "Rubicon." Andie's utterance is true because it gets it right about what happened in a certain part of the world at a certain time. Thus, the correspondence theory needs only a basic reference relation and "names" and "predicates" for the objects, properties, and relations in the world. It appears that at least one of the original motivations—that a theory of truth not appeal to anything nonphysical—is preserved.

Whether this serves as an adequate theory of mental content, or about the meaning of sentences or parts thereof, are issues that would take us into philosophies of mind and language.[23] But note that the problem considered earlier, regarding true statements about unicorns, arises here again. The non-existence of unicorns apparently leaves nothing to be the cause of unicorn-beliefs.

One persistent objection to correspondence views of truth is that they seem to require that we can somehow independently see or verify the connection between some belief or proposition and the real world of objects and structures that are independent of us. This issue emerges in different areas of metaphysics and epistemology. We take it up again in Chapter 3. But it is also at issue in the rivalry between coherence theories and the correspondence view.

Coherence: The Truth and the Whole

Coherence theories promise a very different way of thinking about truth. They arise primarily in the nineteenth century, but there are historical ancestors. A **coherence theory of truth** holds that a belief is true if and only if it belongs to a set of beliefs that is coherent, a set which is an organized or systematic whole. Moreover, as we will see, for some coherence theorists, our beliefs have this "organized whole" character *because* reality is that way. Reality, seen as a *whole*, has an organized and systematic character. For these coherentists, to say that our beliefs *aim* at truth is to say that we aim at acquiring an increasingly all-encompassing set of beliefs. Unlike the correspondence theorist, beliefs don't pair with reality; that is, truth isn't settled by determining whether a

---

23   See Schmitt 1996, Chap. 6, Devitt and Sterelny 1987, and Sterelny 1999 for more about causal theories of language and mental reference.

single belief corresponds to some fact or state of affairs, some bit of reality. It is settled by seeing whether that belief fits into—is coherent with—our organized, systematic belief system.

Metaphysics or Epistemology?

Before considering one classical argument for the coherence view and some recent defenses, a few issues can be clarified. In doing so, we can work with the general but rough characterization of the coherence theory of truth: the truth of a belief is constituted by that belief belonging to a coherent collection of beliefs.

The first issue is whether the coherence theory is a metaphysical theory or an epistemological theory. It might be thought that viewing truth as coherence is our best means of coming to understand or *cognizing* the world. Then we might understand the coherence theorist as saying to us: A genuine understanding or explanation of the world or reality requires us to see things as a whole. And the best way to do that is by seeing true propositions or beliefs as essentially connected, as forming a whole. A rough analogy: If Jessica wants to grasp what William James really thought—if she wants her beliefs about James's views to be true—then she should not content herself with only his published essays, but she should also include his letters, his notebooks and perhaps notes that others took. Thus, we see Harold H. Joachim claiming that "The systematic coherence of such a whole is expressed most adequately and explicitly in the *system of reasoned knowledge*, which we call a science or a branch of philosophy."[24] Genuine truth is seen only in the grasping or cognizing of the whole. Similarly, F.H. Bradley remarks that "My experience is solid, not so far as it is a superstructure but so far as in short it is a system."[25] Bradley continues that in order to have a world "as comprehensive and coherent as possible" he must have continual recourse to the "materials of sense." A coherent system thus requires a continual "upgrading" of belief as a result of perceptual interactions with the world: "And in this way I must depend on the judgments of perception."[26]

Furthermore, we count as more likely to be true those beliefs which "cohere" with other beliefs—that is, which are consistent with our other beliefs,

---

24 Joachim 1906, p. 68.
25 Bradley 1909/1914, p. 210. For arguments that Bradley was not a coherentist, see Stewart Candlish 1989.
26 Bradley 1909/1914, p. 210.

or implied by them, or justified by them. What gives me confidence that that was a male cardinal I just saw in the tree is the coherence of this belief with other beliefs I have: that what I saw was red, and all male cardinals are red, that cardinals are often seen around here, and so on.

Holism and Coherence

A coherence theory of meaning is *holism*. In perhaps the most important philosophy essay of the twentieth century, "Two Dogmas of Empiricism" (1951), Willard Van Orman Quine concludes that meaning is holistic—the meaning of any particular sentence is essentially tied to the meaning of every other sentence in the language.[27] He further concludes that there is no verifying or confirming one sentence at a time.

This aspect of Quine's epistemology has an affinity with coherence theory in this sense. He especially rejects the view that we can understand the "legitimacy" of our knowledge by first identifying a privileged position that rests on experience or sensations as the "guarantor" of our consequent theory about the world, about what there is and the causal network that embeds *real, physical* objects. In this sense, Quine is anti-foundationalist or opposed to what he characterizes as "Cartesian first philosophy." But Quine departs from coherence views of justification in several important respects. His view is too complex to lay out here, but it most certainly is intended to be naturalist, contains pragmatic elements, recognizes the important role of the social and evolutionary character of language, and at times Quine has adverted to "empathy" as part of his understanding as to why we should accept our best scientific theory as our best predictive device and what the real world is like.[28]

To return to Quine's meaning holism, when we set out to test some sentence to see if it is true, we must recognize that the sentence belongs to a "theory." And this theory, a large collection of interconnected sentences of various types, reflects our view of reality. Some of those sentences are closely connected to observations, some not. They are all inter-linked, by logical

---

27 Quine 1961a.
28 Quine's epistemology evolved from 1952 onward while retaining several core commitments, and there is a voluminous library of books and articles about it, including exchanges between Quine and many leading philosophers. See, for example, Dirk Koppelberg 1998; Gila Sher 1996; R.B. Barrett and Roger Gibson 1990; Susan Haack 1990; and Donald Davidson 1990. For an introduction to his epistemology, see Crumley 2009, Chap. 7.

connections of implication and explanation. Consequently, Quine argues, we are testing the theory, not the single sentence. Thus, in Quine's view the *meaning* of any sentence is essentially tied to this background theory. Recall, for example, the relationship between the pressure, volume, and temperature of a gas. Suppose then we test—perform an experiment—the claim that decreasing the volume will also increase the pressure proportionately. But in "confirming" this claim, we are also providing confirmation of the kinetic theory of gases, taken as a whole. And the meaning of the concepts of temperature, pressure and volume are thus interconnected. Or in this example, we are confirming the theory that gasses consist of small particles in motion, and it is their "bumping into one another" that accounts for pressure and temperature. Increase the bumping by decreasing the pressure (think of having the same number of people in smaller and smaller rooms) and you increase the pressure and the temperature (the more people will bump into each other). It is because of his commitment to meaning holism that Quine rejects the "first philosophy" approach and the idea that we can confirm sentences one by one. This is the epistemological side of Quine's meaning holism with respect to confirmation.

Now, some have held that coherence is the nature of truth, meaning and justification (and/or knowledge). Joachim appears to have had such a view about meaning: he claims that the "significant whole" that characterizes coherence is composed of constituent elements, which "reciprocally determine" the contribution each makes to the meaning of the whole.[29] But there is no necessary connection between the three. Quine, for example, committed as he was to holism about meaning, did not hold a coherence view of truth. Nor did he hold a straightforward coherence view about justification and knowledge, at least as those have been typically understood since the middle of the twentieth century.

Coherentists tend to be fallibilists. "**Fallibilism**" means that each one of our beliefs, even ones immediately based on simple sense-experience ("My coffee cup is in my hand"), are revisable in light of further experience. When a shift in other beliefs, perhaps on the basis of new sense-experience, makes for a more coherent system of beliefs, one that excludes that formerly obvious belief, then that belief would no longer count as justified. There is disagreement about such fallibilism, but it is a widely held position. (There are two views here: one about perceptual beliefs—beliefs based on perception about what is in the world—and about sensations, or simple awareness of sensation

---

29   Joachim 1906, p. 66; see also Chap. IV.

contents ["I have coffee-cup-in-hand sense-experience"]. Fallibilism about the former is widely held;[30] the latter is more contentious.)

The importance of fallibilism for the coherentist is that actual systems of belief are always subject to revision: a belief might be counted as true one day and false the next. As Bradley claims:

> Now it is agreed that, if I am to have an *orderly* world, I cannot possibly accept all 'facts' ... And the view which I advocated takes them all as in principle fallible.... If by taking certain judgments of perception as true, I can get more *system* into my world, then these 'facts' are so far true, and if by taking certain 'facts' as errors I can *order my experience* better, then so far these 'facts' are errors... And there is no 'fact' which possesses an absolute right.[31] (emphasis mine)

In Bradley's view, beliefs are true if they belong to a system of belief that presents an orderly and organized world. But their "truth" is open to revision, if some new beliefs render experience more orderly, more organized.

Bradley shares with most other coherentists a "degrees of truth" theory. A real belief system (not an "ideal" one based on complete experience and logical clarity) may be more or less orderly. Thus, there are degrees of truth for a belief, relative to the degree of orderliness of a system. If changes elsewhere in the system make the whole more coherent, the system as a whole becomes more true, and the belief in question gains truth. Bradley holds that the more encompassing a structure or system of beliefs, "the *more* certain are the structure and the facts." Should we reach the "all-embracing ordered whole," then there would be no further revision. As systems approach the "whole," they are more true.[32]

But now we must ask: does coherence with a system of belief make a particular belief more *probable, justified,* or *believable,* on the one hand, or more *true,* on the other? In other words: is a coherence theory of truth really epistemology, without metaphysical import? This sort of question leads to one of the principal criticisms of coherence as a theory of truth.

Suppose that a belief—say, that she just saw a cardinal—was part Felicia's maximally ordered system of beliefs on Tuesday. But on Wednesday, the

---

30 For fallibilism about perceptual beliefs, see Audi 1988 and 1998. Keith Lehrer 1990 argues for fallibility with respect to introspection. See also Crumley 2009, Chap 4.

31 Bradley 1909/1914, p. 210.

32 *Ibid.*, p. 211; see also Bradley 1893, Chap. XXIV, esp. p. 383.

addition of another belief, that Fabio was flying a small red drone around in the trees near her yesterday, makes Felicia change her mind. Her Tuesday belief is no longer the most coherent with her Wednesday set. Must the coherentist say that the cardinal-belief was true on Tuesday but false on Wednesday? And what should the coherentist say about two separate individuals having different but "equally ordered" systems? Suppose that Francisca was bird-watching with Felicia on Tuesday. The belief that there was a cardinal there was, as we've seen, part of Felicia's well-ordered set, but not part of Francisca's, because she already knows about the red drone. On Tuesday, then, does the belief that there was a cardinal there count as true for Felicia but not for Francisca? Isn't there a contradiction here, or at least, a big difficulty for the coherentist?

Here are some related-seeming problems. Consider two inconsistent propositions p and q. It's possible that p and q are incompatible with each other, but that each is compatible with some set $\{R\}$. A coherentist must, it seems, claim that p and q are both true, despite being inconsistent. As a real instance, note that the propositions 'The number of stars in our galaxy is odd' and 'The number of stars in our galaxy is even' are both consistent with every other belief of astronomers; yet they can't both be true. Again: consider two very different sets $\{R\}$ and $\{S\}$; each of these is internally maximally consistent, but there are a number of propositions in each that are denied in the other. A coherentist must, it seems, count every proposition in each maximally consistent set as true, despite the fact that some propositions in one are denied in the other.

In a detailed essay, Francis Dauer argues that there is a way for the coherentist to avoid some of these seeming difficulties. We'll give a very simplified version of his argument, applied to our red cardinal example, which Dauer would respond to by relativization to a community. We can imagine that the community of birdwatchers completely agrees with Francisca that it was a red drone; thus there is a way to see Felicia as "deviant." For Felicia will at some point encounter evidence that her system deviates from the norm of the community. This notion of community could, it seems, be construed rather broadly, up to and including a "community of the whole." Coherentists also respond to these sorts of objections by relying not on a reference to the belief system of one or another person at one or another time, or even of a community of the whole, but rather on an idealized ultimate belief system which people would arrive at given that they had experienced and thought about everything they could; or on the belief system of an omniscient being.[33]

---

33   Dauer 1974.

The objections we have been looking at, broadly speaking, raise the question to coherentists: why think that our coherent thoughts in any way mirror a coherent universe? According to one coherentist tradition, however, this sort of question entirely misses the point of coherentism, which is not that the coherence of our thought does not represent the coherent universe, but rather *constitutes* it. What makes our most coherent thoughts true is not that they correspond to any non-mental external facts. The knowable universe is not non-mental: it's the universe *as experienced*. True belief, then, is that belief which is organized the best.

What we have here, then, is a form of what's called metaphysical **idealism**: the idea that the world—*our* world, anyway—is mind-dependent, or composed of mental objects. Bradley, for example, argues that reality is an ordered system of cognized experience. Thus, our epistemological test for acceptable belief—the coherence test—is in fact a test for truth. To be a true belief is nothing more than *to be* a member of a maximally coherent set.

Brand Blanshard: Why Coherence?

Brand Blanshard's argument for coherence as the nature of truth is the focus of this section. This is not to say that Blanshard's approach is best. The line of argument, however, has various features in common with a number of coherence theorists. It also bears some similarity to a recent defense of a view of coherence truth, as we will see below.

We might preface the argument by looking more closely at certain features of the coherentist idea. Blanshard distinguishes the "immanent" from "transcendent" pulls of belief. On the one hand, because of the *immanent* pull, we want not merely a collection of beliefs. We want a *system* of beliefs. Our (pretheoretical) confidence in our beliefs increases as we recognize an order to them. Perhaps we can put it like this: believing is intrinsically aimed at order, at systematicity. This order includes the logical connections among beliefs and the evidential connections (that this belief gives one some evidence for that belief). Thus, Pauline's belief that there is only honey and no sugar in Portia's kitchen is supported by her belief that Portia thinks sugar is unhealthy. Still another connection is *nomological*—the natural or scientific laws that tie beliefs together in virtue of the explanations they offer. (For example: The best explanation for why the pressure inside this tire increased is that the air inside became warmer; thus belief in the former fact is coherent with the latter supposition.) This set of relations—logical, evidential, and explanatory—can be understood as *explanatory coherence*, and we often judge the greater truth of a system or theory by its explanatory coherence.[34] There are other connections, but perhaps this suffices to provide some sense of the systematicity or order *within* a system of beliefs.

If we desire order, we also desire comprehensiveness. The more all-encompassing our beliefs, the better. Beliefs provide content, and greater comprehensiveness spells more content. To be information hungry is to be belief hungry. Thus, we have the immanent pull of our believing.

But content signals to us "on the other hand." And that "other hand" is the recognition of a decided *transcendent* pull to our believing. The representational character of belief points outside our beliefs. Why have belief at all unless it is to reveal the world around us? The whole point of believing is to put us in touch with something that transcends a set of beliefs, namely the world. The world as it is, *in itself.*

Critics of coherence theories of truth frequently hold that coherence theorists mistake the *test* of truth for the *nature* of truth. Blanshard argues that this criticism misunderstands the issue. The argument has two parts, first that coherence as a test must *presume* that reality is itself coherent, that it is an ordered reality. The second part of the argument attempts to show that if we *assume correspondence is true*, we are led either to skepticism or to a contradiction.

Supposing that coherence is a *test* of truth that leads us to recognize a further assumption: reality is itself coherent, that is, intelligible. Blanshard insists that it makes no sense to assume coherent thought measures up to an incoherent or unintelligible reality. So, coherence is a test of truth only if reality itself is coherent. Blanshard recognizes that this does not reveal the nature of truth. Still, it is imperative, in Blanshard's view, that we recognize the necessary *intelligibility of the metaphysical structure* that underlies our efforts to understand the nature of truth. Reality must be coherent.[35] Blanshard sees it as a sum of necessary and interconnected parts. That is why testing our belief system for comprehensiveness and interconnectivity—for coherence—is a test for truth. Grasping this interconnectivity is understanding reality. Reality thus can be cognized directly and not as a putative representation whose veracity is in need of demonstration.

---

34 Paul Thagard 2007 and 2010, Chap. 4, esp. pp. 90–92.
35 Blanshard 1939, p. 267.

Blanshard asks what follows from the idea that truth is correspondence. In Blanshard's view the coherence of our beliefs includes fundamentally the thoughts we have as a result of our perceptual contact with the world, specifically noting colors, sounds, and smells.[36] This is an important point for the classical and contemporary coherence theorists. Coherent sets of beliefs about the world essentially include beliefs that we have as a causal operation of our senses. Thus, coherence theorists think that a coherent set of beliefs is informed by reality. The standard for correspondence is that we somehow see that thought corresponds with reality. But Blanshard asks how we can see or claim that belief corresponds with reality. "For in order to know that experience corresponds to fact, we must be able to get at that fact, unadulterated with idea, and compare the two sides with each other ... such fact is not accessible."[37] Either skepticism or self-contradiction awaits us.

The first part of this claim—that to verify correspondence we would need to compare our beliefs to naked, unexperienced, fact—is of course controversial and much disputed, but it is not obviously implausible. (The issue arises in philosophy of mind, epistemology, philosophy of language, as well as metaphysics.) It is a position that has been held by a number of philosophers. If cognitive access to reality is mediated by our concepts, then, as Blanshard says, the original—the world as it is in itself, "unbound" by our concepts—forever eludes us, and skepticism awaits. Reality as experienced is always through the frame of our concepts. Thus, we never grasp reality as it is itself and are led to skepticism.

An alternative point of view, however, is that we have direct contact with reality, not merely some distinct representation that needs to be shown to represent correctly. But direct contact with reality, with the world, is not belief/world correspondence; then we've lost correspondence.[38] We are often enough in *direct contact* with particular objects. There is something basic given to us in thought; "basic": unbound or unstructured by our concepts.

The following analogy is not Blanshard's, but consider God's knowledge for a moment. We are told by various philosophers and theologians that God's

---

36 Jonathan Dancy 1985, Chap. 8, is very good on explaining the features of coherence theory (although Dancy focuses on Bradley).

37 *Ibid.*, p. 268.

38 Some correspondence theorists, then and now, also think we have direct contact with reality. Bertrand Russell, for example, distinguished *knowledge by acquaintance* from *knowledge by description* (Russell 1912, Chap. V).

knowledge is *intuitive*; it is not ideational or conceptual. Yet is there any sense in talking of God's thought as *corresponding* to reality? Correspondence only arises when we consider whether some *representation*, some structure of concepts matches or fits or *corresponds* with reality. God's existence is of course not the point here. The relevant point is Blanshard's claim that direct contact erases the "space" for correspondence. Correspondence requires a kind of gap between thought and reality. When you can have your facts directly, truth is not correspondence.[39]

Correspondence theorists will of course object to the argument for various reasons. Most importantly, the correspondence theorist can reject Blanshard's claim that we can make sense of an unmediated contact with the world, and that this blurs the boundary between thought and world. Causal accounts of correspondence of course hold that objects (or states of affairs) cause certain thoughts or concepts. But direct realists about perception—those who hold that we are in direct contact with objects in the world—often hold a correspondence view of truth as well.[40] Like Blanshard, they see some perception as a "direct connection" between the thought and the object; but they see this as producing a direct, immediate, representation or concept of the object. So, it seems, direct connection does not remove the need for a correspondence relation.

As noted above, coherence theorists have no desire to deny the causal connection between world and thought. Blanshard, as does Bradley, accepts that; his argument is both a critique of correspondence as the nature of truth and an argument for seeing coherence as the nature of truth. Of course, these are fundamental and complicated issues, and critics have raised substantial questions. While we can't resolve all those issues here, perhaps it is enough to observe for our purposes that one typical dismissal of coherence—namely, that the coherence theory of truth offers only a test of truth—has a plausible response; so at least that particular criticism of the coherence theory of truth fails to dismiss the coherentist position. That a range of issues have only been touched upon, some epistemological, some metaphysical, and some "metaphilosophical," perhaps illustrates the complexity of this aspect of the nature of truth.

---

39   *Ibid.*, pp. 268–69.
40   For example, Michael Devitt 1991.

When Is a Belief a Belief?

More recently, coherence theories of truth have been thought to face a *specification* problem, as James O. Young calls it.[41] The objection is due to Ralph C.S. Walker, and has been thought to undermine any attempt to sustain a coherence view.[42]

Walker argues that the coherence theorist cannot specify or identify the system of beliefs—what beliefs a person has—without either admitting that truth is correspondence or being caught in an infinite regress. A coherentist holds that truth is a property only of beliefs. So for p to be true, it must be true that "p is a belief." But for 'p is a belief' to be true, then this also must be a belief: the belief that p is a belief. But if the belief that p is a belief is to be true, then this too must be a belief. Because for the coherentist, truth conditions are supplied only within a belief system, the coherentist is off on a vitiating regress. There is no coherentist answer to the question, according to Walker, "Is this a belief." Unless of course the coherentist gives up coherence in favor of correspondence.

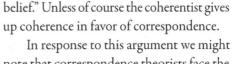

In response to this argument we might note that correspondence theorists face the same supposed problem. Their claim is that p is true only if p corresponds to a fact. When is it true that "p corresponds to a fact"? That proposition is true just in case "p corresponds to a fact" corresponds to a fact. And so on, in the same kind of regress.

It is not clear that advocates of the coherence theory of truth should accept the "specification objection." It is open to coherentists to argue that there are assumptions in Walker's objection that they are not obviously committed to holding.

Coherence theorists hold, in Walker's view, that the truth of any belief is relative to the system of beliefs. In other words, the truth conditions of any given belief are

---

41   Young 2001.
42   Walker 1989, e.g., pp. 99–100.

determined by the other beliefs in the system. If I believe "There is cake in the kitchen," then the truth of this belief is determined by the other beliefs I hold. So, the truth conditions of my belief will be explicated by looking at the other beliefs I hold.

The problem for the coherentist, according to Walker, arises at this point. Since the truth conditions of the belief are given by my other beliefs, we must be able to specify what beliefs I hold. There seems no end to this specification, however. Every time the coherentist attempts to explicate the truth conditions of a particular belief, it seems that an endless supply of beliefs must also be specified. Thus, we can never identify the system of beliefs that determine the coherence of some particular belief.

For example, suppose I believe that there is cake in the kitchen. (It may help keep track if we identify this belief—"there is cake in the kitchen"—as B1). The truth of this belief is relative to my other beliefs. In essence, the belief's truth conditions are given by my system of beliefs. However, according to the objection, there is a "new" belief that I have to consider: my belief (B2) that I *have* this belief, B1, "There is cake in the kitchen." Don't I believe that I believe there is cake in the kitchen? Of course. (We return to this below.) Well, then this new belief, B2, about my belief is part of the system of beliefs also. Thus, (B2) must be taken into account when determining the truth of (B1). You can no doubt see the problem: the specification objection holds that there is a third-order belief, namely, I believe (B3) that I believe (B2) that I believe that there is cake in the kitchen (B1). And of course, *ad infinitum*. Thus, the system of beliefs can never be specified, and it is this system the sets the conditions of truth for any belief. So, the truth conditions of any belief cannot be explicated. Or more simply, whether any belief is true—for the coherentist—cannot be determined.

First worry about the objection. The assumption that if I have a belief, I must believe that I have that belief is very suspect (and is the subject of extended discussions in both philosophy of mind and epistemology). It becomes even more suspect as we move higher up the "order chain." It is very plausible that we have many beliefs without also having, for each of those beliefs, a belief that we have them. Now, if you ask me, "Do you believe there is cake in the kitchen?" I may very well say, "Yes, of course." But this ordinary, commonplace response, which may be explained in any number of ways, in no way yields a *theoretical* commitment to a driving assumption behind the specification objection. This observation is likely enough to set aside the objection, but there is a more important point to be made.

Coherentists distinguish between the system of beliefs a person has and the way the world is—reality. Do I believe that there is cake in the kitchen? Yes. And that I *really do* have that belief *is part of reality*. It does not follow from this that I must also believe that I believe that there is cake in the kitchen. If it does not follow, then the specification objection cannot get started.

It is important to be clear about the relation between "system-relative" truth conditions and reality. The truth of my belief is indeed relative to the system of beliefs that I have. Of course, it may be that "cake in the kitchen" is not part of reality. But don't I then have a false belief?

Here is the key point for the coherentist in answering this question. Relative to the beliefs I have, the belief that there is cake in the kitchen counts as true. There is another perspective, however. That there is cake in the kitchen is not part of reality. So, the coherence theorist can adopt this "reality perspective," as Blanshard does, and say the following: yes, relative to your beliefs, that belief is true, but your belief system is only a partial grasp of reality, of the way the world is (as Blanshard, Bradley and others hold). A system of beliefs that determine the truth of some particular belief reflects *our best partial grasp of reality*. To a fallibilist, however, this "gap" between reality and truth relative to a belief system is not troublesome. Enhancing this partial grasp is the epistemic side of the coherence theory.

Neither of these perspectives opens the door to the specification objection. Yes, truth is determined relative to my system of beliefs. The coherentist, however, need not accept that there is the iterative chain of beliefs that I believe that I believe ... *ad infinitum*, which must be counted as part of my belief system. Well, then what "specifies" the beliefs I have? Where do I find the "catalogue" of my beliefs? Reality. The beliefs I *actually* have are part of reality. On various occasions, I may set out to get a better grasp of this part of reality. That is, I may set out to obtain a better grasp of what I actually believe. This epistemic endeavor of attaining an ever-better grasp of reality is entirely consistent with a coherence theory of truth. This epistemic endeavor is no different for the coherentist than for other theorists.

In holding to the distinction between reality and our best partial grasp of reality as reflected in our system of beliefs, the coherentist has a consistent position. Keeping in mind the coherentist's view of the metaphysical aspect of the relation between the system of beliefs and reality, then dismisses the worry posed by the specification objection. That the coherentist can consistently distinguish between reality and the system of beliefs that reflects reality should not be overlooked.

James Young offers a similar response, which has certain ontological presumptions (that appear different than the presumptions of the present response).[43] As Young claims, "... there is a fact about what system [of belief] is accepted, but their [coherentists'] position is in no way threatened by this concession." Or as he notes two paragraphs earlier, "Coherentists divorce what is true from what is real; it is possible that a fact is the case but that there are no truths about this fact."[44] Again, we can make out the same thought in Blanshard and Bradley. Our system of beliefs is provisional in the sense of *increasing*, and thus there are degrees of truth. Yet there remain aspects of reality not captured by our system of beliefs. In this sense, we can distinguish *true beliefs* from *reality*. It is only by presupposing the correspondence theory, Young claims, that one rules out this line of response.[45]

In a sense, it is not surprising that Young identifies a "presupposing" of the correspondence view in the specification objection. It seems that once the coherentist distinguishes between belief and reality, the thought is that the only plausible view of truth is correspondence. But the coherentist holds and tries to explain that there is an alternative to the correspondence theory's "one fact at a time" approach.

A Pragmatic Conception of Truth

In the latter half of the nineteenth and the beginning of the twentieth centuries, a new view of the nature of truth arose, the pragmatic view, which drew criticism and protests from coherence and correspondence theorists alike.

Classical pragmatism is identified with three American philosophers, Charles Sanders Peirce, William James, and John Dewey, all born in the nineteenth century and continuing their work into the twentieth, with Dewey living until the middle of the century. As in any school of thought, the positions of each of these three differ. Dewey, for example, thought that the scientific method could be turned to any question, although he was most certainly interested in art and culture. Peirce too was deeply concerned about science and its progress, but his later work emphasized the nature of a sign and the existence of *real generals* (a term which he applied to physical law and abstract objects). In James we find more of an emphasis on ordinary *particular* experience, of

---

43   Young 2001.
44   *Ibid.*, p. 97.
45   *Ibid.*, p. 99.

the world of common sense, but he still thought of pragmatism as scientific. Yet all three identified their view as *pragmatism*.[46] And there is more than one common element among them. Still, a notion of truth that is reasonably identified as pragmatic can be discerned among the three.

The ideological background for the classical **pragmatist view of truth** was epochs-old rivalries and dichotomies—between rationalist and empiricist, between correspondence and coherence, between subject and object. These rivalries needed to be set aside, indeed dismissed. Basic to these oppositions were some assumptions that pragmatists held were unfounded—for example, the idea that there was some *first* truth, whether an *a priori* truth or the first encounter with an isolated sensation. From the pragmatist point of view, this assumption is a falsification of experience.

The two founding documents of pragmatism, Peirce's "The Fixation of Belief" and "How to Make Our Ideas Clear,"[47] tell us that belief arises within experience, from a background of already held beliefs. Some new experience produces doubt. Peirce identifies *inquiry* as the movement from doubt to belief, where belief is characterized by a "contented" feeling that overcomes or "appeases the irritation of doubt."[48] Inquiry begins within a context, framed by held beliefs and interests, and is the resolving of the "irritation." This is not Cartesian doubt; as James and Dewey also held, merely putting a proposition as a question is not doubt; there is no drive for resolution, no beginning of an inquiry. "There must be a real and living doubt, and without this all discussion is idle."[49] Decades later, James similarly notes, while glossing F.C.S. Schiller (a pragmatist at Oxford) and Dewey, the "strain" a new experience can put on one's received opinions (or beliefs), producing an "inward trouble." The relieving of this inward trouble is found in a new belief, "some idea that mediates between the [already held beliefs] and the new experience into one another most felicitously and *expediently*. The new idea is then *adopted as the true one* (emphasis mine)."[50] "A new opinion counts as "true" just in proportion as it gratifies the individual's desire to assimilate the novel in his experience to his

46   Peirce in 1905 renamed his view *pragmaticism*, in reaction to what he saw as the opposition to the nominalism in James's development of pragmatism (Haack 1977, p. 378).

47   Both essays are in vol. 5 of *Collected Papers*: vols. 1–5, edited by Charles Hartshorne and Paul Weiss, vols. 6–7, edited by Arthur W. Burks, pp. 5–22 and 23–41, respectively. (Page references are to Justus Buchler 1955.)

48   "Fixation," p. 10 and "How to Make ...," p. 28.

49   "Fixation," p. 11.

50   James 1906–07/1963, p. 29.

[already held beliefs]."[51] This is the function of calling a belief "true," James argues: to marry old belief with new experience. In fact, the *reasons* why we call things true is the reason why they are true: "... for 'to be true' *means* only to perform this marriage-function." And "objective truth" is "nowhere to be found."[52] This needs a little clarification.

The meaning of a term or concept, for the pragmatist, is its *practical* difference. Collette says to Claude, "I'm worried that the iron will rust." Collette's idea, her thought, her belief about the iron is about what *will happen*. Meaning, tied as it is to the practical sphere, is essentially connected to the future. "This is why he locates the meaning [of a proposition] in future time ...," Peirce says.[53] And commenting on Peirce, James observes that even subtle differences between concepts or thoughts are nothing more than a "possible difference in practice."[54]

For the pragmatist, experiences converge. Collette's inquiry regarding the nature of iron is neither random nor isolated. Peirce, emphasizing this convergence more, likened the activity of thought to the "operation of destiny." In one of his more famous (or infamous) remarks, he says: "The opinion which is fated to be ultimately agreed to by all who investigate, is what we mean by the truth, and the object represented in this opinion is the real. This is the way I would explain reality."[55] Dewey later endorses this as the "best definition of truth from a logical standpoint known to [him]."[56] This *real* is not mere invention by us, however.

How are we to have any sense of "ultimate agreement" and hence what is true? Peirce is in agreement with James and Dewey: truths have practical consequences. As James would later say, if there is no practical difference between two statements, then they are at most verbal variations.[57] Dewey too wanted us to see thought not as intellectual, but as practical activity.[58] All three pragmatists hold that there is no end to inquiry. (In his early writings, Peirce appears to hold that there is an actual end to inquiry.) As James would say, "The fundamental fact of our experience is that it is a process of change."

---

51 *Ibid.,* p. 31.
52 *Ibid.*
53 Peirce 1955, p. 261.
54 James 1906–07/1963, p. 23.
55 "How to Make ...," p. 31.
56 Dewey 1939, p. 345 n6.
57 James 1904/1963, p. 163.
58 Dewey 1930, p. 160.

How does this affect our understanding of the pragmatic account of truth? Fitting belief to the facts (correspondence) or capturing the systemic whole (coherence) are not really wrong as much as they are beside the point. There is no standard outside experience; instead the "standard perpetually grows endogenously inside the web of experiences...."[59] James holds, like Peirce, that reality resides within experience. And to the worry about what supports these "intra-experience" standards, James says that "Humanism [pragmatism] is willing to let finite experience be self-supporting."[60] The pragmatist's conception of truth is that it is the continual resolution or "mediation" of old opinion with new experience. The meaning of our ideas or concepts is always the difference they make in our practical activity. (For Peirce, this difference has a future aspect to it: what difference it *would* make in our future activity. This leads to one of the differences between Peirce and James but seems to align him with Dewey.)[61]

But we are not free to hold any belief. Both James and Peirce see experience as constraining belief. And as we have already seen, beliefs are successful ideas, in that a belief is the resolution of doubt. Thus, some particular belief is true because it is another step in an ongoing successful inquiry. In a sense, truth opens inquiry; it does not bring it to a conclusion. Thus, Dewey in his Gifford Lectures protested against certainty because it brought an end to inquiry.[62] And Peirce insists on this rule for philosophy: Do not block the way of inquiry.[63] Truth is what works, what is expedient. Truth is what pushes experience along by reconciling the forward edges of our experience with the contents of the experiences we bring to the present moment.

It is important to bear in mind that pragmatism holds that belief is constrained by reality. James insisted that experience puts us in touch with reality. Similarly, Peirce and Dewey have no doubt about our contact with the world. But *copying* or *mirroring*—or correspondence—is not constitutive of truth. Certainly we have images of the world around us. Hilary Putnam points out, however, in his discussion of James, that it is not the having of the image—or its accuracy—that matters; it's what we do with it.[64]

---

59   *Ibid.*, p. 180.
60   *Ibid.*
61   Haack 1977, pp. 388 ff, esp. 390.
62   Dewey 1930.
63   Peirce 1955, p. 54.
64   Putnam 1997, p. 173.

Perhaps we have enough now to provide an account of the **pragmatic theory of truth**: a belief is true if it provisionally reconciles new experience with old, as a further step in the ongoing process of inquiry, and proves useful to the believer cognitively and practically. Perhaps we can put it like this: for the pragmatist, "experience" is fundamentally a *verb*, a continuing activity or ongoing process. It is within experience that "belief," "meaning" and "truth" get their sense. "Belief is the appeasement of doubt" and "the meaning of concept is its practical difference" and "truth is what works" are not separable constituents. They are the "ecology" of inquiry.

Bertrand Russell is one of the many who excoriated the pragmatist conception of truth, especially as it appears in James's thought. Russell, you'll recall, advocates the correspondence view: propositions are true in virtue of a structural correspondence with some aspect(s) of the world. Russell's opposition was animated in no small part by James's claim that a belief (idea) is true in so far as it helps to put us in a satisfactory relationship with other parts of our experience.[65] But this, Russell felt, was a hugely over-permissive and subjective account of truth; it meant that anything goes. Russell was reacting to James's position that beliefs are tested or verified in experience, that new beliefs are accepted relative to those already held, and that beliefs along the way are all open to revision. The testing—or verifying—of belief is always ongoing. In the pragmatist view, there is nothing more to truth than its role in experience. In this sense, truth is always provisional.

But according to Putnam, Russell interprets James in a way not consonant with James's view.[66] James, like Peirce, expects that truths converge on a perhaps unreachable but ideal limit. Yet we are guided by a fallibilist conviction about our standards. Even our standards for testing our ideas—for determining "what works"—evolve in the course of experience. Again, as Putnam observes, in James's view, the verified is not the true, it is the "half-true."[67]

James does not hold that belief creates facts—"We do not make God exist by believing in him...." Instead, believing brings about behavior that yields a particular result.[68] Notice that Peirce tells us that truth is to be found in the limit of what a *community* of inquirers hold. Of course, each of us starts with our own convictions or beliefs, but even these do not spring into existence out

---

65   Russell 1947, p. 844.
66   Putnam 1997, p. 180.
67   *Ibid.*, p. 181.
68   Robert G. Meyers 1989, p. 98.

of nothing. In Lecture Six of the Lowell Lectures, "Pragmatism's Conception of Truth," James remarks, "True is the name for whatever starts the verification-process, useful is the name for its completed function in experience." If "the true" did not have this value, we would never have worried so much about it. And it is from this "simple cue" that the pragmatist derives "her general notion of truth as something essentially bound up with the way in which one moment in our experience may lead us towards other moments which it will have been worthwhile to have been led to."[69] We would shun truth, he claims, if there "were no *good* for life in true ideas."[70]

Key Concepts

- · correspondence theory of truth
- · states of affairs
- · realism
- · coherence theory of truth
- · fallibilism
- · idealism
- · pragmatic theory of truth

Reading Questions

1. How would you describe the difference between "facts," as Russell and Wittgenstein understood them, and "states of affairs" as Austin understood them? Which do you think better serves a correspondence theory?
2. In a few sentences explain how Austin accounts for statements "corresponding" and when they are true.
3. Explain the importance of the notion of a structured or organized whole for coherence theory.
4. Why does Blanshard hold that coherence is not merely a test of truth?
5. Critics characterize the pragmatic view as "truth is what works." Explain the sense in which this is true. Is this a defect of the view?
6. Choose one of the three views of truth discussed in this chapter and write a short essay explaining its chief advantages.

---

69   James 1906–07/1963, p. 90.
70   *Ibid.*, p. 36.

For Further Reading

A very accessible introduction to Russell's views is Russell 1912. His essays on logical atomism are in Russell 1918–19/1956; although somewhat more challenging, they are still accessible. Wittgenstein's *Tractatus* is considerably more difficult (but fun!); Urmson 1956 is helpful and very clear. Hans Sluga and David Stern 2017 contains excellent essays, two of them specifically about the *Tractatus*. Still one of the best introductions to that work is G.E.M. Anscombe 2001.

Devitt 1991 explains his correspondence view, as well as his criticisms of rival theories and criticisms of correspondence. Davidson 1986 is widely seen as a defense of a coherence theory of truth.

F.H. Bradley 1893 and 1914, H.H. Joachim 1909, and Brand Blanshard 1939 are all very readable. Jonathan Dancy 1985 is very good on Quine, holism, and coherence theory.

Sandra Rosenthal, Carl Hausman, David Anderson, eds., 1999 is a collection of essays focused on different aspects of Peirce, James, and Dewey's thought. Many of the essays draw connections to recent philosophical issues. John E. Smith 1978 is still an outstanding introduction to classical pragmatism; Chap. 2 surveys in detail the views of truth of Peirce, James, and Dewey. In addition, H.S. Thayer 1980 is a critical history of pragmatism, and perhaps still *the* account of that history.

Frederick Schmitt 1996 is a very nice survey and examination of different theories of truth, as is Richard Kirkham 1995. Michael P. Lynch 2001 is an excellent anthology, containing either selections or essays representing the major schools of thought.

CHAPTER TWO

TRUTH II

The Twentieth Century, Necessity, and Possible Worlds

The Twentieth Century

BEGINNING IN THE EARLY TWENTIETH CENTURY, TWO NEW CONCEP-
tions of truth arose. These views held that the long-standing traditionalist
project of identifying the nature of truth was at best in need of revision and
at worst should be abandoned. The traditionalist search for the deep essence
or nature of truth was misguided. **Deflationism** holds that there is no special
property or nature of truth for a theory of truth to reveal. Identifying some
belief or sentence as "true" is redundant or a mere linguistic convenience.
Several prominent twentieth-century philosophers have held some version
of the view, and versions of the view are held by many philosophers today. At
least one person has remarked that some version of deflationism is now the
most widely held view of truth (rather than some version of correspondence).

Much of twentieth-century philosophy was motivated by both a generally empiricist outlook and a preference for a more sparse metaphysics, one that invoked fewer types of objects and properties. Moreover, as noted in the previous chapter, a recognition of the importance of language, specifically our understanding of the nature of linguistic meaning, shaped theories across a wide range of philosophical disciplines. Truth theories were not immune. The idea that *truth* or *being true* names a special kind of property was suspect. As philosophers developed theories of truth that shunned a special "truth property," deflationism became more widely endorsed and accepted.

One influence on the deflationist approach stems from Wittgenstein, who proposed a very different view of the task of philosophy, in his two most influential works, the earlier *Tractatus* (see Chap. 1) and the later *Philosophical Investigations*. In both works, Wittgenstein is suspicious of the idea that philosophy reveals to us the real nature of things, including truth, propositions, meaning. Many regard both works as anti-metaphysical. The important point for our purpose is that in his view we can be misled by language (although he takes different tacks in the two works). In the *Investigations*, he remarks that "philosophical problems arise when language goes on holiday."[1] Later he claims "Philosophy is a battle against the bewitchment of our intelligence by means of language."[2] Wittgenstein thought that the structure of language leads to confusion: "One thinks one is tracing the outline of the thing's nature over and over, and one is merely tracing round the frame through which we look at it."[3] His aim is to "shew the fly the way out of the fly-bottle" by reminding us that philosophy "leaves everything as it is" and is not uncovering some hidden nature. We think there is a deep essence to concepts such as meaning or truth. Instead, we need, according to Wittgenstein, to remind ourselves of the many different ways language can be used and hence the ways in which we might be "bewitched." A simple example (though not one particularly relevant to philosophy) of how language can "bewitch": consider *sakes*. What is a sake, really? We think that there must be one essence common to its different uses: "for the sake of your health," "for your children's sake," "for God's sake." It seems to be something that can be had by other people and other things, but what exactly is it? How many of them are there? Could there be sakes without people? (If this reminds you a bit of the disappearing Cheshire Cat leaving

1   1953, p. 38.
2   *Ibid.*, p. 109.
3   *Ibid.*, pp. 309, 114.

behind only a smile, you might be interested to know that Wittgenstein was very familiar with some of Lewis Carroll's work.) But these are silly questions that shouldn't have been asked in the first place, if we had only attended to the manifest ways that we use that phrase in ordinary language and were not misled by the surface grammar. The search for "essence" or "natures" is of course held by some to be the defining *nature* of metaphysics. But some deflationists about truth think that questions about the nature of truth arise from a similar sort of "bewitchment." Whatever their motivation, deflationists hold that there is no special property or characteristic property that is the essence of truth.

A hugely important contribution, not only to the topic of truth, but also to other areas of philosophy, appeared in 1935:[4] Alfred Tarski's article "Der Wahrheitsbegriff in Den Formalisierten Sprachen," later translated into English as the "The Concept of Truth in Formalized Languages." In the essay, Tarski's principal concern was to understand the notion of truth as it is used in the language of mathematics (and logic). In 1944, he published a second essay on the same topic, "The Semantic Conception of Truth."[5] It is this essay that gives us the name of this view of truth. The **semantic conception of truth** sees truth as essentially tied to a language and relies on the notions of *object language*, *metalanguage*, and *satisfaction* (explained below) to elucidate what it is to be a true sentence. Both of these essays *formalize* the notion of truth, using an advanced logic apparatus.

The semantic conception is not the first version of deflationism, but is an appropriate place to begin consideration of that general movement. Versions of deflationism rely on an important feature of the semantic conception.

Semantic Conception of Truth

The development of formal logic in the late nineteenth and early twentieth centuries provided very powerful tools of analysis and theorizing to philosophers, mathematicians, and logicians. For example, in 1905 Bertrand Russell made use of predicate logic in order to demonstrate a difference in the logical structure of sentences containing names and sentences containing definite descriptions (descriptions that purport to denote a unique individual, e.g., 'the present president of the US'). Mathematicians and logicians are of course interested in notions such as truth and consistency. Prior to Tarski's work,

---

4   Tarski 1935.
5   Tarski 1944.

there was no rigorously formulated account of truth for formal systems, that is, mathematical or logical languages. When Tarski set out to show how truth could be "formalized," he wanted to do so without relying on any semantic notion, such as truth or reference. But he also had in mind apparent paradoxes about truth, including the ancient and notorious "Paradox of the liar." How should we understand someone who says "I am lying" or an instance of the sentence "This sentence is false"? (The sentence seems to refer to itself, saying that it's false; yet that's just what the sentence says. So, it's true. But if it's true, then isn't it false?)

Without entering into the formal apparatus employed by Tarski, we should be able to get a pretty good sense of his notion of "truth-in-a-language." First point: any sentence is true *relative to a language*. In one sense, this is to be expected. Remember, Tarski was working with formal languages, where the domain—what the language is about—can be specified with some precision. Then, for example, "geometry sentences" are true (or false) relative to the language we are using to talk about geometric objects. Some think this is a disadvantage of the semantic conception: it does not give us an account of truth in general. And it is sometimes asked whether the semantic conception of truth can be applied to *natural languages*, languages such as English or Spanish or Italian or Polish. As we will see later, a prominent account of the meaning of natural language sentences utilizes the Tarskian idea.

What is it to be true for a formal language sentence? (We will be rather informal here, since it is the general Tarskian thought that we want.) Start with a domain—the objects or things to be talked about. In arithmetic, we talk about doing things with numbers; in geometry, it's geometric objects. And our "framework" for talking about those objects is a way to name them, both generally and specifically. The axioms, together with some basic logic rules, tell us the sentences we can generate. Now, select some sentence. Let's try the Pythagorean Theorem: "For every right triangle, the square of the hypotenuse is equal to the sum of the squares of the two adjacent sides." This sentence is true if it is *satisfied by* all the right triangle objects in the domain. Why "all"? Because this is a *universally quantified* sentence; it's about all the right triangles. And this places a constraint on the sentence being satisfied. Thus, the Pythagorean Theorem is true if and only if all the right triangles meet the condition set out by the theorem. Tarski tells us (very metaphorically): go find all the right triangles; do they *satisfy* the sentence? Do they meet the condition set out by the theorem?

One more example from arithmetic: There is a successor (a number that follows) of 7 that is less than 10. Notice this is not a universal sentence; it's a "some" sentence, or an "existentially quantified" sentence. It says "There is at least one ..." Is it satisfied? Well (metaphorically again): go look at the numbers. Is there at least one number that follows 7 but is less than 10? Yes, there is. Thus, the sentence is satisfied. (Tarksi's own formulation was more complicated, but we need not worry about that here.)

We now have an account of truth for sentences in a formal language. Universal sentences are "true-in-L" (the formal language we are using) if and only if all relevant objects in the domain **satisfy** the sentence (i.e., their insertion makes the sentence true). Can't get complete satisfaction? It's false. For a "some" sentence—an existentially quantified sentence—it is "true-in-L" if and only if at least one object in the domain satisfies it. Can't get no satisfaction? It's false. "True-in-L" is satisfaction.

Tarski wanted to explain truth without relying on the concept of truth itself or some concept that presupposed the concept of truth. And many think he succeeded in doing so. Some, however, suspect that satisfaction is itself a disguised semantic notion. And Tarski seems to suggest that his account of truth is a kind of correspondence theory; others have similarly claimed that Tarski's semantic approach is a correspondence theory. However, there is no attempt to offer an explanation or definition of "correspondence." Tarski viewed his account as a "material adequacy" condition. Any satisfactory or "adequate" theory of truth should yield the sort of connection offered by T-sentences.

Could you apply this approach to truth in natural languages? Perhaps we can get a sense of what that might be like for a restricted domain for English, say, the domain of *human beings*. As a universal sentence, consider the sentence S_1: "All human beings are mortal." Does every object in the domain— every human being—satisfy the condition? The answer is "yes." Then this sentence is "true-in-English." Or S_2: "Someone knows where Alessia is." Is there at least one object in the domain that satisfies the sentence? Again, if the answer is "yes," then the sentence is true. One more: "Tarski taught at the University of California, Berkeley." This sentence is satisfied if the object in the domain that is picked out by the name "Tarski" has the property or characteristic identified by the predicate "taught at the University of California, Berkeley." He did. So the object named by "Tarski" has the requisite property, and thus the sentence is true. Again, this sentence is *true-in-English*.

Notice that this latter sentence seems to fit with the idea of correspondence. The sentence is true because it is satisfied, which someone might think is a different way of talking about correspondence. But others see coherence at work; after all, it is truth relative to the *whole* language. A sentence is true relative to the framework of the language as a whole. We leave this issue aside.

One further important point. Tarski showed—and required—that the truth conditions of any given sentence in a formal language be derived from a small set of axioms together with a set of names of the objects and a set of primitive predicates, or the names for the primitive properties. Thus, there is a theorem for each and every sentence in the language that spells out that sentence's *truth conditions*. These derivable sentences—theorems—spell out the truth conditions in the form of biconditionals, or if and only if sentences.

Suppose for a moment you could axiomatize English and provide the required list of names (and variable names) and primitive predicates. A Tarskian account of "true-in-English" would provide a derivation, a theorem of this form:

T(S): "S" is true-in-English if and only if....

where "S" is the name of a sentence, and the ellipsis is filled in by the truth conditions of S, whatever those happen to be. These are called the T-sentences of English.[6] Remember: if Tarski's approach works, you could derive a T-sentence for each English sentence. And "true-in-English" is then nothing more than just this very long (at least countably infinite) list of T-sentences or theorems.

("Countably infinite" groups or sets can be counted using the natural numbers: 1, 2, 3,.... You will never run out of numbers, but it is an unending task. And, yes, there are "uncountably infinite groups or sets," for example, the real numbers, as the nineteenth-century mathematician, Georg Cantor, proved.)

Perhaps the most frequently cited T-sentence, "Snow is white," is true-in-English if and only if snow is white. This particular T-sentence looks trivial and uninformative. Yet the *derivation* of this sentence is far from trivial (depending on the axioms). Moreover, consider a T-sentence for the French sentence "La neige est blanche." That is:

"La neige est blanche" is true-in-French if and only if snow is white.

This leads us to see the difference between an **object language**, the language we are attempting to specify the range of T-sentences, e.g., the language of arithmetic, and the **metalanguage**, the language we are using to talk about the object language. Here we have French as the object language and English as the metalanguage. In a formal language, such as that of arithmetic, the object language is a restricted fragment of English, together with the required mathematical concepts.

Tarski noticed that natural languages like English are at once object language and metalanguage. When I tell my friend, "In English, 'see you later' means...," I am using English as the metalanguage to say something about English, the object language. My explanation is a level above the simple "see you later."[7]

---

6   See Richard Montague 1974 for examples of the attempt to axiomatize fragments of English, using modal logic.

7   And it is this distinction between object and metalanguage that allows Tarski to give an explanation of the Liar Paradox. Tarski's idea is that to prevent the paradox from arising, one needs to "step outside" the language into a metalanguage to talk about when a sentence is true (or false). This is Tarski's way of avoiding the self-referential problem in the Liar Paradox. See Bradley Dowden's "Liar Paradox" for a helpful and detailed account of the paradox.

T-sentences, and their derivability, as noted earlier, turn out to be important for deflationism and have been famously employed by Donald Davidson and advocates of a truth conditional approach to the theory of meaning.[8] Similarly the notions of meta- and object language figure in arguments that we will see about realism. It is interesting to note that this seemingly innocuous idea, exemplified by "'Snow is white' is true if and only if snow is white," has been utilized by proponents of every major theory of truth, and some of those proponents claim that it lends support to their preferred approach. Tarski's idea exemplifies something essential about truth. How this idea should be utilized in a theory of truth is another question. In fact, deflationists argue that it shows us that there is not some deep structure to truth, which requires a theory to reveal.

Deflationism

Unlike traditional accounts of truth, deflationism holds that there is no special property or nature of truth to be revealed by a theory of truth. Reference to the nature of truth is meant to convey the thought that there is something that all true sentences have in common, *other than simply being among all the true sentences.*[9] We shall sketch three different deflationist views: redundancy, disquotationalism, and the minimalist theory.

The motivational thought behind these views is that there is nothing *substantial* to truth, and hence they are sometimes known as "insubstantialists." However they are termed, they agree that the traditionalists' search for the deep structure of truth—correspondence, coherence, even pragmatist—is a mistake. The redundancy view is typically considered to be the first deflationary theory to appear.

Redundancy

Announcing that some sentence "is true" can, on at least some occasions, look like it's merely a "repetition device." Samantha announces, for example,

---

8   Davidson 1967.

9   There are "classification issues" that arise when considering deflationism. For example, the minimalist theory of truth, as developed and advocated by Paul Horwich, is sometimes counted as deflationist and sometimes not. For our purposes, the minimalist view is treated here as deflationist, recognizing that Horwich counts "is true" as naming a property. Cp. Frederick Schmitt 1995, pp. 125 ff, and Richard Kirkham, pp. 339 ff.

"It's true: Andie put the remote right here on the table." We see no apparent difference between what Samantha said and simply repeating the sentence "Andie put the remote right here on the table." You might think in saying "it's true" that she is affirming her support, but she could have easily done so by repeating the sentence. "Is true" is redundant.[10]

This much seems essential to the **redundancy theory**: Merely asserting some proposition and saying of that proposition that it "is true" are interchangeable. Thus, there is no real content to the predicate "is true"; it is vacuous. Adding "is true" says no more than repeating the proposition. Samantha might say, for example, "There is no school today." She asserts *that there is no school today*. Or she might have said, "'There is no school today' is true." The "is true" doesn't tell us anything more than her original assertion. As a consequence, to say of some proposition that it is true *does not attribute some property to the proposition*. Perhaps we can borrow the correspondence theory for a moment to explain this latter point.

Suppose that Felicia tells Fabio "The milk carton is empty," and Juan chimes in "It's true: the milk carton is empty." Now, on a simple understanding of the correspondence theory, Juan has attributed a property to the proposition. There is some sort of property that the proposition has, such that the proposition somehow represents some aspect of the world. We might say the proposition has the property "corresponding to." And traditionalists about truth hold that theories of truth are supposed to do just this. For the correspondence theorist, explaining the nature of truth by pointing out the property or feature it has is constitutive of *being true*. The redundancy view denies that there is any such property. Juan might say "it's true" for any number of reasons, e.g., agreeing, emphasizing, drawing attention to the proposition or some other reason. But these are in no way revelatory of the nature of truth. Juan adds nothing new precisely because the predicate "is true" names no property. Indeed there is no property to name. That we can express matters in this way points to a feature of the redundancy theory, namely, that we are misled by the apparent structure of the sentence.[11] But this seems not quite right to some.

Critics of the redundancy view ask us to consider our understanding of the meaning of certain pairs of sentences. For example: Pauline might say in

---

10 The redundancy view is generally traced to Frank P. Ramsey, although there are those who think his view was more than a simple redundancy view. Ramsey 1927; Brian Loar 1980 and Pierre Le Morvan 2004 argue that it's more than a redundancy view.

11 Chase Wrenn 2015, p. 105.

class "First order predicate calculus is truth-functionally complete." Peter, sitting next to her, has no idea what she *means*. When Professor Patrick says "'First order predicate calculus is truth-functionally complete' is true," Peter grasps a meaning that he didn't grasp from listening to Pauline—the sentence said by Pauline is a true sentence.[12]

Nonetheless deflationary critics of traditional approaches to truth see in redundancy theory the core of an idea about how best to understand truth.

Disquotationalism

Disquotationalism is the view that the logico-linguistic function of the predicate "is true" is to remove the quotation marks from the named sentence in T-sentences. Some see disquotationalism as a type of redundancy theory, but it is worth distinguishing them. Willard Van Orman Quine, perhaps the best known advocate of the view, once endorsed Wilfrid Sellars's term for the "perfect theory of truth": the *disappearance theory*.[13]

On some occasions, for various reasons, we want to talk about sentences. But this is only temporary. As Quine says, the whole point is reality: "is true" directs us to reality. Yet Quine recognizes that because of "complications," there are occasions when we want to *mention* a sentence, not use it to talk about reality. If Shep says, "That cat Pyewacket was outside my window again last night," he is *using* the sentence. An aspect of the world is noted—the relation of a particular cat to a particular window at a particular time. On occasion however, we only *mention* a sentence. Thus, when Nicky says, "Queenie said, 'Gillian is in love,'" Nicky is not *asserting* the sentence, or making any declaration. Thus, he is not using it. He's merely mentioning it to convey what Queenie said. Nicky only *mentions* the sentence Queenie *uses*. Why does the *use–mention distinction* matter?

When we mention a sentence (or other bit of language), we use a linguistic device which Quine characterizes as a "momentary retreat from the world."[14] That is, we make a "semantic ascent," talking about sentences instead of about reality. But the ascent is not permanent. T-sentences make use of the device of *disquotation*, according to Quine. "By calling the sentence 'Snow is white' true,

---

12   See also Wrenn 2015, p. 106.
13   Quine 1970, p. 11.
14   *Ibid.*, p. 12.

we call snow white."[15] The truth predicate—the "is true" of T-sentences—is a device of disquotation. In the T-sentence "'Gillian is in love' is true if and only if Gillian is in love," the function of the *is true* is to remove the quotation marks. We move from talking about a sentence, a sentence we merely name or mention, to talking about the world.

Ordinarily we don't genuinely need the disquotation device. But in indirect speech—saying what another said—or talking about many sentences at once, it can be useful to attach the "is true" to the quoted or named sentence. Disquotation moves from the linguistic plane back to the world. It is a way of ceasing to mention or quote a sentence and instead use it. So viewed, disquotation then reveals no special property that we point to with the predicate "is true." It is more a matter of convenience that allows us under various circumstances to move back and forth between language and the world.[16]

Recall that T-sentences only provide us with a notion of truth *relative to a particular language*. The semantic conception of truth yields only "language-indexed" truth. A traditionalist about truth, someone who thinks there is some property possessed by all true sentences, will no doubt dissent from the idea that the most we can capture is truth relative to a particular language.[17] This "language relative" difficulty suggests another concern about the redundancy view. Consider, for example, this sentence:

> "Pierre's statement, 'Les érables perdent leurs feuilles à l'automne,' is true.".

This sentence clearly is acceptable; it is not difficult to imagine a situation where this or a similar sentence might be said in a meeting or even a classroom. Notice, however, what happens, when we "disquote," dropping the "is true" and disquoting. We obtain:

> Les érables perdent leurs feuilles à l'automne.

---

15   *Ibid.*

16   But see Joshua Schwartz 2016 for a very different reading of Quine's view of disquotation.

17   See, for example, Schmitt 1995, p. 127.

Obviously this is not an English sentence. The expectation is, since disquoting is relative to a single language, that we would obtain an *English* sentence as the unquoted sentence. As noted, there is nothing odd about the original sentence. Yet there is no obvious way to fix this type of problem.

A similar point raised about the redundancy theory might be raised here. Suppose that someone in Naval Intelligence[18] says about a particular encoded sentence: "'X{RI O:MDFU' is true if and only if the battleship is east of Manila." A critic of disquotationalism might think that such examples illustrate more than semantic ascent. That is, it is an illustration of the way in which T-sentences correlate object language sentences with truth conditions—and informatively so.

Why is this a criticism of disquotationalism? If the view were correct, presumably all that we would be doing by removing the quotation marks is "re-saying" the same sentence. But at least on some occasions, it appears we are doing more than that. It seems as though we are asking for an account of the truth conditions, and this might be accomplished, characteristically, only by using some different formulation. When Eddie asks Stella after she asserts a calculus theorem, "Can you tell me why that's true?" Eddie is not asking her to repeat the assertion. He is asking her to explain the truth conditions of the proposition. Now Quine might be right: *disquotation moves us from talking about sentences to talking about reality*. By itself, however, this does not imply that the traditionalist about truth is wrong.

Three further examples illustrate specific problems that can arise with the disquoting approach. Consider the following example:

What Fred said at the meeting is true.

Depending on circumstances, this sentence might be what has been called a "blind ascription," that is, the speaker may not know exactly what Fred said, but nevertheless is confident that what Fred said is correct. Clearly the "is true" is not redundant; it serves to note that whatever Fred said, it is indeed *true*. And this can reasonably be counted as ascribing a property to Fred's remark. Similarly, the "is true" in this sentence might be noting Fred's reliability about such matters. Even knowing the content of Fred's "saying," e.g., the budget is

---

18   Quine was in Naval Intelligence during World War II.

out of balance, it still is not obvious that the "is true" is redundant. The function of "is true" in such cases is more than simply disquoting.

A similar sentence illustrates that "is true" allows us to capture certain generalizations, as Quine recognized, that we would not be unable to do without that predicate:

Everything Henry says is true. (Or: Henry always tells the truth)

The function of "is true" and "truth" in these sentences allows us to assert a number of sentences, despite our not knowing or not having access to those sentences. In a sense, "is true" allows us to assert a general truth, which we would lose if we relied solely on disquoting.

One further example:

Sally's statement, "I am hungry," is true.

This sentence is *acknowledging* that Sally is hungry. Removing the "is true" and the quotation marks leaves us with

I am hungry.

This new sentence obviously means something different than the first. But a simple disquotational view is unable to account for the difference in meaning.

We should not lose sight of the general issue as we move through these examples. Deflationists hold that there is no special property about truth; everything we want to say about the world, we can say without the use of "is true" or similar expressions. These examples illustrate why many have doubts that the deflationists are right.

Minimalism

A recent defense of a minimalist theory of truth, one that may avoid these objections, is due to Paul Horwich.[19] As Horwich presents it, this is the view that "is true" names a property, but it is a "minimal" property. We begin by noting two important aspects of **minimalism**.

---

19   Horwich 1990.

First, according to the "Minimal Theory," truth applies primarily to propositions, not to sentences. Sentences *express* propositions; the proposition is the meaning of the sentence. So any sentence is true in virtue of the truth of the proposition it expresses. For example, 'Maples lose their leaves in autumn' is true by virtue of the truth of the proposition it expresses, which we might name in italics: *that maples lose their leaves in autumn*. Notice that this leads us back to the notion of truth conditions. Sentences are true because they express propositions whose truth conditions are satisfied. For example, the sentence 'Maples lose their leaves in autumn' means or expresses a proposition—in particular, that proposition whose truth condition is that maples lose their leaves in autumn.

Second, the Minimal Theory *is* all propositions with a by now familiar biconditional ("if and only if") form:

The proposition that *p* is true if and only if *p*.

That is, the theory defines "is true" or "truth" implicitly. Instead of defining truth as "correspondence with the facts" or "what is verified in experience," Minimal Theory *is* the list of all true propositions having this form. So, for any sentence expressing a proposition, there is the corresponding biconditional in the list of biconditionals that are the Minimal Theory. For example: Pauline says "Jack is an actor." Then the proposition that Jack is an actor is true if and only if "Jack is an actor" is on the list. And every other proposition expressed by some (declarative) sentence has a corresponding biconditional that is part of the list that is the Minimal Theory. According to Horwich, this list is all that there is to truth or "is true." We understand truth to the extent we grasp (some part of) the list. (There are some technical complications that Horwich addresses, which we pass over.) Thus, Minimal Theory defines truth implicitly. Now obviously this is a very long list, an infinitely long list.

A strength of the Minimal Theory is that we can now explain the sentences that pose a problem for redundancy and disquotationalism. Begin with:

Sally's statement "I am hungry" is true.

The proposition expressed by this sentence, the meaning of the sentence, is, say, "Sally is hungry." So, this biconditional is part of the Minimal Theory.

The proposition that *Sally is hungry* is true if and only if Sally is hungry.

And this is the very plausible result that we want. But what about the sentence "Everything Henry says is true"? A fair paraphrase of this sentence is "Each sentence said by Henry is true." This is easy to accommodate in Minimal Theory. Each sentence (said by Henry) expresses a proposition. And for each of those propositions, the appropriate biconditional is on the list. Then "go through" each of the propositions expressed by Henry's sentences. If the truth conditions are met for each of those, Henry always tells the truth.

We have spent some time with Horwich's view, not only because it improves on previous deflationists, but because it is also widely influential and much discussed. However, there are some deep questions that remain unanswered. First, the concept of *proposition* is itself controversial. Some suggest that the notion presupposes the notion of truth. Second, why is it that a particular sentence-token—roughly, a sentence said at a particular time and place—is taken to express a particular proposition?[20] And why is it that some propositions are true? Saying that their truth conditions are satisfied only puts this problem off one step: why is it that certain states of the world satisfy some propositions and not others? A further worry is expressed in various ways by

---

20 Most of Horwich's 2001 book attempts to answer this question.

different commentators.[21] The concept of truth is implicitly defined by the list. Anil Gupta has two observations about this approach. First if we understand a concept, we understand the parts of the definition of that concept. The less our grasp of the parts of the definition, the less our understanding of the concept. Second, and more important, we only grasp a very small part of the list, but most of us have a very good grasp of the concept of truth. More succinctly, how does the list of biconditionals explain our apparent understanding of *truth*.[22] We seem to have legitimate worries about how to explain our understanding of truth and how some beliefs and sentences are tied to the world.

Necessity

We shift now to a different set of topics.

Metaphysics, at least in part, is concerned with the nature of things. Identifying an object as some *kind* of thing is often taken to imply that such an object has certain properties *essentially*. It would not be that kind of thing if it did not have certain characteristics. Mathematical objects may be the simplest example: the nature of a triangle, for example, is to be a closed plane figure having exactly three sides, and it's necessary that every triangle have three sides. It's not merely that there aren't any two-sided triangles: there couldn't be any. Another sort of example: every sample of platinum has the essential property of having the atomic number 78. If it's platinum, it *must* have this atomic number.

Closely related are the ideas of necessity and necessary truth, notions that have been and still are an important part of metaphysics. Plato and Aristotle framed questions and approaches that still animate metaphysical inquiry.

Necessity, Possibility, and Possible Worlds

Intuitively we distinguish between the possible and the necessary, but we also recognize the relation between them. *Necessary* truths could not *possibly* turn out false. Consider "Necessarily a square has four sides." No matter what the circumstances, no matter how circumstances in the world (or the universe!)

---

21   In addition to Gupta, noted immediately following, see, for example, Trenton Merricks, 2007, pp. 189–91.

22   Anil Gupta 1993, pp. 365–66. I have considerably relied on Gupta's essay.

might have been or could be different, it's just not possible to get a square that has something other than four sides.

This thought about circumstances being different leads to one of the most important developments in the twentieth century and one of the most important conceptual tools in philosophy. This is the notion of possible worlds, an idea initially formulated in the eighteenth century by Gottfried Wilhelm Leibniz. But not until the twentieth century was it given a rigorous development, with Saul Kripke often credited with using the notion of possible worlds to provide a rigorous semantics for the notions of necessity and possibility.

What is a **possible world**? Intuitively they are complete sets of circumstances, of states of affairs. That is, think of all the ways our world might have been a little different or even a lot different. Imagine, for example, a world exactly like ours, except that George Washington decides to call off the Trenton Christmas raid because of inclement weather. Or think of more mundane complete sets of circumstances: in this world—the actual world—Alessia's credit card falls out of her wallet, but Andie calls it to her attention, and she retrieves it. But in *some possible world*, Andie doesn't notice, leaving the credit card to fall into other hands. Although Marlon Brando's character, Terry Malloy, in *On the Waterfront*, is fictional, when he utters "I coulda been a contender," he's saying something about what might have happened *had circumstances been different*. The possible world in which he is a contender is (we imagine) a lot like the actual world; but in some worlds very unlike the actual one, he's a ballet dancer, or president of the US. (Could he have been a goldfish or a book?)

Perhaps we can make this notion of a possible world a bit more tangible. To do so requires some mental stretching, making use perhaps of some simplifying assumptions. First start with the objects that are in the actual world; include not only lions and tigers and bears, but tables and chairs, pianos and guitars, all the scientific objects, benzene molecules, cells and amino acids, even fields, planets, and stars. Consider all the properties that each of the actual objects has. Now imagine a proposition that tells us or says for any and every object, it does or doesn't have a particular property. Just one example: In the actual world, Warren Buffett is 5'10" tall. So the proposition *Warren Buffett is less than six feet tall* is true in our world. Yet in some other possible world—in numerous possible worlds—another proposition is true: *Warren Buffett is over six feet tall*. For all the contingent properties, for every object x, and any property F or G or H...., the propositions x has F or x has G or x has H are true in some possible worlds and not others. Now start collecting all the various combinations of true propositions. Just using this one object and the three properties, there are eight different kinds of possible worlds. In general, consider every pair of contradictory propositions, such as *Gerald Ford was a President* and *Gerald Ford was not a President*, or *the University of Nevada was founded in 1874* and *the University of Nevada was not founded in 1874*. Imagine all the different ways "true" and "false" could be assigned to these propositions in these pairs. Any possible world is described by a complete set of propositions true at that world. Informally: each of the possible ways "true" could be assigned to all of those pairs—that's a possible world. So, in some possible worlds, Ford was a President and in others he wasn't. And in others he didn't exist at all! How many possible worlds are there? Clearly, at least a countably infinite number. Perhaps we can't enumerate or catalogue all the possible worlds, but the notion is precise enough for us to use in approaching particular topics in many areas in philosophy and logic, especially in an area known as modal metaphysics or the metaphysics of modality.

In particular, we now have a way of characterizing necessary truths and possible truths. A necessarily true proposition (also called, for short, a "necessary truth") is a proposition *that is true in all possible worlds*. No matter what the circumstances, no matter which maximally complete set you choose, *a square has four sides* is true in every such set. That is, it is true in every possible world. Note that there are also necessarily false propositions: those true in no possible worlds—for example, that $2 + 2 = 5$.

A **possible proposition** (also called a "contingent proposition"), on the other hand, is a proposition that is true in a least one possible world. For example, *Fabio won the lottery* is possibly true, since there is at least one possible world in which Fabio won. But that proposition depends on other propositions being true as well. Obviously, it must be a possible world that has lotteries (remember: there will be many possible worlds without lotteries) and in which Fabio plays the lottery. Note that some possible propositions are not just merely possible—they are also true in the actual world (e.g., *snow is white*). And some possible propositions are false in the actual world but true in some others (e.g., snow is blue).

You might be wondering whether or not logical possibility and metaphysical possibility are the same or equivalent notions. An example often cited to show they are not the same is: *Water is a compound, not an element*. Water *could not be* other than it is, a compound comprising hydrogen and oxygen. Thus, it is metaphysically necessary. Yet there seems to be no contradiction in saying that water is an element, that is, simple and non-compound, as Thales and other ancient natural philosophers did.[23] This distinction is perhaps not surprising. One way to think of metaphysics, as noted earlier, is as a study of the *essential nature* of things. We want to know what makes this thing what it is. Thus, we recognize metaphysical necessity as tied to the nature of things. It seems possible, however, that the nature of at least some things might have been otherwise. So, there is—at least so it seems—no logical contradiction in asserting that some metaphysical necessity might not have been.

Saul Kripke provided the framework for the semantics of several modal logics—logics of necessity and possibility. Traditional propositional logic concerns itself only with true and false; but modal logic extends the reach of logic to sentences that are *possibly* and *necessarily true* (or false).

Kripke and the Necessary a posteriori

Saul Kripke, who published his first significant essay in modal logic when he was just nineteen, has made significant contributions in modal logic, modal metaphysics, semantics and philosophy of language. One of his more interesting arguments reshaped debate about the epistemological distinction between the **a posteriori** (that which can be known only through sense-experience) and the **a priori** (that which doesn't need sense experience to be known).

Underlying this is the thought that it is a *necessary truth* that any thing is identical to itself. Or, any thing is always self-identical. I could not be other than me any more than Socrates could not have been something other than Socrates. (Leaving open the question of the appropriate referent of "Socrates"; see Chap. 8.) Thus, any "identity truth" is always necessarily true.

Kripke holds that this has an important consequence. Suppose we have two (genuine) names for the same object or the same stuff, e.g., "water" and "H_2O." But water is identical to H_2O. That is, water = H_2O. You can't be water and not also be H_2O. Since this is an identity, it's necessarily true. In the language of possible worlds, in every world where we find some stuff that is water, that stuff is H_2O.

Many philosophers pre-Kripke held that if some truth were necessary, then we could come to know it only *a priori*, just by reflecting on the proposition. After all, it could hardly be the case that experience shows us that everything is self-identical, for example. Kripke argues, however, that "water is H_2O" shows us that some necessary truths—identities that science discovers—are

23   John P. Burgess 1999, p. 81.

known *a posteriori*. We find out through experience that water is H_2O, not by simply reflecting on the concept of water. Hence, "water is H_2O" is a necessary *a posteriori* truth.

Of course, it was also held that any truth known *a priori* must be a necessary truth. Again, if some proposition is knowable *a priori*, or by reason alone, then no matter the circumstances it is true. That is, it's true in any possible world, or necessarily true. Kripke argues that there are contingent *a priori* truths: that there are some truths that are contingent (not necessary), but are known independently of experience (a priori). Descartes's famous "I think, therefore I am" is a contingent *a priori* truth. Indeed, Descartes argued that he needed no experience to know this truth; it is discoverable *a priori*. But it's merely a contingent truth that Descartes existed: it's possible (though not actual) that there is a universe without Descartes.[24]

A Few Notes on Modal Logic

Different modal logics provide different logical structures or frameworks for conceptualizing the logic of possibility and necessity. These different logics have been extensively researched. The brief notes to follow are not intended as an introduction to modal logic, but simply to give something of the flavor of those logics to readers already familiar with basic symbolic logic.

Modal logics are extensions of propositional logic (and there are *quantified modal logics*, extensions of the predicate logic). That is, in addition to the axioms of propositional calculus, various *modal axioms* will yield new theorems—new necessarily true propositions about the logical relationships between modal propositions. In addition to letters that stand for propositions and the logical operators, like conjunction or if-then, modal logic adds the box □ and the diamond ◊. These are sentence operators, necessarily and possibly, respectively. In propositional logic, we have atomic propositions, such as *p*, and compound (or molecular) propositions, such as $p \supset q$; i.e., if *p*, then *q*. We can now form the new sentence (proposition) ◊ *q*, which we read "Possibly *q*," or "It's possible that *q*." If the variable *q* stands for the sentence "Stuart stays at school," then we have "It's possible that Stuart stays at school." Or we might have the conditional or if-then sentence $p \supset q$,

---

24   See Kripke 1992; also Crumley 2009, Chap. 9.

and we can form the new sentence $\Box$ $(p \supset q)$. This modal sentence is read as "It's necessary that if p then q."

The two operators are understood as "exchangeable." That is, $\Diamond$ p—possibly p—can also be expressed as $\neg \Diamond \neg$ p. This latter formula is read as "It's not necessary that p is false." The formula $\Box \neg$ p says that it's necessary that p is always false, or p is necessarily false. What sorts of propositions are necessarily false? Self-contradictory propositions are necessarily false, but they're not the only kind of necessarily false proposition. The proposition *Water is an element* is necessarily false, but not logically false.

We can understand different modal logics as telling us which modal sentences follow or can be deduced from other propositions, given a particular set of axioms. The most basic set of modal axioms belongs to the logic system T:

1) $\Box$ $p \supset p$, which says, "If it's necessary that p, then p is true (or p is actual)."

This shouldn't seem too surprising given our earlier comments about necessary truths. A necessary truth is true in all possible worlds. The actual world is one of the possible worlds, so any necessary truth is true in the actual world. Perhaps it is obvious that if some fact is actual—it exists in this world—then it's possible. (Or: Whatever is actual is possible.)

2) $\Box$ $(p \supset q) \supset (\Box$ $p \supset \Box$ $q)$

Sometimes known as a distribution axiom, this says: if it's necessary that if p, then q, then if p is necessary (or necessarily true), then q is necessary (or necessarily true). Again this might seem intuitive once the symbols are clear. Suppose you know that some conditional, an if-then sentence, is necessarily true. That is, this conditional is true in every possible world. Then suppose further that you know that p is necessary—true in every possible world. We find the true conditional in every possible world, and we also find the antecedent of that true conditional in every possible world. Then we will find that the consequent—the q in our conditional—is true in every possible world.

Many other modal systems take these two axioms and add a "characteristic" axiom. Two of the most well-known are S4 and S5. These two systems were first formulated by Clarence Irving Lewis, who had been working on them since 1912, and in his *Symbolic Logic* of 1932, he formulated several systems, including S4 and S5. S4 adds to the two axioms of T:

3) $\Box$ $p \supset \Box$ $\Box$ p

Interestingly 3) says that any necessary proposition is necessarily so. This "iteration of necessity" says, again informally, a necessary truth can't fail to be necessary.

S5—perhaps the most frequently used modal logic—adds the following to T

4) $\Diamond p \supset \Box \Diamond p$

This formula says that if it's possible that p is true, or possibly true in the actual world, then it's necessary that p is possible. Informally: if it's possibly true, it must be possible, or a proposition is possibly true only if there's no way it's self-contradictory. It's worth noting perhaps that S5 includes S4; that is, everything that can be proved as a theorem in S4 is also a theorem in S5. But there are theorems of S5 that cannot be proved in S4. S5 is thus a "stronger" system. In fact, the characteristic axiom of S4 can be proved as a theorem in S5.[25]

Do Possible Worlds Exist?

It's possible that Jack could have been an actor. Possible worlds semantics understands this sentence as true given that *there is* at least one possible world in which Jack is an actor. Possible world semantics thus appears to commit us to the existence of possible worlds. A seemingly straightforward explanation of our modal propositions implies that possible worlds exist! I have a possible world twin—at least one!—that's an actor. What sort of things are these possible worlds?

Genuine Realism: They Are Real

The City University of New York professor, Michio Kaku, writes in one of his several books,

> I am reminded of the passage from Olaf Stapledon's classic work of science fiction, *Star Maker*, "Whenever a creature was faced with several possible courses of action, it took them all, thereby creating many... distinct histories of the cosmos."

25   G.E. Hughes and M.J. Cresswell 1968, p. 49; also Graeme Forbes 1985, p. 17.

A few lines earlier, Kaku quotes physicist Alan Guth, one of the architects of the notion of the inflationary universe: "There is a universe where Elvis is still alive." Immediately after, he quotes physicist Frank Wilczek:

> "We are haunted by the awareness that infinitely many slightly variant copies of ourselves are living out their parallel lives and that every moment more duplicates spring into existence and take up our many alternative futures."[26]

Similarly the noted physicist Sean Carroll has recently argued for the view that there are a plurality of universes.[27]

The idea of unreachable "parallel universes" or universes continually giving birth to new universes is not unique to physics and cosmology.[28] In what many find a startling claim, the philosopher David Lewis developed and defended **modal realism**. Lewis held that possible worlds are concrete worlds like our actual world. No less real, no less *concrete*, many inhabited with "**counterparts**" of you and me, just as actual from the point of view of that world, and utterly unreachable.[29] You may someday travel to the moon, but you will never travel to one of these possible worlds; the Hubble Telescope will never send back a photo to earth of one of them.

If they are wholly unreachable and unobservable, then why believe in their existence? Lewis recognized that concretely existing possible worlds would be met with suspicion. Still he held that there was a pressing reason to acknowledge their existence. Our pervasive talk of things that might have been different commits us to the existence of possible worlds:

> I believe that there are possible worlds other than the one we happen to inhabit [remember: our world is a *possible* world]. If an argument is wanted, it is this. It is uncontroversially true that things might be otherwise than they are. I believe, and so do you, that things could have been different in countless ways. But what does this mean? Ordinary language permits the paraphrase: there are many ways things could have been besides the way they actually are. On the face

---

26   Kaku 2005, p. 169.
27   Carroll 2019.
28   *Ibid.*, p. 15.
29   David Lewis 1973, 1986.

of it, this sentence is an existential quantification. It says that *there exist many entities of a certain description, to wit 'ways things could have been.'* I believe that things could have been different in countless ways; I believe permissible paraphrases of what I believe; taking the paraphrases at face value, I therefore believe in the existence of entities that might be called ... 'possible worlds.'[30]

Lewis provided a fuller account of his modal realism in his 1986 *On the Plurality of Worlds*. There are at least countably infinite many possible worlds. Some vary greatly from this world; some vary only minimally. These possible worlds are physical or spatio-temporal objects, which contain other physical objects. And in some of those worlds you and I have counterparts: the being in that possible world that is most similar to me (or you, if we are interested in your counterpart). Notice that those possible world denizens are not identical to you or me: neither of us exists in any other possible world than the actual one. No spatio-temporal object is in many places at once. Some of them are, however, close variants of their this-worldly counterparts. Here in our world, Roy and Dale have two consecutive classes in the same classroom. In this world, they remain in the same desks for the second class. In a relatively "close possible world," between classes they move from desks on one side of the room to desks on the other side. Similarly, there is at least one possible world in which "counterpart Jack" is an actor.

Lewis held that these possible worlds are of the same kind as this world. Perhaps more important is the notion of "concrete." Lewis is dubious of the abstract/concrete distinction (see Chap. 5). Instead, he notes the following: "In my modal realism, the donkeys and protons and puddles and stars that are part of this world have perfect duplicates that are parts of other worlds." Hence, "... at least some possible individuals are 'concrete'."[31]

Lewis also recognizes the need to say something about the internal structure of these worlds. He claims that the internal structure of these worlds is likely characterized by something like our spatio-temporal relations, e.g., this Potpourri Press cup was made in South Korea in 1991. We leave the details aside to consider another feature: the possible worlds are causally isolated from each other and from us. One world does not affect any other world: you can't get there from here.

---

30   Lewis 1973, p. 84; emphases added.
31   Lewis 1986, p. 82.

"Actual" is always said from *within* a world and refers only to that context of being said. From counterpart Jack's point of view, his is the actual world. Thus, Lewis claims that "actual" is an indexical, like "here" or "yesterday"—the referent of "actual" depends on the time and place of its utterance. Or, as he says, every world is actual at itself.[32] In general, an *actual world* is a world of existing concrete objects having various properties and standing in various relations to each other. Lewis thinks there are many such actual worlds. Another view (below) holds that there is only one actual world: this world.

Lewis thus rejected the idea that possible worlds are but sets of propositions. Possible worlds comprise *actual, existing* states of affairs, that is, objects and their properties. A donkey with its various properties is no set of propositions, even though there are many true propositions about the donkey.

This is a simplified account of Lewis's view. But it is enough to let us see two of the reasons Lewis held that possible worlds exist and are real, no less than *our* actual world. First, Lewis argued that talk of possible worlds has greatly expanded in clarifying philosophical issues. A second reason is that of quantification. Leaving aside technical details, commitment to the existence of possible worlds helps us explain sentences in which we talk about some or all of the various objects and their properties.

Unsurprisingly, there are a number of objections to Lewis's possible world realism. Following some of these would require deeper explanations of the logic and related issues. These are explained in some detail by John Divers in his *Possible Worlds*.[33] However, three can be addressed here.

Other possible worlds, remember, are causally isolated from us. Consequently, we cannot "see" into the distinct worlds, nor seemingly catalogue the individuals in any of those worlds. The matter appears worse: it is urged that we cannot *refer* to those world-bound, non-actual (by our lights) individuals.[34] In other words, how is it that we are able to talk about these individuals? In this world, our actual world, when Sara sees Sam enter the classroom at 10:12, she asserts correctly "Someone is late for class again." Clearly there is some justification for Sara's claim. In virtue of what, however, could Sara talk about counterpart-Sam, who managed to get to class on time (and having completed his homework)? She doesn't see him; no one points to counterpart-Sam and says, "That's Sam, the one that does his homework."

---

32   *Ibid.*, pp. 92 ff.
33   Divers 2002, Chaps. 5–9.
34   Divers 2001, Chap. 5.6; the discussion here is based on Divers.

But isn't it enough to have this description—the one that gets to class on time and does his homework? Unfortunately for the Lewis realist, there are too many such counterparts! Moreover, suppose there are lots of *indiscernible* worlds with our punctually prepared Sam. How is it that "counterpart-Sam" refers to any single (other world) individual?

But there is a way to single out a unique counterpart, the Lewis realist could respond. We already have a description in hand of the counterpart, and could further enrich this description by talking about other parts of the possible world, based on our world. (This strategy is called "recombination": combining parts of our actual world to describe some possible world.) The obstacle seems to be the possibility of multiple possible worlds that are indiscernible duplicates, yet meet the required description (e.g., a punctual, prepared Sam). Yet, it is argued on behalf of the Lewis realist, there is a reason to rule out the possibility of such duplicates, on the grounds of theoretical utility. A theory of modality that rules out the indiscernible worlds is more useful than a theory that doesn't.

So, when Sara says to Sam, "You know, it's possible for you to get to class on time ... with your homework done," the Lewis realist can insist that she succeeds in referring to a single counterpart. And in general, there is no obstacle to talking about or referring to other-worldly individuals.

A second widespread objection is the supposed irrelevance of counterparts. How, for example, does counterpart-Jack tell us anything about this-world-Jack?[35] Knowing that a counterpart of me is an actor does not obviously help me to understand the sense in which I might have been an actor. It is only by thinking about the properties I have *in this world* and the circumstances I find myself *in this world* that I really understand "could have been." It thus seems the content of the sentence "Socrates could have been foolish"—as typically understood—is not about some foolish counterpart.[36]

But this is clearly a mistaken interpretation of Lewis's counterpart theory. It is true that Lewis's strategy goes beyond our normal commonsense "possibility talk"—but in itself this is not a defect of the theory. The Lewis theoretical interpretation of modal claims about actual world Socrates and actual world Jack are about those two this-world individuals. Consider the claim that Jack could have been actor. The technical counterpart "translation" of this claim is

---

35 E.g., E.J. Lowe 2002, pp. 130–31.
36 Divers 2002, p. 129.

along the following lines. (Avoiding symbols) There is a possible world, and in that world, there is an individual that is the counterpart of Jack, and that counterpart is an actor.[37]

We can perhaps go a bit further, making use of the recombination strategy noted earlier. Thinking about me, the properties I have, and the circumstances in which I've found myself is precisely what it means to talk about real, existing concrete possible worlds. Imagine a possible world as much like this one as you wish; fill in the details of "me," and let that possible world with counterpart Jack be just like this one up to the point that he says, "Larissa, you know what? I've changed my mind; I think I will go to the audition tonight." This discussion might be carried further,[38] but perhaps this is sufficient to show that the content of counterpart-theoretic claims can be understood as relevant to our actual world individuals.

One last brief final point: How could we ever *know* about other possible worlds if we are wholly isolated from them? Based on our recognition that things could have been different, Lewis makes certain inferences. This practice is not wholly atypical. So, the short answer is: We know them because certain inferences have led to a theory, which in turn leads us to accept the existence of certain items, as we explore that theory further.[39]

The preceding does not show that Lewis's realism is our best candidate for interpreting modal claims. Perhaps, however, it shows that this robust realism about possible worlds, while widely criticized, is nonetheless defensible.

An Ersatz View: Actualism

The more widely held view about possible worlds is that they are abstract objects and it is known as **actualism**: the view that only actual things exist, with our world the only actual world. Possible worlds are actual, but they are abstract objects, not concrete, as Lewis holds. With one exception of course: our world, the actual world, is also a possible world. Here we sketch Robert Adams's view, but similar views are also held by, among others, Alvin Plantinga.[40]

---

37   *Ibid.*, p. 122 has a relevantly similar symbolization.

38   *Ibid.*, pp. 129–33.

39   For more on "modal epistemology," see Divers 2002, Chap. 9.4.

40   Adams 1974 (all page references are to Loux 1979), pp. 202–03; Plantinga 1976.

Modal Fictionalism

Modal fictionalism agrees with modal realism that possible-world theory provides a powerful explanatory resource. However, instead of thinking of these possible worlds as modal realism does, as inaccessible concrete objects, it treats our talk about possible worlds in the same way as we treat talk about fictional characters, entities, places. The sentence "Princess Leia is Luke's sister" is not "really" or strictly true. Neither is "The North Pole is the home of Santa's elves." These sentences are in fact elliptical. The former is elliptical for "According to the fiction of *Star Wars*, Luke and Leia are siblings," and the latter is elliptical for something like "According to the twentieth-century fiction of Santa Claus, he and his elves live at the North Pole."

Then how should we understand modal claims, such as "Jack might have been an actor"? In the modal fictionalism view, we treat possible worlds as fictional objects, and paraphrase accordingly. Jack's possibly having been an actor is paraphrased as "According to the fiction of possible worlds, there is a possible world in which Jack is an actor." Necessary truths are treated similarly; for example, "It is necessarily true that 2 + 3 = 5" becomes "According to the fiction of possible worlds, in every possible world '2 + 3 = 5' is true."

One advantage of modal fictionalism is that it removes the problem of understanding "in every possible world" or "there is a possible world" as apparently asserting the existence of possible worlds. We are thus able to retain the explanatory power of possible worlds, without resorting to a special type of entity. Still one might wonder about the ontological status of such fictions. It is worth noting that some argue that fictions are themselves abstract objects.[41]

Adams distinguishes two types of actualism: *hard* and *soft*. Hard actualism takes possible worlds to be fictions (see Modal Fictionalism box). Soft actualism—the view held by Adams and described in what follows—holds that possible worlds are *logical constructions* from existing objects and properties in our world. That is, we build up fully determinate possible worlds from the things and properties already in this world. In this view, our world provides "enough" to construct these abstract objects, which we identify as the possible worlds.

---

41   For analysis of a different problem, see Daniel Nolan 2016, Supplement.

As noted earlier, possible worlds are sets of propositions, which Adams identifies as *world stories*. A bit of elaboration on three points is needed. First, we don't in fact construct these world stories (possible worlds). It would be cognitively impossible for us to do so, because there are an infinite number of them, some differing in only the tiniest detail of a kind unknown to us. (Presumably, we have at least an *in principle procedure* for doing so, which Adams explains.) This limitation leaves the actualist no worse off than mathematicians, logicians, and cosmologists. When needed we can construct or at least tell enough of any chosen world story.

Second, and more difficult, is the concept of proposition. The nature of propositions is itself a topic in metaphysics, often included in surveys of the field. Briefly, there are two ways of understanding propositions. They can be understood as complexes of objects and properties, or as is sometimes said, states of affairs. (Unfortunately "states of affairs" is also variously interpreted; here we take the term to refer to arrangements of objects and properties, some of which actually are or obtain, some of which do not: "Jack is an actor" is a state of affairs, but it does not "obtain.")[42] Or they can be understood as representations of those objects.[43] If we understand them in this way, the component parts of a proposition, which function representationally, are concepts.

Lastly, as noted earlier, propositions are held to be the meanings of or what is expressed by sentences. "Snow is white" and "la neige est blanche" are two different sentences, but they have the same meaning. That is, they express the same proposition. And since propositions are linguistic items, they are *representational*. They are *about* aspects or features of the world. The proposition *that Abigail Adams wrote to John that he should "remember the ladies"* is about a particular person and her view about another person's relationship to a particular document. Alternatively we might say that it's about Abigail's relationship to a particular thought *that John should remember the ladies*.

(It is worth noting one issue, which will not be pursued here. In the actualist view, "talk about possible worlds" is in fact "talk about sets of propositions."[44] But a standard way of identifying propositions is the set of possible worlds in which they are true. Thus, we seem to have two perhaps too closely connected notions: possible worlds are sets of propositions, and propositions are sets of possible worlds in which they are true. This seems to some a bit circular.)

---

42 Mark Textor 2016.
43 Ted Parent 2018.
44 Adams 1974 (in Loux 1979), p. 204.

It is the second of these senses that is of interest to us here. Actualism (of the soft variety) views possible worlds as sets of propositions, that is, as abstract objects. But those abstract objects are wholly based on *objects, properties, and relations in this world*. Unlike the modal realist, there are no existing objects apart from this world. Again, the actualist holds the following ontological principle: to exist is to be actual. And "actual" is *not* an indexical. To exist is to be actual. Here in this world. There is no other.

The Lewis realist tells us that we should understand "Jack could have been an actor" as there is a possible world in which a counterpart of Jack is an actor. But how should we understand modal claims about individuals in the actualist view? Roderick Chisholm first introduced the problem of *transworld identification* in his "Identity through Possible Worlds: Some Questions."[45] Consider again "Jack could have been an actor." Some of the abstract object possible worlds will have as a part a concept of "Jack" that is much like Jack in the actual world. But these concepts will differ qualitatively, in virtue of the qualities assigned to them by that particular concept. Despite qualitative differences, we are tempted to say that it is the *same* individual in each world. In the actualist view, then, one Jack can be in many worlds. Compare this to Lewis realism. In the realist view, there is only one Jack, who resides in this world, and his many counterparts, *who are not the Jack in this world*, reside in other actual-indexed worlds.

Now we can see Chisholm's worry. We form conceptions of possible worlds by conceiving a variety of states of affairs or propositions describing some aspect of the world, e.g., Jack proposed to Natasha in New Orleans at the Dream Palace. If "possible world Jack" varies too greatly from actual world Jack, in virtue of what are the propositions about actual world Jack? Indeed Chisholm presented a thought experiment imagining a sequence of worlds in which the Biblical Adam and Moses exchange qualities, one step at a time until they have finally "traded places" with respect to their qualities.[46] First, suppose that Adam rather than Moses parted the Red Sea; then suppose that Moses rather than Adam lived in a garden for a time; now suppose Moses's wife was Eve... and so on. At the end of the sequence, are we still confident that we are conceiving Adam and not Moses?

---

45   Chisholm 1967.
46   *Ibid.* (in Loux 1979), p. 82.

The intuitive idea is that the individual Jack is held fixed and the circumstances vary. This seems to suggest—again, setting aside some technical but theoretically important considerations and argument—that it is a *bare fact* that we are talking about the very same Jack in each possible world. That is, no matter what other properties Jack may have, that *this* individual is Jack is primitive and unanalyzable. If we were to ask, "why is this individual in this possible world Jack?" the answer seems to be "because it is." This does not show that actualism is mistaken. Adams and others have endorsed and defended this sort of view elsewhere.[47]

It draws attention, however, to the issue of *representation* and reminds us of the worry of the relevance of counterparts in Lewis's view.[48] As this shows, both actualism and Lewis realism face the issue of how the preferred interpretation of possible worlds discourse is relevant to a particular actual world individual. And this is a pretty significant issue! Possible worlds are intended to help us understand, among other issues, how to interpret apparently simple modal claims, e.g., "Jack could have been an electrical engineer." Understanding such claims apparently is not such a simple matter after all.

This very brief—and highly "skeletalized"—account of two theories of possible worlds only highlights a few of the issues that remain topics of debate in modal metaphysics.

Key Concepts

- deflationism
- semantic conception of truth
- object language
- metalanguage
- redundancy theory
- disquotationalism
- minimalism
- satisfaction (of a predicate by a term)
- possible world
- necessarily true proposition
- possibly true proposition

---

47   E.g., Adams 1979 and 1981.
48   Lewis 1986, pp. 158 ff; see also Melia 2008, pp. 138–39 and 145.

- *a posteriori*
- *a priori*
- modal realism
- counterpart
- actualism
- modal fictionalism

Reading Questions

1. In a few sentences, explain why T-sentences are not in fact trivial. (E.g., even though "'Snow is white' is true if and only if snow is white" looks obvious, why are such T-sentences important?)
2. Is Tarski's view compatible with coherence theory and the pragmatic theory? Explain.
3. Why is "It's necessary that *p*" logically equivalent to "It's not possible that *p* is false"? Sentences such as "All bachelors are unmarried males" are considered as necessary truths, but they seem to be so because of the meaning of the terms. Can you come up with an example of a necessary truth that is not as obviously dependent on the meaning of subject and predicate?
4. What do you think is the strongest argument in favor of modal realism? What do you think is the strongest objection?
5. Write a brief essay that explains actualism and why it might be thought a better account of modal statements than modal realism.

For Further Reading

Colin McGinn 2015, Chap. 8, is a very clear, accessible presentation of Tarski's theory of truth. (Chap. 9 then explores Donald Davidson's use of Tarski to develop a truth conditional approach to meaning.)

Anil Gupta 1993 is a very accessible summary and critique of Horwich's minimalism.

Burgess and Burgess 2011 is a very helpful and rigorous presentation of deflationism and related issues such as indeterminacy, vagueness, and antirealism.

Michael P. Lynch 2009 presents and defends a theory not covered in the text (*pluralism*); he also reviews and critiques the other theories of truth.

Hughes and Creswell 1996 no doubt is still the standard introduction to modal logic. (This is a complete re-working of their original 1968 work.) This new version includes sections on contingent identity and counterpart theory.

Forbes 1985 is an excellent introduction to interpreting the notation used in modal logic and surveys several issues in modal metaphysics, developing and defending his own views.

John Divers 2002 is a readable, extensive, detailed explanation and analysis of modal realism and actualism. It is extremely helpful in understanding the issues.

CHAPTER THREE

REALISM AND ANTIREALISM

"REALISM" IS A TERM WE'VE ALREADY MET, IN CHAPTER 1. THE WORD refers to the view that there is a world of objects whose structure, properties and relations are independent of any particular set of representations of them. Beliefs, propositions, sentences, statements: are all *representational*; they are about something or have some content. Typically, reality is thought of as a "mind-independent" world, a world that is what it is, independently of our beliefs—our representations—of it.

The concern of this chapter is with this **global realism**, realism about (at least) the ordinary things that appear around us, more or less as they appear. We will also consider challenges to it. **Local realisms** concern some specific type of object or fact: e.g., about numbers—that they exist independently of our beliefs or talk about them; about ethics—that there are moral facts, objective truths. About time, about universals. And about the things scientific theories depend on for their explanations: quarks, gravitational fields, etc. (**scientific realism**). Of course, one might be a global realist in the sense above, but not a realist about universals or the existence of moral facts. It would be natural to call this global realism "metaphysical realism," but this term will have a specific use later. Instead, we simply call it *realism*.

The World of Common Sense: An Argument

"Isn't it obvious? I mean, isn't it just obvious that the world is independent of us?" The world of common sense is a mind-independent world. Various aspects of it (but not all of it) are typically experienced by means of our five senses; the world of common sense is an observable world. Oh, occasionally we might look at something indirectly, via images in a microscope or a telescope. But the objects that we encounter generally are objects that are "available" to us through perception: we see, taste, touch, hear, feel, smell a world comprising myriad objects and their properties. Sometimes those objects are described as medium-sized objects, in the sense that they are larger than very small things like viruses, and smaller than very large things like galaxies. But they may range in size and character from very small ants to very large elephants to rivers and mountains.

But it's obvious that the world of common sense is also a world of artifacts, objects conceived, designed, and constructed by people. From a tiny transistor to a cell phone to a car to the Golden Gate Bridge to the Eiffel Tower: these artifacts are also part of the world. Of course, those objects would not be part of the world were it not for human conscious intervention, so they are not (in a sense) mind-independent. But once in existence, they have certain features or properties, we think, in and of themselves. Some reject this idea that artifacts should be included in our notion of realism, but some have argued that artifacts should be seen as part of reality.[1] As already noted, the "in and of itself" is central to the mind-independence of the commonsense world. Before the first sighting by a human being (and after that), an object, its nature and properties, were there.

So before an object is first sighted by some human being (and after that), the nature and properties of the object are already there, independently of being observed. For example, Morro Bay Rock possessed its nature and properties prior to anyone seeing it. Its size and shape—which prompted Juan Cabrillo

---

1   Michael Devitt 1991 excludes consideration of artifacts. See Amie L. Thomasson 2003 for a sustained defense of "human kinds"—artifacts (and institutions) that result from human invention—as falling within the scope of realism.

in 1542 to name it "El Morro"—are there, possessed by the rock, independent of being observed by anyone.

So far, we have approached the "world of common sense" as if no one had doubts about it. We know, however, that some have raised questions about such a world. Most of this chapter will look at some of those questions. Here we might look at what is likely the principal strategy for arguing for a realist view of the world of common sense. That strategy is an instance of the *argument to the best explanation*.

An argument to the best explanation asks of a particular phenomenon "what would best explain this?" Consider for a moment what is perhaps a *tiny bit* controversial, an argument to the conclusion that American astronauts walked on the moon in 1969. This is the best explanation of the images that we on earth saw on TV. Two rival explanations of those images are available. The first is that somewhere on a sound stage, "the government" and its operatives created a facsimile of a landing, filmed it, and broadcast that filmed facsimile. The other is that the landing *really* occurred. And the latter is the better explanation, because it's simpler, there seems to be much more evidence for it, and it fits with other things we accept. It is the best explanation available, so it should be taken as true.

Can we appeal to a best explanation argument for commonsense realism? One of the first things we might notice is that our experiences show a good deal of agreement with each other—as if they indicate objects that are requisitely independent of us. Different persons at different times usually rapidly come to an agreement about the type of object and its characteristics. George and Bert, for example, both see and agree that there is an oak tree in a certain location, having certain characteristics, e.g., that it's several feet in circumference, that it's surrounded by a large snow drift, that there is a car "plowed into it," even though their individual perspectives on or experiences of the tree vary significantly. The independent existence of this oak tree is the best explanation for this agreement.

In addition, our "multimodal experiences" suggest independent objects that are responsible for these experiences.[2] Not only do I have a visual experience of the cup of coffee, but I also have a tactile experience of the cup, and olfactory and gustatory experiences of the coffee. These experiences "coalesce"

---

2   See, for example, Paul Thagard 2010, pp. 72–76. Thagard's general aim is a bit different than here.

around this cup. And the cup—as an independent object with its own intrinsic properties—*explains* the organizational structure of my experience.

Immediate experience and identification, nevertheless, still might be held to be consistent with the non-existence of independent objects, or of their properties, as experienced. But consider what happens when we *learn* about those objects: the new facts that we become aware of are not implicit in our initial representations. And we find that objects have—as near as we can tell from our beliefs—unexpected properties. It has been suggested that this is the first step away from common sense toward science. Leaving science aside for the moment, consider for example the stellar constellation Orion. Yes, we determine that this arrangement of stars is "Orion." But that these stars pass westward during the spring and summer months seems *independent* of our initial representations. Nor is there any *a priori* reason to suspect that our beliefs are such that the stars Betelgeuse and Rigel will move westward in such a coordinated fashion.

A little closer to home. Many of us learned early on that water not only becomes solid as it freezes, but also expands. The expansion itself is surprising; most liquids contract as they are cooled.[3] But our experience reveals something else—frozen water is "lighter" or less dense than warmer water, and thus the ice floats. (Thus, explaining why ice forms on the top of a lake: the frozen water from deeper in the lake floats to the surface.)

These rather ordinary observations serve to underwrite a view of an *independent* world. Unexpected but regular behaviors of objects suggest that there is something more to those objects than our beliefs about them—if what the "facts" are is up to me, it seems I wouldn't be so often surprised by what they turn out to be. Our epistemic position with respect to the world provides the basis for an inference to the best explanation argument that leads to a metaphysical conclusion:

1. Our experiences of objects and their properties exhibit a stability and regularity across contexts, from one individual to another and within the different modes of experience of a single individual.

---

3   Masakazu Matsumoto 2009 offers a recent theoretical but accessible explanation for this surprising fact.

2. In addition, our experiences of objects and their properties often reveal surprising or unexpected facts about those objects, facts that appear to be independent of our initial beliefs about those objects.

3. The best explanation—the simplest and most comprehensive explanation—of our experiences of these objects is that such objects are both objective—accessible from different perspectives and contexts—and independent of our beliefs.

4. So, we ought to conclude that there is a real world, a world comprising entities, properties that are objective, independent of, and external to us. That is, we should be commonsense realists.

Unsurprisingly best explanation arguments are thought by some to be faulty. Whether or not some explanation is simple or comprehensive is itself in need of justification. (We will see something like this later in the chapter.) This is a legitimate issue that raises many complications. Still this best explanation argument perhaps serves to provide a more detailed account of the commonsense reaction "Isn't it obvious that these objects don't depend on us?"

Scientific Realism

Modern theoretical science occasions revisions to our commonsense view of the world. From the very large to the very small, we acquire a new conception of the relation between the sun and the earth or a new understanding of the structure of the atomic and subatomic world. Science tells us "The world *appears* that way, but in *reality* it is like this." Yet science and common sense are often interleaved, as indicated by explanations of the nature of rainbows, or the boiling and freezing of water, or the static electricity encountered when removing clothes from a dryer. Science provides "microstructural" explanations, which rely on entities that are typically not part of our commonsense experience—theoretical entities. And these explanations invite the obvious question: what reason do we have for thinking that these unexperienced entities are real, that they are objective and independent of our representations?

Scientific realism is a topic much discussed by both scientists and philosophers of science. Here it is possible only to consider a small part of that discussion. Intuitively the idea is that scientific theories aim to tell us the truth about the world. How do they do that? Scientists invoke or appeal to theoretical entities. Thus, we can think of scientific realism as the view that scientific theories contain terms that refer to or designate entities and their properties and relations, and these exist and are independent of our representations of them.

Michael Devitt, one of the principal proponents of scientific realism, offers a slightly qualified version. His version refers to *most* of the *essential* entities, along with their properties, in our *well-established* scientific theories.[4] This qualification reminds us that realists are not committed to the view that scientific theories are always completely right; even the best science gets things wrong. But the realist contends that in general and for the most part, scientific theorizing provides an accurate picture of the world.

Two points need minor clarifications. (1) Theoretical entities are often associated with *unobservable* entities. The distinction between observable and unobservable is itself debated by theorists. Here, however, there is no harm in identifying the notions of unobservable and theoretical, and relying on our intuitive sense of "unobservable." (2) We have so far been using the term "entity" rather than "object." This merely highlights the fact that contemporary theory sometimes appeals to "things" that seem a little different from our ordinary objects. For example, the magnetic field that surrounds magnets is represented mathematically as a vector field, a type of mathematical structure. It is quite unlike ordinary objects like rocks and cabbages. Such details aside, so long as we understand that the "objects" of science may differ from what we ordinarily think of as objects, there is no harm in thinking of theoretical terms referring to objects and their properties.

With these clarifications in mind, here is a gloss of scientific realism. Science aims at truth, and that aim is reflected in its theories. (Theorists disagree about whether or not a particular view of the nature of truth is an essential part of scientific realism.)[5] These theories are groups of interrelated (sometimes complicated and abstract) sentences. And these sentences purport to tell us about what's out there in the world, what types of objects are out there, and about their properties. That theories use specific terms to designate or refer to objects thus connects scientific realism with the notion of truth.[6] A theory enables us to explain some phenomenon. Appealing to some theory as a basis for our explanation works because the theory essentially gets it right. The theory

---

4   Michael Devitt 2006, p. 102.
5   Cp. Devitt 1989 and Psillos 2000.
6   Psillos 2000, p. 707.

is generally correct or right precisely because its terms refer to real things. "Real things": objects and their properties that exist and are independent of our representations of them.[7] This gloss gives us a clue as to how to defend scientific realism: scientific theories generally get it right: They are successful!

I wear a wristwatch, which I've had for some time. I never have to wind it, yet it keeps time extremely accurately. Every three years or so, I take it to my jeweler, who replaces the old battery with a new one. How does this quartz crystal watch succeed in doing this? Richly described theoretical details are readily available, should you be interested; it suffices to point out that passing a small electric current through a quartz crystal causes that crystal to oscillate—vibrate—at an exact number of times per second. Every second. 32,768 times per second, but who's counting? Well, the watch is; by "counting" the oscillations, it "knows" when a second has passed, then making the second hand move. This is perhaps one of the more mundane applications of the success of scientific theory. But still a success.

The Success Argument

The *success argument* for scientific realism holds that a realistic attitude toward the theoretical entities of science is the only plausible explanation for the success of science. In one formulation of the argument, it is suggested that the success of science is *miraculous* unless we are realists, unless we take the theoretical entities of science to exist independently of us.[8] The success argument for scientific realism is likely the principal argument for and likely the most widely discussed argument concerning scientific realism.

The no-miracles version of the success argument can be elaborated further. It assumes of course that "miracle explanations" are no explanations at all, since they leave the "how" wholly unexplained. Genuine explanations bring understanding. To understand why something happened we need to know the entities and properties responsible for the occurrence of the phenomenon. By citing the unobservable objects and their properties, we say *how* some phenomenon occurred. When a theory fails to identify the "responsible parties," when it doesn't tell us the *how*, that theory might well

---

7   Cf. Psillos 2000, §2.
8   See Hilary Putnam 1979, pp. 72–73; see also Anjan Chakravartty 2017; Stathis Psillos 2000.

be discounted. Alfred Wegner, for example, first argued for continental drift in the early part of the twentieth century. In his view, around 245 million years ago, Africa, Europe, and the Americas formed a "super continent," Pangea. Drift over millions of years separated the continents into those we recognize today. Yet Wegner was unable to explain the *how*, what entities or properties accounted for this drift. The "realist explanation" was not yet complete.

The theory was not accepted until the 1960s, when scientists acknowledged the shifting of tectonic plates and the "spreading" of the ocean floors, as magma flows upward through cracks in the earth's crust. Without this appeal to tectonic plates or seafloor spreading, drift would be inexplicable—miraculous. We are able to explain continental drift because the theory appeals to real entities: tectonic plates.

We should further notice that the success of science is closely tied to the *truth* of its theories. At a minimum, the truth of a theory depends on its key or central theoretical terms referring to or designating entities in the environment. The term "electron," for example, refers to a particular kind of entity. So, our scientific statements are true because they identify certain features or aspects of the world. Admittedly our understanding of the electron has changed since it was first introduced, but the realist maintains that electrons exist. Were it not for the reality of electrons and their properties, we would lose our explanation for multiple phenomena, including ubiquitous and familiar phenomena, such as electricity or chemical bonding and the formation of molecules.

Although scientific realism holds that terms "match up" with entities or properties in the world, scientific realism does not require a correspondence theory of truth. Someone who holds a coherence theory of truth may nonetheless be a scientific realist, as is, for example, Paul Thagard. Recall that the central difference between those two views of truth lies in their differing account of truth conditions, not in whether or not the terms refer to real, existing entities.

The success argument then turns on the connection between realism and truth and the assumption that any non-realist explanation is really no explanation at all. Philosophy of science explores these and related issues in considerable detail. While the details won't be fully explored here, it is important to provide some sense of the kind of non-realist view the success argument has in mind.

Instrumentalism

Instrumentalism in the philosophy of science is the view that scientific theories provide us with conceptual or formal clarity, and prediction. This can hardly be denied; but for instrumentalists, this is the only aim of science. Theories are primarily instruments for prediction, thus enabling us to "manage" the phenomena. Instrumentalism thus denies that scientific theories are linguistic or mathematical pictures of reality; their theoretical terms don't pick out independently existing entities. They're counted as successful only on the basis of their conceptual clarity and prediction ability.

In some areas of science, such as quantum theory, it's been suggested that we should treat theories as tools and not necessarily as descriptions of reality. The "objects" that, it seems, quantum theory postulates are very strange indeed: neither here nor there, without location until observed, for example. Can these be real objects? Richard Feynman, Nobel laureate in physics, remarked of quantum theory, "The best we can do is describe what happens in the mathematics, in equations, and that's very difficult. What is even harder is trying to decide what the equations mean."[9] David Mermin, a prominent physics professor, has summarized this instrumentalist—that is, non-realist—version of quantum theory with the pithy "Shut up and calculate." Mermin's idea is that we should view the equations of quantum theory as enabling our ability to make predictions about what we will experience next. This attitude toward theories as predictive and calculative tools is characteristic of instrumentalism. Holding to an instrumentalist view, however, does not imply that one holds that there is no "world beneath" our everyday experience. Niels Bohr, often characterized as instrumentalist, acknowledged the existence of a quantum world, but held that we will likely need to revise our understanding of the relationship between the everyday and quantum worlds.[10]

This perhaps suggests two further points. Realists insist that the aim of science is explanations that rely on theories that are true, or closer to the truth. The non-realist or instrumentalist is instead claiming that we gain an understanding of the world when we see that the mathematical aspects of a theory allow us to predict or account for the experienced phenomena. We recognize and understand the phenomena to the extent that they are

---

9   Feynman 2015, p. 329.
10   Ball 2018, p. 84 ff.

connected or covered by applications of one or more mathematical structures. (We will see something like this in Michael Dummett's view.) The further insistence, the non-realist might claim, on maintaining that science also provide a true picture of the world—and that this is the primary sense of "explanation" or "understanding"—is an addendum to science, a *metaphysical* addendum. It is worth noting that some hold there is not always a clear line between the "science aspects" of a theory and the metaphysical aspects of that theory.

The non-realist might further observe that science has for some time readily made use of theories without knowing *why* they apply to the world. Modern science is sometimes described as the "mathematicization of nature." Yet no one has convincingly explained why it is that mathematics is indeed the language of nature. Eugene Wigner raises precisely this issue in the interestingly titled "The *Unreasonable* Effectiveness of Mathematics in the Natural Sciences" (emphasis mine).[11] Mathematical theories, e.g., non-Euclidean geometries, developed long before their physical applications became apparent. Wigner mentions in particular aspects of topology and complex numbers as important in the formulation of quantum theory. Why should that be? Wigner in fact thinks that there is something virtually miraculous about the application of mathematics to the natural world; he notes it is a "wonderful gift we neither understand nor deserve." But the mathematics "works" in articulating and explaining the phenomena. And the suggested, somewhat speculative point here is that the non-realist can claim that the "true aim" of science is still a matter to be settled and has not yet been decided against the instrumentalist.

Perhaps a better way to understand the relevance of this issue is this. To the extent that the success argument depends on inference to the best explanation, it looks like the argument *assumes* the connection between a theory referring to really existing objects and success. But this connection is what is at issue, claims the critic.

Matters about reference (and success) we will see in more detail in subsequent sections. For the moment, consider that the critic holds that the history of science at the very least leaves open the alleged connection of reference to real entities. There can be success without a theory referring to real entities. For example, it is argued that the chemical ether theories of the first half of the nineteenth century were successful. James Clerk Maxwell, one of the

---

11   Wigner 1960.

century's most celebrated physicists, in fact claimed that existence of the ether was "better confirmed than any other chemical entity in [physical science]."[12] Thus, there is legitimate reason to doubt the connection between real entities and success. Yet the realist needs precisely that connection in order to support the best explanation of the success argument.

While there is more to be said about scientific realism, one further challenge to the view should be noted. Some critics of standard scientific epistemology in general and scientific realism in particular claim that even rocks, trees, and, yes, even the moon are *constructions* by theorists. For example, Sandra Harding, known for her contributions in epistemology, philosophy of science, and feminist theory, claims the following:

> [I]n fact scientists never can study the trees, rocks, planetary orbits, or electrons that are "out there" and untouched by human concerns.... Trees, rocks, planetary orbits, and electrons always appear to natural scientists only as they are *already socially constituted* for the social scientist.... Scientists never observe nature apart from such traditions [discussions by earlier generations of scientists].[13]

Constructivism (or social constructivism) is extremely controversial. It will suffice to note that of the many criticisms, it is argued that social constructivism cannot explain the causal interactions that we want science to explain. Fortunately, that issue need not be settled here. It is to the broader issue of realism and reference and truth that we now turn.

Richard Rorty and Pragmatism

In his important and controversial *Philosophy and the Mirror of Nature*, Richard Rorty wrote:

> To see keeping a conversation going as a sufficient aim of philosophy, to see wisdom as consisting in the ability to sustain a conversation, is to see human beings as generators of new descriptions rather than beings one hopes to be able to describe

---

12   E.g., Larry Laudan 1986, Chap. 5, esp. pp. 112–15.
13   Harding 1993, p. 64; emphasis added.

accurately. To see the aim of philosophy as truth—namely, the
truth about the terms which provide ultimate commensuration
for all human inquiries and activities—is to see human beings
as objects rather than subjects....

In eschewing truth—Truth with a capital "T"—as the aim of philosophy,
Rorty turns to pragmatism as an understanding of how we should view
human beings in their relationship to each other and the world. Thus, Rorty
shuns the rivalry between traditional theories of truth and their consequent
views about realism. Essential to Rorty's pragmatism are several interrelated
claims. First and perhaps foremost, there is no revelatory theory of truth.
There is no deep property of truth awaiting discovery by some theorist of
truth. Consequently, there is no relationship "being made true." Closely
related to this is the thought that we should stop seeking "the world as it
is in itself"; once we let that go, we will let go the debate over realism,
both about truth and the world. More generally, there aren't deep *metaphysical* facts or essences to be discovered about a host of long-disputed
philosophical topics. Rorty thinks, for example, that there is no clear line
between fact and value, nor any clear line between our moral inquiries
and our scientific inquiries. Philosophy, morality, art, science are rooted
in human experience and thus—following James—in our interests and
our goals. Hence, as the quotation at the outset maintains, the aim of
philosophy should be to "keep the conversation going." Rorty adverts to
the hermeneutical tradition in understanding this keeping the conversation
going—that we are cooperatively trying to see how it all hangs together.

   This is only to indicate the lines of Rorty's thinking, not the arguments
he employs. Yet one argument is very similar to that employed by classical
pragmatism. Both Rorty and the early pragmatists think that the inability of
centuries of debate to advance toward some conclusion is at least evidence
that something is wrong with the underlying assumptions of the philosophical
rivalries. The turn to pragmatism, in their view, is not the way to *resolve* those
disputes, but to turn away from them.

For more see Rorty 1972; 1976; 1982, especially the Introduction; 1986; and
1999, especially Part II. An excellent introduction to Rorty is Alan Malachowski
2002.

Dummett's Verificationist Antirealism

The British philosopher Michael Dummett (1925–2011) proposed two new ways to think about the realism debate. First, he held that the many different debates falling under the term "realism" likely have no single feature in common. He held nonetheless that there is a uniform and productive approach to the disparate "local realism" debates.[14] Whether we are talking about the reality of time or realism about mathematics, there is a "method" for thinking about these issues.

His second and most important and lasting contribution regarding local realisms is that we should treat these as *semantic* issues. That is, we should approach these *metaphysical* questions as *questions about meaning and truth*. The beginning of this chapter characterizes commonsense and scientific realism as claims about the kinds of objects and the properties they have. Dummett's own approach is to claim that we have a clearer grasp of the issue if we first consider our understanding of the meaning of particular disputed claims and the way in which we think about those claims as true or false.

To be a realist, according to Dummett, is to be committed to the idea that all particular declarative sentences are true or false (i.e., the realist holds the **bivalence principle**). All of them are *objectively* true (or false) even though there is no possible **verification** (determination of their truth or falsity), now or in the future; indeed the truth (or falsity) of these sentences may be in principle unknowable.[15] Alternatives to this realism might be that unverifiable sentences are neither true nor false, or that they lack meaning. Dummett holds that realism is thus committed to the possibility of the existence of "verification-transcendent" sentences. Realists differ, however, on whether or not these assertions have their truth-value by virtue of the existence of (unperceivable) objects thought to be implied by those assertions. This is a matter of metaphysics; but because realism does not involve having one or the other position, realism is, according to Dummett, not a metaphysical position. The essence of realism is the position that every assertion is true or false, even those with no possibility of testing. Truth or falsity, then, for the realist, is something independent of verifiability. This is a position about meaning, truth, and verification, not a metaphysical position.

---

14   Dummett 1978, pp. xxx ff, and "Realism" (same volume), pp. 145–65.
15   Dummett 1963/1978, p. 146.

As Bernhard Weiss notes, if we were only concerned about what entities exist, we would miss this feature.[16] Realists and antirealists disagree about the *conditions under which we are entitled to say that a certain type of sentence is true.* We might frame the point of contention in this way: "What could it mean to say that some sentence is determinately true or false when we are in no position to verify its truth or falsity?" Dummett thus brings out a feature of the realism debates not previously noticed.

As already mentioned, Dummett's concern is with local realism; four areas are of particular concern: the reality of the past, subjunctive conditionals, mathematical sentences, and, related, sentences about the "unsurveyable domains," as he calls them. Subjunctive conditionals are sometimes called "contrary to fact conditionals." Subjunctive conditionals are sentences such as "If Fabio had left ten minutes earlier, he would have caught the express bus" or "If Felicia had known there was a golf course nearby, she would have brought her clubs." Such sentences look like ordinary "if-then" sentences. But they are "declaring" that something would have occurred if facts had been different. And "unsurveyable domains" refers to the impossibility of finding out whether some event or occurrence will ever occur. Dummett uses the example, "A statue will never be built here." Notice the occurrence of "never" in the sentence: the sentence asserts an alleged truth about a specific location, and that truth is claimed to hold for a never-ending sequence of times. Hence, we can never "survey" this location into the never-ending future to see whether or not a statue is built at this spot.

An alternative way of expressing the realist position is that given any sentence in one of these contested areas, there is a *fact of the matter* about the truth or falsity of the sentence. There is a fact of the matter *even though we may never be in a position to know or tell whether the sentence is true.* According to Dummett, these are *undecidable* sentences for which there is no way for us to decide the truth-value of the sentences. Undecidable or verification-transcendent sentences bring us to the significance of a theory of meaning realism.

Meaning and Verification

In Dummett's view, the realist ties the meaning of sentences to their truth conditions. Understanding a sentence, knowing its meaning is understanding

---

16   Weiss 2002, p. 51.

A statue will never be drawn here.

the conditions under which that sentence is true. For the realist, then, what is it to grasp the meaning of a sentence, such as "sugar is sweet"? It is to recognize or grasp that *sugar being sweet* is the feature of the world. Samantha thus knows what "le sucre est doux" means if she knows that the sentence is true if and only if sugar is sweet. And we might say that she *understands* the French sentence precisely because she knows its truth conditions.

Now the realist, remember, holds that the truth conditions are objective and mind-independent. Thus, for the realist, every sentence is *determinately* true or false. There is a fact of the matter about the truth (or falsity) of any declarative sentence, *even though there is no way in principle to determine whether it is true*. Realism is a commitment to views about meaning and truth.

Dummett, however, holds a verificationist view of meaning: we understand a sentence if we are able to recognize the conditions that would verify a sentence, or justify a person in asserting that sentence. He frequently calls this *justificationist semantics*. In his view an adequate theory of meaning should also provide us with a theory of *understanding*. That is, we should be able to say what it is for any competent speaker to *understand* a sentence. "To understand an expression," Dummett says, "is to know what it means, that is, to grasp its meaning."[17] But there is something more as well. Dummett insisted that understanding a sentence consists in being able to recognize whether that sentence is indeed true.

It is not difficult to see the move from connecting meaning and truth conditions to Dummett's idea of understanding. If one knows the meaning, one knows the truth conditions. If one knows the truth conditions, then one knows—that is, understands—what the world would look like were those conditions to obtain. So, understanding a sentence is knowing under what circumstances the sentence would be true or false.[18] Alternatively, we understand a sentence only if we could determine the truth or falsity of that sentence were we placed in suitable circumstances. Samantha understands "the tea is sweet" only if she understands *when that sentence is correctly assertible* or that she is warranted in making the claim.[19] Both meaning and truth must be seen as epistemically constrained.

Thus Dummett is an antirealist—disagreeing with what he takes to be the central views of realism, on the matters of meaning, verification, and truth. He writes:

The conflict between realism and antirealism is thus a conflict about the kind of meaning possessed by sentences of the disputed class.

---

17   Dummett 2006, p. 15.

18   A reviewer's suggestion helped to clarify this point.

19   *Ibid.*, p. 57.

For the *antirealist* an understanding of such a sentence consists in knowing what counts as evidence adequate for the assertion of the sentence, and the truth of a sentence can consist only in the existence of such evidence.[20] (emphasis added)

For the verificationist there is a range of undecidable sentences. We cannot determine then whether we are justified in asserting them. So, for the verificationist, *it makes no sense to say that such sentences have a determinate truth-value.* Hence, the bivalence principle is false. The realist contends, however, that there is a fact of the matter as to whether or not such sentences are true. That fact of the matter is given by the truth conditions of the sentence. The sentence is true if those conditions exist. Consider for a moment this sentence: There is intelligent life outside the visible universe. There is no way in principle that we could ever determine whether that sentence is true. For the Dummettian antirealist, there is no fact of the matter about the sentence. Not so the realist. There's a reality "out there," independent of us. We can't tell if the sentence is true. But it has a truth-value nonetheless.

Might not someone defend the realist view by appealing to some superhuman intelligence? Dummett addressed precisely this in his Gifford Lectures. First consider the following sentence. Suppose in 1947, Sam claims "The Pyramids of Giza are visible from outer space." Although neither Sam nor anyone else (at the time) perhaps could imagine being appropriately placed to make such a claim, there were circumstances (and indeed are, given the right camera equipment) that would show that the sentence is justifiably asserted.[21] Presumably realist and antirealist might agree about the sentence. Now consider the sentence "A statue will never be built here." There is no circumstance that would allow us to determine whether such a sentence is correctly assertible. The sentence is not about some distantly future time. There is no circumstance, no time, that surveys the unending extent of the referred to times. But couldn't God, or some being with superhuman cognitive powers survey this unending sequence of moments? Dummett claims that he is unable to make sense of such a suggestion. It's not that our powers are deficient, he argues; it's that *no sense can be given to the idea of an unending task being completed.*[22]

---

20   Dummett 1978, p. 155.
21   See NASA's website of images of earth from space, https://visibleearth.nasa.gov/view.php?id=79253
22   *Ibid.*, p. 71.

Surely, however, we understand such sentences. We do so, Dummett claims, by extrapolating from decidable cases, from more easily surveyable to perhaps more complicated. "Tomorrow we will go to the zoo," promise your parents. Or "When you're older, you will understand," they hint. These sorts of cases provide us with the means for grasping the *sense* of the more problematic sentences. The suggestion is that we extrapolate from our ability in these decidable cases to the undecidable ones. But here is what extrapolation will not do: it won't determine the truth-value of undecidable sentences. There is "no legitimate notion of truth" in such cases.[23] It is this that brings us to the notion of a mind-independent reality.

Having identified the source of the dispute between realist and antirealist views on meaning, there is a new question. For the antirealist to press the case against realism, there must be some reason for accepting a verificationist semantics rather than a realist theory of meaning. Dummett has two explicit challenges to a realist theory of meaning, the acquisition challenge and the manifestation challenge.[24] Here we focus on the acquisition challenge. Framing these "challenges" is the idea that claims of understanding depend upon the *behaviors* of a person, especially verbal behavior. Those behaviors include when the person asserts a sentence or how that sentence is used in inferences. Deirdre's claim to understand that Caesar crossed the Rubicon in 49 BCE is most certainly in doubt if she also sincerely insists that several eyewitnesses have posted videos of the event on YouTube.

Importantly Dummett claims that, given the theory of meaning, "it must be comprehensible how we could come to acquire such an understanding of our language."[25] This is the acquisition challenge that Dummett holds that the realist about truth and meaning cannot meet. In his essay "The Reality of the Past," he calls the antirealist argument a "very strong one":

> ... [T]he process by which we came to grasp the sense of sentences of the disputed class, and the use which we subsequently made of the disputed class, are such that we could not derive from it any notion of what it would be for such a sentence to be true independently of the sort of thing we have learned to recognise as establishing the

---

23   *Ibid.*, p. 91.
24   The "challenge" terminology is Bob Hale 1997, pp. 275 ff.
25   Dummett 1978, p. 155.

truth of such sentences.... In the very nature of the case, we could not possibly have come to understand what it would be for the sentence to be true independently of that which we have learned to treat as establishing its truth: there simply was no means by which we could have shown this.[26]

Understanding a sentence requires an explanation of how we "learned to recognize" those circumstances that make the sentence true. We have been "trained," Dummett says, to see or recognize the circumstances that "conclusively justify" the assertion of some sentence. (In other words, Dummett accepts "warranted in asserting" rather than *conclusively* justified.) But the realist claims that the truth conditions of some sentences are verification-transcendent. It is then mysterious, the antirealist responds, how we could have learned to recognize whether those conditions obtain. Why would we say "these are the truth conditions" if those conditions play no role in our learning or using the sentence?[27]

In Dummett's view, there is a second significant consequence for the realism debate. There are sentences—undecidable sentences—of which it makes no sense to say that they have a truth-value. The realist, remember, is committed to every (declarative) sentence being either true or false. This follows from the realist's claim that every sentence has an *objective, mind-independent* truth-value and the bivalence principle. The manifestation challenge claims that we could have never learned to recognize the appropriate circumstances for asserting an undecidable sentence. Meaning and truth thus depend on the verification or justification conditions. When there are no truth conditions for a sentence, it makes no sense—in the antirealist's view—to say that the sentence is determinately true or false. The sentences have no truth-value. There is no fact of the matter about the sentence's truth or falsity. This is antirealism. The *real* extends only as far as our verification abilities take us.

Nor can we save this mind-independent reality by appealing to some superhuman intelligence that can "see" the truth-value of such sentences. The problem is simply pushed back one step. Imagine that some superhuman intelligence sees the truth conditions for a sentence, and sees that they are satisfied (or not). But it would be impossible for us to tell that this has happened.

---

26   Dummett 1978, p. 362.
27   See Hale 1997, p. 275.

Some responses to the acquisition challenge are worth considering.

Consider past tense sentences, e.g., "You had breakfast this morning." This is *beyond verification*; that is, there is no *present* fact about the world that satisfies its truth conditions. We of course want to take those dirty dishes in the sink as evidence for the truth of the sentence, but that does not give truth conditions for the sentence itself. In ordinary cases, the realist can appeal to the "truth-value link." Imagine Lisel says in September of 2017, "I am stranded in Miami." A year later Larissa says that Lisel was stranded in Miami. Because of the truth-value connection between present and past tense sentences, it makes sense—the realist claims—to call the past tense sentence true.[28] The realist is claiming that our command of present tense sentences implicitly contains the *connection* between the present tense and the truth of past tense sentences. Learning the language, in particular learning how truth applies to present tense sentences, already leads one to see how truth applies to past tense sentences.[29] But as Bob Hale points out, this is not a general solution to the problem. Even if this provides meaning and truth conditions for sentences about the past, it does not seem to give a definite truth-value to "A city will never be built here." (The view that sentences about the future, even ordinary ones like "Fred will be here before 3 pm," now have no truth-value, may be a bit surprising, but, for various reasons we will not go into here, has been held by numerous philosophers.)

Setting this drawback aside, there is another problem with the truth-value link idea. The present and past tensed sentences about Lisel being stranded in Miami both involve truth conditions that are "detectable." But this is not quite the antirealist acquisition challenge. That challenge is how do we explain a past tense sentence as *true now* when we are unable to recognize whether the conditions of its truth obtain. Dummett suggests that we remove all the witnesses, all the evidence that shows that the present tense sentence in 2017 "Lisel is stranded in Miami" is true. How then do we understand applying "true" to that sentence? But that is our predicament with respect to Larissa's past tensed sentence. Indeed that is our problem with an entire class of sentences about the past, e.g., "Shakespeare's last thought was about the face of the woman who inspired the character of Juliet." The realist holds that this sentence is determinately either true or false—even though we don't—and can't—know which.

---

28   Dummett 1969/1978, p. 363.
29   See Hale 1997, pp. 276–77.

There is a fact of the matter. But to the antirealist this makes no sense. These sentences have no truth-value, according to the antirealist.[30]

In his John Dewey Lectures, Dummett seems to moderate his position, which might be characterized as follows. The *real* includes the content of Shakespeare's last thought. Still there is no sense to saying that the sentence is determinately true or false. This is perhaps reminiscent of the coherence theorists considered in the previous chapter. Our best notion of truth and meaning may still consist in verification conditions, even though *the real* "contains more" than the content of the set of true sentences available to us.[31] Interestingly, however, Dummett also asserts that parts of reality may be indeterminate. And he suggests that God's logic might be "three valued," (true, false, and undetermined) precisely because reality is indeterminate.[32]

Before we leave Dummett's antirealism, we might ask one further realist question about the world and the distant past. Doesn't the progress of science give us information about the world as it is *in itself*? Dummett argues that science presents us with ever more abstract mathematical models. And it does so *without* telling us how things are in themselves. Try to frame the idea of a world as it is in itself, and we keep running up against a reality essentially mediated by our concepts. Strip away those concepts, strip away the language and "barren mathematical models" are the inevitable result.[33] We can't give a sense to the idea of a mind-independent reality. Thus, Dummett's semantic antirealism—his verificationist semantics—leads to antirealist conceptions of truth and reality: "The conception of 'the world as it is in itself' collapses because, of our own resources, we can give no substance to the expression 'like' as it occurs in the question 'What is the world like in itself?'"[34]

Putnam's Internal Realism

During the two decades from the 1970s to the 1990s, Hilary Putnam was one of the foremost advocates of **internal realism**: the concepts of truth and reference have their application only within a language or theory; truth

---

30 Dummett 1969/1978, pp. 363 ff. and Hale 1997, pp. 276–77; see also Dummett 2006, pp. 90–91.

31 Dummett 2013, Chap. 5.

32 *Ibid.* and Dummett 2006, Chap. 8 ("God and the World").

33 Dummett 2006, pp. 97–99.

34 *Ibid.*, p. 98.

and reference are always *relative to* a conceptual scheme or theory. Internal realism opposes *metaphysical realism*, which Putnam describes as committed to three distinct but related theses: (1) the world consists of a fixed "totality" of mind-independent objects; (2) there is one true theory about this world; (3) truth is some sort of correspondence between expressions and the already structured, mind-independent objects.[35] This "one true theory" view Putnam also refers to as the "received view," especially when it is used to characterize scientific realism; in addition, he refers to it as "external realism." The defining characteristic of this external or metaphysical realism is that our expressions—by means of some notion of correspondence—are true, and we are thus in contact with the already structured, mind-independent world. "Already structured" objects have their characteristics or properties *independently of how we think of them*, and objects are of a particular type in virtue of those properties. Putnam thus calls the world of metaphysical realism a "ready-made world"; that is, the world's objects have their nature and function independently of our inquiry and theories. We discover—we don't constitute—the world via our representations of it. His internal realism opposes this idea of a ready-made world. (Putnam's 1981 lecture is entitled "Why There Isn't a Ready-Made World.")

Putnam wants to show that we are not entitled to claim that our language, which we can think of as a theory, uniquely puts us in touch with an already made, mind-independent objects. We think that our terms are referring to the mind-independent objects and their properties that are "reflected" in the one true theory of the world. Putnam thinks this metaphysical realist idea is wrong. His claim is not that we can't be certain that we have locked onto at least part of the one true theory. Rather, his claim is that objects and properties are only "real" relative to a language.

Now, how would one go about showing this? Neither Putnam nor the realist can escort us outside the language (any more than the metaphysical realist can) and *show* us whether there is or isn't a ready-made world. But there is another way, pioneered by Quine, that proceeds by showing the language-relative nature of reference. Putnam says he can show that our sentences can keep the truth-values we normally assign to them, yet the terms in those sentences will be about very different objects.

---

35   *Reason, Truth and History* 1981; for example, pp. xi and 49.

This is crucially important. In Putnam's view, the metaphysical realist holds that that there is only one true theory of the world. Or better: there is only one true complete theory. (Recall the other two claims—that there is a mind-independent world, and truth is correspondence to it.) The uniquely true theory identifies objects and properties that really are in the world. And the various epistemic arguments for realism are intended to support the unique theory aspect of metaphysical realism. Of course, theories are expressed in the sentences of some language. And the truth of those sentences depends entirely on their appropriately matching up to the world. So, in our language we assign "true" to the sentence "The banana split was invented in 1904 in La Trobe, Pennsylvania" because certain specific events occurred in a specific place at a specific time. Banana splits and Pennsylvania are of course not the fundamental objects of our ontology. Suppose, however, that sentence were true, not because of our usual way of thinking (e.g., bananas, ice cream, etc.), but because of some other way of assigning just those words in that sequence to very different events, objects, and properties. That is, suppose we had a different set of truth conditions that make the banana split sentence turn out to be true. Which assignment of truth-values is the correct assignment?

Your realist inclinations will immediately incline you to say something like, "But look, we can figure this out very simply. Maybe for this one sentence we can't tell, but wait till we add other sentences. Pretty soon we will be able to see which one is right because only one of these assignments of truth conditions will be successfully extended." If this reminds you a bit of the success argument, it is not surprising.

Now we are at the heart of Putnam's strategy (and of Quine's). Putnam argues that we can take our language and assign competing but complete sets of truth conditions to them in such a way that the two interpretations make all the same assignments of truth conditions. We have *competing* truth conditions assigned to each sentence of the language, but they give us all the same truth-values![36] (Remember: truth conditions—what objects, properties, in the world make a sentence true.) To borrow from Quine, when you say "That pesky rabbit was in the carrot patch again last night," there is more than one way to make that sentence turn out true. But simply from what we know of the two interpretations and the objects they designate, and from how we act,

---

36 E.g., Putnam 1978, p. 64.

we can't tell which interpretation, which assignment of truth conditions, is the uniquely correct one.

"So?" your realist inclination prompts you to ask. Putnam (and Quine) have a simple answer: then you have no way of telling which ontology—what there is in the world—is the correct one. Are we talking about re-occurring whole rabbits, or temporal stages of some rabbit spread out through three-dimensional space? (Or, in a moment, cats on mats or cherries in trees.)

This is the task Putnam sets himself in the model-theoretic argument: to show that *from inside the language*, we cannot tell which is the "right" way to assign truth conditions. Hence, we cannot turn to what we count as the true sentences in our theory to tell us the correct ontology of the world. More than one complete assignment of truth conditions—that is, more than one theory—can be assigned so as to get the appropriate set of trues and falses for the sentences of the language that expresses our theory of the world. If Putnam is successful, then the metaphysical realist cannot get what is needed to sustain the view.

The internal realist claims that we must draw a twofold conclusion: (1) truth and reference are relative to a language; hence, the "objects in the world" will vary from language to language; (2) there is no further court of appeal; there is nothing outside language to settle the matter of which is *the* true theory talking about *the* objects as they are independent of any mind or language. Thus, there is no uniquely true theory. And there are no mind-independent objects waiting to be discovered by our best cognitive efforts. Putnam has claimed that metaphysical realism is "incoherent" and that it "collapses."[37]

Two quick qualifications. Putnam is not a *relativist*, as that term is understood. He argues against the claim that "true-for-me" and "true-for-her" is all there is to truth.[38] (Roughly: the relativist denies that there is any sense to *objectivity*, but Putnam insists and argues that the internal realist retains that notion.) Second, Putnam is not claiming that we make the physical stuff that is the matter of our world; we will see this below when we consider Robert Schwartz.

To summarize then: If you can show that you can keep all the same truth-values for a language, but assign different aspects of the world as the truth conditions, metaphysical realism must be mistaken. Or, if there is no unique way to link terms and their referents—the objects the terms designate—then

---

37   Putnam 1978, pp. 123–24 and 130; see also Ernest LePore and Barry Loewer 1988.
38   Putnam 1981, pp. 119–24.

there is the intrinsic possibility of "ontological relativity," paving the way for Putnam's internal realism. (Putnam acknowledges Quine's work in this area; see Box below: Quine and Ontological Relativity.)

We have spent some time explaining the general aim of Putnam's *model theoretic argument*. The argument can seem a bit daunting when it is first encountered. Putnam claims we are unable to tell from the practical and semantic constraints on the language which aspects of the world are picked out by the terms of the language.[39] The strategy, as already noted, is to show that there is always an alternative way of having a sentence turn out true, even though the referents of the terms are not what we would normally expect. Moreover, there is no way to *fix* the referents from *inside* the language. As explained above, if successful, this would be an unhappy result for the metaphysical realist.

A sketch of the argument. Putnam considers the sentence "the cat is on the mat." Our preferred, standard understanding of English is that "cat" denotes the cat and "mat" denotes the mat. Given the standard truth conditions—precisely those the correspondence theorist assigns—if we find the cat on the mat, the sentence is true. And it is so because the intended referents of "cat" and "mat" are appropriately related to each other. That is, one is on the other.

Suppose, however, that the truth conditions of the sentence are specified in such a way that any time the cat is on the mat, there is a cherry on the tree. Similarly, on any occasion that the cat fails to be on the mat, there is no cherry on the tree. We now seem to have *competing* truth conditions for "the cat is on the mat." We want to say that it is the cat being on the mat that makes the sentence true. Yet another aspect of the world—the cherry on the tree—would do the trick just as well. We might say then that the pairs, cats and mats, and cherries and trees always exhibit the same truth-conditional relationship. (Putnam has a formal apparatus to illustrate systematically the general point of cats and cherries.)

Here is the important point. *From inside the language*, one word–world pair is as good as the other. Or, the semantic aspects of the language don't settle which parts of the world should be connected with which parts of the language.

We know of course what the metaphysical realist wants. "Cat" goes with cat, and "cherry" goes with cherry. The realist wants our words (or concepts) to connect to or match up with the world in a particular way, *in a unique way*. Putnam's model theoretic argument is designed to show that such a unique

---

39   Also Putnam 1978, p. 46.

way cannot be vouchsafed, simply through consideration of how the language works, both formally and practically. Or to recur to Quine: we are always re-interpreting within some further background language.

There are distinct but related issues here. Consider the semantic issue first, which is likely the first reaction of many upon seeing Putnam's argument. "Look," someone might say, "I know what I'm talking about—cats!"

The appeal here is to the mental states of the speaker. This will not work in Putnam's view, however, because the referent of our terms depends in part on the environment. Reference depends on more than simply a speaker's concept of the object.[40] But this is the point of Putnam's argument—the formal structure of the language doesn't settle what is being talked about.

Quine and Ontological Relativity

Putnam acknowledges his debt to the work of Willard Van Orman Quine and Quine's "ontological relativity," as well as related issues about linguistic meaning and reference. Quine argued that there is no fact of the matter about meaning and reference. He argued that the referent of a speaker's *observational terms* could not be settled definitively. A speaker of another language might say that a "*gavagai*" (Quine's famous coinage) was present, but the precise referent of that term is "inscrutable." That is, the term may pick out our customary rabbit, or an undetached rabbit part, "this rabbit at this moment," or even a numerical function! We can't settle the matter, Quine argued, because the speaker's mere behavior won't settle a term's referent, and since the theoretical and logical features of a language are open to different "structurings," reference is inscrutable. The *inevitable* possibility of such different structurings Quine called the *indeterminacy of translation* (or meaning). (Putnam's argument relies on similar points.) Quine later drew an important metaphysical consequence, that of **ontological relativity**.

Perhaps the salient point of such relativity is that understanding a language—or theory—always requires us to understand it relative to some background language (theory). A very simple example. How we understand the ordinary symbol sequence "100 + 101 = 1001" and count it as true or false depends upon the background language, i.e., false in Arithmetic-Base-10, but true in Arithmetic-Base-2. Quine's larger point is that ontology—the things we say exist—depend upon the theory we accept. And *crucially*, there is no final court of appeal for identifying what *really* exists: "It is meaningless to ask this [the referent of 'rabbit'] absolutely; we can meaningfully ask it *only relative to some background language*." Pragmatic considerations may go some way in narrowing the options, but even those will leave us with ontological relativity (see below).

See Quine 1960, 1969; the quotation is from Putnam 1981, p. 55.

---

40   Putnam 1981, pp. 22–29; the original argument is Putnam 1975b, esp. pp. 223–35.

Does behavior or circumstance provide a way out of this indeterminacy? Consider the following story: Felicia tells Fabio that the cat is on the mat and to let her in, and Fabio walks to the door, opens it, and the cat darts in and down the hall, while Felicia smiles. Surely that settles the matter. It was about cats, not cherries. Here, however, the Quinean background becomes important. Behavioral evidence is the only available evidence that "fixes" reference; we turn to the behaviors of speakers in a community to provisionally settle the word–world connections. Surely it is enough to say that "cat" picks out the cat, not the cherry.

But Putnam/Quine reply: Fabio's "cat" may have some passing temporal stage as its referent, while Felicia may have a collection of co-located properties as the referent. Neither is "correct"; neither will be deemed inappropriate by circumstances or usage. In fact, if that's the end of the story, neither Felicia nor Fabio will have any hint that the other's language has a different reference. Yet from the *metaphysical perspective*, these are certainly two different worlds—in this sense: the ontologically basic elements differ. Cats and cherries are, in a sense, stand-ins for different word–world connections and different metaphysical structures. The realist's notion of truth is a unique correspondence relation holding between words and regions of the world. Putnam's argument shows—or is at least aimed at showing—that this appeal is not sufficient. The "referring laser" that our word "cat" shines on some cat, unfortunately, can be seen as highlighting not only too many parts of the world, but also *too many differently metaphysically structured worlds*. The metaphysical realist holds that there is a correct and unique correlation between our language and the world. In picking out cats as the referent of "cat," claims the realist, we have hit on the unique real ontology of the world.

In reply, many contemporary metaphysical realists point to one relation that fixes reference: the causal relation. Eloise's concept of elephant refers to all and only elephants precisely because that thought is caused by or brought about by her interaction with elephants (not cherries).[41] But Putnam's reply is that, if our other terms are indeterminate, then so is the notion of *cause*.[42] Elsewhere, in criticizing the metaphysical realist's notion of a ready-made world, he also criticizes the notion of cause, as enabling us to pick out objects

---

41   See Jerry Fodor 1987 for a detailed account and defense of the link between cause and concept; see also Crumley 2006, Chap. 8.

42   Putnam 1981a, pp. 45–46. His argument here is in fact more general, but it applies to *cause* as well.

as they are in themselves. Now, the issue is whether we can somehow pinpoint or explain a "natural," mind-independent sense of "cause." Indeed, he writes disparagingly that the causal theorist relies on a relation that "has the dignity of choosing its own name."[43] Putnam argues that what we count as a cause in any given case is relative to our background interests. He further worries that more recent analyses of cause themselves rely on a very complex theory that is hardly natural.[44]

Perhaps the argument can be summarized as follows. Putnam agrees that we succeed in referring to cats and not cherries. But what explains this success? In Putnam's view, not our intentions, not our mental states. There is no way to check that our words have lassoed just the part of the world we want, in the structure that we want. But then what is left? We can't rely on the purely semantic and pragmatic features—that's the point of the model-theoretic argument. And again we can't get "outside" the language to check. Hence we must always rely on "re-interpretation": explaining our terms and sentences within the framework of some broader theory of language. And this is just *internal realism*. The only way that we can think or talk about anything is from within our conceptual scheme, our set of concepts and the way they "set out" the structure of the world. But from the standpoint inside such a scheme, assertions or presuppositions about existence or property attribution are interpreted realistically. That is, we don't think or say, "The cat's on the mat, *for me*, but of course what I mean by those words is not necessarily what you do, and what kind of reality I'm taking the words to represent is relative, not necessarily shared, and impossible to determine by anybody, and not demonstrably better than any other approach." No; we say, "The cat's on the mat, and I know what I mean by that, and it refers to a real cat and a real mat that were there independently of how I or you or anyone thinks about them."

But the question here might be: given our language and thought, is this really to be called realism? His reply: it's "all the realism we want or need."[45]

The final issue is an epistemic *cum* metaphysical issue. Surely we can see how language as a whole connects the world. This might remind us of the realist's best explanation argument. Isn't our *normal* interpretation of our language the best, since it best accounts for our experience? the realist might ask. Of course, Putnam quickly points out that "best" is a little bit like "cause":

43   Putnam 1984, p. 7.
44   Putnam 1981b/1983, pp. 211–18.
45   Putnam 1978, p. 130.

Both are relative to *our* interests. And that is all we have to settle the matter; we cannot get *outside* of our language to *check*.

This argument has been widely debated and disputed. Some challenge the technical details that have not been brought out here. Others insist that Putnam failed to grasp how the causal theory of reference that he helped develop met the challenge set out by his argument. Some sense of the "final score" is provided by Bob Hale and Crispin Wright in their balanced presentation and analysis of the argument.[46] About particular details of the argument, they argue that Putnam succeeds in some "subarguments" and not others. They think Putnam is right that our mental states alone cannot suffice to explain reference in the sense required by the metaphysical realist. But they also hold that Putnam's response to the causal theorist is unfair. In general, their view is that the "permutation" argument—that part of the argument considered here—is inconclusive.

However, they hold that Putnam "has done enough to issue a very pointed challenge, and one to which it is by no means clear that the metaphysical realist can satisfactorily respond."[47] Happily for our purposes, they focus on the larger *metaphysical* issue. First, Putnam, as an internal realist, has no desire to deny that we succeed in referring to cats rather than cherries. Putnam holds there is a very real sense of objectivity, but it is only found in some version of internal realism. But successful reference occurs within a frame of reference, a frame which will include metaphysical, semantic, and practical aspects. The metaphysical realist needs, they claim, a *"more substantial sense of 'truth'."* There must be facts that explain why it is that a causal theory of reference (if there is one that succeeds) is the right way to conceive the connection between mind and world. That is, they seem to suggest that the metaphysical realist owes us an explanation of the nature of reference such that it would enable us to "lock onto" the world. Moreover, this seems to be an *external fact*, a fact about what the reference relation is in itself. Yet Hale and Wright note that Putnam's argument seen generally is that we can't attain such a perspective.[48] If Putnam's argument is successful, then this is a significant setback for the metaphysical realist project.

---

46   Hale and Wright 1997.
47   *Ibid.*, p. 444.
48   *Ibid.*, pp. 445–46 and 455 n38.

Star Making

Putnam remarks that "the mind and world jointly make up the mind and world."[49] This internal realism of Putnam's is the view that asking what objects there are "only makes sense to ask *within* a theory of description."[50] The idea, however, that we are somehow participants in the *making* of the world strikes many as a rather odd contention. How is it that human beings had a hand in the making of the world? Robert Schwartz takes up exactly this issue in his "I'm Going to Make You a Star."[51] Schwartz advances several considerations to lessen the starkly puzzling character of internal realism, considerations worth reviewing.

We "physically fashion" artifacts, and make a considerable change in the natural world, but all these things, we think, have an independent existence when not being altered by us. Natural objects seem to owe their characteristics, not to us, but to the "world itself." If we are supposed nonetheless to be participants in making the world, it must be in some other way. Schwartz suggests that this may come in the act of symbolization and categorization. Our concepts and categories are thus the indicator of the world's objects and their properties. It is in this way that we take part in making the world, in making even distant objects such as stars.

Like Putnam, Schwartz denies that truth is merely subjective. This is an important point for the anti- or internal realist. Truth is *objective*; but Putnam's view is perhaps more clearly reflected by saying that truth is objective relative to a theory or system of description. "Betelgeuse is a red star" is true if and only if Betelgeuse is in fact a red star. There are *facts*, according to Schwartz. But while the facts may not depend on Ariel or Armin, they come into being relative to a scheme, a system of description (i.e., a way of understanding how language and world link). "Whether there are stars, and what they are like, are facts that can *emerge*, only in our attempts to describe and organize our world. The world is not given to us ready-made with stars...."[52]

Facts, and hence "being objective," emerge in our descriptions or our theory-building or version-making. But how can facts or objects emerge? Schwartz first observes that something is a star because it shares commonalities with other stars. But commonalities come cheap. Focus on one set of

---

49 Putnam 1981a, p. xi.

50 *Ibid.*, p. 49.

51 Schwartz 1986, pp. 427–39.

52 *Ibid.*, p. 435.

properties, you will get one grouping. Focus on another, and you may get a different grouping. Our solar system has nine planets. (Or eight?) Schwartz claims that it is only relative to our theory that we group our sun and the North Star (and Betelgeuse) together but leave out the Evening Star (Venus). We highlight certain features and not others.[53]

Here we see that Schwartz shares Putnam's view that the world is not ready-made. The particular arrangement of "star properties" was not waiting for us to come along with the appropriate label. "Star properties" have their structure and arrangement because of our modes of symbolizing and arranging. Nelson Goodman makes the same point when he remarks, "... but these things and worlds and even the stuff they are made of—matter, anti-matter, mind, energy or whatnot—are themselves fashioned by and along with versions ... facts are small theories and true theories are big facts."[54] Putnam, Schwartz, and Goodman all contend that one cannot separate out those preformed features of the world from our modes of description. Schwartz points out that realists sometimes claim that our versions' or theories' modes of description cannot make anything true. In one sense the realist is right: our sincere assertion does not imply the truth of that assertion. Yet, so Schwartz holds, mind and world jointly make the world. The world doesn't wear its facts on its sleeve; rather our theory construction shapes facts.

How does the non-realist explain our sometimes getting it wrong? Isn't this a pre-structured world pushing back, telling us that we have it wrong? Two aspects of an answer are discernible. First, construction of worlds or theories is difficult. It takes insight and creativity. "Arduous business" Schwartz calls it. Second, it is worth noting that as the world does not wear ready-made structures of facts on its sleeve, neither do our theories. Theories are *elaborated*; we might even think of theory elaboration or version elaboration rather than construction. And the process of elaboration reveals new, previously unrecognized "facts." For many, $a^2 + b^2 = c^2$ is a basic recollection from high school geometry. But *proving* that theorem requires considerable stage-setting and the "elaboration" of other geometric concepts, e.g., similarity and congruence. This process can reveal "truths" that conflict with other beliefs or new theories. The Michelson-Morley experiment of 1887—attempting to detect the medium or ether in which light waves travel—failed, and awaited Einstein's *new* theory to explain the failure. The non-realist thus claims we cannot know in advance whether or how a theory or version might go wrong.

---

53   *Ibid.*, pp. 435–36.
54   1978, pp. 96–97.

We might summarize Schwartz's argument like this. Of course artifacts—things we make, like rocking chairs or smart phones—have the properties they do in virtue of our constituting them. Other parts of the world seem a little more complicated; there seems to be something about them that we *do not make*. How should the internal realist explain this? Schwartz uses the example of New Jersey to illustrate, but one can think of other presumably mind-independent phenomena as well, such as the Grand Canyon or the Rocky Mountains. For any "natural" thing, there are "an unlimited number of features" that category exhibits.[55] Being a member of some category requires having the requisite features, but which are the requisite features "is not written in the stars."[56] And it is our theories that draw out those features or properties. Our theories organize the world, and in so doing, the "facts 'fall out'" of our theorizing, of our symbolizing the world. It is in this way that a star might exist billions of years before any life form, much less any conceptual scheme, existed. And of course we did not compress gasses or route rivers or push tectonic plates to raise mountains. Most antirealists do not deny the reality of a world. Rather they assert that it is in our describing, symbolizing, and theorizing that this featureless world *takes shape*. Our categories give it that shape.

Perhaps this is sufficient to give some further context to the contention that there is no ready-made world. And perhaps this is *the* line of contention between realist and antirealist. There is little doubt that realism, or even the metaphysical realism described by Putnam, is the preferred position of most who struggle with the issue. Indeed the antirealist view is rather jarring when contrasted with the appeal of realism and its arguments. Perhaps the latter part of this chapter has lessened the jarring appearance of antirealism.

Key Concepts

- global realism
- scientific realism
- instrumentalism
- bivalence principle
- verification
- internal realism
- ontological relativity

---

55 Schwartz 1986, p. 435.
56 *Ibid.*

Reading Questions

1. Explain how the inference to the best explanation argument supports commonsense realism and scientific realism.
2. How is the notion of truth connected to scientific realism?
3. What do you think are the best reasons for adopting an instrumentalist approach to scientific theories?
4. How does Dummett's view of the realism–antirealism debate differ from the traditional view, which holds that it is a debate about objects?
5. Explain the verificationist view of meaning (as advanced by Dummett); why does this view of meaning lead Dummett to hold an antirealist position, at least about some issues?
6. How would you explain the importance of Putnam's model-theoretic argument?
7. Write a short essay that explains Putnam's notion of internal realism; identify at least one problem or objection to Putnam's view and explain how you think Putnam could respond.

For Further Reading

Michael Devitt 1991 is an important work from the realist perspective; Devitt explains and defends realism, especially scientific realism, and the causal theory of reference that is an important element of realism; he offers his critiques of various opposing viewpoints. Anjan Chakravartty 2017 is a detailed and helpful summary of the positions and arguments in the debate about scientific realism, including instrumentalism.

The relevant essays from Quine are in his 1969; Chapter 2 of his 1969 is the original presentation of indeterminacy and inscrutability. Paul Roth's 1978 is an excellent account of both indeterminacy and the role it played in Quine's thought.

Dummett's 1978 contains many of his seminal essays, as does his 1996; for those interested in his intuitionist views in mathematics and logic, some essays cover the topic in detail. Both his 2006 and 2013 are very accessible and provide a nice overview of his thought, along with his thinking in some different directions. The 2013 is especially focused on the reality of the past.

Putnam's 1981 is extremely important for his internal realist view, but it also situates that view in his general view about rationality and broader issues, such as culture and morality; also his 1978 situates his thought in that broader context. Volumes 2 and 3 of his collected papers, 1975 and 1983, contain not only the essays noted in the text but many other essays, either specifically or broadly related to the realism topic.

Peter French et al., eds., 1988 is a collection of papers that helped shaped the debate when the realism–antirealism controversy was returning to the scene. A more recent collection of essays on the topic of truth and realism is Patrick Greenough and Michael P. Lynch, eds., 2006.

CHAPTER FOUR

UNIVERSALS

THE NOTED AMERICAN HUMORIST WILL ROGERS ONCE REMARKED, "If there are no dogs in Heaven, then when I die I want to go where they went." About a quite different subject, C.S. Lewis, the Christian apologist and author of *The Chronicles of Narnia* and *The Screwtape Letters*, along with many other works, noted, "Courage is not simply one of the virtues, but the form of every virtue at the testing point."

A common linguistic occurrence is found in both these quotations. We sometimes think about a particular dog or talk about a particular character trait or note a particular color on a particular object. We sometimes say that a particular action was an instance of courage—that the action *instantiates* courage. Often enough we do more than that. Some thoughts are about *all* dogs or are about *all* mammals. Sometimes we want to say something about *all* compassionate or brave acts. Our language enables us to refer to all members of a certain group or kind or to refer to the kind itself: dogs are mammals; dogs are four-footed; wisdom is a virtue; compassion is a virtue.

Closely related to this sort of ability to think and talk *generally*, we find occasion to distinguish between an object and its properties. This can lead to thinking or talking about the *property itself*. Not only do we notice "this red over here" or "that red over there," but we often identify all these occurrences as *instances of the same color*. That is, we distinguish at times—in thought and language—between *red* and all the particular occurrences or *instances* of red. Someone who says "Red is my favorite color" is not talking about any particular colored surface. A small, local coffee shop chain once used magenta for the color of the upholstery in its booths—here a magenta, there a magenta, separate occurrences of *the same color*. No need to confine ourselves to talking about color; consider *courage*. This soldier is courageous, that bystander is courageous in helping someone out of a burning vehicle, and many years ago, a young Chinese man blocked a tank at Tiananmen Square. These and other numerous acts are *particular instances of courage*. All these particular behaviors are grouped together because they evidence the *same attribute*—courage. Moreover, we take the concepts of courage or beauty or magenta as *predicable of* many different objects. That is, we often say—or think—that a particular property or characteristic is possessed by many different objects; we attribute or *predicate* a property of many different objects.

These examples point to two phenomena, which require two technical terms. We refer to—talk about—some kind or property. This type of linguistic reference is known as *abstract reference*. While the term might be unfamiliar, there is nothing out of the ordinary about abstract reference. Our ordinary way of talking apparently makes use of abstract reference in sentences like "Magenta is a color" or "Patience is a virtue." Notice that in such examples we appear to be talking about some quality or property. The other technical term, *attribute agreement*, refers to different instances of the same property. This American Eskimo pup, that piece of paper, and this napkin "agree" in having the same attribute: they are all white. Attribute agreement is our primary concern in this chapter.

These technical terms should not distract from the main point. Our ability to think and talk about an entire class of objects or to recognize the same property occurring in a lot of different places constitutes our ability to think and talk in general terms. And this ability is tied to an important and longstanding metaphysical problem: the problem of universals.

Universals, Particulars, and Instantiation

Aristotle and the Essence of Human Beings

Aristotle clearly had an interest in terms referring to a particular *kind*, such as "human" or "animal." And he had a quite specific account of the nature or essence of a human being: an essence he argues is captured by the term "rational animal." The Aristotelian terminology of genus and species enables us to see the role of each part of the term in identifying human nature. Humans are in the genus *animal*, while their "specific differentia"—the quality that defines their species, and differentiates it from others in its genus—is *rationality*. In other words, while we are similar to other animals in many ways—and thus part of the animal genus—we differ from other animals because of our rational ability, and thus constitute a unique species. The universal *animal* is in each of us, just as it is in the gray wolf or the koala bear. But another universal is immanent in each human, a universal not had by other animals, and that universal is rationality.

Start with attribute agreement: instances of the same property occurring in many different places at the same time. All the different instances are grouped together because—some believe—they share a common element. Indeed this booth is magenta because it shares in some sense the element, *magenta*, with other objects, just as this act is courageous because it shares the element, *courage*, with other acts. We say that the booth *instantiates* magenta or this act of pulling someone from a burning vehicle *instantiates* courage. Courage or magenta is something over and above—separate from, but shared by—all the particular instances. Such an element, if it exists, is a *universal*. A **universal** then is a general characteristic or category which can be instantiated—shared—by many objects or particulars at the same time; it can be predicated of or attributed to many things, called **instantiations**.[1]

This gives us a way to think about particulars, as well. **Particulars**—or, synonymously, what we have been calling "objects" or "individuals"—cannot be instantiated. In this sense, every particular is unique.

---

1   E.J. Lowe 2002, Chap. 19.

Plato, the first to identify universals, used the term *forms*:

> Socrates: We speak of many beautiful things and many good things,
>   and we say that they are so and so and so define them in speech.
> Glaucon: We do.
> Socrates: And Beauty itself and Goodness itself, and so with all the
>   things which we then classed as many; we now class them again
>   according to one *Form* of each ...
> Glaucon: That is so.[2]

Socrates identifies the form as existing separately from the "many" instances.

Philosophers disagree about whether or not universals exist and, if so, what they are. There are three main views on this subject. **Realism about universals** holds that universals exist. This is the view held by Plato and others that universals are a special kind of object, which exists separately from the many occurrences or instances. At the other end of the spectrum is **nominalism**, the view that universals do not exist; only particular things or particular occurrences of properties exist. It turns out that there are several nominalist options. There are also two middle views that call for consideration. One, called *moderate realism*, holds that there are universals, but not as separately existing objects. They exist corporeally, not ideally, in their instances. This view is often attributed to Aristotle. (Some call a Platonic view, by contrast, "extreme realism": the universals, not their instantiations, are *what really exist*.) Another view, first articulated (according to some) by the French philosopher Peter Abelard (1079–1142), is **conceptualism**, the view that universals are just concepts, located in the mind, that are universal because they refer to many individuals.

Universal: A Special Object

Words and Universals

As we've noted, realists hold that a property, such as *redness* or *courage*, is a universal. Words that name properties are typically called *predicates*, a term that you might have seen in the context of grammar, or computer or formal languages (e.g., "predicate logic").

As we will see, some nominalists hold that all predicates are just words.

---

2   Plato 1974, *Republic*, 507b; emphasis added.

But another question arises: does every predicate name a property? Clearly the question is more pressing for realists, and some predicates seem obvious. "Is a candle" counts as a predicate, as does "is red" or "is cylindrical." Other predicates less obviously name properties, e.g., "is a book returned to the store" or "is a color liked by logic students." In Plato's *Parmenides*, Parmenides asks the young Socrates if "hair" or "mud" names a form. Socrates seems disinclined to think so.

Different theorists of course give different answers. One possibility is to recognize as *real* properties only those required for science. And the most extravagant view is to say that, yes, there is a property named by each meaningful predicate. Allowing the unrestricted view, however, can quickly run into problems, seemingly inviting contradictions. Michael Loux discusses this "unrestricted predication" in his *Metaphysics* (2006), Chap. 1.

The realist view holds that universals are independent, existing apart from their instances. A ruby red glass goblet sits on the table. Here is an instance of the universal *red*. Destroy this goblet; smash it to smithereens! You will have destroyed *this instance*, but you will not have destroyed the universal *red*, which exists independently of particulars. Indeed, even if all red things were destroyed—even if there never were, or never will be, any red things—the universal red would still exist.

This independence raises a difficult point, however. Although instance and universal are distinct, *the universal is wholly present in each instance*. This coffee shop booth is no less magenta than that one. And courage is wholly present in this Medal of Honor recipient, just as it is wholly present in this Victoria Cross recipient. By contrast, compare, in this respect, a class—a collection—of things, for example, all the states of the US. Wyoming is one of them, but that class of states is not wholly present in that state. That state is just a part of that class. Similarly, the coffee shop booth is only a (very small) part of the class of magenta objects, past, present, and future.

Thinking of a universal as a kind of pattern or archetype might help us to understand how a universal is wholly present in each instance. Many shirts may instantiate *the same pattern*—shape, form, style. The pattern is wholly present in each individual shirt. (We're not talking about the sewing pattern—the paper shapes that guide construction.) Make as many shirts as you wish of this pattern. Each shirt is an instance of the pattern, and the pattern is wholly present in each shirt. Thus, note two slightly embarrassed individuals who arrive at the social event only to find that they are wearing *the same shirt*! And the pattern never gets used up. No matter how many instances, the pattern is never exhausted. Perhaps this metaphor helps us understand how the entire universal is present simultaneously in many different objects. We can also note that this "not getting used up" feature is a consequence of their immaterial or nonphysical nature.

Those who believe in the existence of universals mostly agree that they are not physical. They aren't made up of elements listed in the Periodic Table; they aren't electromagnetic fields or very special plasmas. Perhaps the most important aspect of this immateriality is that universals don't take up space. And this has an interesting consequence: Lots of different universals can be instantiated by the same object. Not only can one and the same universal be *multiply instantiated*, but multiple universals are or can be in the same place. Consider again that ruby red glass. It instantiates several universals at once: cylindrical, red, and glass. All these universals are simultaneously "in" this particular ruby red goblet. How many universals can be present in any given object? An indefinitely large number. Each genuine property possessed by an object is an instance of a universal. And for each *kind* that this object belongs to, it instantiates that universal.

While universals are instantiated in spatial objects, the separately existing universals—e.g., *beauty* or *magenta* in themselves—are not located in space, the way a chair or a table is. And nonphysical, non-spatial objects are not discoverable by the senses; they are discovered instead by reason or thought. (In the *Republic*, according to some translations, it is "understanding" that enables us to grasp or discover universals.) As nonphysical objects, universals are one type of *abstract object*—members of a category that, according to some, includes a variety of other kinds of nonphysical entities, such as numbers. (We leave aside the issue of whether universals are "in time" or temporal objects. In calling them "abstract," we simply note that they don't have the other attributes or properties associated with physical objects.) Realists about universals accordingly are realists about abstract objects.

Realism

The Transcendentals

Thirteenth-century medieval philosophy saw a heightened interest in a very special kind of universal: the *transcendentals*. These are those properties or qualities that are true of everything. According to Jorge Gracia 1992, a transcendental includes or "covers" not only other objects and properties, but all categories as well, whether substance or quality or quantity. In a sense, transcendentals run through every category. The property of *being* was held to be the highest or most fundamental transcendental; it is true of everything that *is*.

Other predicates, such as unity, good, and truth—and for some, including Aquinas (1225–74), beauty—are "convertible" with being. To say that the predicate "true" is convertible with the predicate "being" (or "is" or "to be") is to say that we have two names for one quality. If something *is*, it is always also *good*, *unified*, and *true*. Or as Aquinas remarks, true, for example, and being "differ in idea," but are the same in reality.

How can it be that beauty or goodness are properties of everything? Here is Aquinas: "Nothing exists which does not participate in beauty or goodness, since each thing is good according to its proper form.... Created beauty is nothing other than a likeness of the divine beauty participated in things." Setting aside for now the reference to a "divine" beauty, Aquinas also seems to acknowledge a "natural" beauty. Everything is composed of form and matter, and the proper form of an object is inherently beautiful.[3]

---

3   Aquinas 1953, p. 88.

Realists incline toward two principal arguments for the existence of universals, and versions of both these arguments appear in Plato's dialogues. Socrates asks Meno, in the eponymous dialogue, to provide the *common element* or *characteristic* that all virtues share. In response, Meno offers a list of several different virtues for different types of people, and Socrates remarks:

> I seem to be in luck. I wanted one virtue and I find that you have a whole swarm of virtues to offer. But seriously, to carry on this metaphor of the swarm, suppose I asked you what a bee is, what is its *essential nature*, and you replied that bees were of many different kinds. What would you say if I went on to ask, And is it in *being bees* that they are many and various and different from one another? Or would you agree that it is not in this respect that they differ....
>
> Then do the same with the virtues. Even if they are many and various, yet at least they all have some common character which makes them virtues.[4]

Socrates' remarks rely on the notion of attribute agreement. We group different particular dogs as one and all *dogs* because they all share a common attribute or characteristic. (They may be different colors, sizes, weights, etc., but they all share the common attribute *being dogs*.) Similarly we identify different virtues (e.g., courage, moderation, wisdom) as one and all *virtues*. Socrates asks for the shared common attribute. Socrates asks the same question in *Laches*, but here about courage:

> And I will begin with courage, and once more ask *what is that common quality, which is the same in all these cases* and which is called courage?[5]

Notice that Socrates claims we need some explanation about why we group all these things together. Why do we count all these various actions as one and alike "brave"? Or why do we group Helen of Troy, Renoir's *Sunset at Sea*, a melody, and a rainbow as all beautiful? Socrates is arguing that there is "something" common to each, and our grasping that common element leads to

---

4   Plato 1961b, *Meno*, 72b, d; emphasis added.
5   Plato 1961a, *Laches*, 191e; emphasis added.

that attribute agreement between any two objects—here, that both objects are large—is best explained by appealing to a very special object, a universal. The universal is the one over the many large items. Parmenides now asks the young Socrates:

> Parm: But now take Largeness itself [the universal] and the other
>   things which are large. Suppose you look at all these in the
>   same way in your mind's eye, will not yet another unity make its
>   appearance—a Largeness [another universal] by virtue of which
>   they all appear large?
> Socrates: So it would seem.
> Parm: If so, a second Form of largeness will present itself over
>   and above Largeness itself and the things that share in it; and
>   again, covering all these, yet another, which will make all of
>   them large. So each of your forms will no longer be one, but an
>   indefinite number.[7]

Parmenides' line of questioning is very simple. The problem Parmenides is raising is this. Universals are supposed to explain the likeness of attributes between individuals. If you need the universal to explain how all the particulars are alike, will you not need still a second universal to explain the apparent likeness between the individuals and the first universal? And if we need this second universal, won't we still need a third universal? And won't this process of needing another universal continue indefinitely?

Realists invoke universals to solve the problem of the one over the many, the problem of attribute agreement. Parmenides' objection, however, suggests that the one over the many problem arises *even for universals*. An explanation that keeps introducing new things that need to be explained hardly seems an adequate solution to the problem.

Explanations, interpretations, and assessments of the Third Man themselves have filled books. While most scholars agree that there is a challenge to the realist position, they disagree over how to understand the argument. The twentieth-century Plato scholar Gregory Vlastos claims that the argument is Plato's "record of honest perplexity,"[8] that Plato knew there was a problem but was unsure of the best way to address it. Some commentators have identified the

---

7   Plato 1951, *Parmenides*, 132a, b.
8   Vlastos 1954, pp. 343–49.

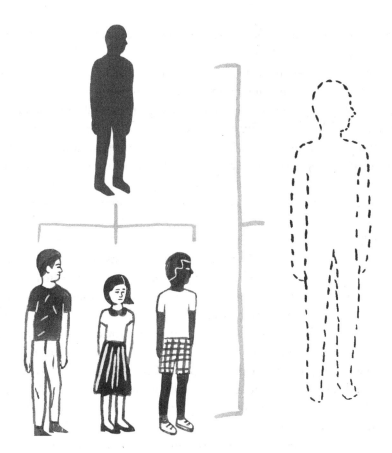

problem as "self-predication," or the idea that the form itself has the property
or attribute it's supposed to explain—so the form *largeness* is itself large, or
the form *man* is somehow "manlike," or the form *beauty* is itself beautiful. We
may not be able to cover all of these difficult issues, but we can look at some
important aspects of the problem.[9]

It might seem that the Third Man Argument threatens only Plato's version
of realism. But various "regress arguments" challenge any realist who holds
that universals exist separately from their instances.[10] Cynthia Macdonald
casts the challenge in the form of a dilemma for realists. Here we modify
her presentation a bit. The dilemma is this: either the universal is *like* the
particulars, or it is *not like* the particulars. To put it a little differently, the
universal "unifies" the instances—makes them all instances of red or instances

of beauty—either because it is *like* the instances, or is unlike them, but has some other relation to them.

Well, if we take the first—the universal is *like* its instances—we are on a very quick ride to the Third Man Argument. (But this doesn't seem right: the form *largeness*, for example, is not itself large. In general, universals aren't instances of themselves.) But let us take the second—focus instead on the *relation* between universal and its instance. Now we have the relation between universal and this instance, and the relation between the universal and that instance, and so on. This relation is the same in each case. But now we seemingly need a universal that "covers" all these *particular* relations between universal and instances.

The following particular instance of the Third Man Argument may make it a little clearer. Consider a large pile of different hats: a derby, a top hat, a balaclava, a beanie, a baseball-cap, a fire-fighter's helmet, and so on. Each hat is different from every other one, but they're all *hats*. So that means (according to realists) that they all participate in the form of hats—each of them is related to a single *Ideal Hat*. Now, the ideal hat cannot be made of silk or knitted wool or cotton, or any other particular material, because real hats made of any one of a large number of different particular materials are all related to it. So what do all those real hats and the Ideal Hat have in common? Well, there must be another form that all those real hats and the Ideal Hat participate in. But now we can run the same line of reasoning concerning this additional form and the Ideal Hat and the real hats, and conclude that still another form exists. And so on, multiplying forms infinitely.

Whichever way we choose, then, to understand universals, a version of Third Man—a regress—seems to pop up. We continually see the need for yet another universal to explain a new group! And that is just Macdonald's point.

A common thread runs through many realist responses to the dilemma. They insist that the initial relation between universal and particular is both explanatory *and basic*. Appealing to the universal tells us something about the world, about the things in the world, and about our ability to think and talk about various kinds of objects. But they also claim that we can't analyze this concept of "instantiation" further. It's a basic essential fact about red or beautiful particulars, for example, that they instantiate a given universal.[11] Some others argue that it is a mistake to think of a form as the *type* of thing

---

11   Macdonald 2005; Donagan 1963; A.E. Taylor 1949. Armstrong 1989 suggests that there is no real regress problem for realism about universals.

that can be reasonably "grouped with" sensible things. The Parmenidean challenge in Plato's dialogue is intended to get us to find a new conceptual understanding of "form," such that we no longer think that the real nature of a form is exhibited through physical metaphors.[12] It is perhaps worth noting that, as we will see, this notion of *basic and unanalyzable* appears in both realist and nominalist views—though the views differ over what counts as basic and unanalyzable.

Before we leave this topic, we might make one further note. The Third Man Argument is widely held, following Vlastos and others, to depend on certain assumptions or "principles." One of these is the notion of self-predication and a second is that of non-identity. The first claims that at least implicit in Plato's dialogues is the claim that any form can be predicated of itself. That is, that the form *Large* (if there is such a form) is itself large or the form *Courage* is itself courageous. The non-identity principle holds that if something—including some form—has a certain character, there must be *another* form in virtue of which we apprehend or cognize that thing having the specified character. Again, it is easy to see how the regress is off and running, given these principles. Vlastos suggests that Plato was unaware of the problem posed by the self-predication thesis. This is not entirely obvious, however. At *Republic* 597c, Plato claims that if two "ideal" beds had the character "bedness," they would not be the Form *Bed*. Plato seems here at least to reject self-predication.

We draw this to a close by remembering that one argument for the existence of forms is that we need to explain in virtue of what we cognize or grasp that some group of particulars is classed as falling under the same concept. In introducing the forms, we had recourse to the idea of a paradigm. Thus we might think of a model and its copies. The paradigm or model in a sense has the character of which instances are copies. Thus, the pattern or paradigm *modus ponens* exhibits or displays a structure had by particular applications of *modus ponens*. Similar to Meinwald's suggestion that Plato thought of different types of predication, this understanding of the model-copy relation suggests an understanding of the relationship between form and particular that does not obviously invite the Third Man Argument.[13]

---

12   See, for example, Mitchell Miller 1986 and again Meinwald 2011.

13   See H.F. Cherniss 1965 and Crumley *ms*.

Universals a Precondition
for Thought and Communication

A further passage from the *Parmenides* is also relevant. Parmenides' series of criticisms of the theory of forms, at least in the dialogue, appears to leave Socrates at a loss. Yet Parmenides seems disinclined to discard the theory entirely, as he says:

> But on the other hand ... if, in view of all these difficulties and other things like them, a man refuses to admit that the Forms of things exist or to distinguish a definite Form in every case, *he will have nothing on which to fix his thought*, so long as he will not allow that each thing has a character which is always the same, in so doing will completely destroy the significance of all discourse. But of that consequence I think you [Socrates] are only too well aware.[14]

A necessary condition of thought and language, according to Parmenides, is that something "anchors" our thoughts. If we are to make any sense of our many references to beauty or to courage or all the various properties we ascribe to things, something fixed, something unchanging must exist. We suppose, for example, that Sara is thinking the same thought, about the same thing—courage—when she says on Tuesday that the soldier is brave as when she says on Wednesday that the teacher showed courage. Julia may disagree with Jack that the painting is beautiful, but they presume that there is something over which they disagree. Parmenides suggests that without forms, without the "anchor," Sara's thought about courage could mean one thing one day, and another on another day; Julia and Jack would not really be communicating at all, since nothing ties one thought to the other. If Julia and Jack are to engage in genuine discourse, there must be something that is the *same* in their conversation. Thinking and meaningful speech require a unity, Parmenides suggests, something that binds together separate thoughts or different utterances. Without the theory of the forms we are unable to account for the apparent fact that thought and language are meaningful.

This view is shared by contemporary writers, as well. C.A. Baylis makes a similar point:

---

14   Plato 1951, 135c; emphasis added.

The existence of communicable knowledge requires shared meanings. Such knowledge, in its simplest form, is knowledge of the *common characters* exhibited by various objects and events.... Our problem is to explain [universals'] nature and their function in knowledge in terms that are neither mystical nor false to the facts of conscious communication.[15]

Baylis underscores the recognition expressed in Plato's dialogue: universals are required to explain successful communication. This perhaps helps us to see the realist insistence on the need for universals. Universals explain not only our *individual* ability to think and talk generally; they also "anchor" the possibility of shared, common knowledge about the essence or nature of things. Nominalists, of course, think that their view also provides an explanation of the meaningfulness of our language and our thought.

A Contemporary View: Universals as Concepts

One contemporary approach to universals holds that we take universals as concepts.[16] Aune calls this a "P-theory," to be contrasted with the moderate realist view of Aristotle and Armstrong. Concepts, as already noted on occasion, are used to classify things. We organize the objects of the world by the concept they "fall under." In appealing to the notion of concepts, Aune argues that these concepts are not "eternal entities," nor do they have rigid boundaries. We should acknowledge that there may be borderline cases of which instances fall under a concept. A concept is still a type or kind in virtue of the fact that it classifies or categorizes individuals.

This allowance for vagueness sets the concept view of universals apart from an Aristotelian view. In that view, a universal is a definite, repeatable property, which many objects may or may not have; it is an all or none affair. But in Aune's P-theory, to say that "Socrates is wise" is not to attribute some repeatable entity to Socrates. Rather, we are describing a particular individual as wise. As Aune says, the sentence says something about what the individual, Socrates, is like. (We might note that this bears some resemblance to the notion of a primary subject or individual, of Aristotle's *Categories*, which we see in the following chapter.)

---

15 Baylis 1951, p. 636; emphasis added.
16 Bruce Aune 2001.

Perhaps more important is that Aune holds that the problem posed by resemblance issues does not arise for the concept theory. I say of Mandy's hair that it is red, of Mauricio's laptop that it is red, and Marvin's apple that it is red. Aune argues that when we learn to apply color words—learn to classify things according to color—we learn to say what *those* things are like.

Aune is thus rejecting the assumption that we classify particulars by reference to something other than the individual or particular itself. Why does this matter? Suppose Mandy says "Jacques' jacket is brown." The advocate of universals claims that we understand this act of *predication* (i.e., saying that the subject 'Jacques's jacket' has the property named by the predicate 'brown'), only if we understand the nature of *brown*. That is, in order to understand what Mandy has said, we must know the nature of the universal brown.

Aune holds that this view of universals is a mistake. Instead, on many occasions, he holds, we understand the predication in and of itself. How does this understanding come about? Presumably we learned this as we acquired the concept *brown* (or any other concept).[17] We acquire concepts in part by learning the conditions under which an individual is described in some particular way. This acquisition of concepts, however, need not be understood as first grasping some other repeatable, definite object.

When do Mandy and Maddie have the same concept *brown*? According to Aune, they have the same concept when that term is a functional counterpart for each—that is, when the term "brown" plays the same cognitive role for both Maddie and Mandy. Could this functional concept exist by itself, like Plato's forms? Seemingly not. But Aune holds that these classifying concepts exist so long as they are part of someone's conceptual repertoire. (Aune is here drawing on aspects of a view advocated by Wilfrid Sellars.[18])

There are echoes of various views in Aune's theory. The Platonic aspect of his view seems to derive from the classificatory nature of concepts. And while Aune does not appeal to the idea, Plato seems to hold in different dialogues that people may be more or less virtuous, more or less beautiful, more or less courageous; yet, we classify them under those concepts. Aune attempts to explain how this is so without the appeal to a specific, definite repeatable entity. Yet, in insisting that we understand predication as *describing what an individual is like* (that is, as describing an individual as belonging to some category or class),

---

17   *Ibid.*, pp. 136–38.
18   For a clear explanation of Sellars's view, see Michael Loux and Thomas Crisp 2017, Chap. 2.

Aune retains an important feature of universals. And importantly, he addresses two key motivations for invoking universals: the desire to understand why we group different individuals in the same class, and the desire to explain the referents of various predicates.

Nominalism

Nominalism comprises several different views, but they all have this in common: they deny the existence of universals. Only individuals or particulars exist. The word "nominalism" comes, via French, from the Latin *nominalis*, meaning "pertaining to a name or names." Nominalism seems to many to have the commonsense advantage of recognizing only individuals and rejecting the need for any special type of object. Instead, nominalism asserts that nouns that apparently pick out or designate universals in fact are words only and can be "rephrased."

The celebrated medieval English philosopher William of Ockham (1285–1347) was a champion of nominalism. He is also responsible for a principle that underlies many nominalist arguments: the principle now known as "Ockham's razor." That "razor," now expressed as "do not multiply entities beyond necessity," tells us to prefer the simpler of two explanations.

Michael Loux provides an instructive contemporary account of this notion of simplicity as a standard for evaluating theories.[19] Loux notes that the aim of a theory, whether in the natural or social sciences or in metaphysics, is *to explain*. A theory is judged to be better because it better explains those phenomena being investigated. But simplicity is one way an explanation can be better. So, given two theories, each explaining the desired "facts," we are inclined to prefer the simpler of those theories. One quick example might help to illustrate. Let's take the example of Newton's laws of motion, which became the basis for classical mechanics. Newton's laws explain motion from the behavior of billiard balls on a table to the motion of a train approaching a station—or, as the former football commentator John Madden liked to point out, the force exerted by a player on an opposing quarterback. The beauty of Newton's law is that, with just three simple principles or laws, it explains so many varied instances of motion and rest. The theory explains them, and it has the virtue of being simpler than its rivals.

---

19   Loux 2006, Chap. 1.

Here's an example of its use in medicine. When confronted with a patient with a collection of different symptoms, doctors first look for a single underlying condition that would explain them all.

Nominalists think their view is simpler because they rely on only one kind of entity—individual objects—to provide explanations of abstract reference and attribute agreement. In their view, acknowledging the existence of universals is a multiplication of entities beyond necessity.

In his writings about nominalism, Ockham went a step further, arguing that appeal to universals inevitably led to contradiction. Like others, Ockham believed that anything that exists is an individual, and that to claim otherwise is obvious folly. So, if a universal exists, it too must be individual: "It ought to be said that every universal is one particular thing and that it is not universal except in its signification, in its signifying many things."[20] Nothing could be both universal and individual at the same time.

It's important to be clear about Ockham's complaint. Anything that exists, he says, is individual. By definition, individuals cannot be in two places at once. Yet universals—supposedly—are in many places at once. So it seemed to Ockham and others that realism bordered on self-contradiction: Something that can't be in many places at once was held by realists to be in many places at once.

Yet this still leaves us with questions. If we are not to rely on universals, what then can we say about, for example, why we call all these things magenta or all these acts courageous? If nominalists claim to offer a simpler theory than realism, how do they propose to explain the apparent fact of attribute agreement? Of the many types of nominalism, we look at the answers provided by two.

Strict Nominalism

Strict nominalism insists that all our apparent talk of attribute agreement, apparently implying the existence of universals, in fact refers to nothing more than individuals. (David Armstrong, an opponent of this view, called it "ostrich nominalism."[21]) Realists, remember, invoke universals to explain the truth of various assertions, such as "Socrates is wise": Socrates instantiates the universal *wisdom*. Similarly "Boethius is wise" and "Pascal is wise" are true because both Boethius and Pascal also instantiate the same universal. The strict nominalist

---

20   Ockham 1974, p. 78.
21   Armstrong 1978, Vol. I, pp. 12–16.

claims, instead, that there is nothing to explain here. We have three individuals, each of which is wise. There is no exemplifying or instantiating to be explained. There is just this individual, and he happens to be wise, and that individual, and he happens to be wise.

Along with the realist, you might be waiting to ask about all these individuals that are wise. Haven't we come across a case of attribute agreement? That is, aren't we grouping these three individuals—Socrates, Boethius, and Pascal—together because they *share the same property*? In other words, isn't there *agreement* among their *attributes*? We know the realist explains that the attribute agreement which allows for this "grouping together" occurs precisely because these three individuals share in or instantiate the same *universal*.

But how will the strict nominalist explain attribute agreement without relying on universals? The strict nominalist insists that there is nothing here to explain because we have come across a basic metaphysical fact. These facts— that there are different objects described using the same predicates—are primitive; they cannot be analyzed further. This thing is magenta, and that thing is magenta, and that's all there is to it. You don't need a third thing to explain this.

In a famous essay titled "On What There Is," the twentieth-century philosopher Willard Van Orman Quine straightforwardly expressed this idea:

> One may admit that there are red houses, roses, and sunsets, but deny, except as a popular and misleading manner of speaking, that they have anything in common. The words "houses," "roses," and "sunsets" are true of sundry individual entities which are houses and roses and sunsets, and the word "red" or "red object" is true of each of sundry individual entities which are red houses, red roses, red sunsets; but there is not, in addition, any entity whatever, individual or otherwise, which is named "redness".... That the houses and the roses and the sunsets are all of them red may be taken as ultimate and irreducible, and it may be held that [the realist] is no better off, in point of real explanatory power, for all the occult entities which he posits under such names as redness.[22]

To say that facts are "ultimate and irreducible" or "primitive" or "unanalyzable" is a way of saying that a particular theory or view takes certain facts or

---

22   Quine 1961, p. 10.

items as basic or as starting points; there is no prior point of explanation. When Newton proposed his view of gravity, critics asked for an explanation of the attractive force of gravity. Newton, however, insisted that there was no further explanation. Matter attracts. Period. There isn't any further explanation of how or why it does it. Strict nominalists thus make two claims. First, they can explain just as well as the realist. Second, that there are numerous *individual* red things or *individual* wise persons is just a fact about the world. An *ultimate* fact—it requires no further explanation.

But Realists of course hold that attribute agreement—counting different objects as having the same property—requires some explanation. If Danny has a red rose and Deirdre has a red rose, our ordinary sense is that the two roses *share* the same color. These are both *instances of red*, realists say, because they share a common element, the universal. Realists hold that strict nominalism simply ignores these apparently obvious facts without *explaining why* our "normal sense" about attribute agreement is mistaken.

Despite the fact that their explanation is more complex because it requires a second kind of thing—universals—realists believe they still offer a *better* explanation than strict nominalism. Why? With the claim that it is just a brute fact about the world that there are only individuals, *and* no explanation why our ordinary view is mistaken, strict nominalism seems incomplete or arbitrary. The realists think they explain our normal intuition, accommodating our sense of the metaphysical makeup of the world.

Nominalism and Resemblance

Another less "strict" version of nominalism, **resemblance nominalism**, claims that we classify together certain individuals or use the same word to describe multiple objects because they *resemble* each other. Still, resemblance nominalists hold, there are only individuals in the world. But like members of a family, some individual objects may resemble one another, while another set of individuals resemble each other in a different way.

In the view of resemblance class nominalism, there is no need to bring in universals to explain attribute agreement. There are just individuals, grouped together. When Julia says "this book is blue," according to the resemblance class nominalist, she is talking about nothing more than individuals. She is saying, in effect, that this individual book is one of many objects that constitute a resemblance class—the class of blue things. Similarly, Deirdre's applauding the *courage* of the men and women of the armed forces does not invoke the idea of a universal. Instead she is referring to that group—that *class*—of individuals that are brave. Again, there is no need for the universal.

We've been slipping in the quasi-technical term "class" as a synonym for "group." This use of "class" is not in the socioeconomic sense, but the mathematical sense. A class is just a specified group: the class of people invited to Julia's party on Saturday, the class of books owned by Deirdre, the class of *wise* individuals, the class of *red* individuals. So, according to resemblance class nominalists, when we say that Deirdre bought a *blue* dress, we are simply noting that the dress belongs to a particular group.

Moreover, a single individual might belong to many different classes. An individual book can belong to the class of individuals that are red, to the class of individuals that are rectangular, to the class of individuals that are expensive, and to the class of individuals that are books about physics.

Thus, according to the resemblance class nominalist, there are only individuals. Individuals belong to different sets, such sets being specified or described by one of our linguistic terms. The realist is then wrong to think that universals must exist in order to explain our apparent reference to or thought about some common or shared element. This appeal is both unnecessary and a mistake, in the resemblance class nominalist's view.

The realist worries, however, that a resemblance class nominalist will get the wrong classes. A simple example might help. When I *think about* dogs—e.g., that they are descendants of the gray wolf—I am thinking about all and only those things that are dogs. My thought is about *everything* that instantiates the universal *being a dog*. Thus, my thought "includes" American Eskimos, Irish setters, shelties, puppies at the animal shelter, puppies I've seen, and puppies I will never see. Pick any two members of this class and here's what is guaranteed: they both instantiate *being a dog*. Instantiating the relevant universal determines the class of things included in my thought. That's how the realist gets the "right" class.

But some have noted that the resemblance nominalist can get some very odd "groupings." Our resemblance class can be a very motley crew—an Irish setter, which resembles a golden retriever, which resembles a bulldog, which resembles the Terrytoons cartoon character, Deputy Dawg, which resembles creatures from the infamous *Star Wars* bar scene, one of which resembles a Yorkshire terrier, which resembles a cat a former neighbor once owned... A cat?

WITTGENSTEIN AND FAMILY RESEMBLANCE

Various versions of resemblance theory provide different accounts of the nature of resemblance. One development of this view suggests that paying attention to our ordinary ways of talking and thinking—the way ordinary language works—may provide some relief to our perplexity.

Ludwig Wittgenstein had influential views about the problem of universals. First, it seems that he should be classed as a nominalist, not a realist. It is the rules of our language that determine when we group objects as falling under the same general term, or as showing the same characteristic. And the language, he argued, does group things by resemblance, but he thought that the usual view of resemblance was often too simple. Often we group things by their "family resemblance." This sort of grouping is an ordinary aspect of daily life. Observe a group of close relatives. What you see is that there is no characteristic that they all share; rather, there is a chain of overlapping similarities. Albert's eyes may be like Betty's, whose nose may resemble Cliff's, whose mouth and chin resembles unmistakably his brother Dexter's, whose.... no doubt you can continue the pattern.

Wittgenstein uses this everyday concept to explain why we take various items and call them by the same name. One of his favorite examples is "game," but we might use any common noun, say "chair." We identify all chairs as chairs, not because they possess some common element, but because we recognize overlapping similarities. (It won't do, for example, to say that all chairs are fit for sitting—so are sofas and loveseats and benches. But we want "chair" to refer to *only* chairs.) Overlapping similarities are the basis of resemblance, and hence enable us to group things together under the same term.

Renford Bambrough argues that in appealing to the notion of family resemblance, Wittgenstein solved the dispute between realism and nominalism.[23] According to Bambrough, Wittgenstein's concept of family resemblance explains why various items are "collected together" in language and thought, thus responding to the realist argument that our intuitions about groups of objects require explanation. Wittgenstein would not count as a realist, however, since family resemblances do not involve universals. There is no such thing as the "ideal chair" whose characteristics are true of all and only chairs.

---

23   Bambrough 1960; see also Nammour 1973.

ALBERT

BETTY

CLIFF

DEXTER

TROPES

Resemblance nominalism explained how two individual things are both (for example) blue by saying that they are both members of the same sets of things, and that these sets are constituted by individuals that resemble each other. But the problem with this is that individuals, each with a complicated collection of characteristics, can resemble each other in many ways. Well, we can specify that the appropriate resemblance is with regard to color: they're all blue. But that just puts us back where we started.

Trope nominalism[24] hopes to solve the problem here by seeing individual things as bundles of **tropes**. What is a trope? Sam's blue shirt has a particular blue on him, and the sky has a particular different blue up there. Even though we can imagine that they are precisely the same shade of blue, there are two tropes here: the one in Sam's shirt and the one in the sky. These aren't instances of a universal; they're particular "things"—individuals. More importantly, nothing is "shared"; each occurrence of blue is just *this particular* blue. Thus, tropes are particularized properties. Borrowing the term from one of America's more famous philosophers, George Santayana (1863–1952), Donald C. Williams named these individuals *tropes*.[25] Now think of ordinary things, like Sam's shirt, as being constituted by a bundle of different tropes, and nothing but them. The suggestion is that they are the basic entities of reality!

But now let us try to see how this is supposed to help with the problem of universals. What we want trope theory to do is to answer the question: why are Sam's shirt, and the sky, both blue? The answer proposed by trope theory is not the realist answer: that they both "participate" in the thing that is the form of blueness. Neither is it the resemblance-nominalist answer: that they are both members of a class of things that resemble each other. The answer they propose is trope-resemblance-nominalism. One of the tropes constituting Sam's shirt *resembles* one of the tropes constituting the sky. The class of blue tropes (for example) resembles each other more than any of them resembles any trope not in that class. So the relevant resemblance class includes all and only the resembling tropes. We avoid the problem of "in what respect" the members of the resemblance class resemble each other. In this class, they're all reds.

And what of nominalism's promised "simpler" view? It's true that there are only particulars in the trope view. But admitting tropes—particularized properties—might not be all that simple. Note that tropes are not physical objects; they are, instead, what some call "abstract particulars."[26] There are two senses in which we might think of them as "abstract." First, some theorists hold that we recognize them by a process of abstraction. That is, we "abstract" away from the other features of an object. In focusing on the blue of the shirt,

---

24   This is a very recent position, but some think that versions of it occur in Aristotle and
      William of Ockham. See Lahey, 1998.
25   Donald Williams 1953, pp. 5–6.
26   Campbell 1991.

I abstract away from its shape or its texture.[27] But there also is another sense for "abstract." Many universals can occupy the same place. So also can many tropes occupy the same place. This apple comprises *this particular red, this particular sphere, this particular sweetness,* along with the other tropes that constitute this apple. So, while the trope view may not require us to posit the existence of universals, the realist might doubt that it is any simpler to think of ordinary objects—a table or a dog or a glass—as bundles of abstract particulars.

But consider an argument Bertrand Russell made in favor of universals: it raises a problem about resemblance nominalism, and also about the trope-resemblance proposal. Russell asks whether the relation of *resemblance* and all its instances require a universal. In the context, how else should we explain our calling all the particular resemblings by the same name? Why do we count these as *resemblance* classes? We apparently count them, Russell says, as instances of the *same relation.* Russell argued that the nominalist is thus unable to escape invoking universals. All the individual resemblings can be treated as the same only if we see them as instances of the universal *resemblance.*[28] Some trope theorists reply that there is a *resemblance trope.* Otherwise, the resemblance-relation is not explained. So is trope-theory an advance?

A similar question might be asked about the *compresence* of tropes to constitute a particular object. We will see this question again in the next chapter, but it is worth noting here. Some critics have asked why some tropes "bundle together" to form an object. One answer seems to be the relation of compresence. Critics wonder how best to understand this relation.

Consider for a moment the red hollyberry candle in front of me. It comprises many different tropes, including color, shape, fragrance. Now we might understand these tropes as internally related. That is, they *had to be a part of this and no other bundle.* To some, this seems too strong. It seems to claim that this candle had to be just this way, and no other. There is nothing incoherent about such a view, but to many, it seems to say that every characteristic of this candle is essential to it. Again, this seems too strong, since we think that certain aspects—tropes—of this candle might have been different, yet it would still be *this* candle.

Alternatively the relation of compresence might be considered an external relation. Suppose Mandy is seated to the left of Jack. The relation "seated to the left of" is an inessential feature of both Mandy and Jack. They would have

---

27   Douglas Edwards 2014, p. 50.
28   Russell 1959, Chaps. IX and X.

been the same individuals had Mandy been seated to Jack's right or indeed if Mandy were not seated anywhere in the room! In this view, however, if we think of the tropes as externally related, this relation itself must be a trope, a compresence trope. However, now we seem to have an argument similar to the Third Man. There must be some further relation which explains why this particular trope is compresent with the other tropes. And this further relation requires yet a new compresence trope.

Now the trope theorist can of course deny that compresence tropes are part of the bundles. But this presses a question that is often asked of bundle theorists: how should we understand why some object is structured in this way? Why are the tropes related to each other in the way that they are? There is something about the way the wax trope, the fragrance trope, and the "burning" trope of this candle are interrelated. Does trope theory assist in our understanding of that?[29]

More can be said about trope theory, and indeed, about the abiding dispute between realism and nominalism. But two "intermediate" views are worth noting.

Moderate Realism and Conceptualism

Immanent or Scientific Realism: David Armstrong

David M. Armstrong, an Australian philosopher who has been extremely influential in metaphysics, epistemology, and the philosophy of mind, argued for a version of moderate realism that is sometimes called *immanent realism*.

Like Aristotle, Armstrong held that universals exist, but not separately from their instantiations; universals always and only exist in the objects. A distinctive feature of his view is that determining which universals exist is an *empirical* matter. That is, science tells us which properties exist. And the relevant properties are those that are reflected in scientific laws; for example, the charge of an electron is a property of electrons, and therefore a universal. Hence, this moderate realism is a scientific realism.

Armstrong thought that the ontology of the world—its structure—was a conjunction of all the states of affairs, that is, all the objects and their

---

29   See Edwards 2014, pp. 54–59.

properties. Immanent universals are necessary to explain the structure of the world, and the physical necessity that we see in scientific laws.

His two-volume work, *Universals and Scientific Realism*, examines the various nominalist views in the first volume and develops his own version of moderate realism in the second volume. *Universals: An Opinionated Introduction* is a tour of his objections to nominalist views and a briefer account of his own view. Interestingly, in the concluding section, Armstrong suggests that a version of trope theory and his immanent realism may both be right, simply alternative ways of talking about the same set of issues.

Perhaps there is a different way to understand the "universal" element in our thinking. Two different views suggest just that. **Moderate realism** holds that our "kind concepts" refer to universals, but universals are "in" the objects. Conceptualism holds that each concept itself is universal because it stands for or refers to a number of individuals. Aristotle is often considered a moderate realist, as are various thirteenth-century philosophers, such as St. Thomas Aquinas, while Peter Abelard's view is often thought of as conceptualism (but different commentators have variously associated him with moderate realism or different versions of nominalism).

Understanding and comparing views such as Aristotle's moderate realism or Abelard's conceptualism is challenging because each uses its own terminological framework. While the intricacies of the terminological framework frequently nuance the views under consideration, it is possible to provide general outlines of moderate realism and conceptualism using the terminology employed elsewhere in this chapter.

Moderate Realism

A sketch of Aristotle's moderate realism emerges in his *Metaphysics*, in a criticism of the realist view he attributes to Plato. In *De Interpretatione*, Aristotle defines "universal" as "that which is of such a nature as to be predicated of many subjects, and 'individual' as that which is not thus predicated."[30] For our purposes, we can interpret "can be predicated of many" to mean "can be multiply instantiated."

---

30   Aristotle 1941c, Sect.1, Pt. 7.

Aristotle, like the realist, holds that different individuals may manifest the *same property*. This chartreuse shirt and that chartreuse blouse both exhibit the property "chartreuse." Chartreuse can thus "be predicated of many" and so denotes a universal. To put it another way, chartreuse is a universal because it is instantiated in this shirt and this blouse.

Aristotle, the *moderate* realist, disagrees with the realist's view that the universal exists *separately* from its numerous occurrences. For the moderate realist, universals always exist in the objects that manifest them or possess them. (The technical term is that the universals are *immanent*, existing only in particular objects.) This has an interesting consequence: there are no *un*-instantiated universals. We have a concept of the universal, but this concept is not a universal itself—it just "stands for" the universal. If we think *chartreuse*, we are thus referring to the universal, wherever and whenever it occurs in one or many individual objects.

It's important to be clear on a major difference between moderate realism and trope theory: in moderate realism, it is the universal occurring in each object. These "chartreuses" are not merely similar. *They are one and the same chartreuse* occurring in different places at the same time. (The chartreuse tropes in those two pieces of clothing are distinct things. Tropes in two distinct places are never one and the same: they are always distinct tropes.) We group objects together—that is, we recognize attribute agreement—when we recognize that the same quality is instantiated in more than one object. But, though the moderate realist agrees with the realist that the best way to explain attribute agreement is in reference to a universal, moderate realism also differs from realism in that the moderate realist rejects the idea of independently existing universals. Instead, moderate realism sees universals as a distinct type of entity, multiply and simultaneously occurring in various objects.

The moderate realist view, then, looks like this in simple outline. A group of blue objects are classified as *being blue* because the same universal exists in each. This is how the moderate realist explains attribute agreement. While the universal can exist in many objects at once, there are only "immanent occurrences," never existing apart from those individual objects. Hence, for the moderate realist, the universal *blue* is occurring here, now, in this book, in that book, in this glass, in that shirt—and when we think *blue* we are thinking about all and only these "immanent occurrences" of blue. The moderate realist keeps universals, but they're "pushed inside" the objects.

(The idea that one and the same thing exists in two different places at the same time is not as bizarre as it at first might seem. Consider a university with two campuses: it exists downtown and in the suburbs simultaneously. The difference, however, is that we should say that part of the university is here, and the rest of it is over there; but *all* of the universal *blue* is supposed to be both in the sky and in Sam's shirt.)

Why does Aristotle think that the universals don't exist separately from their occurrences? His principal criticisms of Plato appear in the *Metaphysics*, one of Aristotle's more difficult works, which examines not only Plato, but his other predecessors as well. Two objections to Plato are worth noting.

First, Aristotle claims that invoking the Ideas, or Plato's forms—our universals—is an unnecessary duplication. Aristotle likens those who affirm the independent existence of universals to a man who wanted to count the things that existed, but thought the counting might be easier if there were more things to count. But the metaphysical task of "counting" or cataloguing the types of objects is hardly made easier by adding more. Aristotle wonders why we should add to or complicate our "counting task," by supposing that there is a whole class of objects undetectable by the normal means. This criticism leads quickly to the second, more important thought behind Aristotle's criticism.

Aristotle apparently held that Plato's view is not explanatory because it's not clear how the *independent* existence of universals contributes to the nature or essence of particular things. How can something *outside* the object be a part of its essence?[31]

Perhaps Aristotle's point might be explained in this way. We sometimes want to know what makes something a given *kind* of thing. For example, we want to know what is that special characteristic or group of characteristics that makes something a dog, and not, say, a coyote. Today we might rely on the genomic differences to tell us their different natures or essences. Having the "dog-gene-structure" is the essence of being a dog. But the essence is something *in* the object. Once we know that essence, does it tell us any more to say, "Oh, by the way, this essence also exists by itself"? Aristotle thinks not. A universal "off by itself" seemingly has no effect on the essence of some individual object. So, Aristotle thinks that if our aim is to understand something about *particulars*, knowing something about a universal *removed from* particulars seems an unlikely path to the desired understanding.

On two counts then, Aristotle thinks that separately existing universals don't help: they don't help with explaining the essence or nature of objects, and they don't help with explaining our knowledge of individual objects.

---

31   A.E. Taylor 1949.

Two points might be made on Plato's behalf. Some have pointed out that the forms as Plato viewed them are not really unnecessary, since they allow him to give a unified answer to ethical, epistemological, and metaphysical questions. That we call widely different actions all by the same name, e.g., "courageous," that we are able to explain differences between opinion and knowledge, that we are able to explain the nature of the objectivity—all of these matters can be given a consistent, unified account by appeal to the forms. Identifying courage as a universal explains why we call "courageous" widely disparate acts, e.g., the act of the bystander who steps in to prevent a mugging of an elderly citizen or the soldier who sacrifices his life. And we are able to explain the differences between believing and knowing about the nature of courage, which in turn is explained by a metaphysical theory, the theory of the forms. We *know* what courage is when we have grasped the form. This theory at once gives us an understanding of the connection between attribute agreement, knowledge, and objectivity. Thus, there is an "economy" to Plato's view.[32]

Second, Plato might agree that it's only when a universal is instantiated in an individual that it makes a difference to the sort of individual it is. Yet Plato might—and arguably did—dissent from the idea that independently existing universals do not contribute to our understanding of individuals or particulars. For example, in the *Phaedo* Socrates argues that we can come across two items that are said to be equal, but we recognize that they are not quite *exactly* equal. This implies, Socrates claims, that we are comparing the apparently equal objects to some independent standard, which Socrates says is the universal *equals*, or the relation of equality.[33] Responses to these objections might be made on behalf of Aristotle, but there is no room to discuss them here; instead, we will move on to one more important facet of moderate realism.

Aristotle held that we acquire our concept of a given universal by a process of abstraction, which is an intellectual rather than a sensory process. But abstraction begins with the sensory process. Imagine that as Deirdre surveys her back yard, she notices several American finches perched on the various trees and bushes. Of course, Deirdre has "sensings" of each of the finches. But something else also happens. Deirdre's intellect extracts or *abstracts* the *intelligible form* of the common nature or essence of this kind, American finch. The intelligible form itself is not something sensible. Rather

---

32   Cherniss 1936.
33   Copleston 1946, Vol. 1, Pt. II, Chap. 29.

it's something apprehended and known intellectually. Deirdre doesn't see or smell or taste the intelligible form, but she does cognize or apprehend or think it. In virtue of possessing this abstracted intellectual form, Deirdre now has the concept *American finch*, a concept standing for or referring to all and only American finches.

Moderate realism thus holds that universal concepts—concepts that refer to many instances—are formed by an intellectual process of abstraction. The universal concept refers to all particular individuals possessing the universal because the abstracted form is the intellectual aspect of that essence. And this provides the moderate realist with an explanation of abstract reference: the concept refers to the universal. When Deirdre says that finches are birds, she is referring to the immanent essence of any and all finches.

The Aristotelian in particular and the moderate realist in general thus think that their view possesses all the advantages of a realism like Plato's, but none of the disadvantages.

Moderate realism is closely related to conceptualism, but, as we will see, they differ in an important respect.

Conceptualism

Heloise and Abelard

The twelfth-century relationship between the philosopher Abelard and his student Heloise could scarcely be rivaled by Hollywood. In fact, Hollywood saw fit to make *Stealing Heaven* in 1988—the story of their romance, perhaps the most famous romance of the medieval period.

In Paris Abelard achieved considerable fame: his attractiveness, his intelligence, and his skill in argument all contributed to his reputation. When he was hired by Heloise's uncle to tutor her, the two fell in love. Abelard's poems to her and their affair became well-known among the populace—and eventually by Heloise's uncle, who tried to separate them. The lovers continued to meet secretly, however, and when Heloise became pregnant, Abelard offered to marry her. Only after a time did she accept, and the two attempted to keep the marriage secret to minimize the damage to Abelard's career.

Heloise's uncle began to spread information about the secret marriage, and Heloise retreated to the safety of a convent. Her uncle, believing that Abelard was trying to end the marriage by forcing Heloise to become a nun, had him beaten and castrated. Abelard retired from public life, entered a monastery and eventually founded a convent that Heloise later headed.

Out of touch with each other for ten years, the two began a correspondence, initiated by Heloise. The letters are a famous moment in romantic literature (Levitan 2007). They range over various topics, including morality, the nature of love, Heloise's and Abelard's feelings about their relationship, and Abelard's request to her that he be buried at her convent. Heloise honored his request.[34]

Peter Abelard contributed significantly to the medieval debate about universals. While most commentators recognize the importance of his work, there is some controversy about how to interpret and categorize it. He is described as a moderate realist, as a nominalist, and as a conceptualist. Here, we will interpret Abelard's view as a form of conceptualism—but clarifying this account will perhaps also illustrate why Abelard's view is sometimes classified in other ways.

To put it simply, Abelard's view is that universals are concepts that exist only in the mind but can refer to many individual non-mental objects. In other words, concepts are particular "things," which exist only in individual minds and enable us to think about objects. Concepts, of course, are not things the way a coffee cup or a camellia bush or a cloud are things; they differ both from each other and from things like camellias and clouds. Contemporary vernacular might call them "mental particulars." Here Abelard holds a view not unlike other nominalists, namely, that everything that exists is particular (or individual). Concepts, too, are particular. Yet, some concepts are also *universal* in the following sense: they refer to more than one individual. As in moderate realism, these universal concepts are reached through intellectual abstraction.

Abelard's view requires us to be careful about the nature of these universal concepts. As mental phenomena, they do not exist apart from the mind. Indeed this is part of what differentiates Abelard's view from realism. The universal concept enables us to talk and think generally, yet it does not exist outside the mind.

Understanding the process of forming a universal concept is central for Abelard. On encountering a particular horse, Dobbin, I form a concept *of that particular horse*. This concept includes the various aspects of *this horse*. It's brown, with a black mane, not very tall, but friendly.

---

34   Wagoner 1997; Marenbon 1997; Gilson 1960.

After seeing several horses, after collecting several sensory images of particular horses, Abelard says that I abstract a common form. This form, or "image" as he sometimes says, is not tied to any particular horse. The image is generalized, so that it stands for all horses. This differs from Aristotle; I don't abstract the intellectual form from the universal or the essence contained by the individuals. Abstraction for Abelard is more like neglecting the individual differences, or *abstracting away* from the particular differences of each of the individual concepts and "seeing" what is left. This abstracted or generalized concept *horse* is universal in the sense that it has been "de-particularized" sufficiently so that it stands for all the various particular horses. The word "horse," when it names this universal concept, is a universal name or word. So, the word names the concept, and the concept stands for all the particulars. As a generalized and hence universal concept, *horse* now refers to any and all horses.

The universal concept *horse* stands for all horses. The English word "horse" and the Latin word "*equus*" refer to all horses, since they name the same universal concept. But does the universal concept stand for many particulars because there is something *the same* or *common* in the individuals? Or is this just a matter of convention or arbitrary grouping, such as "Well, it seems to me that these individuals are alike ..."? Abelard holds the former, that a universal concept is formed because of something in the objects; there is an *objective* reason for universal concepts. We didn't just manufacture the concepts based on nothing. Instead we group or classify individuals because of some common element, or "common cause," as Abelard called it. Abelard further seemed to suggest that it's more than just similarity or "being a lot alike" at work here. But conceptualism also rejects the idea of moderate realism, which holds that a universal exists *in* many different particulars. Thus, Abelard says, "Since there is no *thing* in which things could possibly agree, if there is any agreement among certain things, [that is, if they are both of the same sort,] this must not be taken to be some *thing*."[35]

To put it more succinctly, universal concepts are generalized images, intellectually abstracted from particular sensory images. The generalized image thus explains our ability to refer to many individuals by a universal word, e.g., "horse." And this standing for or referring to many individuals explains why we have a *universal* concept. Such concepts are universal because they stand for a plurality of individuals.

---

35   Abelard 1969/1992, p. 26; Marenbon 1997, pp. 190 ff.

Two principal differences between moderate realism and conceptualism may then be noted. While there is a "common form" that is the basis of the universal concept, Abelard rejects the idea that there are immanent universals. And while both views acknowledge a process of abstraction, the moderate realist believes that it is the universal (or the form) that is abstracted. For the conceptualist, the intellect abstracts by generalizing, by ignoring the differences between particulars.

While conceptualists reject the moderate realist's claim that a universal exists in each object, they also reject the nominalist claim that what might look like a universal essence is just similarity or "being a lot alike" in some respect. There really is something common to the various individuals, says the conceptualist—just not a universal.

To its critics, this seems like an uneasy intermediate view, occasionally flirting with realism, then with nominalism. For it might seem a simple step from "common element" to "immanent universal." And, in the other direction, it might seem a simple step from the conceptualist emphasis on naming a universal concept to the nominalist dismissal of categories as "just names." In its position on this issue, conceptualism occupies a central fault line between realists and nominalists. In attempting to find generality in our thoughts rather than in the world, conceptualism attempts a delicate balancing act. In doing so, it inherits special problems of its own. And these problems perhaps illustrate why most theorists are today either realist or nominalist.

Key Concepts

- universal
- particulars
- realism about universals
- nominalism
- moderate realism (about universals)
- conceptualism
- Third Man Argument
- strict nominalism
- resemblance nominalism
- tropes
- moderate realism

Reading Questions

1. In your own words, explain the attribute agreement argument for realism. How would you assess this argument? Do you agree with Plato or other realists that there is something like an objective standard for beauty or courage? Explain.

2. In the dialogue *Parmenides*, Parmenides asks the young Socrates if he accepts universals for things like mud or hair. Socrates says that he is unsure. (The problem here seems to be that a universal is an ideal form, and how can there be an ideal form of something that is nasty?) And in the *Republic*, Socrates mentions the form of "bed." Do you think a realist about universals ought to accept that universals for these sorts of things exist?

3. Do you agree with the strict nominalists, like Quine, that we don't need to explain why we group red houses, red books, red glasses together? Why or why not?

4. Which form of resemblance nominalism do you find more defensible, the resemblance class view or the trope view? Why?

5. Abelard held the view that it is only words or concepts that are "universal." A word or term is universal because it is used to refer to many individuals. Do you agree with this view? Why or why not?

6. Write a brief essay that explains the advantages of universals over nominalism.

For Further Reading

Three surveys of metaphysics contain chapters on universals. E.J. Lowe 2002 and Loux 2006 are perhaps a bit more advanced. Loux has separate chapters on universals and nominalism. Carroll and Markosian 2010 also contains a chapter on universals. Two worthwhile collections of essays/selections on universals and particulars are Loux 1970 and Schoedinger 1992. The shorter work by Armstrong 1989 presents his assessment of other views, primarily forms of nominalism, and also presents his own moderate realist view, which identifies universals with scientific properties. W.T. Jones 1969b contains a section explaining the medieval thinkers' debate on universals. There are several accessible treatments of Aristotle's view; Copleston 1974 is particularly helpful and readable. The interpretation of Plato's views on universals (forms) is still contested. White 1976, which is readily accessible, and Rosen 2008, perhaps a bit more challenging, offer important and interesting interpretations.

Gracia 1992 is an accessible and careful presentation of the medieval view of transcendentals.

CHAPTER FIVE

THINGS

METAPHYSICS AIMS TO DESCRIBE THE NATURE OF REALITY, OF ALL THAT there is. Perhaps the single most obvious feature of that reality is the existence of *things*, of objects, of individuals. Philosophers often call them "particulars." Particulars range from the very large—the planet Jupiter, for example—to the very small—the molecule or the atom or the neutron or the single cell. Now philosophers are not usurping the role of scientists when they attempt to explain the nature and structure of all things. When philosophers ask about the nature of things, they are trying to understand something about their metaphysical nature. They are not trying to reveal the genome of the *canis lupus familiaris*— man's best friend—but they are interested in finding out what it is to be an individual object, whether a dog or a planet or a tree or a town, or any *thing*.

It may seem odd to think that metaphysics could tell us about the general structure and nature of things. After all, isn't that the business of the sciences—to tell us what makes up things and how they are put together?

Notice, however: we can still ask a few very general questions, which the sciences seemingly don't answer. We distinguish between a thing (or object) and its characteristics (or properties). Just what is the relationship between the thing and its characteristics? (This question will become clearer in a moment.) And a related question: is there something more to an object than just its characteristics? What more is there to this hollyberry candle than its color, scent, shape, and its other features? Are some properties more important than others for an object to be that object or that *kind* of object? That blue-footed booby—it couldn't be a *blue-footed* booby without its blue feet (could it?), but what if it didn't have the characteristic of performing a mating dance? The "metaphysics of things" aims at answering these types of question.

Notice that the metaphysics of things distinguishes between the *type* or *kind* and an individual instance of the kind. No doubt your early science classes taught you that mammals are warm-blooded vertebrates with hair that produce milk for their young. The kind *mammal* has various individual instances, including Millie, the echidna (a relative of the duck-billed platypus), a mascot of the 2000 Summer Olympics. And Millie has characteristics that distinguish or *individuate* her from other echidnas. The metaphysics of things considers both the identity of the kind and the individual.

First Thoughts: Individuals as Substances

Many perhaps take for granted an intuitive picture of individuals or things. We think of cats and dogs, or people and chimpanzees; we think of rose bushes or cherry trees. At some point, we may come to think of molecules. We may wonder if mountains or clouds are things in the same way as chairs or golf balls. No matter our answer to these latter examples, we continue to think of the world as a world of things. And we think of these things—each one having its uniquely identifying characteristics or properties—as the ultimate constituents of the world. We may nonetheless recognize a thing as made up of various components. Yet the puppy's tail, the cat's whiskers, a person's hand—these are parts of the whole, of the individual. The *individual* thing is basic.

Notice that it is not the type that is basic, in this view; it is the individuals. And the individuals or basic things of course have characteristics or properties. The dog is growling, or the rose bush is blooming. Julia is wise, or Jack is frugal. The kitten is calico, the puppy energetic, or the chimpanzee curious. Such characteristics or features are features that *belong* to the individual, not to some part. We don't think, for example, "There goes Jack's brain again, being frugal." Springtime visitors to Washington, DC, during the Cherry Blossom Festival, don't think that a branch is blooming, but rather that the tree is blooming. Moreover, setting aside the Cheshire Cat in *Alice in Wonderland*, we don't think there are disconnected, independent grinnings. We think that we always experience "frugal-ness" as someone or other being frugal, the smile or the grin as belonging to someone or other. It is a cherry blossom or a shirt that is pink; we don't experience pink "all by itself." Our experience of pink is always an experience of the color as *belonging to* some individual thing.

There are then three aspects to this intuitive picture of the makeup of the world: individuals as basic, individuals as being of a certain kind of thing, and features or characteristics or aspects as belonging to or depending on the individuals.

Aristotle's *Categories* provides one of the earliest attempts to describe systematically the picture of the things that make up our world; it is a view that is in many respects similar to the intuitive picture just described.[1] Aristotle identifies the basic things or individuals of the world as *substances—primary substances*, as he calls them—the puppy, the palm tree, the proton, or any other individual thing. Primary substances "underlie" everything else. We can note two senses in which they underlie everything else. First, they are the ultimate constituents of the world, which is made up of individual dogs, trees, and planets (rather than being made up of qualities like "brownness" or of categories like "Chihuahuas"). Second, the properties of these individuals, including relations to other individuals, depend on the individuals or primary substances. You can't have just brown, by itself; you have to have a brown something—a brown dog, for example.

Things Change: Substance, Essence, and Accident

Aristotle's substance view continued to serve as a metaphysical framework much discussed by medieval philosophers, discussed in relation to a wide range of topics including the nature of individuals or things in general, human nature and the soul, and even the nature of God.[2] Reliance on the concept of substance, variously defined, continued through the early modern period. More recently, despite serious criticism offered by Berkeley and Hume, and twentieth-century process philosophy, substance views have seen something

---

1   Aristotle 1941a.
2   Gilson 1940 surveys many of these issues.

of a revival by some contemporary defenders.[3] The notion of substances with attributes—called the **substance or the substance-attribute view**—is a fundamental framework for thinking of individuals, one that has been used to explain a number of features of things or individuals.

First, consider the thought that individuals, for example, belong to kinds. This plant is a begonia, that animal is a white-tailed deer. The kind has an *essence* or a *nature*, some defining property or properties that each member of the kind possesses. You're not a mammal unless you're a vertebrate, for example. In the early twenty-first century, we might appeal to DNA, for example, to distinguish the kind *rhesus macaque* from *lemur*. Sometimes it is an easy matter to identify a defining characteristic—e.g., one defining characteristic of a tricycle is that it has three wheels—while listing those defining characteristics for some objects may be more complicated. Often we note the kind as a way of identifying the essence. Bucephalus is a horse and what makes him a horse is possessing that characteristic of *being a horse*. Alexander the Great is a human being in virtue

of his having a certain essence, a certain defining characteristic, namely, *being a human being*. Of course, if we thought that what makes something a human being or a horse is simply having the DNA definitive of a human being or horse, we might say: Bucephalus is a horse because he possesses the attribute of *having the DNA definitive of being a horse*. Notice, however, that identifying the essence of more complex objects—say, human beings—simply by noting their molecular makeup can be controversial. Various thinkers—among them philosophers, but also theologians, artists of various types, and social scientists—have held that the defining characteristic, or *attribute*, of the *nature* of human beings is more than just some common molecular structural pattern.

Aristotle, for example, thought that the defining characteristic of human beings is the ability to reason, as did Descartes and Kant, each with their own take on this ability. Julia and Sam are of the kind *human being* then because they both possess this rational ability. On the other hand, the twentieth-century German philosopher Martin Heidegger suggests at times that the defining nature of human beings is that we are the being that speaks—we are language-using creatures.[4] The interest here is not to adjudicate between rival conceptions of *human being*. The point rather is to note that an essence or nature comprises certain properties, certain attributes. And two individuals belong to the same kind if they both have the same general nature or essence.

Leibniz: All Our Attributes Are Essential

G.W. Leibniz held an unusual view of substance. In his view, the basic individuals are immaterial, indivisible entities called *monads*. Our familiar objects are composed of monads or societies of them. Monads are characterized as "windowless": because of their nature, they are not affected by the outside world. The apparent interaction between monads or societies or collectives of monads is only apparent. That is, when Andrea tells Andy to close the door and he does, or when one billiard ball hits another and the second takes off, this looks to us as though there is some causal interaction between the two. But this is merely apparent. What we take to be cause-effect sequences are rather unrelated; any change in a substance comes solely from the nature of that substance itself. Observed regularities—the second billiard ball *always* moves when hit by the first—are due to the coordination of the natures of things by divine plan, known as *pre-established harmony*.

---

4   Heidegger 1976; see also Heidegger 1965.

Leibniz held that persons possess only essential attributes; there are no inessential or accidental attributes. According to him, apparently accidental attributes are so only from *our* perspective. From God's point of view, those attributes are necessary parts of who we are. Thus, God knows a complete description of each individual from eternity, and there is no changing any item in that description. Hence, Alexander acquiring Bucephalus at the age of thirteen is an essential feature of Alexander the Great, even though it seems to us to be an accidental or inessential property of Alexander.

Not all attributes are essential, however. Some attributes are inessential or *accidental* to being a particular kind of thing. While both Julia and Sam are human beings, her light-colored hair differs from his dark-colored hair; similarly, their eye color may differ, or their height. Characteristics such as height or eye color or age are *accidental* attributes. Changes to these—Sam dyes his hair; Julia becomes a year older—do not change the kind of thing, only some of its properties.

The substance-attribute framework thus provides an answer to a more general question: what is change? For the substance theorist, change is simply a change in attributes. Lose an attribute, gain an attribute—a thing changes. And with the distinction between essential and inessential attributes, we also have a way of understanding two different types of change. Paint the dining room table a light red. The table has changed. Yet it's still a dining room table, because the altered attribute is inessential. The cherry tree loses its blossoms, but it's still a cherry tree. Sara now sports a tattoo—changed, yes, but still Sara.⁵ On the other hand, supposing for a moment that cellulose is an essential characteristic of wood, burning a spruce log in the fireplace "changes" the essence of the wood. This is essential change, also called substantial change.

Any substantial change involves destruction. The individual becomes a new kind of thing, and the old individual exists no more. During cases of "radioactive change," for example, an atom of one kind can change into a new kind of atom.

---

5   See, e.g., David Ross 1971, pp. 81–83; see also Aristotle 1941e, Book V.

Hierarchy: Animal, Vegetable ... or Artifact

Dogs belong to different (pure or mixed) breeds, but they all belong to the same species. And here we have a simple example of a hierarchy of kinds. Perhaps somewhere along the way, reading a book in botany or biology, you came across a more complete hierarchy: species, genus, family, order, class, phylum, kingdom. We talk about the *animal* kingdom, for example. Is there an analogous hierarchy for objects?

Sort of. Aristotle identified three kinds of primary substances, or things: animals, including human beings; plants; and the basic individuals or elements acknowledged by science. Of course, Aristotle knew nothing of hydrogen or carbon atoms, even if certain kinds of "stuff"—of say, iron, gold, and silver— were well-known. But Aristotle thought there were four "basic elements" composing all physical things. (For modern substance theorists, there are far more elements in this category; a standard version of the modern Periodic Table recognizes about 120 basic elements.)[6]

To these three kinds of individuals or things, let us add a fourth—artifacts. We might think of an artifact as something which requires the skill or intervention of some animal. Thus, we might think of beaver dams or bird nests as artifacts, and hence a type of individual (though some philosophers argue that artifacts are not individuals[7]). Still there seem to be clear cut cases of artifacts, such as things we make or build.

We might then think of our hierarchy like this. Every individual thing is a member of some kind. And every kind is a member of some "family"—animal, plant, basic scientific element, or artifact. Each of these then is a kind of object; each belongs to the "object kingdom."

To recap: a substance is our familiar individual—Bucephalus, Alexander, the rose bush, the table. And the *kind of individual* is determined by the essence or the defining attribute(s) that each possesses. Substance theory enables us to explain the nature of change too, as well as to distinguish essential from inessential or accidental change. It also enables us to classify individuals according to the type of object they are.

---

6 See Aristotle 1941e, Book II.
7 E.g., van Inwagen 1990, Chap. 13.

The Independence of Substance:
A Contemporary View

Substance, as we have seen, is an ontological category. Like *property* or *class*, the term "substance" names a very general and fundamental kind. Perhaps the most important aspect of substances is that they exist *independently*. Unlike properties, they don't depend on something else for their existence. Aristotle and later René Descartes held that if something was identified as substance, it is both necessary and sufficient that it is subsistent—that is, it does not depend on something else for its existence. God, according to Descartes, is the only truly independently existing "object." But we can also talk about what counts as an object in our terrestrial realm. What is it that can exist by itself? Minds and bodies, in Descartes's view. Here we see *substance* as a very general category, defined by the principal attribute by which genuine objects manifest themselves. As you perhaps already know, Descartes divides all objects into two types of substance: minds are essentially thought or thinking, and bodies are essentially extended. Again, no mind nor any body depends on something else for its existence—so no mind *depends* on any body. This of course opens the door to various problems about the relation between mind and body, but that is a topic for another field of philosophy.[8]

We have set aside some "niceties" here: mammals as physical beings or objects require something else for their existence: sperm and an egg, care from a parent, and a hospitable environment, just to name three. But we recognize that there is an intuitive sense in which they are independent. And it is worth trying to spell out this intuitive sense more rigorously. Joshua Hoffman and Gary Rosenkrantz have undertaken this task, defending an independence account of substance, which is consonant with historical views of the nature of substance.[9]

They begin by locating the notion of substance in one of two very general categories. A substance is a *concrete* entity rather than *abstract*. We noted in the previous chapter that realists about universals identify them as abstract objects. Also noted there, realists about mathematics consider numbers or sets to be abstract objects. Hoffman and Rosenkrantz observe plausibly that every object is either abstract or concrete. Properties, relations, and propositions are for them subcategories of abstract objects. As examples of concrete

---

8   See Crumley 2006, Chap. 1.
9   Hoffman and Rosenkrantz 1997.

things, they mention several subcategories, including, importantly, substances, events, time, place, and collections (groups), among others. It is worth noting that spirits are, for them, concrete.

The term for this—the immediate subcategories of *abstract* and *concrete* level—is "Level C." Substance is thus a Level C category, and material objects and "spirits" are subcategories of substance.[10]

Perhaps this diagram will help visualize the hierarchical arrangement:[11]

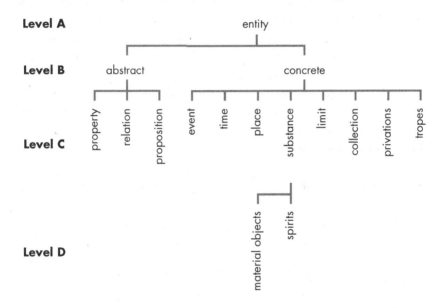

Often the distinction between abstract and concrete is drawn along spatio-temporal lines. On this view, a concrete thing is a thing that enters into spatio-temporal relations: this cup is *on the table*. And abstract objects are entities (or things or objects—here the terms are used synonymously), are those that are not part of the spatiotemporal framework.

Hoffman and Rosenkrantz resist this idea and instead prefer to rely on the notion of *part*, more specifically, *parthood*. They appear to hold that we have a pre-theoretic grasp of the generic concept of parthood. That is, I (presumably) understand, as do you, what it is for a hydrogen ion to be part of the molecule of water. Parts need not be only concrete, however. This book

10   *Ibid.*, pp 47–49.
11   *Ibid.*, p. 48.

before me has an abstract property, being rectangular. A substance then may have both concrete and abstract parts. An object is thus concrete if and only if it is a substance and if at least some of its parts are spatiotemporal parts; otherwise it is abstract.

You are no doubt wondering why they appeal to the notion of parthood in order to identify concrete substances. Their principal worry is that some abstract entities appear to enter into spatiotemporal relations. Suppose that Alyssa is attentive (their example). Alyssa is a concrete object. The property of her being attentive is abstract, yet it appears to enter into spatiotemporal relations. Relying on the notion of parthood thus enables Hoffman and Rosenkrantz to recognize Alyssa as a concrete substance (perhaps a spirit) that has as an abstract part—being attentive.[12] We are thus able to see the way in which substances—what we might call individual objects—can have parts.

Of course, the important point for us is Hoffman and Rosenkrantz's account of substance. Think for a moment of what we might take to mean. Ordinarily, an object not needing anything else to exist. Clearly the pup at my feet or the woman next door need something else to exist; indeed we know they both need lots of things. Food, some shelter, warmth, water, oxygen, and if in fact both are essentially social beings, contact with other animals (of some type). But there is a sense in which *at least for a time* either could exist *by themselves*. Of course, we allow for their proper parts—they both need hearts that pump, brains that control internal homeostatic properties. But what don't they need? Some entity or object in one of the other categories, which exists at that time. For at least during some time interval, the puppy doesn't need me, nor does my neighbor. Nor for some duration do they need other persons or animals. Now, this looks like an independence condition. Neither my puppy nor my neighbor need as a part of themselves some event to occur, whether it is the election of a president or the preparation of a dinner. Neither does either require that it be some particular time, even dinner time! Particular times and places aren't part of them.

This sketch focuses on two instances of mammal, but presumably we could tell a similar story about the red book to my right or the cup approximately 18 inches north of the book.

How does this yield independence? Suppose we have a material object or spirit. And suppose there is at least some time interval. During this time interval, the object (say the woman next door) does not require any item in

---

12   *Ibid.*, pp. 49–50.

the Level C concrete category to exist as *part of herself*; then there is a sense in which she doesn't *need* those items. She is independent of them.

Couldn't it be objected that any object needs something else at some point—the cup needs the artist that drew the cardinals on holly branches that adorn its outside, the book needs the authors Joshua and Gary, the neighbor needs parents? In response, this is no doubt more than the intuition or ordinary experience that motivates the independence account of substance. So, perhaps that *for an interval* is sufficient to formulate a notion of independence.

The final definition of substance Hoffman and Rosenkrantz provide has three clauses, the last of which they identify as an independence condition.[13] The development of their detailed argument in part shows that the other categories, such as event, are not substances. And the rest of the book puts their notion of substance to theoretical work, considering various issues in metaphysics, including what it is to be alive. Perhaps, however, these few paragraphs are sufficient to indicate that a historically prominent understanding of what it is to be substance can be formulated in such a way as to address both traditional and contemporary metaphysical issues.

Things = Substratum + Properties

Sally is a tall red-haired Mid-westerner. The rug is brown, oval, and fuzzy. In each case, we think of a *something* plus its properties; the *something*—the substance—holds its properties together.

Some might think that the notion of a primary substance doesn't quite explain all that we need to know about things. So what holds the properties together? What's the Sally or the rug here?

In response, some have urged a different notion of substance, in this context often called **substratum**—*that which supports or holds together the various properties of an object.* Substratum theorists distinguish between the properties of an object and what it is that holds the properties together. Importantly, this theory does not identify the substratum with any group of essential properties. Moreover, for the substratum theorist, the substance *as* substratum is not the individual, as it is in the Aristotelian substance-attribute view.

---

13   *Ibid.* The definition is on p. 65; p. 66 identifies the independence clause.

Locke on Substance/Substratum

Observing that we find groups of qualities or characteristics occurring together, John Locke, the seventeenth-century empiricist and political philosopher, argues in *An Essay on Human Understanding* that we naturally suspect that something *holds them together*. Qualities aren't "free-floating"; they don't exist alone, by themselves. I now experience or sense individual qualities—red, solid, glass, Christmas-tree-shaped—and I sense them as occupying this same little space. This Christmas decoration comprising these qualities has "something" that holds all these properties together, so that I can talk about *this* Christmas decoration rather than just a number of individual qualities. Locke's explanation of these qualities being joined together is that "we accustom ourselves, to suppose some *Substratum*, wherein they [the qualities] do subsist, and from which they do result, which therefore we call *Substance*." If anyone were to reflect on the notion of substance in general, Locke says that person would find that this notion is only "a supposition of he knows not what support of such qualities."[14]

It is worth noting that Locke's view of a substratum is simultaneously a critique of the Aristotelian notion of substance and a distinct view of the notion of substance, understood in the only reasonable way we can, as *substratum*.

Aristotle thought we experienced or sensed substances directly; but Locke suggests that the notion of substance is an inference. We *infer* the existence of this substratum, based on our "sensible ideas," or our experiencing of apparently "grouped together" sensible properties. As I look at the book lying on the table, I have various sensations, among them orange, rectangular, a certain feel. I find these properties "together" on numerous occasions: I found—experienced or sensed—them together last evening, this morning and now again this afternoon. And I suppose or *infer*—as you might also—that there is *something that holds them together*.

At least initially this seems a reasonable inference. We don't experience properties disconnected from objects. I find this orange and this rectangular together, or I observe the yellow and a slightly curved, cylindrical shape together; and the red, slightly sweet-smelling, and spherical stay together. That is, something seems to hold together the properties of this book, of that banana, of this apple—something that properties are *of*. This something—*we infer*—is the substratum, which we call "substance," according to Locke.

---

14   Locke 1975, Bk. II, xxiii; E.J. Lowe 2005, Chap. 3.

So far we have been thinking of the particular substratum of a particular object. When we ask what the idea of "substance in general" is, we find, according to Locke, that we can give nothing other but this sense of *support* to the idea. This is all we are left with if we take away all the qualities or characteristics that apply only to specific objects. *Substratum* is, he says, we know not what. If we take away our ideas, which arise through our senses, caused by the qualities or characteristics of things, we are left only with this idea of support.

Substratum theorists tell us that the metaphysical structure of things is that they are "compounds." The pup at my feet, the book on the table, the cup, the crickets outside are to be understood as things, each comprising two kinds of components or constituents. Things are constituted by, made up of, a substratum and various properties. Michael Loux characterizes this as a *reductionist* picture of objects: the substratum theorist *reduces* objects to this general structure of substratum and property.[15] While the substance-attribute view agrees that a thing has properties, that view, at least as understood by Aristotle, takes individual objects as basic. Instead, substratum theorists find something more basic than individuals or our ordinary objects, namely, the substratum and the qualities attaching to a substratum.

Substratum theory also provides a way of distinguishing two objects. Imagine that Danny and Deirdre have the same book—same color, shape, markings, etc. What is it that distinguishes the two books? According to the substratum theorist, each has its own unique substratum. The particularity or individuality of any object derives from the substratum of that object.

So the substratum view tells us what it is to be an individual thing and how individual things may be discerned. Individual things are "composed of" substrata and qualities. And each individual thing has its own unique, identifying substratum.

But What's It Like? Worries about Substrata

Very quickly, however, we confront a difficult question. A substratum holds the qualities or properties together; it supports those qualities. Does the substratum itself have any qualities? It would seem not. How could it? If the substratum had its own properties, something would be needed to support or hold together those properties—another substratum, which would presumably

---

15 Loux 2006, Chap. 3.

have its own properties as well. So we would need another, and another.... This would seem to lead to a never-ending regress.

But then what? We seem forced to conclude that *substrata have no properties whatsoever*. Pointing out that a substratum has the property of *holding properties together* does nothing to dispel the difficulty, since this is but another way of describing the *property-less* "we know not what" that holds properties together. Following the substratum theorist's idea leads us to a very peculiar metaphysical entity. All we can say about this "thing" is that it holds properties together somehow. Bishop George Berkeley would later suggest that this substratum looks a lot like, well, nothing.

A related difficulty emerges. Substrata were supposed to serve to distinguish or uniquely identify objects, but we cannot use them for this. And this seems to lead to an odd conclusion: if we accepted this view, we would not be able to distinguish what common sense tells us are two objects with all the same properties. How could we? Imagine, for example, apparently two identical books—same size, color, markings, etc. The properties are the same, so those do not *individuate* them. And now the substrata won't help either—they don't have any properties that would serve to say "here's one and there's the other." How can a "featureless" substratum accomplish the uniquely distinguishing or individuating function? It would seem substrata can't. Substratum theory is thus unable to explain a very basic metaphysical intuition of ours. It does not tell us why what appear to be two identical items are in fact *two*. So, there seems to be something fundamentally wrong with the substratum view.

Indeed, it looks even worse! It's not just that substrata aren't able to differentiate similar objects, but that the substrata of very different kinds of things seem to be interchangeable. The substrata of the pie and the piano, of the piano and the pup, of the pup and the palomino, would all also seem to be wholly interchangeable. Nor does there seem to be any difference between the substrata of Julia and Jack. How could this be? Differences, notice, apparently come from having different properties. But there can't be any *difference* between substrata because substrata don't have any properties!

(You will notice that we aren't relying on where an object is located, or its "space-time" location, to differentiate among objects. We would like our "identifying feature" to be something *internal* or *intrinsic* to an object, not its location, which is an extrinsic property.)

The metaphysical picture of substratum theory seems to have collapsed because of two apparent problems. First, a substratum is itself without properties; it supports properties but does not itself have properties. So, we are seemingly unable to explain anything about substrata. What are they? Well, they hold properties together ... but that's all we know about them. Apparently we are led then to a second problem. If substrata are themselves "property-less," it is not at all clear how objects are to be distinguished from one another—not only very similar objects (this book and that one) but even wildly different ones.

To be fair to substratum theorists, some contemporary thinkers have defended versions of this view, under the heading of "bare particulars," or sometimes "thin particulars." For example, it is argued that "thin particulars," while not themselves things, are nonetheless of a special ontological or metaphysical type. A bare particular "makes" an object *this individual*. Thus, to ask what sort of properties they have is a mistake. Worrying about the property-less aspect—and assuming that they need to have qualities in order to be distinct from one another—is to misunderstand the claim that thin particulars are distinct.[16] This version of the substratum view then suggests a different way of thinking about what it is to be a real individual object. There are particulars—bare or thin—that are without properties and unlike the particulars of our normal acquaintance, yet are what makes some object an individual object, distinct from any other. Property-less yet real.

A different approach to this problem is rather abrupt: dispense with substrata! and just keep the properties! So let's see what things look like if we get rid of substrata and keep just the qualities ... objects are *bundles* of qualities.

Bundle Theory

Fictional Objects

In an 1897 editorial in the *New York Sun*, Francis Church famously penned the line, "Yes, Virginia, there is a Santa Claus," answering an eight-year-old girl's question about whether Santa Claus exists. He wrote, "The most real things in the world are those that neither children nor men can see." But even many children nowadays think of Santa as fictional.

We often refer to fictional characters. How are we to understand what—if anything—we are referring to in this ordinary practice? Are fictional characters *objects*? If so, in what sense? Do they "exist"? If they don't exist, in any sense, what are we talking about, when we talk about them? How can we

---

16   Sider 2006.

say true things about them? One widely held view is *abstract artifact* theory, and a recent elaboration and defense is that of Amie L. Thomasson.

In her 1999 *Fiction and Metaphysics*, Thomasson argues that fictional objects, including fictional characters, are abstract artifactual objects. Like other artifacts, fictional objects are created by one or more human beings. And they are created *in* the literary work penned by the author(s). Oedipus, Romeo and Juliet, Don Quixote, and Sherlock Holmes are one and all *creations* of their authors. In this, they "existentially depend" on both the author and the literary work or works.

But they are also *abstract* objects. They are not concrete objects, having some location in space and time. Do they exist? Yes: they exist as much as any other artifact. But they exist only in those possible worlds where the elements on which they existentially depend also exist—Iago exists, but only in the possible worlds where Shakespeare exists and wrote the play *Othello*.

R.M. Sainsbury's 2010 *Fiction and Fictionalism* critically examines a number of views about the nature of fictional characters, including abstract artifact theory. Sainsbury also explains and defends *irrealism*, the view, which he opts for, that we should not think of fictional characters as objects.

Empiricism moves in a dramatic direction after Locke. Locke's empiricism led him to invoke the notion of a substratum as our best understanding of the idea of substance. A more trenchant empiricism, however, insisted that the evidence of our senses simply did not entitle us to invoke any notion of substance or substratum at all. The senses reveal no hidden substance or substratum, but only qualities: the lavender of a late spring lilac bloom, a summer scent of cantaloupe or watermelon, the orange of a carrot, with its crunchy texture—no substratum, just a bundle of qualities.

Berkeley and Hume on Bundles

In 1710, George Berkeley gave an early version of the bundle theory:

> As several of these [qualities] are observed to accompany each other, they come to be marked by one name, and so to be reputed as one THING. Thus, for example, a certain colour, taste, smell, figure and consistence having been observed to go together, are accounted one distinct thing, signified by the name apple.[17]

---

17   Berkeley 1965, Sect. 1.

But Hume is often credited with the full and explicit version of the theory. In the opening pages of his *Treatise of Human Nature*, Hume writes:

> I wou'd fain ask those philosophers, who found so much of their reasonings on the distinction of *substance and accident*, and imagine we have clear ideas of each, whether the idea of *substance* be deriv'd from impressions of sensation or reflexion [introspection— observation of one's own mind]? If it be convey'd to us by our senses, I ask, which of them? and after what manner?[18]

Hume continues that if substance *were* discovered through the senses or through subsequent introspection, it could be nothing more than a quality itself. And this leads to the conclusion, according to Hume, that we encounter not substances and their attributes but bundles of qualities: "We have therefore no idea of substance, distinct from a *collection of particular qualities*, nor have we any other meaning when we talk of reason concerning it."[19]

Berkeley's skepticism about material substance and Hume's skepticism about the notion of substance in general led them to a view, still held by many in one form or another, known as the **bundle theory**—the view that objects are nothing more than collections, or "co-locations" of qualities. There is no substance, no essence; nor is there any property-less substratum that holds together or supports an object's qualities. For example, two candles sit in front of me. Each is cylindrical, each six inches high and three inches in diameter. But one is red and the other green. The qualities *constitute* or *make up* the candles. That's all there is to these two candles. A certain shape, height, weight, scent, color. And what is true of these candles is true of every object, animate or inanimate.

But wait—if things are only their qualities, and nothing but their qualities, there is a surprising consequence: *any change of quality changes the identity of the object*. An apparent advantage of the substance view is that it explains how an object changes but remains the *same* object. Yet, according to bundle theory, if Julia paints the bookcase red, we have a different object from the white bookcase we had before!

Why this counterintuitive but apparent consequence of bundle theory? In the bundle theory view, all qualities are "equal": there is no distinction between

---

18   Hume 1978, I, i, 6; first emphasis added.
19   Hume 1978, I, i, 6; emphasis added.

essential qualities and accidental qualities. Every quality is just as important as any other quality. In fact, *every quality is essential to the object* because that's what it is to be an object—to have a particular group of qualities. To be *this* object is to have *these* qualities. So, any change in quality yields a very similar, but brand new, object. To put this a bit more formally, the identity of an object is determined solely and wholly by *all* its qualities.

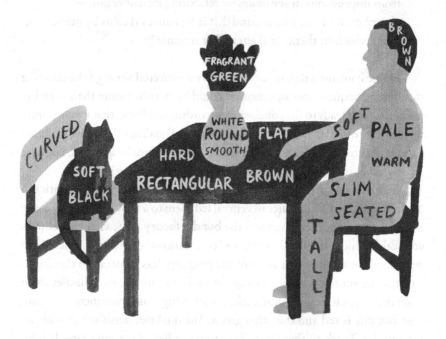

This of course differs dramatically from our two previous views—and from our intuitions about the identity of an object. When we see Julia's newly painted bookcase, we don't think that Julia has created an entirely new object. This was the apparent advantage of the substance kind and substratum views: we could continue to think of the bookcase as the *same* bookcase because either the essential properties remained or the substratum remained. Bundle theory then departs considerably from our more commonsense view of objects.

Someone like Hume has a response to this apparently extreme consequence. The bundle theorist notes that when we pause to consider the notions of substance or substratum, we cannot get a clear sense of such a notion. Our sensory experience simply fails to reveal anything in the world that corresponds to our commonsense notion of objects. And reflection on our actual sensory experience reveals that objects are comprised solely of their properties, and of *all their properties*. This object—whether bell, book, or candle—is all and only this group of qualities. Consequently, any change in properties yields a new object. Hume accepted this highly counterintuitive consequence of bundle theory, saying that a series of very similar things does not constitute one continuing object, and that we merely imagine some unseen continuing substance.

Further, we do not experience any select properties as *essence*. As Berkeley suggested, take away the qualities, and we are left with ... nothing! Hence, in this sort of empirical view, it's not surprising that my knowledge of objects is knowledge of nothing more than a bundle, a bundle of qualities. Of course, not all advocates of bundle theory accept Hume's version of empiricism. Nonetheless, versions of empiricism much like Hume's often motivate such a view.

Bundle theory seemingly differs from the substratum and substance views in another respect: we might wonder how it is that the bundle theorist identifies *kinds* of things. Imagine two dogs, say, Snoopy and Spot. All of Snoopy's properties make him this dog and not some other. That's the point of bundle theory: to be Snoopy is to be this bundle. Similarly with Spot. Without a distinction between essential and accidental properties, however, bundle theory doesn't provide us with a way of identifying what makes Snoopy and Spot this *kind* of thing, namely, a dog. According to bundle theorists, however, we can choose a set of properties ourselves and simply decide that so long as a bundle has these properties, it is a dog. Hence the radical nominalism discussed earlier.

This need to decide that certain properties define the kind *dog*, or any other kind, varies from our typical view. We tend to think there is something internal or intrinsic about the fact that "dog-defining qualities" are found together. That is, we commonly think of these qualities as *essential*, and as internally unified, regardless of our decisions or beliefs. Bundle theory rejects this notion of essence or of "kind-defining" properties and directs us only to all the properties equally. This gives us little guidance as to how to determine the kind, apart from whatever customary or conventional decisions we make.[20]

Critics of bundle theory have also noted the problem of distinguishing between two (or apparently two) objects that have all the same qualities. Common sense seems to say that two objects can have exactly the same properties, yet remain distinct. Bundle theory seems to lead—mistakenly, critics contend—to a different result. Again, imagine two candles, identical in all

---

20   Macdonald 2005, pp. 91–95.

respects: same height, color, diameter, weight, scent. They have the same properties. Now ask the simple question: according to bundle theory, what makes them two things instead of one?

You might suggest that we can distinguish objects because of their spatial location. Could we imagine two distinct objects sharing every characteristic, and occupying exactly the same space at the same time? Wouldn't that really be one object?

This may seem unsatisfying, however. If Deirdre and Sara are identical twins, we don't think they are two *because* they occupy different spaces. They are two because *internally* or *intrinsically* something differs. Similarly for objects: critics argue that there must be something "inside," as it were—an intrinsic "thisness" that makes this thing and that thing two different things...[21]

Various replies have been proposed to this problem. Unfortunately we cannot follow most of them here since following the ins and outs of the replies and objections to those replies require a technical framework that we leave aside. There is still doubt about the success of the bundle theory in replying to the "identity problem."[22] But a brief sketch of one possible solution is available.

A Bundle of Tropes

Normally we think that this red of the candle and that red of the book are but instances of the same kind of quality. Trope theory, on the other hand, claims that there is no kind *red*, but only different, "particularized" reds—different ones for every object. These particularized qualities are called *tropes*. (See Chapter 4, where we began discussing trope theory.) We distinguish the two candles because each has its own particular properties, and these particular properties occur nowhere else.[23] Similarly, Julia's book differs from Jack's seemingly identical copy because hers is nothing but this "one-time only" group of particularized properties—tropes. So, the trope theorist can explain how objects are individuated.[24] It is not surprising, however, to find that one of the standard questions posed to trope theory is the same as that posed to bundle theory in general: "what holds the bundles together?" Substratum

---

21   Loux 2006, Chap. 3.
22   Loux 2006, Chap. 3.
23   Donald Williams 1953.
24   But see Casullo 1988 for a contrary view.

and substance theorists already have an alternative they prefer. Rather than re-explore this terrain, perhaps we might look in a different direction ... some very different directions.

Are There Any Objects?
The Special Composition Question

A student once told me that the desk he was sitting at was actually three distinct objects: the desk, or the desk/writing surface, the chair in which he sat, and the hinge that attached the desk to the chair and allowed it to swing up to make for easy exit.

Peter van Inwagen raised the following question.[25] Under what circumstances does a collection of objects (that we are agreed are individual objects) combine to form a new composite object? His answer is rather striking, since it says that most things we call objects are not objects at all! Plants, pups, and pumas are objects; you and I are objects. But not the laptop or the table on which it rests. Not the ruby red crystal goblet or this house. And, of course, not any desk in a classroom or any part of it.

Mereology is the study of the relations between parts and the wholes those parts form, as well as the relationship between the parts of such wholes. Van Inwagen's question is a mereological question, known as the **Special Composition Question**. Van Inwagen expressed the question a little more technically:

Suppose one had certain non-overlapping material objects, the x's, at one's disposal; what would one have to do—what could one do—to get the x's to compose something?[26] Notice the assumption in the question that the x's, the non-overlapping objects, are indeed objects.

Three different *families* of views are held in response to the SCQ (Special Composition Question). The first is *nihilism*, and there are indeed a range of views here. For example, "extreme nihilism" holds that there are no objects at all; there are no things in the world. There's stuff, or "gunk" as David Lewis termed it, an infinitely divisible stuff that has no smallest parts; hence, gunk is undifferentiated. A very similar view holds that there is but one object, The World, or the "Blobject." It, like "stuff," has no parts. A less extreme view

25   van Inwagen 1990.
26   *Ibid.*, p. 23.

holds that there are basic objects in the world, say, some basic kinds of physical object, but they never compose to form compound objects. Thus, there are basic physical objects arranged "laptop-computer-wise," but there is no laptop computer. Van Inwagen argues for an *organicist* view: the only compound objects are those that are said to have a life. (He considers this a moderate view.[27]) Trenton Merricks adopts a limited organicist view.[28] Aristotle, millennia earlier, might be seen as holding a similar view. What kinds of objects are there? Basic physical elements and those *individuals* that can be characterized as having an intrinsic final end or goal. These turn out to be plants, animals, and human beings: living things.

The second view might be called a moderate view, or a commonsense view: basic objects join together to form new, compound objects. There are tables and chairs, guitars and computers—and a host of other compound objects. Many claim or at least imply that the "obviousness" of such objects is insufficient to admit them into a rigorous ontology. Presently we will turn to a defense of "ordinary objects."

The third and final view is known as "universalism," sometimes "permissivism." Universalism is committed to "unrestricted composition": any two or more objects compose a new object. Alternatively, whenever there are some things, there is at least one thing that they compose.[29] Their distance from one another, their disparity in kind or quality, is of no relevance; if you can name it or describe it, it's an object. Fido's collar, the Lake Ponchatrain Causeway, and the Empire State Building compose an object. As does a "trog," the tree in my back yard, and the pup walking round it.[30]

While the focus of this section is a response to van Inwagen's challenge to ordinary objects, it is worth noting the general line of argument that leads to the perhaps counterintuitive positions of nihilism and universalism. Consider first ontological nihilism.

Nihilists need not deny that our experience is delusory. They can accept there's a structure in the world, but that structure is not because of existent *things*.[31] If Sandra tells Gail, "That's a chrysanthemum," this can be paraphrased away as "It's chrysanthemum-ly." Our subject-predicate grammar misleads us,

27 *Ibid.*, pp. 77 ff.
28 Merricks 2003; see Chap. 4.
29 The second is from Gideon Rosen and Cian Dorr 2002, p. 153.
30 "Trogs" are a type of example offered by Daniel Z. Korman 2015, Chap. 3.
31 See, for example, Hawthorne and Cortens 1995.

the nihilist contends. Of course, many will ask why we think we are misled. And here we return to a familiar metaphysical neighborhood: ordinary objects *cause too much ontological trouble*, whether it's trying to answer the special composition question or trying to explain "co-located objects"—e.g., a table and a swirl of subatomic particles. Another worry, for eliminativists who hold that there are only basic objects in the world, is that composite objects add nothing to the causal nature of the world. The causal powers of basic objects are sufficient to explain any changes in the world. Merricks, for example, explains that the atoms that make up a "baseball" are more than sufficient to explain the breaking of the "window." Of course, he denies that there are baseballs. It is merely an example to show that referring to the objects of common sense *adds nothing to the world*, at least insofar as one very important feature is concerned: the causal nature the world.

The universalist approach, on the other hand, is indeed permissive. This view holds that any describable entity is an object, as already noted. If you can name it, that's an object. Why hold such a view? Simplifying, the general idea is that if there is some putative case of composition (or "fusion"—two (or more) objects composing a new object), that does *not* produce a new object, then we must be able to point out why that is the case. But we are unable to do that. Alternatively, if one arrangement of particles counts as an object, then a slight variant would also count as an object; but this process can be continued *ad infinitum*. So every arrangement of particles is an object.[32] So, the "logic of composition" requires us to admit any fusion as an object, including trogs and this one: Eiffel Tower-Mandy, the barista at the local coffee bar, and the plaque at the summit of Mount Whitney.

One type of objection to universalism, or "universal mereological composition (UMC)," is that it is difficult to understand how such objects could be said to have properties, when we normally think of properties as having contraries. Consider televisions for a moment. This one is an older TV with an analog tuner, that one has a digital tuner, and the one over there is high-definition. And now we have 4K. But there seem to be no similar contrary properties possessed by the UMC object. Indeed we are able to describe the structural properties of the various televisions. However, there seem to be no structural properties associated with the UMC objects. This is a brief account of a much longer argument, but perhaps it suffices to give an idea of the way in which one might argue against universalism.[33]

---

32   Theodore Sider 2001, pp. 120 and 124; and Chap. 4.9 generally.
33   For the longer and detailed argument, see Crawford Elder 2008.

It might be noted that it has also been argued that we view composite objects as *fictions*. Since universalism and nihilism, it is held, are equally coherent options, and there is no apparent way to decide between them, we might treat sentences about composite objects as not literally true but as *apt* or *adequate*, depending on the circumstances.[34]

These are extremely cursory accounts, and nuances of the positions have been set aside. Here the aim is to see if some sense can be made of a defense of ordinary objects in response to van Inwagen's eliminativist argument. He considers four ways we might "compose" a new inanimate object: contact, fastening, cohesion, and fusion. Mere touching, he claims, is insufficient, as is fastening. When Dominique builds a small bookcase (what we would call a bookcase), and Danny takes a small piece of wood with his name painted on it and nails it to the bookcase, we seem to have no way of saying whether we have one object or two.

Similarly, cohesion fails. If Fabio welds together six different pipes to form a continuous length of pipe, how many objects are there? Van Inwagen offers the example of two people shaking hands, after one has just managed to get fast-drying glue spread on his palm. As he notes, despite this "painful experience," there is not now a new object.[35]

As van Inwagen notes, perhaps one can insist that in the cases so far considered, a discernible border still exists—between the board on the bookcase, between the lengths of pipe, and between the two hands. We can then imagine certain situations in which the boundary between objects has "disappeared" through some sort of fusion, by somehow arranging that they grow together. Van Inwagen holds that if object A and object B are two objects, they are necessarily *these* two objects; then fusing them does not change their identity. On the other hand, if they are one object, then they are one object regardless of the fusion. He asks us to imagine Alice and Beatrice fused together (we ignore the somewhat gory details). He claims that the fusion changes nothing about the nature of these objects.[36]

Amie Thomasson argues that there is a generally unexpressed argument that underlies objections to ordinary objects.[37] The central claim in that argument is that there must be some uniform answer to when basic objects compose

---

34 Rosen and Dorr 2001, p. 166 and pp. 168–71.
35 van Inwagen 1990, p. 58.
36 *Ibid.*, pp. 58–60.
37 Thomasson 2007, esp. p. 127.

a new object. But it is not obvious why the "composition conditions" for composite objects could not vary according to circumstance, or to the general frame in which existence questions are asked. For example, the intentions of a creator might be relevant to the art object as *object*, while clearly such intentions are not relevant to why a stick or a stone is an object.

The general thrust of Thomasson's answer is that the proponent of a negative answer to the Special Composition Question and the defender of the existence of ordinary objects, or inanimate composite objects, differ regarding the approach to the nature of the existence question. In her view, eliminativism about ordinary objects holds that we should view existence questions as "category-neutral." She argues, however, that a better way to understand such questions is as relative to some particular categorical frame. To get a sense of the difference here, consider the question about the existence of stones or books or tables or nightclubs or universities. When we ask if there are nightclubs or if this institution is a university, we are not doing so *sans* context. We do so relative to certain conditions that must be fulfilled to count as a nightclub or university. Similarly, we are able to "negotiate" the conditions for counting as a table; we can distinguish between a child's toy table and a dining table. The eliminativist, however, apparently insists that we take a "category-neutral" stance, asking something like, "Are there tables?" But in doing so, there is the presupposition that there is some (relatively) theory-free domain that figures as the background for answering this question.[38] Although Thomasson does not put it this way, in a sense this stacks the deck against ordinary objects. It does so because it assumes a certain framework theory, e.g., whatever basic objects science settles on together with a certain logical apparatus. It is not at all clear, however, that the defender of ordinary objects ought to accept this theoretical background. Some eliminativists about ordinary objects worry about *arbitrariness*, but the defender might wonder why it is that accepting a number of different ontological categories is arbitrary, except in respect to a certain preferred theoretical background.

Thomasson recognizes that there is a significant range of questions to be considered, such as vagueness, whether scientific theory undermines the idea of ordinary objects and indeed the purposes of scientific versus metaphysical theories. Perhaps, however, this is sufficient to indicate one way of defending ordinary objects against a generally negative answer to the Special Composition Question.

---

38   Thomsasson 2007, especially Chaps. 6 and 7.

ferent Directions: Whitehead and Heidegger

An ancient Chinese tale tells of a teacher and a young student. One moonlit night, the teacher points to the moon and proclaims, "That is the moon." The young student moves closer and begins to inspect the teacher's finger. "No," protests the mentor, "you've mistaken my finger for the moon." Some twentieth-century philosophers became convinced that the history of metaphysics, with its emphasis on things and substance, had mistaken the finger for the moon. Traditional metaphysics, whether rationalist or empiricist, missed the real nature of reality in focusing on things and substance. Two of the more dramatically "counter-traditional" metaphysical views looked to *process and event* and the *Being-ness* of things or beings.

Whitehead: Process and Reality

Alfred North Whitehead (1861–1947) was a British philosopher, logician, and mathematician, co-author with Bertrand Russell of *Principia Mathematica*, a work that was very important for the fields of both mathematical logic and the foundations of mathematics. As a Harvard philosophy professor, he supervised Quine. A justice of the United States Supreme Court once remarked that he knew of no one that had more influence on American university life than Whitehead.[39] Perhaps his most lasting philosophical influence in metaphysics is a view known as process theism, the view that God is not an eternally fixed being, but one that undergoes changes through various interactions with creatures and creation. He writes:

> That "all things flow" is the first vague generalization which the unsystematized, barely analysed, intuition of men has produced.... Without doubt if we are to go back to that ultimate, integral experience ... the flux of things is one ultimate generalization around which we must weave our philosophical system ...
>
> But there is a rival notion, antithetical to [this] ... The other notion dwells on permanencies of things ...[40]

Here we see contrasted two views of the essence of things.

---

39   Irvine 2013.
40   Whitehead 1929, pp. 240–41.

Whitehead thought that the essence of things was their *becoming*, that things essentially flow. Reality, for him, was *process*, as suggested by the title of his most important treatise in metaphysics, *Process and Reality*. It is the *event*, not the thing, that is the most basic aspect of reality. The instant or the moment is an abstraction. *Duration*, not instants or moments, is the nature of reality, and duration is how we experience the world. In fact, throughout *Process and Reality*, Whitehead refers to his philosophy as the "philosophy of organism": what we think of as a "thing" is not static, and so is better described as an organism. The *being* of the organism is a process, a process of growth, of development, of *becoming*.

Our interest here is his view of the nature of reality generally. Whitehead thinks there is a better way to understand the world than as relatively static individual substances. He thus conceptualizes or "frames" reality differently than do the substance-attribute views of Aristotle or Descartes. Reality comprises the "creative flow" of **actual entities**, the basic units of reality. All our familiar objects comprise "societies" of actual entities; that a rock or this rabbit consists of a society of actual entities. Understanding actual entities in their creative flow will help us to understand Whitehead's view.

We can use an understanding of the self as an analogy for understanding actual entities and their "creative flow." My self is fundamentally an *experiencing* self. But let's think about where this self of mine has been, and where it's going. Right now—its present—is a *duration*—not an instant, but a very short length of time. To be experiencing is to be experiencing through a "space" of time, a duration. If we are to understand our world, we must understand it through the notion of duration.[41] My present experiencing is the *novel expression* of my past experiencing. In other words, this present experience takes over and takes from and unites those past experiences, but it does so in a way that is novel—different from all of my previous durations of experiencing. Because every experiencing is new, it is creative. Because every experiencing expresses past experiences, experiences are not isolated or "atomistic" bits separate from other "experience-ings." Whitehead's notion of experience differs from Hume's in one important respect. Any particular experience is always part of a process, which includes as an essential part a "re-expression" of our previous experiences.

This novel expression of past experience only lasts for a brief duration, however. It gives way to still another, future experience. And that future

---

41   Whitehead 1925, pp. 71 ff.

duration of experience will be a taking over of this and all other past durations and a novel expression of this flow of experience. This flow of experience continually manifests itself in novel experiencings. And the "me" in all this, the subject, is these novel experiencings, or the "flow" of these experiences. In a moment, we will see the sense in which they are united, according to Whitehead.

Whitehead's notion of an actual entity as a novel experiencing subject shares some kindred aspects with William James's view of consciousness.[42] James, one of the most important American pragmatists, is considered by many to be the father of American psychology. James holds that moments of consciousness last only for a brief duration, but are taken up or subsumed by the next moment—that is "All real units of experience *overlap*."[43]

Affinities—Ralph Waldo Emerson

Ralph Waldo Emerson (1803–82), the American philosopher, essayist, and poet, has been called both the father of American literature and the father of American religion. Emerson's principal occupation was the writing of essays and lectures which he presented throughout New England. His writings reflect diverse influences—from Plato to the German idealist F.C.S. Schelling (1775–1854) to Hinduism.

His essay "History" reflects his view that no thought of one person is "foreign" to anyone. Seemingly this is because all minds are interconnected and that all can share the same thoughts. Plato's and Euclid's thoughts are my thoughts, reflected in my thinking, and of course, reflected in all minds. This view has obvious affinities with the Hindu doctrine of Atman, according to which individual egos are but particularized manifestations or reflections of the whole. In other essays, Emerson notes the interconnectedness of conscious minds and nature. Though there are significant differences between Whitehead's and Emerson's views of nature, the themes of interconnectedness and of an individual as a reflection of the whole are discernible in the work of both thinkers.[44]

---

42   Flanagan 1992.
43   James 1951a, p. 162; also 1951b.
44   Emerson 1987.

In Whitehead's view these temporally extended bits of experience—the durations—are actual entities. Each is a welling up or an upsurge of a prior flow. And each new actual entity expresses that prior flow in a novel way. The actual entity wells up, and it will fall away—cease to exist—only to be creatively "re-expressed" in still a new novel bit of experience, a new actual entity. Thus, every actual entity is a novel expression of the actual entities that preceded it. Because of this, Whitehead claimed that "each actual entity is a locus of the universe."[45] This reflects Whitehead's view that any actual entity is in fact a microcosm of the universe, and understanding that actual entity is to understand the interconnections among all actual entities.

One further aspect of this creative flow of experience, which is my *self*, needs notice. Any experience takes in, or is related to, all of the other novel experiences out there, "outside" of me. My self, in any chosen duration, is related to all the other experiencings. My experience is interdependent with those of others, just as it is interdependent with my prior and future experiences. Sam's experience takes in Sara's experience, just as hers takes in Deirdre's. As Whitehead notes, "we must say that every actual entity is present in every other actual entity."[46] Why does he think this? Since all actual entities are interconnected, Whitehead apparently thinks that a "complete picture" of any actual entity necessarily includes all other actual entities. You can't grasp some actual entity without seeing its "relations," its "family." And its family is all other actual entities. (Carlo Rovelli, a noted quantum physicist and author, similarly suggests that each individual reflects every other.[47])

The becoming of an actual entity is a complex process, involving both *eternal objects* and *feelings*. Eternal objects are very similar to universals, although Whitehead wished to avoid the controversial history of that topic, and so chose the term "**eternal objects**." These are qualities that determine the character of some actual entity. And the actual entity has *come to be* when it takes on this determinate character, that is, when the eternal objects have "combined"—Whitehead calls this "ingression"—to make the actual entity.

Whitehead's terminology is unfamiliar, in part because he is trying to describe a *metaphysical* process, and he wants to avoid the "baggage" of the more common terms in the history of philosophy (e.g., substance, universal). Yet we can get some sense of Whitehead's view of the "coming to be" of an

---

45   Whitehead 1929, p. 97.
46   *Ibid.*, p. 65.
47   Rovelli 2018, Chap. 8.

individual. Every individual, whether cup or coconut or koala bear, has specific qualities. Cup, coconut, and koala all manifest "roundness" to some degree, while the koala is furry, the coconut hard, and the cup fragile. (Whitehead's notion of eternal objects is roughly that of our universals; and roundness appears to be an eternal object.) Like tributaries coming together to form a river, an individual finally *comes to be* when all its qualities are there. The cup *becomes* because a variety of streams of influence or streams of qualities now come together in a particular way. The cup becomes because it reflects particular qualities in a novel way. Also, the koala bear becomes because it now reflects the qualities that "make it up" in a novel way. It is perhaps a little easier for us to think of the koala bear as *becoming* or *in process*, than it is to think of a cup as a process. But in Whitehead's view, all actual entities are in process, whether they are animate or inanimate, animal, vegetable, or mineral.

It may seem that Whitehead suggests that an actual entity is but a combination of eternal objects, without any unity, and thus his concept is similar to bundle theory. Whitehead, however, thinks that there *is* unity to the actual entity, but we must look for it somewhere other than where substance-attribute theorists would look.

Central to Whitehead's view is abandoning the substance view of essence that we find in Aristotle or Descartes or Kant: "It is fundamental to the metaphysical doctrine of the philosophy of organism that the notion of an actual entity as the *unchanging subject of change* is completely abandoned."[48] In the substance view, the *essence* of a thing—its essential qualities—remains the same, or else the object becomes a different thing. For Whitehead, unity of an actual entity is to be found in *process*. More specifically, the essence of an actual entity is the final end or aim of the process, the becoming.[49] Whitehead calls this end "the subjective aim." The unity of an actual entity is the unity of the process: "Process is the growth and attainment of a final end."[50] It's important to note that Whitehead does not mean that there is some final stage to this process, as graduation is to the process of receiving a college degree. Rather, the whole of the process, the becoming itself, is the subjective aim. (Perhaps the education analogy is useful here: we think of our education as an ongoing, continuing process, one that does not end with the awarding of a degree. Similarly the

---

48   Whitehead 1929, p. 65; emphasis added.
49   *Ibid.*
50   *Ibid.*

subjective aim is continually ongoing, as is the "developing" process of any actual entity. As long as the actual entity exists, it is in process; it is *becoming*.)

Indeed the actual world itself is a process, one made up of the actual entities. And here is perhaps one of the most remarkable features of Whitehead's view: *feeling*. Every actual entity is a *drop of experience*. This experience manifests itself as *feeling*.

Given that all our familiar objects comprise "societies" of actual entities, that a rock or rabbit consists of actual entities, does this mean that feeling is everywhere? Whitehead's answer is "yes," but we must realize that not all feeling is conscious. Sam may sense the rose or be aware of his feeling of sadness. These are paradigms of feeling, as conscious events. But Whitehead holds that the feeling is "two-way": the rose "feels" Sam, just as Sam feels the rose. The difference in feeling is a difference in degree, not in kind.

We can get a sense of this similarity of feeling by thinking about Sam and his experience. Sam is an experiencing creature. A full understanding of that experience requires understanding all Sam experiences, including the rose. Sam's experience reflects the *actual world*. Whitehead claimed that every actual entity "houses" the world within itself. And it does so because of its feeling, its feeling of the actual world.

But how are we to understand the rose *grasping* or feeling Sam? Or, for that matter, any actual entity? The rose reflects an actual world *that includes Sam sensing the rose*. The feeling of the rose is thus an expression of the relatedness of the rose; it expresses its connection to the world. The rose, no less than Sam, houses the actual world in itself, as any actual entity does. Its feeling is a reflection of the actual entity in its relation to the world. Notice also that feeling will thus sometimes be a physical feeling, since the relations between actual entities are physical. Indeed, Whitehead identifies physical feeling as one of the two most basic types of feeling.

And this leads us to another important difference between the "categoreal scheme" of Whitehead and that of the substance theorist. For the substance theorist, substances are related to each other primarily extrinsically. A substance is still itself apart from its connection to any other substance.

Whitehead sees the matter differently. All relations—that is, the *connectedness* between actual entities—are intrinsic. In other words, the actual entity is what it is precisely because of its feeling. It comes about because of the prior flow of experience, and that prior flow is manifested in its feelings, its relation to the other actual entities.

Whitehead thought that we had a better *metaphysical* understanding of the world if we abandoned the substance view and instead turned to a view of process, in which actual entities are what they are because of their becoming. *Process and Reality* not only presents a very different metaphysic that can be difficult to grasp, but it is also very terminologically challenging. And we have barely indicated the depth of that work. Nonetheless, we might close this section by noting just a couple of questions. Whitehead acknowledges that he wants to stretch the language. We might wonder, however, whether using the notions of feeling or experience to describe the interconnectedness of things is the best way to go about it. More precisely, we might wonder what more Whitehead has told us about the *cause* of something by talking about feeling or reflecting the relatedness of things. Whitehead also stresses the novelty or creativity of actual entities. But does suggesting that every entity has its own "point of view" capture the essence of creativity in the universe? Lastly, we might wonder about the building blocks of the system, the actual entities themselves—are we really clear what an actual entity is? At one point, Whitehead suggests they are like the monads of Leibniz, only "becoming." And he says there is nothing more to the actual entity; it's as basic as you get. Knowing that it is a drop of experience may still leave us puzzled a bit, in light of the above.

Despite these questions, Whitehead—in both *Process and Reality* and *Science and the Modern World*—raises a number of challenges to a long-held tradition and to the assumptions underlying much of western metaphysics. For now though we turn to another twentieth-century challenge to traditional metaphysics.

Big "B" Being: Heidegger and the Metaphysics of Being

Maha–ya–na Buddhism and Heidegger

Some have found similarities between Heidegger's view and the metaphysical views explicit in particular Asian philosophies. One place to see such a similarity is in Maha–ya–na Buddhism.

One difference between Hinaya–na and Maha–ya–na Buddhism is the ontological status of elements of our experience. For the former, these are passing, temporary phenomena, yet real. The Maha–ya–na view differs. In this view, there is an underlying reality, but the world of our experience is not real.

As Heinrich Zimmer says in his classic work on Indian philosophy, "This one reality, in its ontological aspect, can be termed only *bha–ta-tathata–*, 'the suchness of beings, the essence of existence.'" Zimmer notes that the Maha–ya–na philosophers distinguished three aspects of things: quintessence, attributes, and activities. While the latter two might change, the quintessence of a thing is indestructible.

Thus, the "final truth," as Zimmer calls it, is the "being thus," the "suchness."[51] In this "being thus," we might see some similarity between the Maha–ya–na Buddhist notion and Heidegger's concept of Being.

Martin Heidegger (1889–1976) thought that metaphysics had forgotten an important question, the question of the meaning of Being. Heidegger's project, as he saw it, was to rethink the traditional metaphysical categories, thus overcoming the historical oppositions in metaphysics and epistemology, such as subject-object and mind-body. More than that, he wanted to enable us to ask again the question of Being—to come to understand Being.

Heidegger insisted on our recognizing the difference between beings and Being. (Or as William Lovitt, both a translator and interpreter of Heidegger, once said: "little 'b' beings and big 'B' Being."[52]) Our everyday preoccupation with things "hides" from us the *Being* of these beings. We are preoccupied with the *ontic* level—the level of individual physical things—rather than with an *ontological* understanding of Being. Philosophy, too, shares this preoccupation; the metaphysics of substance is also restricted to the ontic level. But Being *as such* is not some further thing, nor should it be understood as the most general universal. In Heidegger's view **Being** is that which "gives" the things of our everyday world their being. It is the "presence-ing" of things. In a sense, the more fundamental ontological question for Heiddeger is not the nature or the essence of things, or even the question of what should be identified as a thing or "primary substance," but rather that things *are*.[53]

Understanding Being is the peculiar task of human being or *Dasein*, as Heidegger called it. It is only through Dasein that Being can be understood. This understanding is not a purely intellectual understanding that humans can achieve themselves by "figuring out" Being, but is better conceptualized

---

51   Zimmer 1951, p. 517.
52   Heidegger 1977; see also Lovitt and Lovitt 1995.
53   See also Wisnewski 2011, Chap. 2.

as a *disclosing* or the *revealing* of Being that humans can be open to. In an early essay, "On the Essence of Truth," Heidegger notes that our naming of things draws them out so that they can be present to us, where we can let them be.[54] Indeed, a function of the poet, according to Heidegger, is this naming. Truth, then, is not the corresponding of sentences to the world, but is this drawing out of the presence of things. Better perhaps, it is letting be of the world, so that the Being-ness of things can reveal itself or become present.

In Heidegger's view, as Being discloses or reveals itself to us, it also withdraws. This is because we always engage Being through a framework, through a particular style of representation. Perhaps the account of the poet Petrarch climbing Mont Ventoux in 1333, with his "only motive ... the wish to see what so great an elevation had to offer," comes close to what it means to letting the Being of the world reveal itself. Yet even Petrarch inevitably relied on some frame or style of representation. These are not styles of representation or frames for encountering Being that we devise ourselves. Instead, Being presents itself in different ways in different epochs. Our modern period is "technological," a period characterized by the domination of nature.[55] (Indeed, Heidegger's views have led to Heideggerian interpretations of environmental ethics.[56]) Heidegger often used the German word *Gestell*—a frame or shelf—to highlight the way in which we frame or understand things. Since we encounter things through a particular style of representation, Being withdraws. In other words, we grasp Being only partially, failing to grasp Being as such, Being as it is in its "pure" presence.

In his seminal work, *Being and Time* (1962), Heidegger's primary concern is with Dasein, as this is, by definition, the type of being that can ask about the "meaning of Being." At our most basic ontological level, human beings are the *only* type of being that can ask about this most general characteristic of the world.[57] Heidegger calls this sort of inquiry into our finite essence "fundamental ontology."[58] He describes human beings as Dasein—as essentially finite creatures, who are always tied to some context.

Our basic mode of encounter with things of the world is as "ready-to-hand." The hammer, like anything we might use for work or play, is ready-to-hand

---

54 Heidegger 1965, pp. 317–52.
55 Again, see Lovitt and Lovitt 1995.
56 E.g., Zimmerman 1997.
57 Heidegger 1962a, especially the Introduction.
58 *Ibid.*, especially the Introduction and 1962b.

when it is there for us as we are engaged in our projects, in a world. But when we approach things as philosophers, scientists, or observers, we experience them more distantly, as present-at-hand. We also see things in this mode, as present-at-hand, when we cannot engage with them as we normally do — when the hammer breaks, for example, and loses its function. Our most basic encounter with things is not as "knowing" them or "theorizing" about them, but engaging a world with them. Heidegger thought that seeing things as part of our interaction in the world overcame the untenable separation between subject and object, between knower and known.

In later works Heidegger places more stress on language, both how language hides Being from us and how we can come to see or engage Being by getting clearer about how our language operates. More precisely, we have to follow the cues language gives us. Done correctly, this can help us get closer to seeing the true meaning of Being or Being as it is in its original revealing.

In *What Is Called Thinking?* (1976), an early work from his later period, Heidegger attempts to trace the meaning of "thinking" back through language to its pre-Socratic origin. He hopes to find the source or the "originary" understanding of Being. Before Plato's categories of "form" and particular, or Aristotle's notions of substance and attribute, gave shape to the style of thinking that dominated western metaphysics, Heidegger finds a different style of thinking. Seeing thinking in this earlier setting, especially in the few extant fragments from Heraclitus, before our thought was shaped by the categories of traditional metaphysics, we find thinking, which is not first and foremost theorizing. It is rather a kind of "thanking," a primordial way of acknowledging or encountering Being.

It is easy to see a religious sensibility or background in his later work. Being gives us, gives human ("little b") being, its fundamental gift, the encounter with a world. In some more challenging works, there seems to be the suggestion of a coming Event, an appropriation of Dasein by Being. This event strikes some as a kind of redeeming act. Others have resisted this religious interpretation of Heidegger. Yet there is little doubt that the mystery of the relation between Being and Dasein evokes a spiritual atmosphere.[59]

---

59   E.g., Philipse 1998. It is also worth noting that Heidegger thinks that a basic error of Western metaphysics is to mistake *Being* for a being, namely, God. Being, however, is ontologically more fundamental than God.

Heidegger's critics have sometimes suspected that there is less to his work than the often difficult vocabulary makes it seem. Defenders object that Heidegger viewed himself as overthrowing the metaphysical tradition, thus requiring a new vocabulary, a set of terms that made it possible for him to "think the unthought," to see what was underneath or behind the layers of centuries-old conceptual categories of western metaphysics. Heidegger thought we saw *things*, but missed *Being*.

Nonetheless, there is still room for questions. For example, in the essay on truth noted earlier, Heidegger seems to think that the "disclosing" or "revealing" of Being is the essence of truth. This, however, does not follow from his argument. A functioning oven is part of the required background for baking a cake. But it does not follow that an oven is the essence of what it is to be a cake. Similarly the presence (or presence-ing) of beings—of things—may be part of the requisite background for us to talk meaningfully about truth. It does not follow, however, that this disclosing is the essence of truth.

Conclusion

Things are the most familiar part of our world. Natural and social scientists, artists, and writers have all offered viewpoints for understanding things. Yet those viewpoints perhaps do not settle metaphysical questions as much as invite them. And as the various positions indicate, how we understand the nature of things cannot be divorced from our understanding of the world as a whole—or from an understanding of ourselves.

Key Concepts

- substance-attribute view
- substratum
- bundle theory
- mereology
- Special Composition Question
- actual entities
- eternal objects
- Being

Reading Questions

1. The substance view holds that certain properties constitute the essence or nature of a kind of thing. Explain what this means. Do you think things have "essences"? If so, what is our best guide to identifying these essences? Science? Philosophy? Something else?
2. Explain the similarities and differences between the substance-accident view and the substratum view. What do you see as the main criticism of this latter view? Do you agree with this criticism?
3. Try to explain the connection between Hume's empiricism and bundle theory. Explain and evaluate one criticism of bundle theory.
4. Why is Whitehead's view thought of as a *process* view? In a few sentences, explain the importance of the notions of creativity and feeling in Whitehead's metaphysics.
5. Do you think Heidegger is right to claim that beings and Being are different, and that we always understand the latter from some incomplete particular perspective?
6. Which view presented in the chapter gives the best account of *change*? Explain.

Bonus round: Meinongianism, named for Alexius Meinong (1853–1920), roughly holds that for every possible combination of qualities or properties, there is a corresponding object. A gold mountain just west of Fresno is an object, as is the fountain of youth in Florida ... But they just don't exist. What do you think: Does any consistent combination of qualities constitute an object? Are there "nonexistent" objects?

For Further Reading

Aristotle's most important works on substance are *Categories*, *Metaphysics*, and *Physics*, 1941a, 1941b, and 1941c, respectively. There are many useful and accessible introductions to his work: A.E. Taylor 1949 and 1955, Veatch 1974, and more recently, Irwin 1989. And Jones 1969a and Copleston 1946 remain excellent sources.

More recent accounts and defenses of the substance-accident framework are Lowe 2002, Macdonald 2005, and Loux 2006. Each of these also includes accounts of both the substratum view and the bundle view. Lowe 2005 is a very clear account of Locke, including his views on substratum and personal identity, and is easily accessible to the beginner. The two criticisms of bundle theory noted in the text can be found in various places, but a good place to start is James Van Cleve 1985. Macdonald contains those and additional criticisms of the bundle view. A defense of bundle theory is Albert Casullo 1988, who develops a view, not discussed in the text, of objects as momentarily existing. Loux 2006 explains the conceptual route between bundle and substratum views. Donald Williams 1953 defends the trope view and is generally credited with "baptizing" modern trope theory. Campbell 1991 is a detailed presentation and defense of tropes as abstract particulars; some of the arguments may be a bit advanced for the beginner, but it repays the extra effort that might be required.

In addition to the two works already noted, Martinich and Stroll 2007 offers a theory of fiction, examining other theories of fiction as well, and broadly connecting the theory to recent issues in philosophy of language.

Whitehead 1929, *Process and Reality*, is the *locus classicus* for a systematic statement of his metaphysical views. His 1925 presents a number of these ideas and places them in the broader context of the history of philosophy and scientific developments. Both are challenging, especially *Process and Reality*. Two classic secondary works are Sherburne 1971 and Victor Lowe 1962; the more recent Mesle 2008 is a relatively brief and very accessible introduction to Whitehead's view.

Heidegger 1962a is of course the main work; his 1976 and 1977 provide generally accessible accounts of his "later" view. 1965 is an important, if earlier, statement of his view of truth. Lovitt's commentary in Heidegger 1977 is helpful, as is Gray's in Heidegger 1976, for understanding the later view. Zimmerman 1986 and 1990 are very helpful book-length treatments of Heidegger's views. The 1986 notes the parallel between Christian views and Heidegger's view of authenticity. A somewhat more recent work, which also notes the "Christian connection," is Philipse 1998. Wisnewski 2011 is also a helpful introduction to both Heidegger's early and later works.

Heinrich Zimmer 1951, edited by Joseph Campbell, is a readily accessible account of the philosophies of India, as the title indicates. D.T. Suzuki 1963 is also a classic and accessible study of Maha-ya-na Buddhism; Chap. V considers the doctrine of suchness.

CHAPTER SIX

THE NATURE OF MIND

THOUGHTS, WISHES, HOPES, FEARS, EMOTIONS AND SENSATIONS—THESE we take as part of the facts of life, as part of the world. Of course, we aren't always "paying attention" to our mental life, cataloguing every thought or feeling as it happens. Still we often notice some features of our mental lives. Danny notices that the pain has diminished since he took the aspirin. Sara thinks this is the best tasting cake her mother has ever made. After being pressed by friends, Julia "becomes aware" that she really is angry at Jack. When asked—perhaps asking ourselves—we can catalogue or identify our thoughts or our beliefs, our desires or wishes, what we know, or what we fear. All of these mental states—beliefs, desires, hopes, fears, sensations, emotions—make up our mental life. And for many, these mental states seem very different from ordinary physical happenings or states.

It Takes Two

Why do we think these two—the physical and the mental—are different? And why do some of us think that they aren't? Perhaps a good place to start is the different ways we describe and experience them in everyday life.

Getting Physical

Notice the sorts of things that we say about the physical. Julia is wearing a *blue* dress; the cake *tastes* sweet; the desk is too *heavy* to move; that music is too *loud*. In addition, we notice the *location* of things, their *shape* and *size*, or their *motion*. Or we might notice the absence of motion: "Sam hasn't moved from that chair since dinner."

Two sets of characteristics define the physical for us. Our senses give us one: color, sound, taste, feel, smell, shape, motion (or lack of it). And from science we learn a second set: electrons and protons have a charge; quarks have flavors; there are not only "particles" but "fields" too. From an early age we learn a simple scientific account of those sensory characteristics, e.g., sound—"vibrations" in the air that cause vibrations in the ear; or color—light waves of a certain length striking our retina; or smells—molecules traveling through air, striking our olfactory organ.

These observations provide us with a general way of characterizing the physical: the physical is what science studies. **Physicalism** is the view that everything is ultimately physical; only physical things and properties exist. Physicalism is sometimes called *materialism*.[1] It is a type of monism (i.e., a system that holds that everything that exists is the same type of thing).

Dualism

Propositional Attitudes

"Propositional attitudes" are an important type of mental state. As creatures with minds, we have beliefs, desires, hopes, fears. We know things and doubt things. All these (and others) are identified as propositional attitudes.

---

1   This philosophical term does not mean what it does in ordinary language: a preoccupation with money and ownership.

Why *propositional?* This type of mental state has a distinctive feature: content. Such states are *about* something. For example, you believe *that* the Declaration of Independence was signed in 1776 or *that* the blue-footed booby is found in the Galapagos. Or you hope *that* the blue-footed booby will perform its mating dance; you know *that* 1776 was an important year. The content of the belief or the hope or the fear is given by a sentence or a proposition; these are sometimes called "that clauses."

As noted, there are different types of *attitude* one might have toward a proposition—e.g., belief, desire, hope, fear, wishing, knowing. Two of the more important attitudes are beliefs and desires, since we frequently appeal to a person's beliefs and desires to explain behavior. Epistemology focuses especially on *knowing that* and the justification of or rationality of *belief.*

Our mental life, however, can seem like a different kind of thing from a table or a coffee cup. **Dualism** is the view that the nature of the mental is indeed something very different from the physical; the mental is nonphysical. The dualist holds that a complete inventory of the *physical* world would leave something out. Science provides an understanding of the behavior of quarks or the nature of the Big Bang, but no matter how much we learned about physical things, we would still not have a story about a very important part of the world, the mental. So, we might ask the dualist to tell us a little more about these "mental things."

We've already said what, according to the dualist, the mental is not—it's not physical, not colored or fragrant, without shape or extension. My *belief* that the Radiators are playing on Decatur doesn't have a shape or a velocity, any more than my *desire* to have Julia drive us to the Quarter is loud or colored. Of course, we might say, "I'm thinking as fast as I can how to do it," or "Deirdre seems to be feeling blue," but dualists count these as metaphors. Similarly, we might characterize a pain as "sharp" or "burning." These also are metaphors for the dualist; you can't cut anything with a pain, and a burning sensation is no fire hazard. Physical characteristics don't describe or characterize the mental. But, then, what features does the mental have?

The two principal characteristics of the mental are content and feeling. Many of our mental states are *about* actual or possible events or states of affairs; that is, they have content. Jack fears that Julia won't drive; the content of that fear is that Julia won't drive. Sam believes that Twitter is better than email. The content? That Twitter is better. Thus, one quality or characteristic of some of our mental life is that the mental is *about* something, or mental states have content. Willing and choosing, thinking and judging are states with content as well. Danny wills (chooses/decides) going to Baskin-Robbins; the content is that he goes to Baskin-Robbins.

Do all mental states have "aboutness"? Some philosophers think so. But maybe not: for example, you feel sort of sad, but not about anything in particular. Similarly a pain, say, a headache, doesn't seem to be about anything.

Being about something doesn't seem to capture everything about our mental life, however. Some of our mental life is better described as a "felt" quality or as having a qualitative aspect. It is difficult to describe this aspect, but for some mental states, *there is something that it's like* to be in that state. A bit of chocolate tastes a certain way, which can be distinguished from the taste of a strawberry. Anger feels different from frustration; being a little blue can feel much different from depression. Most are very aware of the difference between liking something and loving something. It just *feels different*. These qualitative aspects of the mental, the felt quality, are often referred to as **qualia**, a term meaning a state or condition or property. Qualia, or the synonym "raw feels," are the felt quality or the qualitative aspect of some mental occurrence.

The two principal aspects of the mental then are its *aboutness* or its content and its *what it's like* or *qualitative* character. Some try to understand one in terms of the other; here it's enough to observe that both of these properties seem to describe the mental.

Two Types of Dualism

Epiphenomenalism and the Knowledge Argument

Epiphenomenalism is a type of property dualism, but for some time was not widely countenanced in the philosophical world. It holds that physical events cause or bring about mental states and properties, but mental phenomena are just *epiphenomena*. They don't cause anything; the mental is just an accompaniment of the physical.

Frank Jackson's "knowledge argument" (referenced in the text) thrusted epiphenomenalism back onto the philosophical scene. In an argument that occupied a very small portion of an essay (1982), Jackson asks us to imagine a neuroscientist who has learned everything physical there is to know about vision. The hook: she only sees in black and white, until one day, surgery enables her to see in color. Jackson claims she learns something new by virtue of her color-experience. She now has knowledge that physical theory was unable to give her. And if this is right, Jackson claims, there is more to the mental than what physicalist scientific theories can tell us.

Dualism comprises two main types: a dualism of *substance* and a dualism of *properties*. **Substance dualism** is the view that there are two distinct kinds of substances in the world: bodies—the physical—and minds—the mental. **Property dualism** is consistent with substance monism; it might claim that there is only one kind of substance—the physical—but distinctly mental properties emerge from particular physical arrangements.

Substance dualism tells us that we encounter two *types* of things or entities. There are not only physical objects, but mental objects or entities. But what sort of thing are mental objects? I know what makes an iPad or a peach ... but what makes a mental object? Can I bite one? Do they go bump in the night? Clearly not.

You've probably guessed: mental objects are individual *minds*. We may eat a peach—or even a brain—but never a mind. We are nonetheless aware of minds, or at least aware of what's going on "in" our own. This ability to "look into" our own mind is typically called *introspection*. Introspection reveals content (I just realized *that darn Sam is late again*), attitude (I fear *that he is late*), sensation (that stings), and process (assenting or affirming). And we know our minds by our awareness of them, or our awareness of having a particular thought or a particular sensation or an awareness that some mental process is occurring.

Non-Cartesian Dualism

Does substance dualism need to hold that mental substance is *immaterial*? Of course Descartes thought so, arguing that the mind possesses only nonphysical mental properties. The *essence* of a mental substance is these mental properties—and mental substances have no extension or mass or velocity. Many contemporary nonphysical substance dualists similarly argue that minds are immaterial or nonphysical.

Not all contemporary substance dualists, however, are committed to the immateriality of the mind. For example, E.J. Lowe, the author of several books and many articles on metaphysics, argues for a *non-Cartesian substance dualism.* A self or *subject of experience* is the subject of all and only its own mental states. This self, however, is not identical with the body or any significant part—such as the brain—of the body. This subject of experience is, in Lowe's view, a *human person.*

It may be true, according to Lowe, that a person could not have such experiences or mental states without also having a body; hence his *non-Cartesian* view. Unlike Descartes, Lowe insists that the "mental substance"—the person—may also have physical properties. But it is the person, not the body, that has the experiences. And the person is not identical to the body.

Lowe argues for this view by showing that the *identity conditions* of the body—the conditions that make a body *this* body—differ importantly from the identity conditions of the person. One of the principal arguments Lowe offers is the "replacement argument": "I"—the subject—could survive the replacement of all parts of the body, but clearly the body could not. Thus the subject of experience is not identical to the body.[2]

Minds—mental objects—of course do not have physical properties. We sometimes say they are "located"—Sara's mind is where she is, Sam's where he is—but not all substance dualists agree about that. But this leads us to a catch. One to a customer! Doubtless some of you want to note that it's easy to see what makes one body separate from another. But what makes this mind different from that one? And why are these *my* thoughts that I'm thinking, and not my neighbor Gloria's?

Substance dualists make the plausible assumption that if there are thoughts or sensations or processes, those thoughts or sensations must be had by some *subject.* And that "subject" is the mind; it is what holds all thoughts and sensations together. While there are arguments to this effect that we could follow, we will content ourselves with this assumption: if you are aware of it, it's your thought, and it's in your mind. Of course Sam and Sara could share the same type of *thought contents,* e.g., they both believe that Abigail Smith was married to the second president of the United States. But Sam and Sara have their own individual thoughts. And in general all persons possess a unique and individual mind, and this is a particular and unique mental substance.

Property dualism draws the line between physical and mental in a different place. Property dualists often hold that there is only physical substance,

---

2   E.J. Lowe 2006; Foster 1991; Swinburne 1997; Baker 2000.

and hence every object is a physical object.[3] Some physical objects turn out to be rather special, however, in that they have not only physical properties, but *mental properties*, too. Brains, for example. (Or the nervous system, including the brain.) Because of the complex configuration of approximately 100 billion neurons, especially the 20 billion or so in the cerebral cortex, mental properties (or features) arise. In addition to possessing physical properties, like weighing about two pounds, being sort of gray and white in color, the structure and functioning of human brains also gives rise to another kind of property, mental properties. But unlike the color or the weight of the brain, which could be explained by appealing to more basic physical properties, mental properties cannot be given an ultimately physical explanation. We can tell an evolutionary story of how they came to be. We can know that certain physical arrangements in the brain are associated with certain mental states. But the mental state is *more than* something physical. The right "dopamine arrangement" and we're *feeling* fine. But you can't say everything there is to say about that mental property simply by talking about the underlying physical structures and processes. Hence, we have in mental properties a distinctly different *kind* of property.

Both substance and property dualism share the idea that the mental is *irreducible* to even a very complicated neurophysiological story or theory. You can't explain the nature of the mental by explaining the physical; inevitably the physical account leaves out something essential about the mental.

Arguments for Dualism

Why believe in dualism? There are two principal arguments, the *introspection argument* and the *conceivability argument*, which we will discuss in a moment. Some have found dualism is preferable for the reason that it is necessary for survival after death or for free will.[4]

Lying behind this thought that dualism is necessary for free will is the assumption that a wholly physical world is purely mechanistic—a world in which things happen "automatically" because of the laws of physics and of what occurred before. And such a mechanistic world leaves no room for free will. Similarly, the claim that a person survives death is held to require dualism, most likely substance dualism. We know that the body doesn't survive after death; if something survives, it must be nonphysical.

---

3   Jacquette 1994, Chap. 1.
4   Crumley 2006.

The free will debate is itself vexed—we shall go into this in detail in Chapter 10—and it is not obvious that free will requires the truth of dualism. Nor is it obvious that the truth of dualism would preserve free will. There is nothing inconsistent about thinking that a nonphysical world is as determined and law-governed as the physical world. Let your beliefs and desires be as nonphysical as you choose: still mental laws governing those beliefs and desires may "dictate" subsequent action just as physical laws "dictate" certain subsequent events in the physical realm.

A physicalist might also hold that a person could survive the death of one's body. Supposing that the mind is simply the brain and its trillions of neural connections, the physicalist might find nothing inconsistent in our learning to write the computer program for all the neural connections in the brain, and running that program on a very special computer and that this could constitute survival after death. We just move "you" from one physical system to another. Perhaps this is not what some have in mind by survival after death. (We shall consider what constitutes a continuing person in Chapter 9.) But it is questionable whether survival requires the existence of a *nonphysical* soul. (But is substance dualism *sufficient* for survival after death? The Reading Questions at the end of the chapter ask this question.)

Two other arguments—the introspection and conceivability arguments—are more important for the dualist. The broad outlines of the first, the introspection argument, are already in front of us. Our senses tell us about the world of physical objects. And introspection tells us of the world of the mental, revealing a world of meaning or content, of feeling or "what it is like" to experience this or that. But introspection does not reveal a world replete with physical properties—it reveals a world *devoid* of physical properties. Physical descriptions seem out of place. Leibniz claimed that were we somehow able to walk around inside a brain that we would see moving parts, but we would not see thought or memory; mental "things" just don't seem physical.[5]

Of course, if something doesn't have physical properties, then it seems very reasonable to think that it isn't a physical object. So, introspection reveals that the mental is *nonphysical*. The substance dualist will go on to note that minds, as the subjects of these mental events, are not physical, while the property dualist will be content with noting the nonphysical nature of mental properties, such as having content or being a sensation of a certain type.

---

5   Leibniz 1979, p. 536.

The appeal of the argument is undeniable. It fits with our everyday experience: it certainly appears from our own introspection that my feeling or your belief or Danny's emotion is very different from physical things and their properties. But does this argument make a compelling case for the nonphysical character of the mental? Critics press a crucial point: this introspective power—why should we think that it's so good at telling us what is really there? And critics point to this analogy: perception.

Look around you, they invite you. Notice what you see: people, trees, tables, cups, and water. In other words, you see medium-sized physical objects. Now they ask, what don't you see? That's right: you don't see protons and neutrons and leptons and hadrons; you don't even see the bigger things that make up our world, like water molecules. So, these critics claim, maybe your introspective power is like your visual power. Just as your visual power doesn't reveal the real, deep-down nature of physical objects, maybe introspection doesn't reveal the deep-down nature of the mental. Maybe once you get "down there," you find that the mental is, after all, millions and tens of millions of neurons, in wonderfully coordinated symphonies of excitation and inhibition, reaching out and touching other neurons. My *thought* that if Julia doesn't come soon, the riverboat will leave without us, and my *sadness* that we'll miss the Rads' last concert, is *nothing but* complicated brain activity.

This challenge by critics doesn't show that dualism is wrong, but it highlights a plausible reservation about the introspection argument. Accepting the dualist conclusion requires more assurance of the correctness of the dualist view of introspection. That is, we need some further argument from the dualist that introspection reveals all there is to know about the mental.

The *conceivability argument* deserves to be called famous. To many, it is *the* metaphysical argument for dualism.

The physicalist is making a claim about the necessity of the physical or the impossibility of having anything exist that isn't ultimately physical. The physicalist is saying that *it has to be this way*, not simply that it just happens to be this way. The claim is that it's the nature of the world to be ultimately physical. It's *necessary*.

This makes the dualist objective very clear: undermine the physicalist claim by showing that it's *logically possible* for minds to be nonphysical. This "showing" constitutes the conceivability argument.

How do you show that a claim of impossibility or necessity is false? By showing that its contradictory—its opposite—is *possibly true*. Recall that logical possibility is a much more general notion than physical possibility. It's *physically* impossible to travel faster than the speed of light. It is not, however, *logically* impossible. My father used to ask why something couldn't go faster than the speed of light; why couldn't you get something going 300,000 km/sec, and just give it a little push? That push to get it going faster is logically possible, but the laws of nature in this universe prevent speeding, and speeding counts as anything faster than 300,000 km/sec.[6]

We rely on a variation of the conceivability argument given by Descartes. For convenience, the steps are listed singly:

I can conceive of a mind existing separately from a body.
If I can conceive something, then it's conceiv*able*.
If it's conceivable, then it's possible.
So, it's possible for a mind to exist separately from any body.
If it's possible for minds to exist separately, then physicalism is false.
If physicalism is false, then dualism is true.
So, dualism is true.[7]

This argument is sometimes met with incredulity: how can you prove that minds exist and are nonphysical just from some ideas about possibility and necessity and some definitions? You can't prove that something exists just by thinking about ideas!

There is some point to this objection, but some context is needed to evaluate it. Notice first that only two options—physicalism and dualism—are in play. If someone believed that only spirits or minds, and not physical objects, existed—a view sometimes called *idealism*—they wouldn't accept considering only these two options. But Descartes and most contemporary substance dualists admit the existence of physical objects. So, the issue separating dualist from physicalist is whether there is something *other than the physical*.

More important—and a bit harder to grasp since it is a *metaphysical* issue that is disputed—the conceivability argument takes the physicalist view to involve a "necessity claim": *it's not possible for "you"(some object) to exist at all and not be physical.* (In other words, *it's necessary that any existing object is physical.*) So, showing *that it is possible for a nonphysical thing to exist* is enough

---

6   This example also appears in Crumley 2006.
7   For examples of the conceivability argument, see Chalmers 1996; Campbell 1984; Crumley 2006.

to show that physicalism is false. And the only other option—dualism—is true ... that is, the mental is not physical.

Critics point to the pivotal moment of the argument—the move from conceivability to possibility. Conceiving something does not imply that it's logically possible, according to the critic. I was once told by a logic student that she could conceive a square circle. Granting for a moment that she could have such a conception, a "square circle" is a self-contradictory notion and hence, by definition, not logically possible.

Something similar, according to the critic, is going on here. It *seems as though* a mind separable from a body is conceivable. You may consider the *idea* of a mind as much as you like and never find the *idea* of a body or brain. Yet your inability to discover the necessary connection may reflect only a *cognitive limitation*. Centuries ago, people knew about static electricity discharge (call that SED) from shuffling across rugs and touching doorknobs, for example. But they didn't know that lightning was (high-powered) SED and were able to conceive lightning that wasn't SED. But this argument for the falsity of the lightning = SED theory is obviously no good:

> Lightning that's not SED is conceivable.
> If it's conceivable, then it's possible.
> So, it's possible for lightning to exist separately from SED.
> If it's possible for there to be lightning without SED, then the
> lightning = SED theory is false.
> The conceivability argument is then not compelling.

It took scientific experiment to prove the lightning = SED theory. (Remember Ben Franklin and his kite?) Similarly, physicalists would presumably need science to prove their theory right. They have tried to make good on this promissory note; we will see how below. First, though, we will pause at one problem that has bedeviled dualists for some time. A princess even took up the matter with Descartes!

How Did I Do That? Mental Causation

Minds move matter. Danny wants to let Deirdre know he thinks her talk is going well, and he believes he knows how to let her know—he leans his head to the side, and when he thinks she's looking, he winks. Sam decides that the coffee needs warming so he puts it in the microwave. Julia intends to wave at

Jack: her arm raises, her hand opens, and her fingers begin to wiggle. All these believings and intendings and decidings are mental in nature, according to the dualist. But they have physical effects: they move bodies.

How can something that has no physical properties whatsoever suddenly *bring it about* that hands move, feet shuffle, fingers wiggle, eyes wink?

This problem is the *causal interaction problem*. How do two completely different substances interact?

In 1643, after reading Descartes's *Meditations*, Princess Elisabeth of Bohemia (1618–80), the granddaughter of James I of England, raised the interaction problem in a letter to Descartes:

> Excuse my stupidity in being unable to comprehend, from what you had previously said concerning weight, the idea by which we should judge how the soul (nonextended and immaterial) can move the body; nor why this power ... ought to persuade us that body can be pushed by something immaterial any more than the demonstration of a contrary truth (as you promise in your physics) confirms us in the opinion of its impossibility.[8]

Note that Elisabeth asks how an immaterial substance could move a material body. Later she is more explicit: how might something immaterial impart *motion* to material objects, e.g., parts of the body.

To put the matter slightly differently, we tend to think of causes producing certain effects by means of a mechanism or a series of steps. Critics insist that in many cases we have a pretty good understanding of how one physical event might cause another. A cue ball causes another billiard-ball to move by bumping into it, transferring kinetic energy into it. A burner produces boiling water in a pot by transferring heat energy to the pot, which then transfers it to water molecules. Similarly, we have a pretty good understanding of the sequence of electrochemical steps that lead from neural activity to the contraction of muscles in the arm, hand, and fingers, and the subsequent wave.

We have no clear understanding, however, of the series of steps that might lead from thought to physical change in a body. Critics think it is utterly mysterious how a set of nonphysical thoughts and desires could bring about Jamoca® Almond Fudge neural signals that lead to body movements.

---

8   Cited in Tollefsen 1999, p. 70.

Different dualist responses to this problem are available. One scholar suggests that Descartes had the "opposite" understanding of mind-body causation. That is, Descartes thought our understanding of the mental causing physical events is our basic and fundamental understanding of what it is for one thing to cause another. In a sense, we take our experience of the mind causing behavior and apply that to the physical world.[9] A twentieth-century philosopher, C.J. Ducasse, held that the way that the mental brings about bodily changes or movements is basic and unanalyzable.[10] It is a fact about nature, just as is gravitational attraction. More recently, John Foster argues that so long as there are laws governing mental-physical interactions, there is nothing mysterious.[11] That physicalists are suspicious of these claims is perhaps best revealed by looking in more detail at physicalist views of the mental.

Physicalism

Physicalists hold that everything, object or property, is ultimately physical, differing, however, over exactly how the mental and physical are related. The most basic ontological distinction within physicalism is that between those who think that at least some mental things we talk about are *real*, and those who think that our usual "mental talk" is about something *unreal*. Call this latter group *eliminativists*; they hold that it's best to eliminate or get rid of the mental from our best theories about the world.

But many, if not most, contemporary physicalists think that the mental is something real. Within this group, the most active fault line is between *reductive* and *nonreductive* physicalism. We begin with the currently most widely held version of reductive physicalism.

Reductive Physicalism—The Brain Version

At the beginning of the twenty-first century, a work that received some attention in the popular media, *Why God Won't Go Away: Brain Science & the Biology of Belief* (2001), identified religious and spiritual experience with *brain activity*. The authors "took pictures" of the brains of subjects undergoing

---

9   Garber 2000, Chap. 8.
10   Ducasse 1960.
11   Foster 1991, Chap. 6.

mystical experiences.[12] Of the many sorts of experience people have, spiritual experience may seem the paradigm of something nonphysical. Unsurprisingly the book proved controversial.

At about the same time, a neuroscientist said in an interview, "That's what the brain is: just a piece of meat that has chemicals and electric charges. The mind, of course is just a special version of that."[13]

What is asserted here is that the mental *just is* what happens in the brain. This gets us to the heart of the central version of reductive materialism, generally referred to as the **type identity theory**. This is the view that every type of mental state is nothing more than some *type* or pattern of brain activity. That is, if Sam and Sara both believe that Li Po is a great poet, then the very same pattern of brain or neural activity is occurring in each of them. Deirdre and Danny both desiring to read Emerson's essay "Self Reliance" is *nothing more than* the same type or pattern of brain activity occurring in each.[14]

We then have two ways of talking about one thing. Our commonsense use of mental terms—belief, desire, love, pain, hope, fear—designates the same thing that a sophisticated neuroscience will talk about using its theoretical terminology. Whether Lois Lane says "Clark Kent" or "Superman," she is referring to the same individual. Similarly, something like the terms "visual awareness" and "synchronized neural firings in the visual cortex" name the same thing (at least according to certain researchers).[15]

But why is it called *reductive* physicalism? Identity theorists tell us we have two theories of the mind, our familiar commonsense view and the increasingly rich and sophisticated neuroscientific theory of the brain. As this latter theory becomes more complete, we will be able to replace the commonsense explanations of our behavior with more comprehensive and detailed neuroscientific explanations. *Wants* (*desires*), along with *beliefs, hopes, fears*, etc. figure importantly in our commonsense explanations of ordinary behavior. An adequate neuroscience will explain the very same behavior, perhaps by describing different sorts of neural networks.[16] This *replacing* of one theory's explanations with another theory's—that is *reduction*. And we don't lose our ability to explain anything in the process. Indeed, identity theorists claim

---

12   Newberg, D'Aquili, and Rause 2001, p. 5.
13   Dreifus 2002.
14   For influential statements of this theory, see Smart 1959, 2004.
15   Smart 1959.
16   E.g., Paul Churchland 1988, 1996, 2013.

that in the end we will be able to explain more! It's not that common sense about the mind is wrong, any more than it's wrong to say that the water in the pot gets hotter. But, in each case, there is a scientific theory that gives us a more accurate, precise explanation of the phenomenon or behavior we wish to explain.[17]

The origins of identity theory can in part be traced to ancient Greece, but Thomas Hobbes is probably the first modern philosopher to hold a version of the view. For a long time it was observed that the location of brain injuries or surgery corresponded to types of mental impairment. In the mid- and late-1950s, Ullin Place and his professor J.J.C. Smart published papers explaining and defending versions of the identity theory; the two are generally credited with originating the modern identity theory.[18] (The version explained here, however, is more in line with Smart's 1959 and 2004 view.) Interestingly, Place bequeathed his brain to the University of Adelaide, where he had been Smart's student, and his brain is on display at the university! Advances in brain research have exploded in the last twenty years.

Apart from the evidence offered by various surgical and experimental procedures, identity theorists invoked two basic ideas for accepting their view. First, it is simpler: A world that is through and through physical is "ontologically simpler" than a world that has either two kinds of substance or two kinds of property. This leads to perhaps their more important argument. Science continues to explain more and more of our world. If some form of dualism is true, however, then the mental would be scientifically inexplicable. But given the extent of scientific success and explanation, it's more reasonable to believe that *the mental is scientifically explicable*. So, dualism—it's reasonable to believe—is false, and physicalism *à la* identity theory is true.[19]

This is an important but controversial argument. The ancient Greek philosopher Heraclitus wrote that "nature loves to hide"; perhaps the nature of the mental loves to hide, as well ... even from science. The dualist suspects that the identity theorist's optimism is at best quite premature. Below we will get some idea why.

Identity claims are very strong claims. And identity claims can be falsified—shown to be incorrect—simply by finding some difference between those things claimed as identical. If Sam brings Sara a book and tells her "This book

---

17   Smart 2004; see also Crumley 2006, Chap. 3.
18   Place 1956.
19   Smart 1959.

is your book," Sara can reject this identity by pointing out a difference: "No, it isn't; the author signed my book; this one isn't signed." Similarly finding some characteristic that applies to minds (bodies) but not bodies (minds) is enough to show that the alleged identity does not hold.

Various differences have been suggested, and we have already seen some of them. Mental states don't take up space or have a size. On the contrary, says the identity theorist, it may seem a bit odd, but it's true: Sam's belief occupies a certain space, and if you take its "size" to comprise the relevant neurons, then it has a size. Or to the claim that physical things aren't *about* anything, or don't have a meaning, the identity theorist says, "Again: odd, but, yes, relevant brain activity *is about something*."

Surely, however, brain activity isn't introspectable, but we can introspect our mental states. Doesn't that serve to distinguish the mental from the physical? The identity theorist replies that we are in fact introspecting neural activity. We may not have the language (yet) to describe it as such, but it is still neural activity.[20]

You might suspect that "what it is like" or "how it feels" truly describes the mental, but these descriptions aren't true of patterns of brain activity. Isn't this a difference then—tell me all you want about neurons and electrochemical changes in the brain; tell me all you want about a flood of the neurotransmitter dopamine, but that just isn't the same as *feeling* happy or *feeling* sad, is it? So, mental states have qualitative aspects; brain states don't. Alternatively, *qualia* can't be explained just by explaining complicated neural activity. (The knowledge argument, discussed in the box "Epiphenomenalism and the Knowledge Argument," trades on just this point.[21])

Perhaps it is sufficient to point out that qualia arguments highlight this question: Is it plausible to think that we might have a scientific theory so detailed that even the felt qualities of various experiences—tasting ice cream, feeling a tickle, being angry or joyful, having the visual sensation of magenta or indigo—could be fully explained by understanding the physical? It took a while, but we finally understood why water is *wet*. It took a while, but we finally understood how just by the right (complex) physical arrangement, rather than by some *élan vital* (vital force), we could say "It's alive." So, is it plausible to think that after we learn (much) more about the brain, we will

---

20   For example, Paul Churchland 1988; also 2013.
21   Jackson 1982.

finally be able to say, "Oh; so that's why it feels this way"? In fact, this challenge arises, not just for reductive physicalism, but for any version of physicalism that acknowledges the reality of qualitative states.

Nonreductive Physicalism

A Mental Code

In 1975, Jerry Fodor's *The Language of Thought* brought a seismic shift to philosophy of mind.

Fodor—drawing on philosophy, linguistics, and psychology—argued that the mind is essentially *computational*. The "mental basis" of our beliefs and desires and other propositional attitudes is not whatever spoken language we use, but a *language of thought*, or "mentalese." Unique mental symbols and rules for combining and "transforming" them into new sequences, similar to the rules of syntax that structure a spoken language, are the computational basis of our propositional attitudes. *Thinking* is a series of unconscious computations. To have a belief that the Rads start playing at 11:11 is to be in a certain computational relation to an inner string of symbols, a mental sentence. Unlocking this "mental code" is a task for cognitive science and allied disciplines.

Fodor allies this representational or computational theory of mind with functionalism. It has stalwart adherents and equally stalwart detractors (e.g., Daniel Dennett 1978, Chap. 6).

If you've seen the original *Star Wars* movie, you perhaps recall a scene in which R2-D2 is about to be left behind, and the little "fellow" lets out a mournful R2-D2-cry. Could a complicated machine think at all, much less think "hey, don't leave me"? What about those fantastic creatures in the bar? Jabba the Hutt? Those creatures don't have anything like a human brain!

Almost as soon as identity theory began to gain credibility, other *physicalists* were expressing doubts. Their complaint was this. Identity theory seems extraordinarily *chauvinistic*; it limits mental states to human beings. But that can't be right. There's no reason to think that some other sort of nonhuman, even extraterrestrial, creature might not think. My dog and I may both believe, after watching it roll, that the ball is under the deck; we may both lie on the

ground, seeing the ball under the deck. How likely is it though that we have the same type of brain activity? In principle, with the right arrangement of neurons or some other physical "stuff," almost any physical thing might think. So, identity theory would be wrong about *reducing* the mental to patterns or types of brain activity. You couldn't reduce the mental to one type of physical pattern *because there are too many physical ways for any particular sort of mental event to come about*. Puppies desirous of their toys; robots and Transformers thinking; dolphins and gorillas believing; E.T. being sad; Vulcans being logical—and the list *in principle* goes on. This objection to identity theory is known as the *multiple realizability objection*. As a result of this objection, many physicalists are functionalists.

Functionalism is the view that we classify—name and describe—mental states by their *function*—what leads to or causes them, what they're connected to, and what happens as a result. (Most functionalists are physicalists, although functionalism does not require this; a dualist too might specify mental states by their *functional role*.)

In a simple case, my belief that the ball is under the deck has three types of connections. It's caused by my senses; it interacts with my other beliefs (e.g., well, for sure I'm too big to crawl under there, and I can't reach it); and it leads to some other state or behavior (I grab the garden rake and use it to pull out the ball).

It is important to be clear why functionalism is thought of as a *nonreductive* theory. If the ultimate nature of the mental is functional, many different physical bases might serve. Consider a rough example, my pup and I coming to have the belief that dinner is ready and our subsequent behavior. Upon hearing someone in the next room say "Dinner's ready," we each have the same input. This input interacts with various memory beliefs, together with the common desire "let's eat, I'm hungry." And for both of us, there is a common resultant behavior: both of us rouse and head to the kitchen. Functionalists claim that it's the *functional role* of this belief that tells us what it is to be this type of mental event. Now notice. My pup and I share the same belief despite having different brain activity. Extend this idea to many different kinds of physical systems. So long as the physical "stuff" is something that can support the functional role, the *kind* of physical "stuff" doesn't matter, whether it belongs to computer-driven robots, other terrestrial animals, or other extraterrestrial creatures. Consequently—and this is the key point—there is no way to *identify* some mental state with a *unique* type or pattern of physical activity. *Wanting to go home* is a type of mental state, but it cannot be uniquely identified with a type of *human* neural activity. The physical type may vary, even within our own species. Desiring to see the rock band the Radiators on the riverboat may be realized by one type of brain activity in Julia and a different type in Jack. And if we don't have identity between mental pattern and physical pattern, then we can't *reduce* the mental to the physical.

As stressed above, functionalism is compatible with physicalism. A functionalist might well hold (in fact, many do) that each mental state in an individual at a particular time (identified as to type by its functional role) is identical with some physical state of the individual. But the functionalist will insist that *types* of mental state need not be—most probably are not—identical *types* of physical states. So this physicalism is not type-identity theory. Philosophical jargon distinguishes between a type of things—e.g., dogs—and a *token* of a type—e.g., Fido. A functionalist who is a physicalist, then, would advocate not type identity theory, but rather **token identity theory**.

An interesting but controversial consequence of functionalism is that in principle computers could think. This is analogized by thinking of the brain as the hardware and the mental as the software or the program. An actual R2-D2 would really think, as would an actual Data (the android in *Star Trek: The Next Generation*). HAL of *2001: A Space Odyssey* and "Skynet" of the *Terminator* movies are examples of computer systems having mental states, as is Optimus Prime. The computer "brain" has some means for receiving input (analogous to our senses), processing or transforming it, and producing some output. Given this rough view, a suitably embedded computer *really has* mental states.

If the possibility of a thinking computer is a conceptual consequence of functionalism, would showing that you can't have thinking computers imply that functionalism is wrong? Many have thought so. John Searle's famous— some would say infamous—*Chinese Room argument* attempts to show that computers could never think, no matter how sophisticated the hardware or program.[22] Having a mental life, according to Searle, requires content or mean- ing. Thinking is more than the mere manipulation of symbols; it's *recognizing* the connection between a symbol and the referent of the symbol. But no computer does this. No computer, according to Searle, does anything other than "process" symbols by means of certain rules or instructions. The computer never "sees" what the symbol is about. On the other hand, the symbol string "Jamoca® Almond Fudge" has a meaning for Deirdre precisely because she recognizes a connection between that symbol string and that stuff in that five-gallon drum there.

Searle illustrates the argument by asking you to imagine being in a room, with an instruction book containing rules (in English) for sending out cards with various Chinese symbols on them, given certain inputted cards with Chinese symbols (and Searle imagines that "you" in this example can't speak or read Chinese). The rules only tell what to do when you see various symbols and their combinations, not what the Chinese symbols mean. A Chinese speaker outside the room passes in a card that says, in Chinese, "What is the world's longest river?" and after a while, a card comes out that says, in Chinese, "It depends how you measure river length, but by usual measuring methods, it's the Amazon." From the outside, it might look as though there was a competent speaker of Chinese inside the room. But you know nothing of Chinese, and won't learn anything. Searle invites you to agree that if all you had was the rule book, together with the stacks of Chinese symbol cards, *you would never come to understand Chinese.* Since you don't know what the symbols are *about,* you'll never grasp the Chinese language.

---

22   Searle 1984, Chap. 2.

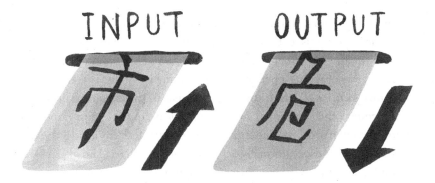

Disagreements over this controversial argument have continued for over a quarter of a century. Critics insist that Searle misunderstands the nature of programs, that his "Chinese room" is too oversimplified, or that he's looking for meaning in all the wrong places. For example, it is argued that it is in the causal interactions between a robot and its environment that meaning would arise. You don't understand what the symbols mean, but the whole Chinese room, including you and the rule book, do. Searle, however, continues to insist that neither anything in the room, nor the whole room and its contents, understands Chinese.

This argument is relevant to functionalism because the Chinese room, as a whole, can exhibit language-related functional states just like those in humans have; yet, he insists, there's no language-related mentality in the box. If Searle is right about this, functionalism would be false. And this accounts for part of the controversy surrounding the argument.

We'll close this section by briefly revisiting the dispute between functionalists and identity theorists. Many turned to functionalism because of the multiple realizability objection. But identity theorists think there's a way around that objection. Their idea is that reduction is possible within a restricted range. Thus, there is, for example, human pain and Vulcan pain and lobster pain.[23] So, there is "pain-in-humans" or "pain-in-Vulcans" or "pain-in-lobsters." And these types of pain can be identified with *restricted* patterns of physical activity. Of course, functionalists insist that this cedes their point—even though the mental is tied to the physical, it's not the physical stuff that tells us the nature of the mental. We discover the nature of the mental in its *function*. In other words, we only know that "pain-in-humans" and "pain-in-Vulcans" should be treated as mental states because of the function of these states.

---

23   Spector 2013 (on lobster pain).

But functionalism too faces a fundamental criticism. Function seems to mischaracterize or miss entirely a whole aspect of mental states—their qualia. In a recent radio ad, a doctor is asked about pain. He responds that pain is the body's way of telling a person that something is wrong. This is of course a very nice *functional* definition of pain; it tells us the purpose pain serves. And of course, this functional view seems to leave out the most important feature of pain: pain *hurts*! Function cannot capture feel. And, indeed, pains, sensations, emotions are normally defined by how they feel. And qualia—the "how it feels" of particular mental states—appear to be an intrinsic feature of those mental states, not a feature determined by functional connections to other elements. The pain Danny feels because of his toothache, is not captured by his subsequently desiring relief or inferring that he should call the dentist or asking Deirdre to bring him an aspirin. Critics of functionalism—and physicalism generally—insist that the real nature of pain is simply that it. hurts. Functionalism defines mental states extrinsically; yet the nature of some mental states—qualitative states—seems to be intrinsic.

Critics—noting the "how it feels" aspect of some mental states—have some eye-catching arguments. One thought experiment asks us to imagine the one billion citizens of China *functionally organized* just like a human brain, attached to a bionic body, with appropriate devices for sensory input and motor output. When something heavy is dropped on the body's toe, information is sent to various members of the Chinese population, and they send other information to others (according to the instructions of the organizers), and eventually these vast networks of information-passing result in motor output from the bionic body: it says "OUCH!" and quickly pulls back its foot. Of course, it is claimed, despite its having the "same functional organization," no one would think that such a "brain" is conscious.[24] Defenders insist that, technical difficulties aside, yes, it would be. The emphasis on the huge size of this operation makes it difficult to see the forest for the trees. If it were not so big,. we'd have no problem attributing consciousness, complete with qualia, to this thing.[25] Critics are thus wrong to suppose that there would be *absent qualia*, the name of this type of objection.

Still another striking thought experiment called *inverted qualia* or *inverted spectra* is intended to show that an intrinsic feature of some mental events simply cannot be captured by functionalism. Imagine Sam and Sara looking at

24   Block 1978.
25   E.g., Lycan 1987.

a rose. Sara has the sensation of red, while Sam, who suffers from "qualia inversion," has the sensation of green. Similarly, when Sarah looks at the clear sky, she has the sensation of blue, but Sam has the sensation of yellow. Otherwise their behavior and their thinking are exactly alike. Both admire the beauty of the rose; both want to leave it on the plant. Both stop at red lights and go on the green. Crucially, both call the color of the rose "red," because that's the word both have learned to use corresponding to that sensation. Functionalism seems to require saying they are having the same sensation. Yet this seems counterintuitive—there's a difference between green and red sensations.

Functionalists' responses are quite varied and detailed. One prominent functionalist grants the qualia objection, acknowledging that functionalism only explains the nature of mental states like beliefs and desires, not qualitative states. Others attack the idea that Sam and Sara are really functionally the same, if they are indeed having different sensations. That is, defenders claim that if there really are two different sensations here, then there is a functional difference.[26]

Does function have a feel to it? This blunt question perhaps captures the contentious point of these arguments. Some would be inclined to say that there are feeling states, qualitative states: the issue is whether or not identifying the function of such states can capture this feeling aspect.

Eliminativism

Dualism, identity theory, and functionalism each agree that there really are mental states and mental properties. They just disagree about the ultimate nature of those real states and properties. But not everyone shares this position: various philosophical arguments and empirical findings have led some to adopt a view known as **eliminative materialism**. The central position of this view is that some significant class of what we might think of as mental phenomena do not exist.[27] Some eliminativists claim that states like belief and desire—states that are claimed to exist in our commonsense view—are in fact not real. "Folk psychology"—what they call our commonsense view of our mental states—is, they claim, a radically false and misleading theory.[28] Other eliminativists suggest that our notion of sensation is at best confused,

---

26   Harman 1999, Chap. 14.
27   For more, see Crumley 2006, Chaps. 6 and 10.
28   Paul Churchland 1981.

and sensation terms do not pick out a clearly defined kind of state.[29] And at least one prominent theorist has claimed that all of our everyday references to the mental are mistaken, whether talking about a hope or a wish or a thought or a sensation.[30]

As startling as such views might initially appear, eliminative materialists have offered a number of arguments that, while disputed, are not easily dismissed. Suppose for a moment that our view of the mind is an *empirical* theory. Like any other theory of the world, it's susceptible to confirmation or refutation by evidence or experiment or by considerations of what makes for good theory.

Eliminativists note that other "folk theories" have not had a good track record—the theory of witches, for example, or "folk physics" (e.g., the sun moves round the earth, is smaller than the earth). Here's a bit of folk science you probably believe. In the same room, touch some ceramic tile, and then touch some wood. You'd say that the tile is colder than the wood, right? Wrong. Science reveals that real temperature is the mean kinetic energy of molecules, and if both wood and tile have been in the same room for a while, then they have the same temperature. (The difference is in heat conductivity: tile conducts heat away from your finger much faster.) Your folk theory of temperature includes radically false beliefs. There is no such thing as the "temperature" of something, that you can feel.

But why think that folk psychology should be grouped with other folk theories that have been definitively refuted? Empirical approaches like cognitive neuroscience explain even more of our mental life, while folk psychology, which has hardly changed since Socrates' day, seems to give us very little that we expect from a good theory. Using folk psychology, which features entities like belief or hope or desire, we still can't predict anyone's behavior better than they could centuries ago, and neither we nor the ancients could predict very well. Neither does it provide much in the way of explanation: "Why did you paint the living room that color?" "Well, I like it." If we take seriously findings in neuroscience, it becomes harder to see how belief-desire psychology turns out to be true.[31] For example, eliminativists suspect that understanding brain activity will require sophisticated theoretical and mathematical tools, and consequently, notions like belief and desire just won't be all that helpful

---

29   Dennett 1991.
30   Skinner 1990.
31   Paul Churchland 1981.

in explaining human behavior. This is unsurprising, they think, since our talk about hopes and fears or beliefs and desires evolved largely as a result of ignorance of the real—neural—causes of our behavior. A science that starts at the "bottom" with synapses and neurons and neurotransmitters may develop theories that ignore descriptions like "Danny fears that the taxi will be late," just as modern chemical theory ignores phlogiston or modern thermodynamics ignores caloric[32] ... *because there are no such things!*

Similarly, some have thought that our notion of sensation is at best unclear; moreover, some think that there is no way to settle whether a sensation is of one type or another—there is no "fact of the matter" about such sensations. Thus, for example, Daniel Dennett argues that we have no way of identifying whether one sensation is the same as another. You simply don't know whether your "spectrum" is the inversion of someone else's. Maybe it doesn't even make sense to think that it does. Dennett draws on various empirical findings that suggest that our conscious life is not always a reliable guide to what is actually happening in the world and "inside" us.[33]

One version of eliminative materialism, developed by Paul and Patricia Churchland, accepts the idea of sensation, insofar as it is reducible to complicated neural states, but rejects the existence of mental states, such as beliefs and desires. They acknowledge that the brain takes in and processes information or content; our brains indeed have a representational function. That is, our brains give us a "picture" of the world around us. But they reject the idea that "Jack believes the ball is under the deck" is an accurate way to describe or explain the content of the neural representations or the way our brain employs such representations. The Churchlands disagree with the suggestion that understanding our cognitive life is best accomplished by utilizing a folk psychology that depends on a notion of propositional attitudes—beliefs, desires, hopes, and the like—whose content is given by sentences. Our brains represent the world around us, but not as described by the commonsense view of the mental.[34]

Perhaps you are familiar with behaviorism (or at least with a well-known aspect of it, behavior modification or behavioral conditioning). Although historically its development came before other physicalist theories—Ullin Place was looking for an *alternative* to behaviorism when he began developing

---

32   The fluid substance that was thought, during the eighteenth and part of the nineteenth centuries, to be responsible for heat, and to flow from hotter to cooler things.

33   Paul Churchland 1981, and Dennett 1991.

34   Patricia Churchland 1986; Paul Churchland 1988, 1996, and 2013.

identity theory—there is a reason we have postponed its discussion. Depending on the version of behaviorism, it can be viewed as reductive or eliminative.[35] A definition that encompasses both views might run as follows: **behaviorism** is the view that the best explanation of behavior is to be found in environmental causes (stimuli) in our environmental history, and the subsequent conditioning that leads to patterns of behavioral response.

Reductive behaviorism, sometimes called analytic or logical behaviorism, is the view that the causes of behavior are environmental stimuli; mental terms refer to *tendencies or dispositions to behave in certain ways under certain conditions*. In this view, mental terms, such as "belief" or "desire," are reducible to descriptions of complicated behavioral dispositions; hence our commonsense conception of the mental turns out to be scientifically respectable.

Eliminative behaviorism, or "ontological behaviorism," similarly adopts a view about stimulus and response, but it rejects the existence of the mental. B.F. Skinner (1904–90) rejected the idea that we might understand the causes of behavior by invoking beliefs, and even expressed a skepticism about sensations. Even as neuroscience was developing rapidly, he argued that the study of the brain would be useless for good psychology.[36]

Skinner was behaviorism's most prominent proponent, although John Watson pioneered the view.[37] Skinner's *Walden Two*, a "scientific novel" published in the 1940s, imagined the benefits of behaviorism by imagining a small society, Walden Two, structured according to the principles of behaviorist psychology. And Watson famously claimed that with a fully mature behaviorist psychology, we could take ten infants and produce musicians, ship captains, scientists, or any other personality type desired. Deirdre's writing talents, Sam's passion for poetry, Sara's scientific abilities are only the consequence of being exposed to certain stimuli and conditioned to respond in certain ways. This is no different from any other animal behavior; indeed "conditioning" birds to play a piano or dogs to run in a particular direction is no different in principle than producing Sam's or Sara's unique interests.

Perhaps the most important motive for behaviorism is the thought, shared with eliminativists, that appealing to mental states simply isn't explanatory. In trying to explain terms like "wants" or "loves" or "believes," we are caught in a circle, always appealing to still other beliefs or desires. We are never

---

35   Crumley 2006, Chap. 2.
36   Skinner 1990.
37   Watson 1930; Skinner 1974.

really able to explain intelligent behavior—our ability to operate successfully and in sophisticated ways in the world—if we rely on our mentalistic view. Behaviorists think that the real causal explanations are to be found instead in one's genetic makeup plus—and especially—one's environmental history, the sum total of a person's interactions with the environment. Indeed, Skinner thought it was futile to look inside a person. No matter what inner state one might find, tracing the history of that state led outward, to the environment. If you want to understand why Deirdre goes to the opera and Julia hangs out at the Dream Palace, awaiting the Rads' next show—all you need to look at is their respective past histories.[38]

While behaviorism was the dominant psychology paradigm in the United States for the first half of the twentieth century, by the mid-1960s, the information-processing paradigm—or cognitive psychology—had more or less replaced it. In part, this was due to serious criticisms of behaviorism, which, according to many, did not receive adequate answers.

Many suspect that replacing mental terms with references only to behavioral dispositions is an impossible task. The behaviorists wanted to interpret assertions that S likes X as something like this: "Under conditions C, when presented with X, S will do A." So we might understand "Sam likes SpaghettiOs" as "If you put SpaghettiOs in front of Sam, he tends to eat them." You may already see at least one problem: what if Sam *wants* something else? What if he's simply not hungry? What if he *wants* to hide from Sara his craving for SpaghettiOs? What if he *wants* to consume less iron? What if he *fears* ...? The problem is that the process of filling out the schema seems (a) endless and (b) to involve still other uses of mental terms. We are unable to get away from our references to the mental.

Next, turn to the claim that inner causes are not explanatory, even if those inner causes are various types of brain state. We can accept the claim that brain states result in part from environmental influences. This claim, however, is not enough to demonstrate that brain states are never the cause of behavior. Because there was some prior, external cause of brain activity, it does not follow that the brain activity is not a cause of subsequent behavior. Indeed, we often cite *causal chains*—a series of causes—as leading to some event. Yet those more *proximal* causes are no less causes because some cause brought them about. Analogously, consider the "cause" of Julia, namely, her parents. Imagine now the claim that Julia's parents are not themselves causes

---

38   Dennett 1978, Chap. 4; see also Crumley 2006.

since they themselves are the result of some earlier cause, namely, grandparents. This claim is at least open to skepticism on the grounds that it misunderstands a series of causes. Yet Skinner's claim about brain states seems just as suspect.

Skinner does not, of course, deny that brain states exist, or that they have a causal role to play in the body. What he does deny is that a scientific explanation of *behavior* (not just muscle-contraction, for example) doesn't involve brain-states. Whatever brain states are involved when someone has a conditioned disposition to behave in some way, that plays no part in real explanation.

But here is an objection that is perhaps more important: environmental conditioning seems unable to explain *novel behavior*. Past history may explain why Jack is waiting at the corner bus stop every morning at 7:37. But how are we to explain an entirely new experience? Perhaps on the way to the bus stop he notices a small dog limping, with no one else around, and he picks up the dog, carries it home, and calls the owner? Of course the behaviorist can say "Well, there's *something*, some set of interactions; some set of 'pet-compassion interactions' in his past...." This seems, however, explanatorily unhelpful. The behaviorist doesn't really tell us how this current behavior was produced, but rather notes "something" must have done it. But this seems much too easy, and perhaps a bit empty. Imagine that you want an explanation of why Pauline is addicted to Queen Anne milk chocolate cherry cordials. The behaviorist tells you that there must have been "Queen Anne" addicting interactions in Pauline's history. Yet we might wonder whether the behaviorist has really explained anything. Again, this type of explanation seems a bit too easy, and perhaps a bit empty.[39]

What's a Belief?

What is it to have the belief that *this chapter is coming to a close*? The dualist tells us that to believe that this chapter is coming to a close is to have a non-physical mental property. For the substance dualist, the belief is the property (or state) of an immaterial mind. Property dualists, on the other hand, tell us that this belief is a mental property had by some brain.

Identity theory, a version of reductive physicalism, tells us that this type, this pattern of mental state, is at bottom nothing more than a type or pattern of neural activity. Pushed by the multiple realizability objection, identity theory concedes that the human pattern of neural activity identical to the

---

39   Dennett 1978, Chap. 4.

pattern *believing that this chapter is coming to a close* likely differs from the Vulcan Mr. Spock's type of "brain activity," which in turn clearly differs from R2-D2's or Optimus Prime's types of *physical activity*. Each different type of physical activity is the belief type *that this chapter is coming to a close*. There are beliefs, according to the identity theorist; they are just patterns—(perhaps restricted) types—of neural activity.

Functionalists—as nonreductive physicalists—are at ease with all these different types of physical bases for the mental. For them, a belief is not to be identified with the physical "stuff," but with the functional or causal role: what typically brings about this sort of belief, what other mental items does it interact with, what kind of behavior—output—does it typically produce? The belief that *this chapter is coming to a close* is a special type of functional state, connected to sensory inputs (e.g., your visual impression of the words on the pages), other mental states (e.g., your belief about the length of this book's previous chapters), and of course behavior (e.g., putting down the book).

Reductive behaviorists think it's a bit misleading to talk about a belief as some sort of inner state. For them—the logical or analytic behaviorists—the belief that *this chapter is coming to a close* is just a way of talking about a tendency to act in a certain way, and it is likely manifested in an arbitrarily large but finite number of behavioral dispositions.

Eliminative materialists claim there isn't any such type as *your belief that this chapter is coming to a close*. Appeal to beliefs and desires is an old, tired, retreating folk theory that will eventually be replaced by the theories arising from the new cognitive and neuroscientific disciplines.

And that brings this chapter to a close.

Key Concepts

- physicalism
- dualism
- qualia
- substance dualism
- property dualism
- type identity theory
- functionalism
- token identity theory
- eliminative materialism
- behaviorism

Reading Questions

1. Explain the difference between substance and property dualism.
2. Do you think there is an adequate *dualist* resolution of the mind-body interaction problem? Explain.
3. Is substance dualism necessary or sufficient for survival after death? Why or why not?
4. What do you think is the best argument for identity theory? What do you think is the biggest problem for identity theory?
5. What are qualia? Explain the problem qualia present for physicalist theories, such as identity theory and functionalism. Do you think there are aspects of the mind that cannot be explained by appealing only to the physical? Explain.

For Further Reading

Over the last several decades philosophy—and other disciplines—witnessed an explosion of interest in questions related to the mind. There are too many introductory texts to list here. Paul M. Churchland 2013 has doubtless become a classic; Jaegwon Kim 2010, John Searle 2005, John Heil 1998 are comprehensive introductions to the field, each examining the various positions and each explaining the author's own views. Dale Jacquette 1994 surveys the issues and defends a property dualist view. Also, Crumley 2006 surveys the several theories considered here. Borst 1970 contains several of the seminal papers in development of philosophy of mind. Fodor 1981 is still a nice overview of the twentieth-century history of philosophy of mind, explaining the issues and problems that motivated competing theories. Two valuable collections of essays are Rosenthal 1991 and Heil 2004. William Lycan's anthology, which first appeared in 1990, and now in its third edition with Jesse Prinz 2008, is a classic anthology. Sterelny's 1990 is still one of the best accounts of the representational theory of mind. And Chalmers 1996 is still very influential, not only for its defense of a form of dualism, epiphenomenalism, but also for opening new concerns and areas of research in philosophy of mind.

CHAPTER SEVEN

PERSONAL IDENTITY

"I haven't changed. I'm the same as I was before—
only in a different way."
> Judy Holliday (as Gladys Glover), *It Should Happen to You*

IN LEWIS CARROLL'S *ALICE'S ADVENTURES IN WONDERLAND*, THE TITLE character tumbles down a rabbit hole to some strange adventures. She happens upon the Caterpillar, who inquires, "Who are you?" This question leaves Alice at a loss: "I—I hardly know, Sir, just at present—at least I know who I *was* when I got up this morning, but I think I must have been changed several times since then." Alice's puzzlement about her present *identity* raises an interesting topic in metaphysics.

Metaphysics aims to identify both the things that populate our world and their nature. There is one type of very familiar "thing" whose nature we often take for granted. And that "thing" is persons. Like Alice we might under various circumstances be led to ask exactly what features constitute the identity of persons. What is it that makes some-"thing" *this* person, rather than some other? For some the identity of a person is to be found in having a soul. For others it—personal identity—is found in having a particular unique configuration of DNA. For still others it is having that body. Answers to the question of *personal identity* are not limited to these three, however.

We might also be led to ask whether some particular person *at this time* is the *same* person as that one, earlier. For instance, you might wonder whether that woman you saw in the supermarket today is the person whom you briefly met at a party a year ago. The issue here is not what we think when we say, "Fred has changed so much since high school that he's not the same person." Fred now and Fred then are literally the same person. What is meant here is whether this person, Fred, is literally the person also called Fred that you knew in high school.

The imagined technology of television programs such as *Star Trek* raises the question in more dramatic fashion: When you flip open your communicator and command "Beam me up, Scotty!" not everyone is so sure that it is *you* that reappears moments later in the starship *Enterprise*. So, we might then ask about not just how many changes, but also exactly what kind of changes you might go through and still be you. Forget about Alice and *Star Trek* for a moment: scientists are hard at work developing new microchip implants for the human brain—in addition to the implants that have already been developed![1] Microchip implants could extend the range of our senses, allowing us to detect more than our "normal" senses allow.[2] Would you now with a normal functioning brain, and the you, say, twenty years from now—with a head-full of microchips replacing your brain—be the same person?

We can distinguish several sorts of questions about identity, corresponding to several senses of the words "identity" and "identical."

When we say "X and Y are identical," we might mean one of two things. We might mean that X and Y, despite being two separate things, have exactly the same characteristics. Two new dimes are in this sense (just about) identical. But we might also mean that "X" and "Y" are two names for one thing. In this second sense, George W. Bush is identical with the forty-third president

1   Snyder 2012.

2   Moyer 2013.

of the United States, and Fred, whom you have just bumped into, is the person you sat next to in third grade. To distinguish the two kinds of "identity," philosophers call the first kind **qualitative identity** (X and Y have the same qualities) and the second kind **numerical identity** (X and Y are one and the same). And—to make things more confusing—there's a third use of the word "identity" that means the qualities or personality or whatever it is that constitutes the important nature of an individual—make you what you are, as in "My Italian roots / love of music / work with dog rescue are basic to my identity." Notice that this sort of "identity" can change over time in what is numerically the same person: a few years ago, Ella wasn't interested in dog rescue. Let's call this sort of "identity" **individual identity**. And, more confusing still, we can ask about what makes for personal identity, where this question is about what counts as a *person* (as opposed to some other sort of being). An answer to this might imply that we count—or don't count—fertilized human eggs, or chimpanzees, or robots, or silicone-based aliens from the planet Zarkon, as persons. We'll call this **personhood identity**.

Persons and Identity

Two obvious and very broad characterizations of persons come very quickly to mind. We think of persons as having a mental or psychological life. More generally, we might characterize this as a conscious life, or simply, consciousness. People have memories, desires, opinions, wishes, fears, sensations, and emotions. They know things, make plans, have hopes and goals. All of these, and others, we tend to think of as mental, as psychological. So, we might identify persons with some aspect of their mental lives, or perhaps the sum total of their mental or psychological life. This sort of idea about identity may have implications for what makes for identity in several of the senses listed above.

But a different point of view produces different sorts of multiple implications. No doubt our most immediate and default means of *identifying* people is by their bodies. Indeed we can tell at a glance that this is Julia because she has Julia's body; we can tell that this is Jack because he has Jack's body. And we know that this is the same Julia we spoke with last Sunday because it's the same "Julia body." No need to investigate mental lives. Thus, one might think of identity as fundamentally body identity.

A variation of the psychological view, proposed by John Locke, provides a starting point for examining these different views.

I Remember Me: A Psychological View

John Locke is perhaps best known for his *Second Treatise on Civil Government* and its influence on the thinking of the framers of the US Constitution and other advocates of the rights of the governed. His contributions to metaphysics and epistemology are significant, too, including his memory criterion of personal identity. Locke argued that a person's identity consists in the chain of remembered experiences. Here, we should note, he was speaking about numerical identity. In particular, he was worrying about what features account for a person remaining the *same* or *identical person* over time, even through various changes. But a second sort of question can be raised about numerical identity: What constitutes the identity of a person; what features or properties make some being *this* person and not some other? These two questions are sometimes characterized as a **persistence question**: what makes this the same person as that one earlier; and an **individuation question**—what makes someone this person and not someone else at the same time.[3]

My remembered experiences make me who I am; your remembered experiences make you who you are. (They are important, perhaps, to all senses of "identity" listed above.)

Now this needs a little clarification, but first consider the intuitive motivation for adopting Locke's memory criterion for persistence. Normal growth or changes in the body do not affect or determine who one is, we suppose. Changes in size or hair color, loss of some body part, we think, still leaves you *you*. Your body keeps discarding old tissue, and building new, so after one year, virtually 100% of the atoms in your body have been replaced. But you are still there. We suspect, therefore, that something else determines persistence identity. In a movie early in Tom Hanks's career, *Big*, Hanks plays a character who is magically transformed from a child into an adult. The "big" version of his character persuades his closest friend that he—in his "big" form—is the same person, by recounting—*remembering*—various experiences. Similarly, the 2000 movie *Bedazzled* imagines the hero—after a bargain with the devil—occupying successive, very different bodies (in some very different circumstances) in order to win the heart of his true love. Another movie, *13 Going on 30*, imagines the dramatic change in a teenager who wakes up to

---

3   These designations due to Macdonald 2005, Chap. 4.

find herself in the body of a thirty-year-old woman—yet her "psychology" remains the same.

A less fictional and a more heartbreaking example is perhaps illustrated in later stages of Alzheimer's. Those suffering from the disease no longer *remember*—family members, friends, or even what they were doing a few moments ago. Indeed it's not too far amiss to say that they don't remember themselves. Some suspect that as the memory of personal experiences disappear, the earlier *person* disappears, as well. We might want to say, then, that *in a literal sense* this Sally, deep into Alzheimer's problems, is not the Sally we knew—is not numerically identical with her.

Locke argues for this idea: a person's memory is determinative of personal identity. The *person* is whatever the person's memory encompasses. We have, then, a psychological or **memory criterion** of persistence identity: a person's identity is determined by conscious memories, or, a little more clumsily, by the memories contained in consciousness. Locke himself was not intent on distinguishing between one's memories and one's consciousness. He notes, for example, that a person's identity "extends" as far as consciousness extends. Thus, he seemingly intends memory and consciousness to be indistinguishable, at least as far as personal identity is concerned. Perhaps this works for individuation identity as well. Deirdre, then, is a different person than Sara insofar as her memories differ from Sara's. Deirdre remembers jumping off Rainbow Bridge into the American River the day before graduation; this memory, however, is not "shared" by Sara. They are thus two different persons. Similarly my current memories constitute my identity, just as your memories constitute your identity. And if, for example, Sam's memories include those of Nestor—an ancient Greek king who participated in the Trojan War, according to Homer—then Sam is indeed *the same person as* Nestor. (What is meant here is not merely that Sam *remembers that* Nestor met Telemachus after the Trojan War; what is meant here is that Sam *remembers* meeting Telemachus after the Trojan War.) Thus, there seem to be some puzzling implications of the view. Locke himself acknowledged that some of his "suppositions will look strange to the reader."

Locke dismisses the idea that *substance* plays a role in determining identity. Locke seems to consider substance, in this context, as the "whole particular," a combination of physical and mental. In ordinary cases, consciousness is a part of the whole particular. But a person goes wherever that consciousness goes. So in Locke's view, my consciousness might find itself attached to the body that we recognize as Carrie Underwood, yet my identity is unaffected. So long as consciousness extends or includes the memory of any past action, it is the same person:

> For it being the same consciousness that makes a Man be himself to himself, *personal identity* depends on that only, whether it be annexed only to one individual Substance, or can be continued in a succession of several substances.

The same consciousness, in Locke's view, can occur in different bodies, different substances. What matters for identity is consciousness:

> For it is by the consciousness it has of its present Thoughts and Actions, that it is *self* to it *self* now, and will be the same *self* as far as the same consciousness can extend to Actions past or to come....[4]

So in Locke's view, if Sam wakes today and remembers the French toast he had for breakfast yesterday, the "Sam remembering" is the same person as the "French toast-eating" Sam. Personal identity is not dependent on the body or some immaterial thing. I am me because of the thoughts and memories that I have when I am conscious. Period.

Our ordinary view considers that temporary losses of consciousness, including sleep, are no threat to one's identity. But if Locke is right and my identity is determined by my consciousness, when my body falls asleep and there is no consciousness, I temporarily cease existing.

There is a more challenging worry about the memory view: we are of course forgetful. I remember but a few things from my experiences in second grade. Indeed for most of us, experiences from but a few weeks ago are no longer remembered; they are no longer part of consciousness. Yet we are inclined to think that, yes, it is us that did these things, even if the experiences have been forgotten. Deirdre no longer remembers her going with her cousins to see *The Lion King*, but we think she is still that same person. A person *persists continuously over time*, we think, even if that person has forgotten certain events or experiences. But Locke's view seems to disallow this. This is but a version of one of the earliest criticisms of Locke.

---

4   Locke 1975, Bk. II, Chap. XXVII, Sect. 10.

Thomas Reid: The Brave Officer and Locke

Thomas Reid (1710–96), associated with the Scottish school of Common Sense, and one of Hume's earliest critics, thought he saw a consequence of Locke's view of identity that he suspects Locke did not see:

> "It is, that a man be, and at the same time not be, the person that did a particular act."[5]

Reid supposed a brave officer, who as a boy was flogged for stealing from an orchard. In his first military campaign, he acted bravely, and later became a general. Now Reid supposed that the brave officer remembered his childhood punishment. But later as a general, he remembers only those military actions, not the childhood punishment.

Notice the apparent consequence for Locke's view: The general *is* the brave officer, and the brave officer *is* the young boy. But the general *is not* the young boy. The general remembering the younger brave officer makes the general the *same person* as the brave officer. And that brave officer, because he remembers the punishment, is the same person as the youthful offender. Seemingly, then, the general is that offender—he is the brave officer who is the young thief. Yet the general has no memory of the theft. So, he is not the thief. And now the general is and is not the young thief.

Reid's puzzlement is now clear. Locke's memory criterion conflicts with our normal "transitivity" intuition about identity. It leads to apparently self-contradictory claims.

This type of criticism led defenders of a psychological criterion to a *continuity* view.

Indeed, in Locke's view, it looks as if there may well be multiple persons occupying Sam's body! For example, suppose that Sam now remembers walking through Aldo's, while visiting New Orleans five years ago. Call Sam's body, then, BODY X. Now, body X contained someone who was remembering playing in a little-league baseball game 15 years earlier. So body X contains the person who played in that game. But since Sam doesn't remember playing in

---

5   Reid 1975, p. 114.

that game, that person is not Sam. It appears to follow that body X contains both Sam and someone else!

Perhaps an obvious solution to some of these difficulties is to suggest that it is *continuity* or overlapping sets of memories that determines personal identity. A *chain* of memories—overlapping sets of memories—enable us to trace the connection between earlier and later memories. Thus, Reid's general is the same as the young boy because the general remembers his actions as a brave officer, and as a brave officer, he remembered the orchard thievery. This *continuity* version of the memory criterion of personal identity—overlapping sets of memories constituting the identity of a person—has prominent defenders.[6]

But consider Alzheimer-afflicted Sally, mentioned above, who has no memories of any past, is numerically identical with no earlier person. There's no overlap between her and any earlier person. Of course, her earlier individual identity is now, we might think, totally destroyed; but still, that person back then, with the different individual identity, was numerically Sally. She's just changed a whole lot.

The memory continuity criterion invites a branching or **fission objection**, that is, we can imagine a person "dividing" into two equivalent beings. The fission objection is a version of the *duplication* problem. Imagine that someday we can transfer the "mental life" of someone near death (call this person U) into a complicated cybernetic system.[7] Suppose further that for some reason, the "transfer engineer" is overly cautious and makes two cybernetic "homes" for U's mental life. U suffers bodily death, but two creatures remain that lay claim to U's memories. Call them U-1 and U-2. You can see the problem. U's mental life is continuous with both U-1 and U-2. But $1 \neq 2$! Identity means one ... and only one! How are we to decide? Can we?

Bernard Williams suggested this "branching problem" many years ago:

> It is logically possible that some other man ... should simultaneously undergo the same changes ... What should we say in that case? They cannot both be Guy Fawkes [our U] ... Moreover, if they were both identical with Guy Fawkes, they would be identical with each other, which is also absurd.[8]

---

6   E.g., Shoemaker and Swinburne 1984, pp. 67–132.
7   Daniel Lyons 1998.
8   Bernard Williams 1973, p. 8.

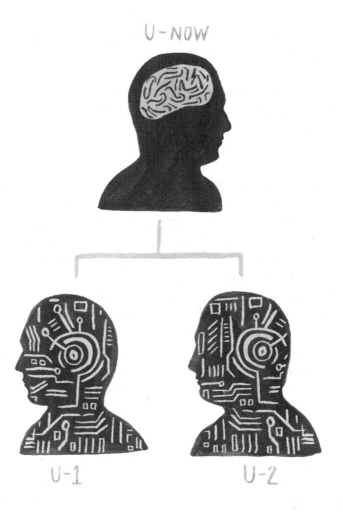

Advocates have two types of response to his fission problem. Roderick Chisholm (1916–99), extremely influential in both metaphysics and epistemology, claimed that U is *in fact* identical with one of U-1 or U-2. We just can't tell which. That is, suppose that you somehow undergo fission: U "branches" into U-1 and U-2. Chisholm claimed U is *in fact* one—and only one—of those branches. The other is someone mentally very much like U, but not *identical* to U. We will just never know which one. So, in Chisholm's view, there's a metaphysical answer to the question. It's just that the metaphysical answer brings with it an epistemic problem, namely, that we can't tell which of U-1 or U-2 U now is.

This response sometimes strikes people as arbitrary. Yet Chisholm held that we are not identical with a body, but rather a "self" that continues in some one of the bodies. That we are unable to *decide* which body "contains U" does not lead to the conclusion that U is not one of them:

> In such a case there may be no sufficient reason at all for deciding that you are or that you are not one or the other of the two different persons. But from this it does not follow that you *will* not in fact be one or the other of the two persons.[9]

Others are less sanguine about Chisholm's approach and suggest that neither U-1 or U-2 is U. Sadly (you might think), U no longer exists. These two branches are in fact two different people who happen to share many of the same memories. This leaves but one option. Fission—branching—brings an end to U.

Occasionally some wonder why branching brings an end to the original U. Why can't U be two? It seems fundamental to our notion of identity that a person can't be in two places at once; one can't be both at home, watching reruns of *Gilligan's Island,* and simultaneously sitting in the library, reading about personal identity.[10] But someone might urge: what if the person is a nonphysical thing? Can't a nonphysical thing be in two places at once? (Another chapter considers *universals,* objects that can be in two places at once.) But that won't help here—to be you is to be some *particular* thing, not some universal.

Still some are tempted to ask, couldn't some person be "distributed" throughout space? Consider a company that outgrows its original offices and moves into two new offices (call them O-1 and O-2) in separate buildings. Does O-1, or O-2, or neither, contain the original company? Clearly both do. A company can exist in two places at the same time. (Note, in passing, that a company can also be an intermittent object—a status that was worrisome when it appeared to follow from Locke's view of persons. A company can cease to exist for a while, then start existing again. Maybe people are like companies?)

But perhaps it's better to think that *part* of the company is now located in each new office. We are not wondering about U dividing into *two parts of one thing.* The branching problem treats U-1 and U-2 as *two distinct persons.*

We have then three options available to us upon branching: 1) U comes to an end; 2) U is one of U-1 or U-2, but we can't tell which; and 3) the unattractive "option" of saying that U, U-1, and U2 are all the same person.

---

9   Chisholm 1976, p. 112.
10   Parfit 1986, p. 199.

These difficulties have led many to think that in the end we should abandon a memory criterion of personal identity. And they turn to the other seemingly obvious criterion of personal numerical identity: that of having the same body.

Same Body, Same Person

Identifying and re-identifying persons by means of their bodies is no doubt the everyday norm. Sara sees that *Sam* is walking towards her because she recognizes the body. Yet she doesn't think "Oh, here comes Sam's body"; she just sees Sam.

This routine practice suggests a view of personal identity as consisting in having the same body: same body, same person. This is the **body criterion** of personal numerical identity, and perhaps it answers both the persistence and the individuation questions. Of course, we should be reluctant to interpret "same body" in some ways. Bodies change over time. Bodies grow—and shrink—in various ways, in height or weight. Hair color changes, sometimes naturally, sometimes helped along. A person may lose a toe or a finger, an appendix or even a limb. In order to understand "same body, same person," we need to understand what exactly is meant by this "same body" criterion of identity. One thing it can't mean is *exactly the same physical stuff*. It's almost certain that not a single atom of a person's body stays there for more than a few years.

Same Body—Having the Right History

Bodies come from somewhere. The body that each of us has right now has a history. The history of the body that is "me," or that body that is "you," can be traced. Initially this history leads to a body of a few hours ago or a few days or months. A complete history will of course lead back to the originating zygote. This body then, like any other human body, has a continuous history, beginning with its origin. Of course, we don't tend to think of zygotes as bodies. Still, from whatever point at which we are willing to say that we have a human body, "this body" has a continuous history.[11]

Perhaps we can use this idea of a continuous history to give us a clearer sense of "same body." Intuitively, we think that a body is the same body as

---

11 E.g., Forbes 1985.

before because it is *continuous with* all the previous moments or times in that body's history. We can trace back successive moments of Sam's body to the first moments in the history of Sam's body. *Continuous* implies that there is an uninterrupted chain of "moments" of Sam's body. Indeed if we could somehow draw a line on a graph or chart, a line representing the history of Sam's body, it would be a continuous or uninterrupted line. We might impose a grid on that graph of Sam's "body line," which allowed us to talk about Sam's body today or last week or last decade. We should not be misled, however: Sam's body remains continuous.

How does this help us with an account of personal identity as same body? First, we have an idea of what makes me *me* and you *you*—our respective and different bodies. Second, it also gives us a way of answering the persistence question: it provides a way of explaining or defining continuous identity through the *same body*. That is, a body now is the same body as a body then, if they are both "located" in this continuing, uninterrupted "body history." Julia's identity is determined by her body, and *you* are your body. And Julia is the same person today that she was six days or six months or six years or six decades ago because of this continuous, uninterrupted "body history." It doesn't matter which two points we choose from this body history; we get a definitive answer to the persistence question.

You might worry that this can't be the "same body" simply because a body has a shape and size, along with other physical attributes. Change the shape and size, you might ask, and haven't you changed the body? Wouldn't this be a different body? Doesn't "identity" mean "exactly the same"?

An analogy might help allay this sort of worry. Suppose Andy returns to Graeagle to revisit his childhood home on Chilula St. The paint color of the house may have changed; a room might have been added; the living room window might have been replaced by a larger window; the roof might have different shingles. Despite these changes in color, shape, size, "décor," we could trace this house back to the very same house of Andy's earliest days. In principle, some group, making an odd documentary, could have taken turns with their iPhones video-recording every moment of that house, from the time cheap wooden stakes and twine first marked out its foundation until now, as Andy pulls up alongside the curb. And time-lapse video would show that Andy is now looking at a house *continuous with the origin* of the same house of those bygone baby bassinet days. We might even suppose that a large number of small renovations have resulted in a house which has no material in it that was there in the old days.

Similarly Andy's body now is continuous with the origin of the body that—let us put it like this—was first Andy. Something may have been added, something taken away. Still we can trace the continuous, uninterrupted history of this body. And this body is Andy. And as long as this "body history" remains continuous and intact, we'll know where to find Andy: go find Andy's body.

We have some understanding then of "same body, same person." Still, even if we accept that bodies persist over time, we might still want to know if there are good reasons for thinking of a body as determinative of identity. Two natural suggestions occur to us almost immediately. The first is already suggested: we count and distinguish persons by their different bodies. That's all we see. A second natural suggestion is that we engage with the world as bodies. Julia's acts—visiting a library, watching a movie, showing a child how to do long division—are the actions of a body. It might be further claimed that our fundamental orientation in the world is a bodily orientation. Directions, spatial relations, perceptual relations are part of our bodily connection with the world. The French phenomenologist, Maurice Merleau-Ponty, explored this idea at length in one of his seminal works, *The Phenomenology of Perception*.[12] Some would go further, insisting that our psychological lives, our thoughts and feelings are tied to our bodies (which, of course, include our brains and the rest of our nervous systems). In recent decades various authors on consciousness and our emotional and mental life have argued that even our mental life must be understood as tied to the body.[13]

"Beam me up, Scotty?"

Should you be willing to walk into that transporter of the fabled starship *Enterprise*? Even if someone that looks, walks, and talks exactly like you shows up at the other end of the transporter travel, perhaps it isn't you after all.

Suppose the transporter works by making a "blueprint" of you at this end, and at the other end, that blueprint is used to assemble "you" out of completely different matter. Would you still think it's you? Derek Parfit first imagined a transporter case like this.[14]

---

12   Merleau-Ponty 1962.
13   Damasio 2000; Edelman 1992.
14   Parfit 1986, Chap. 10.

Or suppose that the transporter disassembles you into sub-atomic particles which it whisks to your destination, and again, a blueprint is used to put you back together out of those particles. Why would you think it's you at the other end, rather than just a duplicate?

According to one expert,[15] the writers on Star Trek were inconsistent about how the transporter actually worked. In some episodes it appears that the transporter sends the person's actual matter through space; but in others, it appears that it just sends a blueprint. This might make a difference about whether you'd like Scotty to beam you up to the *Enterprise*, or whether you'd rather just be left to face the Klingons on the surface of the planet Wombax.

Perhaps you might insist instead that none of this matters because you are nonphysical—but then that might make you wonder whether Scotty's transporter beam could lock on to "you" at all.

The above illustrates that your view of the transporter depends, at least in part, on your view of personal identity—and that thought experiments involving the transporter can help clarify these views.[16]

If I Only Had a Brain

In the movie *The Wizard of Oz*, Scarecrow wishes his head weren't just stuffed with straw:

> I could while away the hours, conferrin' with the flowers
> Consultin' with the rain.
> And my head I'd be scratchin' while my thoughts were busy hatchin'
> If I only had a *brain*.

Brains play a significant part in our lives, as Scarecrow tells us. Despite the apparent simplicity of the same body criterion, various considerations suggest to some that it's not the body, but the *brain* that matters for personal identity. Once again science fiction may not outrun real possibility by that much.[17] But to prevent our discussion from seeming a bit "creepy," let's treat

---

15   Krauss 1995.

16   These and other similar transporter cases are outlined in Carroll and Markosian 2010, Chap. 5. See also Merricks 2001 and Corcoran 2001.

17   Tyson 2010.

this as a bit of science fiction—one that illustrates a rationale for a view of personal identity in the real world.

Can we imagine losing parts—even significant parts—of the body, yet still being ourselves? Not only might we lose a limb or an eye: imagine losing the whole body, except for the brain. If we could find a way to preserve the brain—to allow it to continue functioning—then we might think that our identity is still preserved. Recent philosophy sometimes describes this preservation *sans* body as a "brain in a vat." As long as our brains continue functioning, we continue. Our identity therefore is determined by or constituted by a functioning brain: persons remain the same over time, if their brains continue. Deirdre is the same person today as she was yesterday if she has the *same brain* she had yesterday. And here we can understand "same brain" in like manner as we understood "same body."

We see the brain as constituting personal identity, again, because it is fundamentally implicated in that "part" of us that seems to matter most, namely, our psychological life. Emotions, desires and goals, actions and their motivations all seem inextricably tied to a functioning brain. Thus, it is claimed, personal identity is determined by the brain.

MORE SCIENCE FICTION

As before, we can test the thought that the brain really carries what we think of as personal identity—versus the same-body account—with a science-fiction story. Imagine that Sam's brain and Sara's brain are swapped. Now consider the Sam-body with the Sara-brain. This person has Sara's memories and personality traits, but Sam's body. Is this person Sam or Sara?

Here's a more complicated science-fiction thought-experiment, this time with a bit of connection with reality. The reality: In the 1950s, neurosurgeons began performing a special kind of brain surgery, commissurotomy, in order to help patients suffering from debilitating epileptic seizures. This operation severed the corpus callosum, a network of fibers that allows normal communication and coordination between the two brain hemispheres. Roger Sperry and Michael Gazzaniga studied extensively the effects of this surgery on the patients, finding that the two halves of the brain, when separated, could function independently.[18]

Now to let reality meet science fiction: Imagine for a moment that we can not only "split" brains, but do so in such a way that each hemisphere retains the same psychological life—same memories, same knowledge, same hopes, desires, goals, wishes. And now combine this idea with that of transplanting the separate hemispheres. Again—not entirely disconnected from reality: some very young patients can have half their brain removed, but grow up functioning almost normally.

Let us imagine first that Kiersten, through some medical emergency, is told by doctors that, along with the rest of her body, half of her brain is dying, but that they have been able to "reconfigure" the other hemisphere so that it contains her entire mental life. This half will be transplanted into a new body. If Kiersten is an advocate of the same brain view of identity, she should not be particularly alarmed about whether or not *she*—Kiersten—will continue to live. After all, she will continue as long as her brain continues.

Same brain theorists typically do not require that the *entire* brain continue. Rather, they require first that the "new" brain be a continuant of the original brain. Same body theorists and same brain theorists are alike in this respect. It is the *same* if there is a continuous history. Second, same brain proponents assume that the relevant functional aspects of the brain, such as memories, cognitive abilities, and values, continue. Kiersten survives, then, so long as the brain (or brain hemisphere) is continuous with her "original" brain and the relevant functioning remains.

Now imagine a variation. Kiersten is dying from cancer that has spread all over her body except for her brain; the doctors decide that they can save

---

18   Godwin and Cham 2013.

her by transplanting her brain into another body (brain-dead, but with the rest of the body okay). But they'll make sure she survives this risky operation by having a "backup": one separable functioning hemisphere into each of two bodies—another case of "fission." So Kiersten's medical emergency will produce two independent yet psychologically equivalent hemispheres. (Imagine that doctors desire a "backup" in case one of the transplants fails.) Now suppose that prior to the surgery Kiersten wonders what will happen if both transplants succeed. What should Kiersten think is about to happen to her?

One thought, widely held, is that Kiersten is about to cease to exist! Just as we saw above with the case of U-1 and U-2, a fundamental principle of identity is that $1 \neq 2$. And we now have Kiersten-left and Kiersten-right. But she can't be both. So, Kiersten ceases to exist, and is replaced by these two new "Kierstens." So fissioning of the brain can also lead to identity problems.

(Cases such as this and others are variations of a case originally imagined by Sydney Shoemaker.[19] Considerations of the "Brownson" case—the name given by Shoemaker to one transplant recipient in his original scenario—can even be found in the pages of *Psychology Today*.[20])

Notice: the same brain view encounters the same problem as the memory criterion: we can always imagine there being two beings that have exactly the

---

19   Shoemaker 1963, pp. 24 ff.; see also Shoemaker and Swinburne 1984.
20   Burton 2012.

same identity-determining characteristics, each of which comes into being at the same moment.

We have been concentrating, for the moment, on persistence identity, but the split-brain phenomenon also raises questions about a person's individuation identity. Because the right hemisphere of the brain controls the left side of the body, and the left hemisphere the right side, real people who have had the split-brain operation sometimes exhibit strange behavior. One, for example, was observed to be pulling up his pants with one hand, and pulling them down with the other. Does one of these actions represent the real intentions of that person? Or do we now have two persons in one body?

Does Being Me Depend on the Absence of Competition?

The duplication problem (or fission or branching), along with the various responses to it, highlights an important issue for identity. Identity should, it seems, depend on internal or intrinsic features of an object or person.[21] Continuity of psychological states or continuity of a body or brain requires only that we look at some feature of the person. We don't need to check and see what is happening in the vicinity.

Yet the two-hemisphere transplant case seems to raise the suggestion that identity can depend on *extrinsic* or *external* conditions. If both transplants are successful—if there are post-transplant *competitors*—there's reason to think Kiersten ceases to exist. On the other hand, Kiersten continues if but one transplant survives; so her identity is preserved.

Now imagine that after the operations, one of the transplants, the right hemisphere, awakes before the other. What should she think? Well, she will certainly recall herself as Kiersten. But whether she really is Kiersten seemingly depends on the success or failure of the other transplant. Kiersten must wait to find out who she is! She is either Kiersten or "Kiersten-right." It seems odd that the "first-awake, post-transplant" Kiersten should have to see what happens to *someone else* to find out who she is! Fission cases produce competitors. And the notion of competition seems to lead to the idea that identity depends on extrinsic features, which seems to have odd implications.

---

21   For example, Wiggins 1967, Chap. 1.

Survival vs. Identity

Faced with these sorts of difficulties some wonder whether numerical *identity* is what we really care about. Might we care about something else that does not require identity? Some philosophers have wondered whether what we really care about instead is survival.

Survival

This survival view first became prominent in Derek Parfit's influential *Reasons and Persons*.[22] And this novel suggestion attempts to avoid the difficulties of identity while retaining something important.

How does survival differ from identity? A person, according to Parfit, is constituted by beliefs, goals, and values, around which actions and projects are organized.[23] Sometimes the person envisions these goals and values in some detail. Or they may only be drawn in broad strokes, such as wanting to be a millionaire, or wanting to be your own boss, or wanting by the time you're thirty to know more about poetry than anyone else. Here Parfit seems to be talking about individual identity, and perhaps personhood identity.

A person cares, rather, that *this set* of beliefs, goals, values, and projects continues. Personal numerical persistence identity doesn't matter. That is, when we shift the emphasis from identity to survival, the persistence question gets a very different answer. *I survive*, in some sense, if these projects of mine, together with my beliefs and values, continue to exist, and in some way, my "survivor" can continue to carry out these projects or fulfill these aims or act according to my current beliefs and values. Or as David Lewis describes the view:

> When I consider various cases in between commonplace survival and death, I find that what I mostly want in wanting survival is that my mental life should flow on. My present experiences, thoughts, beliefs, desires, and traits of character should have appropriate future successors.[24]

---

22 Parfit 1986.
23 Perry 1976.
24 David Lewis 1976, p. 17.

Suppose, then, that Deirdre wants to major in mathematics to become an actuary, raise a family, and help rescued animals. She identifies with these projects and values. As long as she is able to pursue fulfillment of those projects, she might well be indifferent to whether *this* body or *this* brain continues.[25] In this survival view, Deirdre should be unfazed by the possibility of multiple survivors. Still a critic might note, as Lewis does, that prior to any transplant operation, Deirdre might reasonably—and compellingly—wonder which *one* will be *me*? But a more central question is this: if Deirdre's goals and values survive—say, in her children—but she dies, is that all she should be interested in? No, say critics: she wants to survive.

Substance and Souls

Animalism

In recent decades, a view intriguingly known as *animalism* has attracted a number of defenders, most notably Eric T. Olson.

Olson holds that human persons are fundamentally animals; we are not essentially persons. The concept of person describes a characteristic of humans, but not a defining characteristic. The kind of being we are is determined by our biological properties, and the continuing of some individual is coincident with the continuing of various biological processes. As animals, we temporarily have certain psychological characteristics, but these are ultimately due to our biological or animal nature. Our identity is not determined by our psychology, as the subtitle of Olson's book indicates: "*Personal Identity without Psychology*."

Animalism insists that *person* is not a kind of substance. This view is considered to be opposed to Lockean or psychological continuity views. Indeed there has been considerable exchange over the past decade or so on the rival virtues and vices of Lockean and animalist views.[26]

Perhaps you wonder why we have not considered a view that has been around, in one form or another, for a long time: that sameness of *soul* determines sameness of person? Of course, if we are to accept it, it will help to know what a soul is, and when we have the same one.

---

25   Perry 1976.
26   Eric T. Olson 1999; Shoemaker 2008.

Plato, according to many commentators, held that persons are their souls. In the *Republic*, several of the arguments apparently identify a person with a soul and its characteristics. The *Phaedo*, Plato's dialogic and literary recounting of Socrates' last hours, explores several ways to think of the soul and whether those accounts of the soul might support a notion of immortality or survival after death.[27]

Aristotle's view of the soul depends on his more general view of form and matter. As we will discuss in more detail below, matter and form provide a way of thinking about the nature or structure of each individual object, including persons. In his view, various objects—living ones—have a special type of form, namely, a soul.

These ancient philosophers' views of the soul have had substantial influence on subsequent metaphysical views. Plato influenced early Christian thinkers, such as St. Augustine. Aristotle influenced St. Thomas Aquinas, who relied on and synthesized the Aristotelian metaphysics to provide a coherent framework for Catholic thought in particular and Christian thought in general—a framework still very much in evidence in present day views.[28]

Form and Matter: "Stuff" and Organization

In thinking about an object, we might adopt one of two perspectives. We might think about the "stuff" of an object, asking, for example, "Where's that wooden candle holder you used to have?" Along the same lines, we might naturally ask of Michelangelo's masterpiece sculpture, the *Pietà*, "What is it made of?" We do not marvel, however, at the mere fact that the statue is made of marble. We marvel at the marble stuff because of the way it is shaped or carved—*because of the way it's organized*. There is an "organizing principle" to this rather large clump of marble. Similarly the candle holder: it's not just that it's made of wood, but that the wood is shaped or structured in this particular way. This piece of wood might have been organized or shaped in some other way; for example, it might have been fashioned into a small bowl.

We have only one object in each case: a marble statue and a wooden candle holder. Yet we "analyze" each object as comprising what it's made of—the "stuff"—and how that stuff is put together. **Hylomorphism** is Aristotle's view that any individual object or substance can be analyzed as a unity of form

---

27   Plato 1961c; see discussions in Burger 1984 and Rosen 2008.
28   Gilson 1940, esp. Chaps. IX and X.

and matter. The "stuff" of an object is its matter. The form is the organizing principle of the object, or how the stuff is arranged or put together. Not just the candle holder, but the candle too is a "unity" of form and matter—the matter is the wax, while the form is the structural arrangement of that clump of wax. Again, it is important to emphasize that candle, candle holder, and statue are each *one* object composed of matter and form. And this is true of any object—it is constituted by its matter and its form.

Soul as Form

Some objects, like the statue or the candle holder, have their forms given to them, imposed by an artisan or a sculptor. We are interested in living things, however. And these seem to have their form *intrinsically*. Living things are of a certain type because of their form. The matter of the lilac bush or the matter of a monkey or the matter of a person is organized according to an innate principle. To be a monkey, to be a "monkey kind of thing" is to have a monkey form. The form *informs* or organizes the matter and guides the development of the matter. Aristotle called the form of any living thing a "soul." Although he distinguished the types of soul characteristic of plants, animals, and people, our focus is the human soul or the form of persons.

The kind of soul distinctive of people is the *rational soul*. Rational souls guide both the physical development and sentience—our sensory ability—of human beings. More importantly, the rational soul structures our rational features, our cognitive or intellectual characteristics. We are thinking creatures in virtue of our having a rational soul. Indeed people are *rational animals*, according to Aristotle. They belong to the genus of animal, but are a distinctive species, namely, thinking animals. (Aristotle understood thinking as an attribute of people, not of nonhuman animals.)

So a person is a basic or primary substance, a single object composed of soul—that is, form—and matter. If we ask, however, what makes a person *this* person and not *that* one, we get an interesting answer from Aristotle. His view might be more easily understood if we return for a moment to our simple candle holder.

Imagine that a candle holder company machines many teak candle holders of the same size, shape, finish, and weight. The form—the shape, the arrangement—of the teak clumps is the same. The form doesn't distinguish one candle holder from another. So, it must be the wood, the matter, that distinguishes.

That is, *this* candle holder is made from *this clump* of teak and *that* candle holder is made from *that clump* of teak. More technically, it is the matter that *individuates* candle holders. Matter, not form, individuates.

Analogously, Sam and Sara are of the same type: rational creature. Thus, they are alike in form. Sam and Sara differ, however, in their matter. Then while persons are basic or primary substances, a unity of matter and form, the individuating principle is the matter of the person. Perhaps what we have here is a body criterion for individuation numerical identity. Yet Sara remains the same person over time because she remains *this unity* of matter and soul. Then, it seems, we have a different test for persistence numerical identity.

You might wonder why the sameness of a person over time is not also determined by the matter. Were this same matter to lose its organizing principle, to lose its form (soul), we no doubt would be disinclined to call this the "same person." Indeed it's not just the calcium, water, and other chemical elements and compounds that make a *person*. It's that these chemicals—this stuff—are organized in a particular way, by a form—a soul—of a certain kind.

Summarizing then, in Aristotle's view a person is the body plus soul. Different matter distinguishes individuals, but a person persists because the unity of form and matter remains. What we want to know from Aristotle, then, is: Is this how we tell it's the same person? Fred now and Fred-as-a-child back then do not have the same matter (though there is a spatio-temporal continuity, with small changes, as we've noted). But do they have the same form? If form is rationality, then every human is endowed with this universal characteristic. But if we're looking at individual types of rational thought, then it's for sure that Fred now and Fred-as-a-child are wildly different.

Medieval and Contemporary Understandings of the Soul

Plato's view may seem a little more typical: namely, soul constitutes identity. Jack goes where his soul goes, just as Julia goes where her soul goes. And Julia is the same person today as yesterday if and only if she has the same soul. In a widely held and well-known, if controversial, set of views, persons continue in the after-life if and only if their souls continue. Thus, no amount of bodily change or even "bodily disintegration" damages personal identity. How are we to think of this type of soul? We look—as a start—to Thomas Aquinas.

Aquinas utilized the Aristotelian framework for understanding the soul: the soul, as form, organized the matter. Like Aristotle, Aquinas too held that the person was a basic substance, a unity of form and matter.[29] Of course Aquinas, as a Christian, was also concerned about an issue that troubled Aristotle far less. Aquinas needed a metaphysical understanding of persons and personal identity that guaranteed not only survival after death, but that it was *this person* that survived.

Aquinas, like Aristotle, held that persons are numerically individuated by their matter. We have different ways of characterizing this matter—flesh and bones or a continuing genetic structure—but the matter is the body as physical. Whether we describe it in modern or medieval terms, it is the matter that is the individuating principle. And, to an extent, Aquinas followed Aristotle's view about the numerical persistence of individuals: He would say that Sam, for example, persists as long as there is a continuing unity of soul and matter.

Now, however, consider Sam's eventual death. Aquinas held, consistent with the Christian view, that his soul continues to exist, even though his body ceases to function or even disintegrates. He further held that eventually the soul would be reunited with a "resurrected" body. Christian thinkers continue to puzzle over the nature of this resurrected body.

But another question arises for Aquinas. We know that the *person* Sam is "restored" when soul is reunited with the resurrected body. What becomes of Sam while soul is separated from body? In the Thomist[30] view, Sam is distinguished from Deirdre by virtue of his matter. And Sam remains the same person as long as the unity of soul and body continue. There seems to be a gap, however, in Sam's existence between the time the soul slips his mortal coil and the time it is united with a resurrected body.

Recognizing the difficulty, Aquinas seems to admit that it is *not* Sam that exists while his disembodied soul exists: "The soul, since it is part of man's body, is not an entire man, and my soul is not I."[31] Of course, this runs counter to the views of many Christian thinkers, as Goetz and Taliaferro observe. Similarly, Brian Davies, a noted Thomist scholar, also holds that "my soul is not I" for Aquinas. Davies argues that, in the Thomistic view, the survival of the soul is not the survival of a human being. It is only an *intellectual* being that exists.[32] Yet Aquinas' view that Sam is not his soul does not seem to bode

---

29   E.g., Leftow 2001, p. 137.
30   "Thomist" is the conventional adjective form for St. Thomas Aquinas.
31   Aquinas n.d., Sect. 924.
32   Davies 1992, pp. 216–17.

well for *Sam's* existence post-mortem, at least during that time that body and soul are separate.[33]

If Davies is right, then a consequence of Aquinas' view is that there is a gap in the existence of the person, from death until the soul is united with a resurrected body. (By analogy, imagine that a house burns down, and nothing is left for a while except the original blueprints, from which the same house is reconstructed later.) Perhaps Davies's interpretation helps Aquinas. One might still wonder what it is that is special about the soul and not some other part of the person. Would preserving all, or even some special part of the body, be sufficient, as well? Clearly, Aquinas would reject this possibility. Otherwise, Sam would have become a "split person," existing both wherever his soul is and wherever the preserved parts of his body are. Indeed, Davies notes that for Aquinas, the *human person* Sam exists only after the soul is reunited with the body.[34]

A different view of personal identity as constituted by the soul, and one that seems closer to the conventional religious view, is found in Richard Swinburne's *The Evolution of the Soul*. Swinburne has written extensively about theological and related philosophical issues (see Chapter 10). Swinburne argues that, while the soul is *part* of a person just as the body is part of a person, a person's soul constitutes personal identity.[35] Souls individuate persons, and the continued existence of the soul explains the persistence of persons over time.

Swinburne views souls as immaterial, as nonphysical subjects. Those items we typically identify as mental, such as beliefs and desires, or intentions and hopes, are in fact *states of the soul*. The beliefs and desires give a structure to the soul. The way in which beliefs and desires are related, how they affect our acquisition of other beliefs and desires, how they affect the judgments a person makes, and consequently, the person's behavior—this complex network of belief and desire determines the structure of the soul.[36] This evolved structure constitutes a person's character. Swinburne summarizes the nature of the soul thus:

---

33 For a different view, see Stump 2003, Pt. II.
34 Davies 1992, pp. 217–19.
35 Swinburne 1986, p. 147.
36 Swinburne 1997, Chap. 8.

Souls are immaterial subjects of mental properties. They have sensations and thoughts, desires and beliefs and perform intentional actions. Souls are the essential parts of human beings, and humans have sensations etc. and perform intentional actions in virtue of their souls doing so.[37]

This description of what souls are, however, does not yet answer the question of personal identity—what makes a soul *this* soul, and how *this* soul constitutes *this* person. Swinburne claims that souls are connected to a body: Julia's soul is connected to her body, and Jack's to his body. A body, however, is not an essential part of the person; it is only contingently a part of the person, and so it contributes nothing to the person's identity. Julia's body—while a part of her—is not Julia. Again, Julia *is* her soul.[38]

Yet this still leaves us wondering how we are to link souls to personal identity. If it's logically possible for a soul to exist apart from the body, our normal way of identifying Julia, or distinguishing her from Jack, is no longer available—these two souls are in principle separable from their respective bodies. Indeed, one who doubts the truth of dualism will wonder how it is that we "track" or identify a person's psychological states. So what is it that makes one soul *this* individual soul and *that* soul that individual soul?

Swinburne argues that there is a fundamental *thisness* or *haecceity* to each soul. *Haecceity* is a Latin term coined by the medieval philosopher John Duns Scotus (1265–1308). In English, it means *thisness*. For Scotus, haecceity is the source of the unity of the soul.[39] The thisness of a soul is a basic, unanalyzable feature of souls, according to Swinburne. In a sense, because a soul exists, it always exists as *this soul*. To put it roughly, any soul has essentially its special "I'm this one" feature.

Some contemporary views of haecceity or "individual essence" hold that an object's thisness is itself a property. In addition to having properties, such as being the author of *Huckleberry Finn* or having been born in Florida, Missouri, Mark Twain also had the individuating property *being identical with Mark Twain*.[40] Of course, this is a quite special property, and whether this type of property exists is still the subject of debate.

---

37 Swinburne 1997, p. 333.
38 Swinburne 1986, p. 146.
39 Cross 2014.
40 Robert M. Adams 1979.

Swinburne recognizes that some critics may think that the haecceity view is "irrational." Two things (souls) can't just be different; they must differ in some respect, or in some characteristic. Indeed our normal way of distinguishing individual things is by means of some property or characteristic. These two glasses are distinct: although both are ruby red, both crystal, both eight inches tall, *something* physical distinguishes them. Similarly, we normally distinguish persons' bodies by means of some physical characteristic. In the case of physical objects, then, like glasses or bodies, we can point to physical differences, which make them *distinguishable* from all other physical objects. But what will we point to with an *immaterial* object like a soul? If souls are identified with sets or collections of nonphysical mental characteristics, isn't it possible that there would be two apparently identical souls, having all the same mental characteristics, and thus indistinguishable?

Swinburne's main positive argument can be laid out simply. First, consider a world in which Deirdre's soul is attached to her body and Danny's soul is attached to his. Now, Swinburne asks us, imagine a world in which Deirdre and Danny switch bodies. But these two worlds are obviously different, he suggests: "What could be more obvious?"[41]

It may be obvious that these two worlds are different, but how is that supposed to address the *thisness* of souls? Assuming that the worlds are different, it is not Deirdre's or Danny's bodies that make them different. All that changes is the souls connected to these bodies: *this* soul (Deirdre's soul, say) is now attached to a different body, Danny's. And similarly for Danny's soul. If soul changes are sufficient to make the two worlds different, then it would seem that each soul must have a thisness. One soul must be intrinsically different from the other. For Swinburne, there would be a difference in worlds even if the mental characteristics are the same for each soul. Thus, the difference between these two hypothetical worlds can only be explained, in Swinburne's view, by the thisness of souls.

But there are still questions one might have about the *disembodied* souls. Could such beings come into contact with one another? We might wonder about the "contact mechanism," since disembodied souls will not have our normal perceptual apparatus. And *thisness* is similarly a nonphysical, imperceptible characteristic.

---

41   Swinburne 1997, p. 341.

Some will dissent of course from the idea that life after death is the life of a disembodied soul; it is the life of a soul in some new (?) body. *Thisness* is a metaphysical fact, it might be further claimed, recognized only by God perhaps. Swinburne does not address the details of life after death, however.

Soul Concerns: Soul Trains and Soul Copies

In a little monograph read by many beginning philosophy students, John Perry imagines a series of conversations over three evenings occurring between two friends, one of whom is about to die.[42] Perry raises two concerns about souls of interest to us here. The first concern is the individuation of souls: there appear to be no clear "identifying characteristics" for a soul. What difference would there be whether a body had just one soul, or series of souls all having the same characteristics—a soul train—moving through?

Swinburne of course has a response to the problem of the soul train. Souls are by nature individuated. This is what it means to say that every soul has an intrinsic thisness. There is in principle, then, a *metaphysical difference* between souls—that is, uniqueness is one of a soul's metaphysical properties.

The second concern for our purposes is raised by the following hypothetical case. Imagine that you die. Your soul—that is, your self—goes to heaven. Upon your arrival, imagine that God—perhaps because yours is such a remarkable or extremely praise-worthy soul—makes a duplicate of your soul. That is, whatever the mental or psychological characteristics possessed by your "original" soul, God manufactures or creates an identical soul. This newly minted soul possesses all the same properties. And so our familiar and fundamental principle of identity reappears: $1 \neq 2$. By being so enamored of you, and making an identical "soul mate," God has effectively killed you off. Again recall that when it comes to identity, competition can be deadly.

Leaving aside whatever other worries a theist might have about this thought experiment, notice that Swinburne's view has a ready, if controversial, response to concern about soul competition. *Not even God can make a soul competitor*. Not even God can make $1 = 2$. The *thisness* of a soul guarantees that it can't be copied in the way imagined.

---

42   Perry 1977.

Key Concepts

- · qualitative identity
- · numerical identity
- · individual identity
- · personhood identity
- · persistence question
- · individuation question
- · memory criterion
- · fission objection
- · body criterion
- · hylomorphism

Reading Questions

1. What do you think is the strongest objection to Locke's view of personal identity? Do you think the continuity view fares better? Explain.

2. Suppose someone claimed, drawing on the movie *Bedazzled*, that as someone occupies several different bodies in turn, even though some memories are retained, there is still a different person with each new body. Different bodies would yield different sensations, even different emotional reactions—hence, a different person. How might you defend the "same consciousness, same person" view against this sort of claim?

3. First, explain the problem presented by fission or branching cases. Suppose you were the person about to undergo a transplant of a hemisphere, should you be concerned about competitors, that is, duplicates? Explain.

4. Briefly describe Swinburne's view of personal identity. Describe what you see as a major problem with this view. How might Swinburne's view be defended from this objection?

5. Suppose a human person were to receive a bionic part in place of some human body part. Now suppose that someone claims that this bionically modified being is no longer a *human* person, perhaps a bionic person, but not a human person. Given that some discussions now suggest that the implanting of microchips in a person will soon

become commonplace, what do you think of this claim? That is, is a bionically enhanced person still a human person? Would a human "Luke Skywalker" cease to be a human person with a bionic hand? How much of a human person's ordinary human body could be replaced by bionic parts, yet still be a human person? Try to identify the principle behind your answer.

For Further Reading

David Wiggins 1967, perhaps a challenging work for the beginner, identifies a number of important aspects and arguments for both identity generally and personal identity. John Perry 1977, as noted in the text, has served as the introduction for many students to the problems of personal identity; it is both rigorous and readily accessible to anyone. Perry 1975 is an anthology containing some of the more important readings on personal identity. Shoemaker and Swinburne 1984 is an exchange between a materialist, Shoemaker, who nonetheless views himself as a "neo-Lockean," and a dualist, Swinburne. Shoemaker defends the psychological continuity view, based in part on his functionalist view of the mind. Swinburne defends the same soul view; Swinburne's notion of the soul comprises various aspects of our mental life, as noted in the text. This same soul view is also detailed in his 1986, 1994, and 1997; as noted in the text, Swinburne defends a *haecceity* notion of the soul. Amelie Oksenberg Rorty 1976 includes contributions by David Armstrong, Derek Parfit, and David Wiggins, all of whom have significantly contributed to recent discussions of personal identity. Parfit 1986, while about much more, contains an extended and influential discussion of personal identity. Bernard Williams 1973, similarly influential in discussions of personal identity, defends the same body view. Corcoran, ed., 2001 contains a number of essays, authored by philosophers who have played pivotal roles in these discussions, on identity and related matters. A sometimes challenging book, which surveys historical and contemporary views (including animalism) as well as standard objections to these various views, is Harold Noonan 2003. Dwayne Godwin's and Jorge Cham's "Of Two Minds" in the "The Mind in Pictures" section at the back of the March/April 2013 issue of *Scientific American: Mind* is an annotated and illustrated introduction to matters related to split brains.

CHAPTER EIGHT

FREE WILL

(A Few) Great Moments in the History of Literature on Fate and Free Will

Free will or its lack is not the sole province of theologians and philosophers. Is a life controlled by fate or mechanism, by necessity? Can one choose—freely—an action that has some significance in one's life? Some of our greatest poets and dramatists have put just these issues before us.

For example, in Homer's *Iliad* (eighth century BCE), Agamemnon rejoices that Odysseus and Achilles are arguing about who is the best warrior—because he thought this fulfilled Apollo's prophecy that Troy would fall when such a "contest" occurred. If the prophecy was being realized, then *fate* was in control.

In Sophocles' well-known play about Oedipus' attempt to escape his fate (c. 429 BCE), it is suggested that while our "choices" are up to us, their outcome is not. Oedipus' parents, hearing a prophecy that their son will kill his father and marry his mother, have him left outside to die—but he is adopted, grows up with no knowledge of his parentage, and ends up unintentionally doing exactly what was predicted. Indeed, we find throughout Greek literature the suggestion that necessity controls our lives—represented, for example, by the Three Fates of Greek mythology, who spin, measure, and cut the thread of our lives.

Several centuries later, in John Milton's *Paradise Lost* (1667), a different view appears: Milton endorses free will, but he links it to rational behavior. Adam, for example, says to Eve: "But God left free the will, for what obeyes / Reason, is free, and Reason he made right" (IX 351–52).

Diane Kelsey McColley 1972 connects this conception of free will to Milton's understanding of the human relationship to the divine, noting that "Man's disobedience ... was not the revelation of his nature, but the violation of it; that is, the voluntary resignation of his free will resulting in the loss of spontaneous love" (p. 107).

THE EARLY SIXTEENTH CENTURY SAW ONE OF THE GREAT DEBATES IN intellectual history. Erasmus of Rotterdam (1466–1536), the great Renaissance scholar, and Martin Luther (1483–1546), the leader of the Reformation, grew further apart as the debate progressed, even though other scholars tried to effect some reconciliation between them. Many hoped that Erasmus and Luther would find themselves allies in their criticism of the Roman Catholic Church. But it was not to be; they differed too much over the subject of their debate. What lay at the heart of their dispute? The nature and extent of free will.

We won't be following either the theological or philosophical turns in Luther's and Erasmus's contentious dispute. That debate signals, however, the centrality of the conviction that we have free will. The pull of free will can be traced back to the *Meditations* of the Roman emperor Marcus Aurelius (121–180), and it is the focus of St. Augustine's late fourth-century work, *On the Free Choice of the Will*.[1] That we have free will is the default position for many. Indeed, this belief plays a central role not only in how we *understand* our own and others' behavior, but in how we *treat* people. The philosopher, John Searle, once held that we *cannot* give up our conviction that we have free will, even though "Our conception of physical reality simply does not allow for radical freedom."[2]

---

1   Marcus Aurelius 2006; Augustine 1993.
2   Searle 1984, Chap. 6.

One picture of human nature presents us as conscious, rational beings who act on the basis of what we know, believe, desire, or hope. Further, at least some of our actions are of our own choosing. We aren't forced to perform these actions: they aren't simple reflexes. At least some of our actions are the result of *free will*.

No sooner have we completed this description, however, than we hear a competing picture, apparently drawn from science. The world, we are told, is a structured, largely predictable world. Everything in it is governed by natural laws, which are revealed to us by scientific investigation. If you take a bowling ball to the top of a church steeple and drop it, it's going to fall—*it has to fall*. In this picture events don't just happen, but must happen. Given the laws, given past events, this new event *must* happen the way it does. This is a *mechanistic* or *deterministic* picture of the world. If we are part of such a world, then our actions are events no different from dropping the bowling ball.

In the second picture all of our actions are fixed by something beyond us; the first presents at least some of our actions as the result of free will, of our choosing to do them. In a moment, we will be more precise about these notions of free will and determinism. Right now, notice that the conflict between these two seems to have implications for another important notion, that of moral responsibility. It is because we attribute "authorship" or "ownership" of an action to a person that we hold that person morally responsible for the action. This deterministic interpretation of the world seems to say, however, that a person isn't the "author" of an act. Rather, that act is authored by—caused by—a very impersonal set of laws and circumstances. So, the outcome of the free will issue has very broad implications. We return to this below.

Before clarifying the notion of free will, we need to set aside one sense of "free." The notions of freedom and liberty appear often in historical, political, and cultural contexts. But in this context, we are not interested in political freedom. And, in our context, the word "libertarian" does not describe a political view. Whether we have free will is a *metaphysical* question, not resolved by consulting experts in political science or political history, or political philosophy, for that matter. The metaphysical question of free will is only about the control of at least some of our actions: are at least some of our actions "up to us," or are all actions "controlled by" a set of laws and prior circumstances?

One more qualification. Libertarians—people who believe that we have free will—do not claim that *all* our actions or behaviors are the result of free will. They willingly admit that some, perhaps many of our actions are indeed determined. Proponents of free will claim only that on some occasions, some agents' actions are free.

(Don't be alarmed by the term "agent." Here the term is used in one of its senses: an "agent" is simply a person or being using a certain power to bring about a certain end. And *agency* is the having this power or this ability to make something happen. A *person's* action and an *agent's* action are for our purposes synonymous.)

Free Will and Determinism

Our intuitive sense of the notion of free will can be characterized more precisely. An agent has **free will** (or an agent's action is free) if and only if the agent *could have done otherwise*, under the same circumstances. With all the same circumstances at the time the person performed some action, that person could have done something else. Imagine an action that we would normally think of as coming about as a result of free will, say, going to a library and deciding to check out *Dial Emmy for Murder* instead of *Death by Honeymoon*. You check out *Dial Emmy*. This is a free act, we suppose, because it was open to you to do something else. You could have checked out *Honeymoon*. You could have done otherwise ... even if all circumstances had been the same.

This picture fits closely with our commonsense view. We think free will is having different paths or options open to us. We may choose one option, but we *could have done otherwise*; we could have chosen the other option. A somewhat different version of free will has recently been developed. But we will be working with this notion of free will: a free agent is one who, on at least some occasions, *could have done otherwise*.

Why Believe in Free Will?

Sartre and Free Will

One of the most dramatic assertions of human freedom comes from a philosopher who asserted that humankind was a "useless passion."[3]

Jean-Paul Sartre (1905–80), the French existentialist philosopher, argued for a view of human nature that includes a capacity for almost boundless

---

3   Sartre 1956. This quotation is from p. 784; those following are from pp. 710, 567, 707, 566, 640, and 725.

choice. Indeed, in his view, human beings are responsible for not just some but all of their actions. "I am responsible for everything ... except for my very responsibility," he writes, because choice—and therefore responsibility—is a fact about human *being*, or our being in the world. In other words, Sartre claims, "I am condemned to be free." I cannot escape this freedom, and not because some "higher power" has made it so. Rather my "condemnation" is that nothing can or will relieve me of the responsibility for what I do. Sartre says of any individual human being, "The weight of the whole world is on his shoulders: he is responsible for the world and for himself as a way of being." For Sartre, whether or not we "could have done otherwise" is not the real question. Freedom is not merely "a *property* of my being. It is very exactly the stuff of my being."

How does Sartre arrive at such a conclusion? Sartre's ontology, his inventory of the basic features of the world, recognizes only consciousness and things. As conscious beings, we find ourselves "thrown into" a world in which there is no God, and which has no meaning apart from what we ourselves give to it. Even our own past is significant only because we assign meaning to it.

We are thus always in the process of making, even remaking, ourselves, according to Sartre. And the way we accomplish this is by choosing personal projects. It is only in the choosing and the carrying out of these projects that a person has a character. Unlike the typical approach to free will, in which character can constrain or even preclude freedom, Sartre holds that our freedom makes our character, and we make it from "nothing." This is the corollary of the Sartrean claim that existence precedes essence: "Freedom is existence, and in it existence precedes essence." In other words, at first we are nothing—and who and what we become depends on our choices.

Sartre was a member of the French Resistance during World War II. He had a long and complicated relationship with Simone de Beauvoir. The author of plays, novels, essays, and his most important and most challenging work, *Being and Nothingness*, he was awarded the Nobel Prize for literature in 1964, but declined to accept it.

What reasons do people have for thinking we have free will? There are two principal arguments: one based on the notion of responsibility or accountability and the other based on our experience—how it seems to us—when we undertake some action. Both arguments are controversial; still, they illustrate how deeply connected free will is to other important views.

We hold people *responsible* or *accountable* for many of their actions. Some years ago I gave an informal talk on free will to adult members of the local community; of the about fifty people in attendance, only one person in the audience thought it was likely that we were not in fact responsible for our actions. To the rest, accountability for our actions not only undergirded our understanding of human behavior, but was also a part of the basis for our moral judgments! Bad behavior results in blame; good behavior merits praise.

We move quickly from accountability to free will. We hold people responsible for their behavior because we think *they could have done otherwise*. Deirdre blames Danny for being late because he stayed at the bowling alley an extra twenty minutes. He could have left on time; he didn't have to bowl the few extra frames—*he really could have done otherwise*. Imagine, however, a different scenario. Imagine that Danny is late because he is arrested and hauled off to jail in a case of mistaken identity. Deirdre now cannot hold him accountable for his lateness; she can't blame him. It was not in his control that the police mistook him for someone else. Indeed Danny was held against his will! *He could not have done otherwise*.

This example is easily generalizable. A necessary condition of accountability or responsibility for our actions is that we could have done otherwise. Of course, we are not talking here of reflex behaviors or internally or externally compelled behaviors, or "accidental slips." Leave aside, then, those behaviors and focus on what we normally consider to be actions that deserve moral praise or blame. We seem committed to the following simple argument. If we are accountable for our actions, then we have free will. Since we believe we are accountable for our actions, the conclusion follows: we have free will. Call this the **responsibility argument for free will**.

You might be wondering if this argument might be turned around. That is, if there's good reason to think that we do not have free will, then we aren't accountable or responsible for our actions. As we will see below, some hold just this view.

Nonetheless, the idea of accountability for our actions seems inescapable for many. And this inescapability has led to the insistence that we possess free will.

The other argument most commonly made for the existence of free will is the **experience argument for free will**. The main idea: it sure seems like a lot of our actions depend on our choices; nothing, it seems to us, *makes us* perform those actions. My experiencing *myself* as the source of my actions, rather than some force other than me, is the key to the experience argument.

I'm very much awake, in command of my faculties; I'm not ill or taking medication. So, if circumstances are normal, my experience—how it seems to me—is a fairly reliable guide to what is actually happening.

We are now able to see the argument from experience somewhat more explicitly. Assuming circumstances are normal, my experience is a fairly reliable guide of what is actually happening. In such normal circumstances, sometimes I experience my actions as something *I'm in charge of*—actions that I freely perform. But this is just my freely performing this action. Hence, based on my experience of this action and the reliability of my experience, I have free will.

Critics still ask whether or not such experiences are genuinely reliable. They might point to other "experiences" that were thought to be reliable, but weren't. For example, B.F. Skinner, the noted twentieth-century behaviorist psychologist, held that our experience of ourselves as "free" was an illusion founded in our ignorance of the real causes of our behavior.[4] In response, libertarians claim that these experiences aren't like that at all. The experience is, as it were, "transparent." We will pick up on this idea below. For now, it is enough to know that the "reliability" of our experience of free will is controversial.

Together the experience argument and the responsibility argument seem to underlie the conviction that we have free will. Still, some see the attractiveness of a competing picture—the deterministic picture.

Determinism

We have an intuitive idea about determinism: *you can't escape the law*. Of course, the sense of "law" here is physical law, the laws of nature, with which we are all very familiar. A historically prominent notion of determinism is that every event has a cause; no event occurs *ex nihilo* (from nothing). Various philosophers, theologians, and scientists still make use of this account of determinism. But a different version is becoming more common: **determinism** is the claim that *every event is the necessary outcome of physical laws and prior circumstances or events*. In other words, events are *necessitated* by a combination of physical law and antecedent conditions. Given certain reasonable assumptions about the notion of cause, one can see that the historical understanding leads to the

---

4   Skinner 1974, Chaps. 8 and 12; see also Crumley 2006.

more contemporary view of determinism.[5] For our purposes, we will work with this more recent view. It's worth taking a look at it in a bit more detail.

Events are familiar enough: Caesar crossing the Rubicon, Washington crossing the Delaware, World War II, Sara dropping Sam off at the train station—all of these are events. But we want to broaden the notion to include some "happenings" you might not normally consider as events. Any object has characteristics or qualities or properties. The rocking chair has the quality or property of being red. Danny has the property of wearing a magenta-colored shirt. The broader sense of event is *any change in the properties of an object*. Change the color of the rocker, have Danny put on a different shirt—those are events. Some events are very complex, made up of other events; World War II, for example. Other events are relatively simple: you pick up your smart phone. The history of the world up to *now* just is all the events that have occurred—from the Big Bang to *The Big Bang Theory*.

Now consider something that you might not have thought of as an "event": *deciding* to go to the library instead of taking a nap. This deciding is sometimes called *volition*. Among a person's many properties are obviously physical properties—height, weight, eye color, chemical makeup, which parts of the brain are activated at a given moment—*and* a person's mental properties. You know these properties: your beliefs and desires, your feelings and emotions, the things you know, your fears, and yes, your "decidings" or volitions. But changing these properties, e.g., changing beliefs, changing your desire ("On second thought, I want the apple pie."), changing your mind: these are one and all events! *Deciding* or *forming an intention* or *volition* is an event.

The implication of seeing mental changes as *events* is not far to seek. If any event is necessitated by a combination of prior events or circumstances and natural law, and deciding is an event, then even deciding or forming an intention is necessitated; it's *determined*. If determinism is true, for any given mental event, *it had to happen*. There's no "could have been otherwise" about it! All of us know what's going to happen if I take any object to the top of the steeple, hold it out over the edge, and let it go. It's going to fall; that *has to happen*. It's necessitated by natural law and prior events. According to determinism, this is no less true of mental events.

In the early nineteenth century, the French mathematician and astronomer Pierre-Simon Laplace (1749–1827) gave vivid expression to determinism that you may have heard described as "Laplace's demon":

5　E.g., Blanshard 1961.

We may regard the present state of the universe as the effect of its past and the cause of its future. An intellect which at a certain moment would know all forces that set nature in motion, and all positions of all items of which nature is composed, if this intellect were also vast enough to submit these data to analysis, it would embrace in a single formula the movements of the greatest bodies of the universe and those of the tiniest atom; for such an intellect nothing would be uncertain and the future just like the past would be present before its eyes.[6]

Laplace's hypothetical "vast intellect" (his "demon") could predict the outcome of any set of circumstances. The knowledge that would be possessed by such an intellect is merely the reflection of the *metaphysical* fact that each and every event is constrained by law; no event escapes the law.

If determinism is right, there are no open futures. Danny's deciding to go see the Radiators down on Decatur Street or his deciding to spend another twenty minutes at Café du Monde eating beignets while reading his Facebook page is just as determined as whether a piece of litmus paper turns red in the presence of an acid.

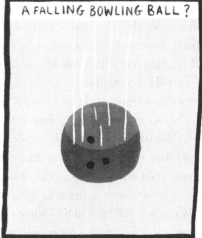

IS EITHER OF THESE FREE?

---

6   Laplace 1995, p. 2.

This view of the world certainly seems to leave no room for free will. Determinism implies that there is only one possible future at any moment; natural laws and prior circumstances determine that unique outcome. But if there is only one possible outcome, if the event that happens is necessitated, there is no "being able to do otherwise." And if there is no being able to do otherwise, then—by definition—there is no free will. Determinism precludes free will.

Some determinists also accept an apparent implication, namely, that we are not in charge of our actions, and hence should not be held morally responsible. They are sometimes known as *hard determinists*, a term coined by William James.[7] (It is not always easy, however, to settle whether someone should be classified as a hard determinist.[8])

The thought that determinism and free will are mutually exclusive is presented in a powerful, controversial, and much-discussed argument by Peter van Inwagen, known as the *consequence argument*.[9] The conclusion of this argument is the claim that the truth of determinism would rule out free will. The technical framework employed by van Inwagen we must leave aside, but the sense of the argument is reasonably straightforward. The argument assumes the *fixity of the past*—we can't change what's happened; what's done is done. Notice—all the laws of nature and all the events prior to any of our births are part of an unchangeable past. Since we can't change those, and what happens now is *determined* by already set laws and past events, then what we do is similarly fixed. There is no "could have done otherwise." Hence, if determinism is true, there is no free will. Those who accept this argument, both determinists and free will proponents, are known as *incompatibilists*. **Incompatibilism** holds that determinism and free will can't both be true. The consequence argument is thus an argument for incompatibilism.

In a subsequent section, we see that some have tried to avoid this result; they have tried to argue that determinism and free will are compatible (and hence, that moral responsibility is compatible with determinism).

Que sera, sera!—The song "Que sera, sera," suggests a kind of *fatalist* view: "Whatever will be, will be." Some confuse determinism with **fatalism**, the view that any event that happens is metaphysically necessary. Determinism says

---

7   James 1978.

8   E.g., Marsden 2003, Chap. 26; Blanshard 1961, see n. 4; Paul Edwards 1958.

9   van Inwagen, 1986, Chap. III.

only that if you start with these laws and this set of prior events, a particular outcome must follow. Fatalism is the much stronger view asserting a metaphysical necessity rather than the physical necessity of determinism. Fatalist views are also sometimes accompanied by the thought that we should simply resign ourselves to the inescapability of what will happen. The philosopher Richard Taylor argued for fatalism, going so far as to suggest that we will lead calmer, more peaceful lives if we accept fatalism as a metaphysical fact. Taylor also appears to reject any real distinction between determinism and fatalism:

> Fatalism is the belief that whatever happens is unavoidable. That is the clearest expression of the doctrine, and it provides the basis of the attitude of calm acceptance that the fatalist is thought, quite correctly, to embody. One who endorses the claim of universal causation, then, and the theory of the causal determination of all human behavior is a kind of fatalist—or at least should be if he is consistent.[10]

In an intriguing presentation of his argument, Taylor asks us to imagine an ordinary man named Osmo, coming across a book in a library entitled *The Life of Osmo*. As Osmo reads *The Life of Osmo*, chapter by chapter, he comes to see that it describes accurately each year of his life. But the book ends three years hence with the death of Osmo in a plane crash! Osmo resolves to avoid the circumstance that brings about the death of "Osmo-in-the-story," yet three years later he nonetheless finds himself boarding the doomed plane. Taylor argues that, though the rest of us might not be able to read our own biographies in advance, the events of our lives are just as determined as Osmo's.[11]

However, philosophers usually want to distinguish between determinism and fatalism. The latter view is often thought to be that things are "fated" to happen no matter what—that is, regardless of our decisions or any other antecedent events. Determinism, on the other hand, holds that things will happen *given* antecedent decisions or other events. (But these antecedent events are themselves determined.) So a fatalist would say: you'll be killed no matter what you decide. A determinist would say: you'll be killed or not, depending on (among other things) what you decide.

---

10   Richard Taylor 1992, p. 55.
11   Richard Taylor 1992, Chap. 6.

But we must leave fatalist visions of the universe, and focus on determinism, as defined above.

But What If We Believe in Dualism?

Dualism—the idea that minds are different in kind from the physical world—has been thought to be a way to save free will. Free will seems to be in jeopardy because of causal determinism. But this causal determinism seems a characteristic of the *physical* world. Determinism is, after all, tied to *natural law*, the laws that govern physical objects and events. Suppose now, however, that our wills are something *nonphysical*. Following this line of thought, willing or forming intentions would not be subject to the laws of nature. Hence, our wills would not be determined. We can take a moment to spell this out in more detail.

First, a dualism defense of free will holds that choosing or deciding or willing is a nonphysical mental event. In the dualist view, natural or physical law does not apply to mental events. A mind or mental event—such as deciding—doesn't have physical properties, according to the dualist. Natural law, however, applies to physical objects in virtue of their *physical* properties. Gravitational attraction between objects depends on their *masses* and the *distance* between them. Chemical compounds are formed according to certain rules depending on the *charge* of the constituent parts; it's no accident that it takes two hydrogen atoms for every one oxygen atom to yield the molecule water.

But minds don't have physical properties, if we assume dualism. My belief that Jamoca® Almond Fudge ice cream is sold only at Baskin-Robbins doesn't have a charge or a mass, nor is it some distance from my desire to eat something chocolaty and sweet. Nor does my subsequent intention to go to Baskin-Robbins have a force determined by its mass and acceleration. The mental and the physical are different *kinds* or have different *natures*. So, the mental is the wrong sort of "thing" to be governed by physical law.

Is dualism then the way to save free will? There are problems with this defense of free will. Dualism does not rule out the existence of *mental* laws "necessitating" the forming of certain intentions, given prior beliefs and wants. And the sort of generalizations that we often make about behavior might be an indication that such laws plausibly exist. Note how many of our common-sense observations rely on such generalizations: if Danny wants to see Deirdre, and he believes she will be down in the French Quarter listening to the Rads tonight, then Danny will decide to go to the French Quarter. Of course, there are a number of complex issues that arise here. Thus, simply appealing to the nonphysical character of the mind won't guarantee that the will is free.

It is sometimes believed that a special creation of humans by a divine being put us outside the causal realm. But an appeal to a divine being as a creator does not really help the dualist here. Creating essentially nonphysical beings does not obviously require giving such beings free will. Any creator the dualist might imagine could have made the mind just as deterministic as the physical world.

What Does Science Say about Free Will?

No Free Will? What about the Criminals?

In the past hundred years, some have suggested that once we recognize that our actions are exclusively caused by biochemical events in the brain, we will need to make compensatory changes in our criminal justice system. Earlier in the last century, B.F. Skinner gave this argument, based on his behaviorism. And now more brain science researchers—those who think free will is an illusion—suggest that we need to see responsibility, even *criminal* responsibility, differently.

In his "The Lucretian Swerve: The Biological Basis of Human Behavior and the Criminal Justice System," Anthony Cashmore, a biologist, claims that as we know more about the chemical basis of our actions, it will become "increasingly untenable to retain a belief in the concept of free will." Cashmore, however, does not think we should unlock the prison gates. We will still need to incarcerate individuals. Our understanding of criminality will need to change, however; we will in fact need to adopt a more utilitarian view of societal punishment—that is, to use it to isolate those likely to offend again, and to discourage future crime.

In her *Mapping the Mind*, an engaging introduction to the brain and its relation to our mental life and our behavior, Rita Carter 2010 intimates a similar point: as we find out more about the brain, our view of culpability, including criminal culpability, will need to change.

Well, that depends on who you ask. Ask Michio Kaku, well-known theoretical physicist, and he'll tell you that modern quantum physics implies that we have free will "in a sense."[12] Nobel laureate Gerald Edelman, author of numerous books on the brain and consciousness, claimed we have a "degree of free will," but such freedom is not "radical."[13] (He apparently believed that indeterminism produces free will only rarely.) Harvard psychologist Daniel Wegner believed free will is but an illusion.[14] On the other hand, Seth Lloyd of MIT suggests that even laptop computers have a kind of free will.[15]

Science proceeds by doing experiments, by testing claims. Is there a way to "test" the existence of free will? In one of the most famous experiments "involving" free will, physiologist Benjamin Libet discovered that subjects reported being conscious of a decision to move a finger only *after* the activation of that part of the brain responsible for sending the movement signal.[16] Many have thought this is genuine scientific evidence *against* free will. The conscious mind—presumably where choosing occurs—seemed not to be in control after all; it seemed to follow what the brain—the physical part—had already done. And if the physical part is in control, that would seem to indicate that it's *determined*, and this counts against free will.

---

12   Kaku 2011.
13   Edelman 1992, p. 170.
14   Wegner 2003.
15   Seth Lloyd 2012.
16   Libet 2004.

Not everyone accepts the deterministic interpretation of Libet's argument. Alfred Mele argues at length that the brain activity prior to the flexing should not be identified with a "decision."[17] Perhaps surprisingly, Libet does not draw the conclusion that freedom is an illusion: he argues that his experiment showed there was time for the subjects to consciously veto movement of the finger after the signal had already been sent but before the finger moved.

And those philosophers who take seriously developments in science are in no greater agreement than the scientists themselves. In 2007, Searle returned to the issue of the "neurobiology of freedom." He argues that we cannot give up our conviction that we have free will. Indeed it is our awareness of the "gap" between our prior mental states and the action we finally take that is constitutive of our experience of free will. But though he examines the alternatives in great detail, he does not ultimately suggest a solution. That is, he does not offer a way to resolve the conflict between the idea that the total state of the brain at one point *determines* the next total state and our experience of this gap.[18]

Robert Kane, a champion of free will, argues that quantum indeterminacy opens the door for free will.[19] (We return to his view below.) On the other hand, Paul Thagard, philosopher and cognitive scientist, claims that recognizing that consciousness or minds are nothing more than brain processes at work leads us to see that free will, at least of the sort promised by dualism, is an illusion.[20]

We have selected only a few, but we could continue mentioning philosopher and scientist alike, some advocating, some rejecting free will, in light of developments in the sciences.

We might not be able to say definitively "what science says." Still, we can sort out matters a bit so that we can see how different thinkers have arrived at their respective claims. Let us begin with determinism and modern physics.

Indeterminism and Free Will

Some have suggested that free will advocates won't find solace in either scientific *in*determinism, the notion that science does not reveal a deterministic world, or the uncertainty and unpredictability of quantum physics. Why not? If determinism is wrong, doesn't that help free will?

---

17   Mele 2014, esp. Chap. 2; also Balaguer 2014, Chap. 7.
18   Searle 2007, Chap. 1.
19   Kane 2002b; 1998, Chap. 8.
20   Thagard 2010, Chap. 6.

Not exactly. We've already seen why determinism seems to preclude free will. But now consider the *randomness* that modern physics seems to bring. According to contemporary science, some events occur randomly: they just happen and there is no rational way to predict their occurrence. Specifying a random sequence or a chance event turns out to be very technical and no easy matter to explain,[21] but suppose this is an example: When you shoot a photon at a barrier with two slits in it, it's (according to some) completely random which slit it will go through. Now shoot photons at the rate of one per minute; given the right arrangement of the slits, it will pass through the right slit half the time. Now put a robot in back of the right slit, with a photon-detector. When it detects a photon, it will push a button. Now, there's a 50% chance the robot will push the button during any one-minute period, but it's completely unpredictable whether it will push the button or not during the next minute. Does that mean that this robot has free will? Obviously not. We wouldn't consider the robot free because of this *unpredictable and random* behavior.

Now imagine that every five minutes or so Sara does something strange. At noon she says "Crustacean!" At 12:05 she walks backwards in a circle. At 12:10 she puts her left index finger into her right ear. At 12:15 she closes her left eye for a full minute. You ask her why she's doing those things, and she replies, "I don't know. I really don't." She goes to a neurologist for very advanced tests, and he discovers (here's where the science fiction comes in) a random signal generator in her brain that fires every five minutes, causing random behavior. Not determined—that means random, right? And this is random, right? But it surely isn't free will.

Genuinely free action isn't random. So believers in free will apparently face a dilemma: a determined action isn't free, but the alternative, a random action, isn't free either. The unpredictable or random character of quantum phenomena on its own simply cannot solve this problem.

Defenders of free will are not without their resources, however. Let us start with the idea of randomness.

The philosopher Robert Kane, a libertarian advocate, has made use of this idea in a quite remarkable way. He suggests that we are at times confronted with differing options, each option supported by good reasons. These differing options correlate with indeterminacy at a subatomic level. Yet there is nothing to determine one option over the other. While the option we choose is

---

21   Eagle 2014.

"random," it is not arbitrary, since each option is based on good reasons. Our choices in these types of situation form our character. As long as a person "embraces" the character formed by such choices, Kane holds that subsequent choices are free. The original "self-forming actions" are undetermined. But the consequent actions are caused by that "self-formed" character, and are consequently free. Kane thus embraces the notion of randomness at two levels (at the quantum brain level and the equally good option level), but claims this leads to free will.[22]

Kane's view perhaps suggests a way of responding to the apparent conflict between the scientific view of the brain and our feeling of free will. Science recognizes different "levels" of phenomena. We might talk about an atomic level, a biological level, or our "higher" everyday, commonsense level of cabbages, kings, and continents, starfish and stock markets, clothes and clouds—the last having both meteorological and virtual instances. Each of these different levels has its own properties. A dress may be blue, but protons are not. Electrons are charged, but not a cabbage.

The properties that arise at these "higher levels" are sometimes called *emergent properties*, because they arise from the complex organization of more basic or lower-level properties. At the atomic and molecular levels, we find properties that physics and chemistry tell us about. Biochemistry tells us about molecules combining in ever more complex ways, resulting in complex biological properties arising. At the neural level, at the level of brain structure and function, we find still more complex neural properties *emerging from* or coming about because of the way biological structures—neurons—are organized or related. At the most complex level, psychological properties emerge. Because of—some contend—the structure of the brain, its complex organization—consciousness, thought, emotion come about.[23] That is, mental properties emerge.

Building on this, some have suggested that while determinism may be true at the neural or "micro-level," it doesn't follow that determinism is true at the macro-level, the level of conscious thought, of decision and choice. Thus, free will could be an emergent property of a very complicated kind of organism.

---

22   Kane 1998 and 2002b.
23   E.g., Edelman 1992; LeDoux 2002.

Agent Causation: A Different Type of Causation?

Suppose God Exists.
Is His Omniscience Incompatible with Our Free Will?

This question has been troublesome for theistic philosophers since St. Augustine. But Nelson Pike's 1965 "Divine Omniscience and Voluntary Action" brought wide and renewed attention to the problem.

God's omniscience implies that he *foreknows* everything. And if he foreknows now that Julia will leave tomorrow to visit the Galapagos to see the blue-footed booby, then Julia *must* leave tomorrow. Otherwise, God would not now have knowledge, and his belief about her departure would be false. But God can't have false beliefs—omniscience precludes that. So, Julia *can't do otherwise* than what God foreknows. So, she isn't free. God knows everything we will choose, and we have no free choice.

Eternalism and *Ockhamism* are two of the main types of response. Eternalism, a view that can be traced back to Boethius and that was also championed by Aquinas, holds that God is outside of time. All times at once are present to God; God never looks *back into the past* or looks *forward into the future*. Hence, it would be wrong to say that God *foreknows* (because "past" and "future" do not accurately reflect God's knowledge). Since God does not foreknow, there are no "divine constraints" on human action. Making God *atemporal* presents its own problems, however; how, for example could God intervene in time?

William of Ockham's suggestion, later revised and defended by Marilyn McCord Adams 1967, distinguishes two kinds of fact: *hard* and *soft*. The former do not depend on any reference to some future time. Thus, a hard fact about the past: In 212 BCE a Roman soldier killed Archimedes, the Greek scientist and mathematician of antiquity. A soft fact makes reference to some future, e.g., Archimedes was killed 2,288 years before the 300th anniversary in 2076 of the signing of the Declaration of Independence.

The Ockhamist solution claims that God's omniscience extends only to hard facts, not to soft facts. God knows *today* that Julia will leave *tomorrow* for the Galapagos is then a soft fact—and it in no way restricts Julia's ability to do otherwise.

This intriguing issue is still much contested and this brief summary only begins to address the challenges of the topic. See "For Further Reading."

Determinist views, and even some libertarian and compatibilist views, hold that causation is always *event causation*: one event causes another. Only events are causes and only events are caused. Indeed reference to events is integral to the definition of determinism. But another type of causality has been suggested. Roderick Chisholm's 1964 address, "Human Freedom and the Self," continues to be seminal in contemporary discussions of free will. Chisholm argued that we need to see free acts as the result of *agent causation*.

Chisholm remarked on the dilemma for free will that we mentioned above. To accept indeterminism—the idea that our actions had no prior cause *of any sort*—was no help. To do so is to abandon the idea that we are responsible for our actions. Now there had to be a way in which the person, the *agent*, was the cause, but could have done otherwise. And for this he thought we should recognize a different type of causation, that is, agent causation.

Agent causation is a causal power that each of us has, a power distinct from event causation. The self is not just a ripple in a causal stream. The self's choosing is not just another event in the deterministic stream of event causation. As Chisholm noted at one point, agents have a power that some of us might think belongs only to God—we are, each and every one of us, self-moved movers! That is, the power to bring about an intention is unique to agents, and the only source of this power is the agent—not some external cause, or even the *caused* brain events, but the agent. Now Chisholm recognized that *uncaused* acts were not genuinely free. And he held that even human action is caused. But Chisholm claimed that persons—or selves—are the cause of an action, not some sequence of prior events governed by natural or physical law. This self chooses which action to perform, and since the choice is not determined by a prior set of events, the agent *could have done otherwise*. Because the agent is the cause *and* could have done otherwise, the action is free in the requisite sense.

Invoking a different kind of causal power—agent causation—allowed him to avoid "metaphysical indeterminism"—that a free act has no cause whatsoever. It also allowed him to avoid determinism. Tracing back the causes of the agent's actions stops at the agent. When this happens, a person could have done otherwise.[24]

Others have since followed Chisholm in ascribing to agents this different kind of causal ability. Timothy O'Connor explicitly says that fundamental to *agency theory*—agent causation views—is the basic tenet that there are two

---

24   Chisholm 1964.

very different kinds of causal powers. First, event causation is identified as the power one object has to act on another. These powers are of course governed by natural law and exemplified by objects. But there is another kind of causal power, which applies "uniquely to intelligent purposive agents."[25] O'Connor sees these powers as *emergent causal properties*—as manifested in our "reason explanations," that is, appeals to the beliefs and desires of the agent. In his view, the "free choice" of an agent occurs along the following lines. A person has certain desires and beliefs (the "reasons"). The person also "represents"— conceives, or thinks of—various possible courses of action. The agent-causal power then brings about a choice, "an executive intention." Our free will thus lies in our special ability to form certain intentions.[26]

It is important to note the nature of this different causal power, in O'Connor's view.[27] There are two different types of reason in his view. First, there are reasons that make it likely (or unlikely) that the agent will perform some action. But these types of reason don't determine what the agent will do. This indeed is the very nature of deciding. Imagine, then, Aphrodite trying to decide whether to attend the poetry reading this evening. She considers reasons both for and against, e.g., she believes there will be a reading of "Prufrock," that Andie will be there and that he too enjoys that poem. On the other hand, she expects she will be driving through heavy rain, that she should reread her physics text. The critic of agent-causality can maintain, however, that if probabilities are all that's at work, Aphrodite's decision is a matter of luck.[28] But O'Connor maintains that the agent-causal power is just this: to settle on or to determine an intention. This is a primitive causal capacity that agents have, in O'Connor's view.

You may well have begun formulating at least one of the questions so often asked by skeptics of this position. This is all very much a mystery, says the critic. We have some idea of what it is for one event to cause another, but what is this mysterious "agent causation"? This has been called the *mystery objection*.[29] Defenders of the view have a response: whether you think of event or agent causation, both are mysterious. If libertarians have a hard time explaining agent

---

25   O'Connor 1995, p. 177; see also O'Connor 2002, esp. Chaps. 3 and 4.
26   O'Connor 2001, p. 55.
27   O'Connor 2011, esp. pp. 323 ff.
28   *Ibid.*
29   Carroll and Markosian 2010, p. 72.

decisions are determined by causes. Compatibilists are sometimes known as *soft determinists*, another expression coined by William James.[34]

Compatibilists draw our attention to the causal influence of *deliberation* or *rational deliberation* on many of our actions or behaviors. When there is this influence, compatibilists say, we are free, in a sense compatible with determinism and responsible for our behavior. Understanding the difference between behaviors brought about by deliberation and compelled behaviors is crucial for understanding the compatibilist project.

Our behavior may be compelled by some external physical force, or compelled by some internal "physical force," e.g., some neurological disorder, or because of some psychological disorder. Psychologically compelled or coerced actions may be rare; we perhaps associate them with various disorders, such as obsessive-compulsive disorders, or physical disorders, such as when someone *can't help but* arrange items so they evidence some sort of proportion or symmetry, or *can't help but* knock on a door in a particular fashion. Kleptomania is the compulsion to steal; the kleptomaniac doesn't decide to do it. While these behaviors appear to be in some sense intentional, such behaviors are in fact out of the person's control. Indeed, real patients suffering from a particular disorder will sometimes say that it *felt like* they had to perform some particular behavior. Sara's bizarre behavior imagined above is compelled.

Much more ordinary, however, is external compulsion. Sam sat down because he was pushed into his chair. Sara arrived late because her car got a flat tire. The common element in all compulsion—internal or external—is that it's behavior that is not the result of the agent's decision. In fact, it would have happened even if the agent had decided not to act that way.

Many of our behaviors seem not like that at all—they aren't compelled, and we don't experience them as such. We don't experience those behaviors as coerced. Rather, sometimes we mull things over, as we might say, weighing the pros and cons. After doing so, we come to a conclusion, the outcome of our deliberation, about large matters or small. We are standing, say, in a Baskin-Robbins, having to choose among 31 flavors, carefully deliberating, and then

---

34 Note that "soft determinism" is not the view that things are mostly determined, or just sort of semi-determined. It's a fully deterministic view. A soft determinist is a determinist who is also a compatibilist. A "hard determinist" is a determinist who is an incompatibilist, and hence denies the existence of free will and moral responsibility. James, by the way, condemned soft determinism, as he found it in Hume, as "a quagmire of evasion under which the real issue of fact has been entirely smothered" (James 1956, p. 149).

say, in a loud and clear voice, "Jamoca® Almond Fudge, please." Sometimes it's just a bare decision, without any mulling-over at all, such as when Andy just picks one of his shirts to wear, rather than the other, for no real reason at all. The compatibilist model of "free action" is the model of action brought about by a decision on the part of the agent.

This view of free action is compatible with determinism, according to the compatibilist. There is an identifiable cause—the decision—that brings about the relevant behavior. And as we have noted, the compatibilist may allow that this decision may itself be determined.

Of course critics of compatibilism claim this is too easy. They want to know in what sense a person could have done otherwise. Imagine for a moment that Danny has told Deirdre that he will take her to the airport on Friday. Later he is invited to join as a contestant in a bowling tournament during the time he was to take Deirdre to the airport. He will have to decide; he will have to *choose*. Suppose that he chooses the bowling tournament and texts the news to Deirdre. Is this choosing—on the compatibilist model—a case of free action?

Critics of compatibilism think not. The critics claim that if determinism is true, then Danny isn't choosing at all. Danny's decision is caused by reasons, his desires, his beliefs; and these are one and all determined by relevant natural law and prior events. And the outcome of Danny's deliberations is *necessitated by* all these prior events. The decision to bail on Deirdre and bowl instead was the necessary outcome of Danny's psychological state, his reasons, desires, and beliefs, and these were necessitated by other things. It is simply not true— say critics—that Danny could have done otherwise—if determinism is right. Stretching back far beyond Danny's birth are a chain of events, which lead to but one possibility: Danny's choosing bowling. The German philosopher Arthur Schopenhauer (1788–1860) neatly summarizes the problem: "A man can surely do what he wants to do. But he cannot determine what he wants."

The Schopenhauerian thought captures the problem, according to the critic of compatibilism. If Danny's reasons *necessitate* his visiting bowling alleys instead of visiting the airport, and if other events *necessitate* his having those reasons, there is no room for free will.

Compatibilism responds in the following manner. Again, suppose that an agent, Deirdre, after weighing the various reasons for and against two options (which we will call A and B), does (A)—she goes to a party with Danny— rather than (B), going alone. Deirdre does A because she willed or chose to do A. The compatibilist maintains that *had she chosen to do B, she would have done B*. Deirdre's action is thus free because she did what she willed or chose.

There is a general compatibilist principle here. This is referred to as the *ability analysis of "can."* To say that an agent *could have done otherwise* is to say that the agent would have done otherwise *if the agent had chosen or willed to do otherwise.* Now we can understand why the compatibilist emphasizes an absence of compulsion. If there is no compulsion or coercion or constraint, what an agent does depends only on what is willed or chosen. An action is free because it's voluntary, that is, determined by the agent's will or choice. This makes no mention of whether or not the agent's will or choice is itself determined. According to the compatibilist, it doesn't matter that it is.

Compatibilists who are also determinists (and most of them are) would add that, given the aims and goals of a person, given that person's preferences, the weight attached to particular reasons, this particular decision, and thus this particular act, had to result. As Deirdre thinks about what she wants to accomplish this weekend, and she tries to decide whether to drive to Pensacola for the weekend or attend the Seurat exhibit at the museum, the relative value she attaches to certain activities, given her desires and goals, lead her to choose staying home and attending the exhibit. Character shapes the outcome of deliberation—who Deirdre is, what she values, believes, and desires guides or structures her deliberation. And given that character and those values and beliefs and desires, she had to choose that action. Schopenhauer also held that character determines our deliberation. He quotes the German poet Goethe: "We cannot escape ourselves."

But the compatibilist might also hold that character is sometimes not simply given to us, that perhaps in some way, we can shape our character. Harry G. Frankfurt points out that we have both *first order desires*—the desire to take a cab to the French Quarter, for instance—and *second order desires*: desires to have (or not have) certain kinds of first order desires. I have a desire, say, for a Godiva truffle. But I may also have the desire to *desire* to eat more vegetables and avoid eating expensive chocolates. The former is a first order desire; the latter is second order, a desire about my desires. Frankfurt claims that we have free will when we act on the desires we want to guide our behavior. And this is the important point, according to Frankfurt: free will is not "escaping" determinism, but rather acting on the desires we want to have. In a sense, then, who we are, what type of character we have, is a function of these second order states.[35] Whether this is sufficient to allay incompatibilist suspicions is a question we will have to leave aside.

---

35   Frankfurt 1971.

We might, then, think of compatibilism generally like this. The determinism side explains the *what* or the *content* of our deliberation. But the "free will side," the responsibility side, focuses on the fact *that* we deliberate.

Two Compatibilist Approaches to Responsibility

The idea that there is a connection between our choices or willings and our responsibilities for our actions can be traced back two millennia. Michael Frede traced it back to the first- and second-century Stoic philosopher Epictetus. His *Discourses* influenced both Marcus Aurelius, a Roman emperor in the late second century, and some early Christian thinkers. Frede held that we are able to assent or dissent from some impulse. It is in virtue of our choosing that we are responsible for the actions which result from that choice.[36]

Frankfurt and Alternate Possibilities

The conclusion of the Consequence Argument and our notion of moral responsibility seem to conflict. If "could have done otherwise" is a necessary condition of moral responsibility, and the argument leads to the conclusion that determinism and this sense of free will are incompatible, then there is no consistent way of adhering to moral responsibility and determinism. Thus, some compatibilists turn to the notion of "uncoerced deliberation" as a way of doing that. But isn't there another way? Suppose one rejected the idea that "could have done otherwise" is a necessary condition of moral responsibility. If there was an argument for that claim, wouldn't that be a way to keep moral responsibility and determinism?

Harry Frankfurt, in a classic essay, argued that "could have done otherwise" is *not* necessary for moral responsibility.[37] In that essay, he identified the *Principle of Alternate Possibilities*, and then proceeded to argue that the principle is false. The principle—usually abbreviated as "PAP"—says simply:

PAP: A person is morally responsible for what he has done only if he could have done otherwise.

The logic of the argument is straightforward: find a case where a person could not have done otherwise, but would still be held morally responsible. Frankfurt

36   Frede 2011, pp. 44–48.
37   Frankfurt 1969.

thus asks us to imagine a special kind of case. These cases are now known as **"Frankfurt examples"** or "Frankfurt-style counterexamples," and there are many of them. They are all intended to show that a person could be responsible for an action even if that person could not have done otherwise. A variant of Frankfurt's original example will suffice here.

Suppose that the villain Victor wants to be sure that Ned will actually commit some nefarious act. Varying a bit the plot of a 1960s movie (*The Manchurian Candidate*), imagine that Ned has agreed to assassinate the just-nominated presidential candidate as he begins his acceptance speech. Victor, however, leaves nothing to chance. Thus, he has a microchip surreptitiously implanted in Ned's brain. Victor holds a switch, which wirelessly activates the microchip. The effect of the microchip is that if Ned chooses to do A, assassinate the nominee, Victor will do nothing, and the microchip will remain inactive. But should Ned reconsider at the last moment and instead begin to choose to do B—bolt from the scene—Victor will hit the switch, and the microchip will prevent Ned from choosing to do B. The activated microchip blocks Ned's ability to choose and subsequently do B, thus leaving A as the one and only alternative.

Consider now Ned's responsibility in the two cases. Obviously if he starts to choose to bolt from the scene, and the microchip is activated, thus blocking that option, we would not consider him responsible. However Nefarious Ned came to be at that place with his apparent intention, if the microchip never "intervened," he would not, in this scenario, have assassinated the candidate. Something else—Victor + switch—not Ned, brought it about that Ned chose and performed A. But what about the first case? What about Ned never beginning to choose to do B, to bolt from the scene?

Frankfurt argues that Ned is responsible, *even though he could not have done otherwise*. It is not difficult to see Frankfurt's line of reasoning. The microchip is never activated; Ned is not prevented from "beginning to choose to do otherwise." All of Ned's actions, up to and including his squeezing of the trigger that fires the fatal round, are a result only of Ned's intentions. Thus, Ned is morally responsible. But again—Ned had no alternative. The microchip blocked his access to any alternative. Ned is then morally responsible even though he could not have done otherwise.

The argument leads to the conclusion that the Principle of Alternate Possibilities is false. And if that is so, then a form of compatibilism about determinism and moral responsibility is unaffected by the Consequence Argument. Once the principle is rejected, nothing stands in the way of holding that moral responsibility is compatible with the truth of determinism. And remember: compatibilists accept determinism. But they also believe we are often morally responsible for some of our actions. Frankfurt's argument thus seems to give them both determinism and responsibility.

As hinted, much has been written about Frankfurt's argument and what it does or doesn't show. Many instances of Frankfurt-style counterexamples have been proposed, resulting in new analyses. Here the *indeterministic world objection* will be considered as a way of illustrating one serious concern critics have.[38]

The objection argues that free will is required for responsibility; PAP should still be considered true, and the Frankfurt case fails to show otherwise. Critics explain the two possibilities in the following way. The first possibility: Imagine that Ned begins to reason about whether to assassinate the candidate, and whether he chooses A or B depends on the outcome of his deliberating. While Ned is deliberating, Victor cannot know how he will decide. Victor cannot know, that is, whether Ned's deliberation will result in choosing action A or action B. Now, if Victor waits until the choice is made, flipping the switch is irrelevant to determining moral responsibility. Ned indeed could have chosen otherwise. Nothing blocks Nefarious Ned's having to choose between A and B. Thus, in this case, Victor and his microchip have no effect on the truth of PAP.

Consider now the other option: Villainous Victor is taking no chances and hits the switch *before* Ned concludes his deliberation. Then, as noted above, the cause of Ned's choice is not Ned, but Victor and the microchip. So, Ned is not morally responsible.

This objection asks us to think through how the "Frankfurt example" is supposed to work. This is not a question about the physical constraints of the Ned case. Rather, the objection targets whether the example obscures certain conceptual details, e.g., has Frankfurt genuinely imagined a case that accomplishes what he says it does. And the critics claim that he has not because the conceptual assumption does not hold under scrutiny. That assumption is fundamentally tied to the idea of *making a choice*. Making a choice *is* the end of a deliberation; there is no conceptual gap for the microchip to make a causal difference. Without such a gap, critics claim, Frankfurt has failed to show that PAP is false. Whether or not the critics have isolated a flaw in the Frankfurt argument, we leave the matter here, and turn to a proposal that agent-causality and compatibilism are in fact compatible.

---

38   See Robert Kane 2006, Chap. 8, and esp. pp. 87–88.

A Compatibilist Agent-Causality

Ned Markosian argues that the agent-causal theories should accept that determinism is compatible with their view of free will and responsibility.[39] Central to Markosian's view is the thought that there can be *double causation* of some event. That is, the agent can be the cause of an event, as well as external physical causes. We can briefly consider two of Markosian's cases. In the first case, imagine Imran, who has good manners, responding appropriately in various social situations. Yasmine politely asks him to pass the salt, which he does. Markosian identifies both the request and the "agent-causing" as the double cause of this action.

Now consider Zane, who performs a series of actions as he grows up, which are caused by him, and shape his personality. His own personality, however, does not make it the case that it is *physically necessary* that he perform the right action. It is incredibly likely, but not *determined* by his personality. In college a "gifted and inspiring teacher" alters his personality ever so slightly. Zane has shaped his personality in such a way that he is open-minded. The teacher brings a little *lagniappe*, a little something extra to Zane's personality, thus making it physically necessary that Zane do the right thing. Subsequently, on his way home one day, Zane passes a burning building and then causes himself to run inside, thus saving hundreds of children. Again, Markosian thinks Zane is morally responsible for his heroic act. Notice again: Zane's action is physically necessary, and this physical necessity is brought about by an external cause (the teacher). Still, it is "up to" Zane to choose to run inside the burning school building.

What might be said about these cases? First, as Markosian notes, the notion of double causation is dubious to some, but leave that aside.[40] What might the agent-causalist say about these two cases? In Imran's case, the agent-causalist might wish to distinguish between the cause of Imran's deliberation and the cause of the passing of the salt. Although Yasmine's request brings about the deliberation, it might still be held that there is no external cause in Imran willing or choosing to pass the salt. It at least appears, then, that the agent-causalist might have a way to dissent from Markosian's analysis.

The second case is likely more difficult. Indeed it may be a borderline case where we cannot say whether or not Zane is a hero, worthy of significant praise.

---

39   Markosian 1999; see also John Carroll and Ned Markosian 2010, Chap. 3.
40   For doubts about the possibility of double causation, see Jaegwon Kim 2010, Chap. 7.

That is, it may not be possible to sort out the actual determinants of Zane's action. And without a way of sorting out these details, we simply cannot say that this is a case of double causation. Perhaps this is sufficient for the agent-causalist though. If it is a borderline case, then Markosian has not yet shown that determinism and free will are compatible.

In drawing attention to the notion of double causation and its role in our thinking about free will, Markosian has still highlighted a very important issue. Perhaps we need to get much clearer about what it is to identify some event or "agent-event" as the cause of an action. And whether one always excludes the other—or are the two compatible.[41]

A CONCLUSION?

Since Epictetus and later Stoicism, we have seen a tension between a world whose events are necessary—events that are wholly determined by initial conditions and physical law—and reason, our rational nature, which seemingly enables us to act on the basis of reasons and to choose independently of prior mental states. In turn, it is difficult to reconcile determinism and moral responsibility. Our *metaphysical* convictions about the nature of the world and of us make it difficult to reconcile free will and determinism, and even more to reconcile determinism and responsibility. It is not yet clear how such a reconciliation can be effected, nor if it can be.

Key Concepts

- free will
- responsibility argument for free will
- experience argument for free will
- determinism
- incompatibilism
- fatalism
- agent causation
- compatibilism
- Frankfurt examples

---

41 For more on mental causation, again see Kim 2010, Neil Campbell, ed., 2003; see also Crumley 2006, Chap. 9.

Reading Questions

1. Briefly describe the two main arguments for the existence of free will. Which of these two seems most compelling to you? Explain.

2. In your own words, explain what determinism is. Again in your own words, briefly explain why determinism seems to rule out free will.

3. What is the consequence argument for incompatibilism? Briefly outline the argument. If correct, what view or views does this argument, rule *out*? Briefly explain.

4. Do you think science shows us that free will is an illusion? Explain. If not, do you think science *could* show us that free will is an illusion?

5. Explain how the compatibilist view of "free action" yields a notion of free will that is compatible with determinism. Who do you think is right, incompatibilists or compatibilists? Why?

6. Choose one of these views—agent causation or compatibilism—and write a brief essay explaining what you think is the best argument for it.

For Further Reading

Timothy O'Connor 2014 provides an extensive bibliography of both historical and contemporary works on free will and related issues.

Martin Luther's *The Bondage of the Will* is his extensive analysis and critique of Erasmus's view of free will and is accessible to the casual reader; Luther 1957.

The best contemporary introduction to free will is Robert Kane 2006. As noted in the text, his 1998 is a defense of free will, which depends in part on "indeterminacies" found in neural processes. There are of course many book-length defenses of free will, including Timothy O'Connor 2002. Laura Ekstrom 2000 is a defense of libertarianism, which does not rely on agent causation. John Martin Fischer is a principal advocate of compatibilism; his 1995 is widely considered one of the most important defenses of that view. Daniel Dennett 1984 is a very accessible—and, like much of Dennett's work, entertaining—defense of compatibilism.

Daniel Wegner 2003 principally draws on research from psychology and cognitive science; Derk Pereboom also argues that our notion of free will is an illusion; his 2014 expands on his earlier work and further argues that our lives can be significant and meaningful, despite the absence of free will.

John Martin Fischer 1989 contains Nelson Pike's 1965 essay and Marilyn McCord Adams 1967, along with Plantinga 1986 and Hoffman and Rosenkrantz 1984, with several other important essays on omniscience and free will. Fischer's "Introduction" is an excellent, longer introduction to the issue. Hasker's 1989 is a book-length treatment of many of these issues; he argues for a unique view of God's knowledge of the future. Robert Kane 2011 is an excellent collection of recent essays on various topics regarding the free will controversy; the essays are authored by theorists who have made significant contributions to the issues and arguments.

CHAPTER NINE

TIME

THE NATURE OF TIME—ITS REALITY OR UNREALITY, ITS STRUCTURE, and the intriguing possibility of time travel—is an important area of metaphysics. In raising questions about time, we confront one of the most central aspects of our experience. Few things seem more apparent than the flow of our experience. We seem to experience a constantly changing present: as the future draws near, it becomes the present and seemingly disappears into the past. Yet there is pressure on this view, not only from philosophers, but also from science.

Albert Einstein's view of relativity led him to accept a dramatically different view of time. Any past time and any future time exist, no differently than the present exists. This gives rise to what is known as the **block universe**—the universe is viewed as four-dimensional, in which all times are equally present. Hilary Putnam once offered a proof that all future times are "real" and exist "now."[1] Imagine a three-dimensional block as a series of planes, stuck together. Each of those planes exists no less than any other. For example, one plane in that block universe is the "present" in which I am writing these words. As you are reading these words, in your "present," this plane of my typing is in your past. But it is no less "there"; indeed the future plane in which you read the words I'm writing now exists just as much as my present plane. Brian Greene, physicist and science writer, compares this block universe to a loaf of sliced bread. Making use of a variant of that analogy, imagine pulling a thread (your life?) through those loaf slices. As the thread moves from one slice to the next, the "past" slice does not cease to exist. Indeed slices not yet reached by the thread exist—future slices exist, in just the same sense as the slice exists where the thread "head" is located.

Four-Dimensionalism

Is there a way of understanding the you that is reading this now as but a proper part of you, a "stage" of you, and "you" properly understood is the totality of these stages? Some theorists think so. To understand this more clearly, begin with a simple three-dimensional object. The loveseat against the opposite wall occupies a region of space. It is extended in three dimensions. But in no (proper) part of that region do we find the whole loveseat. Now complicate the picture a bit. We think of our world as four-dimensional: three spatial dimensions and a temporal dimension. So we might think of the "temporal life" of an object as extending through a region of time. In this sense, the three-dimensional loveseat that we see at any one point in time is in fact only a part or *stage* of the whole. The loveseat—the *whole* loveseat—is only found in the totality of its *temporal* stages. At any selected time we encounter the loveseat in but one of its stages. What's true of the loveseat is true of any object. An object comprises all its temporal parts, and only a part of the object is present at any time.

Four-dimensionalism is the view that a whole object is found only in the whole of the time through which it extends or occurs; moments or sequences of moments are but temporal stages of the object. This view is true of persons as well. Felicia sipping a strawberry milkshake in the neighborhood diner is but one temporal stage of Felicia. To point to Felicia in the diner is to point to but one temporal part of her. In this sense, four-dimensionalism

---

1   Putnam 1967, esp. pp. 242 and 246–47.

leads to a view of identity over time, known as *perdurantism*, or more simply *perdurance theory*. (Not all four-dimensionalists understand the theory in this way.) The identity of any object consists in the whole of its temporal parts. This has the consequence that although Felicia is the whole of her temporal parts, no temporal part is identical to any other. Four-dimensionalism is thus committed to an ontology of temporal parts.

A standard argument for four-dimensionalism is that it supplies an account of change of a certain type of properties of an object over time. This problem is known as the problem of temporary intrinsics. Objects have intrinsic properties, that is, properties that do not depend on any features of the world outside the object. A person's shape, for example, changes over time. And four-dimensionalism seems to explain how we can say, "Look at the muscles Fabio has now!" We are talking about Fabio as the whole of his temporal parts. But our comparison is between different temporal stages, e.g., Fabio at some time eight weeks ago and Fabio at the present time.

It is interesting to compare this account of change with that of the substance-attribute theorist. Recall that the latter view holds, unlike the four-dimensionalist, that the whole of an object is present at every moment that it exists, while its (inessential) attributes change. One way to bring out the difference between the two views is to ask about the relationship between the different temporal parts and *that which continues* in the substance theorist's view. There is of course more to be said about both views; they clearly present rival metaphysical pictures of the world.

An extremely important account of four-dimensionalism is that of Theodore Sider 2001. For a different use of the term—as simply a denial of presentism— see Michael Rea 2003, esp. pp. 246–48; the essay is an excellent summary and analysis of the variety of issues in four-dimensionalism.

Yet this picture of the universe seems very much at odds with an important feature of our ordinary experience: time flows; time passes. Our conscious experience flows, seemingly carried along by time. The flow may seem temporarily faster or slower. But time continues to flow. Our present *ceases to exist* as it passes and becomes past; our future *does not yet exist* as it flows toward us to become our new present, and then past. Time is becoming—the nonexistent future becoming the existent present becoming the past. The block universe contravenes our experience, as it seems to imply that time doesn't flow or pass.

Not every physicist accepts the block universe.[2] Some have attempted to reconcile the science with our experience of time, giving rise to an alternative picture, that of an open or growing universe. Still the block universe remains a startling and challenging picture. It seems to tell us something very fundamental about the nature of our world. Importantly, some philosophers have argued against the metaphysical reality of time. Independently of special relativity theory, philosophers have argued that our sense of time passage, of the ineluctable flow from future to present to past, is a dramatic mistake. Among the most famous and discussed of such arguments is that of John McTaggart (1866–1925), a British idealist philosopher. His 1908 paper, "The Unreality of Time,"[3] argued that the idea of stretches of time successively being future, present, and finally past is self-contradictory. The argument is still very much at the center of discussions about the metaphysics of time by both those who defend it and those who reject it.

Although McTaggart developed his argument independently of the theory of relativity, his categories for thinking about the structure and characteristics of time are remarkably coincident with a scientific view of the nature of time. And that argument provides a departure point for an exploration of the metaphysics of time.

Time Isn't Real

Underlying McTaggart's argument is the thought that time—as we understand it—is real *only if* our concept of time accounts for or explains *time changing*. Now McTaggart claims that we have open to us two ways of thinking about time. More precisely, we have two ways of *ordering* time.

The first is our "time passes" conceptualization. We order—locate—events as past or present or future. The flow of time depends on a distant future event *becoming* not-so-distant future, then near future, then present, then near past. This "flow" continues until that once distantly future moment becomes but part of the remote past. And time flows continuously. Thus each moment changes continuously, from future to present to past.

Thus, the temporal quality, the temporal "determination," of any event changes. Our ordinary linguistic descriptions of events seem to reflect this temporal property of events. We might say of some event, "That's past, water under

2   See Dan Falk 2016; see also Lee Smolin 2014.
3   McTaggart, 1908.

the bridge." Or during the Christmas season, we might tell a young child that Santa will be arriving soon. The event of Santa's arrival has this temporal quality—in the near future. But we are also acknowledging that this temporal quality is *changing*. Santa's arrival is about to change from near future to present. This *temporal change* is, for McTaggart, essential to the reality of time, as we typically understand it. Time is real if and only if any event has this temporal character. McTaggart dubbed this time-passes ordering of time the **A-series**. This is a dynamic view of time, or more simply, *dynamic time*.[4]

The second way of thinking about time is a static ordering of events. This way of describing the temporal character of events simply places them in relation to one another as "before" or "later" than some other event. One event, say the Revolutionary War, is before another event, the Civil War, which itself is before World War II. Absent from this characterization of events is identifying the temporal character of an event as future or past. Consequently, there is no becoming present or becoming past. It is simply to point out the arrangement, the ordering of events. Given this understanding of the ordering of time, McTaggart holds, we forego the notion of time passing or the flow of time. The number line of arithmetic perhaps provides something of an analogy. On the number line -1 is before 3, which in turn is before 7. But in seeing this order or relationship between numbers, we see no flow or passing from one place on the line to some subsequent place. McTaggart called this static ordering the **B-series**. Adrian Bardon calls this *static time*.[5]

In recent decades a "new" version of the B-theorist has emerged. They hold that the temporal structure of the world is wholly given by the B-series ordering, and that all times equally exist. These new theorists explain the truth of tensed sentences, e.g., "John Adams was the second president," by relating particular utterances of such statements to contexts, in particular, the context in which the statement is made. J.J.C. Smart, for example, would explain the truth of a tensed statement—a statement that involves an apparent reference to past, present or future—such as "John Adams was the second president" in the following manner. The tensed statement "John Adams was the second president" is true, Smart would say, if and only if this *tenseless* sentence is true: John Adams is the second president before or earlier than this utterance.[6]

---

4   Bardon 2013, Chap. 4.
5   *Ibid.*
6   Smart 2008, pp. 226–28; see also Mellor 1981, Chaps. 2 and 4, and Oaklander 2004.

The Unreality of Time: The Argument

McTaggart holds that the reality of time requires the passing or changing of time. The reality of time depends, according to McTaggart, on a coherent explanation of how time could change. He then proceeds to argue that the B-series ordering cannot explain or account for change. In itself, this would not show that time is unreal, since the A-series ordering of time is the manifestation of this sort of change. Unfortunately—for the realist about time—the concept of the A-series leads to contradiction, in McTaggart's view. And since that notion is self-contradictory, there is and can be no reality corresponding to the A-series of time. Thus, according to McTaggart, time is not real.

McTaggart begins by arguing that the B-series simply cannot account for the requisite change. He asks us to think about the various candidates for change and argues that none of them provide an explanation of temporal change. Perhaps the most obvious candidate is that of an event. The nature of events is itself a topic in metaphysics. We can see, however, McTaggart's point without perhaps a detailed exploration of the metaphysics of events.

Imagine, then, a simple event, say, Maddie making coffee on a Tuesday at 5:30 am. We might imagine distinct or different events, but *this* event of Maggie making coffee doesn't change.

A bit more detail will help. At 5:30 am Maddie pours water into the well of her Black and Decker coffee maker, puts four tablespoons of Yuban coffee in the basket, and turns on the machine. There is our event. It is *this* event, the event we have identified. But there is no change possible; any change and it would be some other event. Suppose Maddie instead uses a Hamilton coffee maker—this isn't a change to the event, but rather the occurrence of another, a different event. Of course, it is a very similar event. But it is not *this* event. And the same is true of Maddie pouring in less water or using more coffee. Or programming the coffee maker to begin at a later time. One and all are similar events. Yet *different* events, essentially different events.

"Wait!" it might be objected. "McTaggart misunderstands how events change," the objection claims. "Think about the actual brewing of the coffee—at one time the coffee pot is empty, then a third full, half full, and finally full. Surely this is a *changing* event." This objection invites us to consider the structure of events more carefully perhaps; significantly, McTaggart explicitly considers this type of objection. He insists that the coffee pot one-sixteenth full, one-third full or one-half full are in fact distinct events. We have only uncovered, according to McTaggart, a sequence of unchanging events, related to one another as *earlier than* or *later than*. As a simple analogy think of a movie film. Each frame of the film is fixed and unchanging. Of course, we can and do run through these frames very rapidly. But the content of each frame is forever unchanged. Each frame is static and unchanging. As each frame in the film sequence remains unchanged, so each component event in our now complex event of Maggie brewing coffee is forever fixed and unchanging.

The B-series presents us with sequences of events, related to each other as *earlier* or *later*. That order is fixed and unchanging. Equally, any sequence comprises *unchanging* events. Thus, the B-series precludes a notion of change, at least understood as "event change."

McTaggart is of course making an assumption about the *identity* of an event. In particular, he assumes that every feature of an event is an essential feature. Imagining changing any feature of an event is not to change *this* event; rather it is imagining a completely different event. There is some plausibility to this thought. The event of Jack walking into class wearing the Onno's t-shirt is different than the event of Jack walking into class wearing the Radiators t-shirt—even if everything else is exactly the same in the two cases. Now someone might object that we have but two instances or tokens of the same type of event, namely, Jack walking into class. Yet our being able to classify events more or less specifically, e.g., Jack wearing shirt *x* to class, Jack walking into class, or the beginning of class, does not change McTaggart's underlying point. He can argue that the identity conditions of an event—what makes an event this event and not that event—are fixed. Of course we often classify events hierarchically: "making coffee" is a broad category that has as subcategories "making coffee in the morning" and "making coffee after dinner." But within the subcategories are distinct events. Making coffee in the morning with a Black and Decker coffee maker is distinct from doing so with a Hamilton coffee maker. There is then some reason for counting any change in aspect to be an essential change, thus giving us a different event.

Nor can a proponent of B-series change appeal to the object changing. Indeed, as just noted, a change in the object yields a different event. Jack walking into the classroom with a tattoo of a palm tree on his arm is a different event than Jack walking in *sans* tattoo. Changes in object violate the identity conditions of the event, at least in McTaggart's view. (The identity conditions of an event are not necessarily the same as the identity conditions of the object. It would still be Jack [most would say], tattoo or no tattoo. The same Jack can be and is an element of different events. But changes in Jack nonetheless change the event.)

This suggests an issue worth noting. It might be objected to the argument just given that it dismisses object-based change too quickly. Consider the coffee pot: at one time, empty; a little later, half-full. Granted we have two different events here, but what changes is not an event, but an object. The same object is a constituent of two events, events differing in the property of that object (and, of course, the time). Allowing for the continuing existence of objects thus makes change intelligible. Whether McTaggart or the "object-based change" view is correct perhaps depends on a conception of object. One might think of objects as a set of temporal parts or along a more traditional line, which holds objects to be continuing or "enduring," which undergoes a change in properties. It may be that McTaggart held something more like the temporal parts view and needs some further argument for that view of objects. At any rate, back to McTaggart's argument.

A similar response can be made to the objection that the *time* changes within the B-series. Again, McTaggart insists *times don't change*. Monday morning at 2:32 is *always* Monday at 2:32 am. We can imagine Monday at 2:31 am or Monday at 2:33 am. But this is just the *earlier than* and the *later than* characteristic of the B-series. Nothing has changed about the time "Monday morning at 2:32." Again, recall the number line. Instead of some numerical unit, such as integers, think of times. Those times are fixed and unchanging, just as the places of -1 or +7 are fixed on the number line.

Whether we consider events, objects, or times, McTaggart argues that there is no way to introduce change into the B-series. And without change, without passing time, there is no time. Thus, if our concept of time is to designate real time, we must look to the A-series to find the requisite framework for change. Unfortunately, this leads to contradiction, in McTaggart's view.

Why does he think that the A-series leads to contradiction? McTaggart claims that any event has *every* time determination. That is, any event we choose is at once past, present and future. Consider a particular event: it is (in the A-series view) future, then present, then past. All three states are somehow supposed to be inherent in this event. This is plainly incoherent, according to McTaggart: it is self-contradictory to say that an event is past, present, and future. If the A-series ordering of events is self-contradictory, then there is no reality designated by or corresponding to the A-series. It is thus a mistake to see *real* time as comprising the flow of future into present into past.

It might seem that we experience some specific event as a passing present, as the *now* of our experience. That is, we think of one particular event as "passing through" these various stages, and for a time it is future, then, "moving" into another stage, it is present, and finally it moves into the past stage. It's almost as though we think of an event as a ship passing through a series of a locks in a "time canal" (e.g., the Panama Canal). First this "event (like a ship in the canal)" moves into the future lock, then the present lock, etc. The event remains the same and leaves the "future lock" behind when it moves to the present. Thus, there is seemingly no contradiction.

The difficulty with this way of thinking is that "being in the future" is not an external, removable relation of the event. As an example, suppose that when Fred's car breaks down next week, that's the fifth time it has broken down. The event itself is that car's breaking down then; but being the fifth time is the relation between that event and four other breakdowns. That event would still happen, still be the identical event, if it was related to three previous breakdowns, or five, or none. So that attribute of the event is not essential. It's merely an external, removable relation of the event. But, for an event to have a real property, a property which makes it the event it is, it can't be merely a relation. But clearly being past, being present, and being future are relational, removable properties. But the A-series is committed to every event having all three of these relational but incompatible properties simultaneously.

But this can't be: an event can't be past *and* present *and* future. And this contradictory feature of the A-series is true of any and every event.

If this much is right, then the A-series conception of time leads to a logical impossibility, that is, something having contradictory qualities at the same time. Thus, time as ordered by the A-series can't be real. Real things cannot have self-contradictory properties.[7]

Tenses and Truth Conditions

Some recent interpretations of McTaggart's argument focus on the notion of truth conditions of our use of tensed statements.[8] We say of some event that it will be or that it has happened, or that it is. For example, consider the sentence about the future that Sara *will* graduate from college in 2024. That this graduating is *future* is what makes the sentence true now. But that sentence won't be true in 2024. For then the graduating will be present, not future.

7   For an important interpretation and defense of McTaggart, see L. Nathan Oaklander 2011.
8   See, for example, J.J.C. Smart 2008 and Bardon 2013, Chap. 4.

So, when is it true? It is true that Sara will graduate in 2024 when her graduating is future *in the present*. The sentence "Sara will graduate in 2024" is true when that graduation event is future, from the point of view of our present.

You might think that this is as it should be. McTaggart's argument, however, explains why this account of the truth of this sentence about the future leads to an infinite regress, and is thus unsatisfactory. All the "futures" and the "presents" and "is true whens" can perhaps be a little confusing, so taking matters a bit slowly might help.

In this approach to McTaggart's argument, we need an explanation of how we are to understand the truth of tensed statements. We consider a sentence about the future and recognize that the sentence is true when that future event is future *in the present*.

The problem, however, becomes apparent now. We now have a new true sentence to explain: "Sara's graduation from college in 2024 is future, in the present." We have to explain what makes a more complicated, tensed sentence true. But now, however, we require an explanation of the truth of this more complicated sentence: "'Sarah's graduation from college in 2024 is future, in the present' is present." We need to explain what makes it true in the present that that graduation is future in the present. Now you can see that we are on our way to an infinite regress. Whenever we specify the truth conditions of a tensed sentence, a new sentence will appear—and we will need to explain the truth conditions of that new sentence. But this is an unending process. Thus, we never have an explanation of how it is that tensed statements are true.[9]

While no self-contradictory claim is generated, still McTaggart can claim that we have no real understanding of an A-series time order. An explanation that never ends is no explanation at all. The never ending regress of tensed sentences requiring still another account of what makes each new sentence true would not seem to provide a complete explanation. Without such an explanation, we have no understanding of the notion of time passing or change. And without an explanation of passing time, we have no sense of a real time that corresponds to the A-series. Thus, McTaggart concludes that time is unreal.

As already noted, the "presents" and "futures" and "making-true" can seem daunting. Perhaps we can distill the essential claim of the argument in the following way. We can only claim the A-series ordering "picks out" or corresponds to an objective, real time if we can give some explanation of this ordering. Now, at least a part of that explanation is being able to say

---

9   Following Bardon.

what we mean when we say that some event is past or in the future. The most straightforward way of doing so is saying what makes such assertions or claims true. We are met with an apparently insuperable obstacle, however. We give the truth conditions of an A-series sentence. Yet as soon as we do, we find ourselves having to provide the truth conditions of a new A-series sentence! We are met with an infinite regress of ever more complicated A-series sentences. The process is never-ending. The unfortunate consequence of this infinite regress? We can't really say what is meant by any A-series sentence. Oh, we can use those sentences, and often do. But we can give no more real content to such sentences than we can to "It's literally raining cats and dogs." Without being able to provide the real content, the real meaning, it doesn't look like our "time passes" sentences are talking about an objective or real time.

Time Is Unreal

But the A-series is precisely the description of the passing of time. Without the movement from future to past, there is no flowing of time. Yet time is real only if time passes. The B-series alone, according to McTaggart, is not sufficient for *time* to exist. We have an ordering of events. The block universe gives us an ordering of events. But it doesn't give us time. At least not the aspects of time (such as change) that we hold to be features of our experience and of the world. Indeed, a not infrequent reaction upon first seeing diagrams of the block universe is that it can't be right: Time passes; they aren't all there at once!

Saving Time

The depth of McTaggart's challenge to our normal conception of time is in part reflected in the variety of responses and objections to his argument. Some of course insist that time indeed passes and thus that the A-series presents the temporal ordering of reality. Others accept McTaggart's argument against the A-series but maintain that the B-series adequately accounts for change. Still another view acknowledges that time passes but only the present is real.

McTaggart's argument drew response from some of the most noted philosophers of his time, among them Bertrand Russell. Russell argued that the B-series rightly understood accounts for change; we do not need to invoke A-series properties in order to explain change, according to this Russellian view.[10]

---

10   Oaklander 2004, Chap. 16.

He pointed to the change in truth values of propositions as reflecting that change. For example, consider the low fence separating a garden from my front lawn. On Friday, say, the fence is red, and this proposition "The fence is red" is true. *Later*, say on Sunday, I paint the fence white. Then "The fence is red" is false. That proposition has *changed* truth values, according to Russell. That is, Russell does not argue that the event changes; rather we find the passing of time in the change of truth values of the propositions. McTaggart, however, dissents.[11] To understand why, we need to recall his view of events.

An event for McTaggart doesn't change. That the fence is red on Friday, later white, is not one event changing. We have two *different* events. Similarly we have two different propositions—one expressing the fact of the red fence, the other reflecting the fact of the white fence. But there is no change in the truth value of a proposition. Propositions, including their truth values, are fixed, once and for all. Thus, the proposition "the fence is red on Friday, June 23, 2015" describes one event, while the proposition "the fence is white on Sunday, June 25, 2015" describes a different, second event. Events, remember, are constituted by objects, properties, and *times*. If propositions refer to, get their truth values from, events, then propositions do not change their truth value any more than there has been any change in the event of the fence being red on Friday, June 23, 2015 has changed. Thus, McTaggart thinks that Russell has not succeeded in accounting for *time changing* by appealing to B-series change in truth values of propositions.

Do (some) propositions change their truth values? Some theorists, including Russell, hold that they do. On Tuesday, it's true that Julia is at the dentist. Yet that same proposition—Julia is at the dentist—is false on Wednesday. On the other hand, other theorists hold that propositions do not change their truth value. Instead it is *timelessly true* that Julia visits the dentist on Tuesday, March 7, 2016. "Julia visits the dentist on Wednesday, March 8, 2016" is false. Timelessly so. There is no time at which this proposition is true. McTaggart appears to subscribe to this second view, that contingent propositions have timeless and unchanging truth values.[12]

Why accept McTaggart's view propositions? McTaggart further notes that Russell's approach can work only if there is an A-series. That is, "the fence is red" changes truth values only if we can give some sense to the notion that

---

11   McTaggart 1927, §313.

12   See, for example, Roderick Chisholm 1976, Chap. 4, for a defense of this second view.

this proposition is false *now*, but was true *in the past*. So, McTaggart thinks Russell's objection depends upon the truth of the A-series ordering. But the point of the objection was to explain change without appealing to the A-series.

A Little Relief: Prior and the A-series

A.N. Prior offered one of the more widely noted responses on behalf of the A-series.[13] Prior invented and developed tense logic and was a strong advocate of the A-series view of time.

Prior argued that some of our thoughts or expressions about our experience require acknowledging the passing of time. In "Thank Goodness That's Over," he considers a person, say Andie, remarking, after a headache has passed, "Thank goodness that's over." Prior asks how we are to understand the content of Andie's remark. In his view, Andie is not "thanking" a temporal ordering in which the headache occupies several *earlier* B-series positions. That is, Andie is not saying something along the lines of "I'm glad I am in this location in the temporal order and the headache is in some different *earlier* and *fixed* temporal locations." Instead, Andie is grateful or relieved that the headache *has passed*. The headache no longer occupies him now; and that "headache-now" is in the past. It was present but is now past. According to Prior, it is only the A-series that reflects the content of Andie's expression of relief.

There is no denying that many of our expressions about our experience reflect a commitment to the passing of time. We might, for example, consider nine-year old Alyssa eagerly anticipating art class beginning in two hours, becoming more excited as that future time draws closer, being happy when it arrives, and bemoaning its passing: "I wish we were still doing art instead of social studies." It should also be noted, however, that at least some of our commonsense expressions mislead us about the nature of reality. McTaggart can accept that Andie and Alyssa (tacitly, at least) conceptualize the world as a world in which time flows. Yet the point of McTaggart's argument is that Andie and Alyssa—and the metaphysics of passing time—are mistaken.

Still, Prior's argument presses this question: how are we to explain our experience as that of flowing or passing time? D.H. Mellor takes up this challenge on behalf of McTaggart and the discarding of the A-series. In Mellor's view the

---

13   Prior 1959.

apparent passing of time is a reflection of our *remembering* some experience.[14] Prior argued that our sense of relief is about a *once present* experience. But Mellor claims in response that this is not the only way to think about "Thank goodness." Andie's remark occurs *after* the headache, as the headache is earlier than the remark. Of course we normally see the end of the headache as the cause of Andie's relief. But this alone does not suffice to show the reality of the passing of time, or the existence of an A-series ordering of time.

Mellor argues that the heart of this issue is the *presence* of experience and the related notion of our memory or recollection of experience. Larissa's present experience, for example, is of the vireo warblers darting among the palm trees. *Earlier* she had a different present experience, say, of the cessation of the thundershower. Any experience, in Mellor's view, is manifestly present. And Andie's judgment "That's over" is true only if his present experience is "headache-free." We are not normally conscious of the temporal aspects of our experience. On some occasions we are. Andie is aware of just that, according to Mellor, when he judges that his present experience is pain free.

Does this account help us understand the seeming passing of time, reflected in the A-series? Elsewhere, Mellor ties our sense of the flow of time to recollection, to the mechanism of memory.[15] Our sense of the flow of time is tied to the increase in the quantity of recollections we have of events located *earlier than* our present experience. Imagine Deirdre perceiving a vireo warbler sitting on the bird feeder. This is her present experience. *After* that experience, she perceives the bird flying and the empty bird feeder swaying. And she might recollect her experience of the vireo warbler sitting on the feeder. Deirdre might say to Danny that "a vireo warble *was just* here." But a new present experience is of only the bird feeder swaying. And now one last present experience—the bird feeder still. Deirdre has an increasing number of recollections between the experience of the bird sitting and the experience of the still but empty feeder. This ever-increasing series of reflections is, in Mellor's view, the explanation of our sense of the flow of time. (Interestingly recent research in the neuroscience of memory and the way the brain "remembers" appears to support something very compatible with Mellor's view in particular, and a B-series account in general.[16]) And this explanation doesn't rely on the positing of an A-series metaphysics of time.

---

14   Mellor 1981, esp. pp. 48–54.
15   Mellor 1981, Chap. 10.
16   NeuroscienceNews.com. 2018.

More recently, philosophers have suggested that the sensations that Prior notes are evolutionary adaptations. The feeling of relief is actually a by-product of a kind of homeostatic response to some stressful or painful situation. It's a by-product of the body "recognizing," for example, that it need not produce as much adrenaline.

Bardon offers a concise example of this. I am anxious at 2:15 about the tooth extraction at 2:30. I am distressed by the discomfort during the extraction. Finally at 2:45 I am relieved that *that's over*. "That's it." Bardon claims. There is merely an ordering of "time dependent emotional states."[17]

Of course there are other defenders of the A-theory and the passing of time.[18] But perhaps this is sufficient to indicate that critics of dynamic time— the A-theory—have alternative ways of explaining important aspects of our sense of time.

Eternalism and Presentism

The A and B ordering of times generate two very different ways of thinking about time, one of which we have suggested in our mention of the block universe. The other, a view that has been called the "common sense" view by one of its proponents, raises many questions but nonetheless has its determined defenders.[19]

Eternalism

Einstein's theory of special relativity leads to the view that all times equally exist. Julius Caesar crossing the Rubicon with his legion in 49 BCE is no less real than this present moment when, say, Fred is at his twenty-first birthday party. While we cannot say and do not know what they are, all future moments are likewise as fully existent as the Roman legion crossing the boundary of Northern Italy and Fred's twenty-first birthday party. In the eternalist view, there is no difference in the ontological status of future, present, and past.

Einstein's theory tells us that time is relative to a frame of reference and the velocity of that frame. In fact, there is no privileged *now*; there is no perspective from which we can say, "This moment is *now* for the entire universe."

---

17   Bardon 2013, p. 108.

18   See, for example, E.J. Lowe 2002, Chap. 17.

19   Ned Markosian 2004, p. 47.

(This is sometimes called the Galiean view, or Galilean spacetime. Robert Geroch dubs such a view a "democratic framework."[20]) Rather, any set of moments may constitute the now, depending on one's frame of reference. So, every time—from some perspective—is a "now time." And since all now times exist, all times exist.

In this view—known as **eternalism**—49 BCE, now, and August 17, 2023 are, along with every other time, equally existent. Advocates of eternalism are B-theorists, and we can see why from the previous paragraph. Eternalism holds that time is but the ordered sequence of always existing times.

Some might object to eternalism in the same way that they would object to other B-series views. Still others worry that eternalism precludes free will. Suppose for a moment that eternalism is true. Suppose that Julia is trying to decide where she will spend Easter vacation next spring. If we think that her decision is free, then there must be options available to her; her future must be an open future (see Chap. 8). But eternalism apparently commits us to the view that all the next-spring events exist *now*, as Julia is trying to decide. These events include where Julia will be. If those events "already" exist, how is it that Julia has options available to her?

In one sense the eternalist response is simple and straightforward: come next Easter, Julia is on her way to her *freely chosen* destination. Explaining this response requires making a perhaps subtle distinction. Notice first a feature of determinism that is at issue here (again, see Chap. 8). That deterministic view says that, given a certain past, that past, together with certain facts about our world, necessitate, or will necessarily bring about, one particular future outcome. But eternalism, while it is consistent with this deterministic view, in no way requires it.

Indeed, the eternalist can tell a story about our "time slice planes" in the block universe being fully compatible with Julia having free will. That is, consider Julia thinking about where to go next Easter. There are of course a series of time slice planes between now and when Julia finally chooses her destination. Each of those slices is but another moment in Julia freely choosing. Thus, in the time slice a week from now, Julia rules out vacationing in Santa Barbara. And in the time nine days hence, she rules out—freely—visiting the Painted Desert and Petrified Forest in Arizona. Lastly, eleven days from now, she freely chooses to visit her cousin in Salisaw, Oklahoma and relaxing on the ranch. On each of these occasions, we can stipulate that Julia's choice is entirely

20   Geroch, Chaps. 3 and 4.

free and not caused by the events and facts that preceded it. And yet, this account of Julia's decision is fully compatible with the eternalist view of time. Eternalism—like other block universe theories of time—is equally consistent with both a deterministic view and one in which events of free choice occur.

Presentism

Presentism is the view that only the present exists; alternatively, any object that exists is a "now existing" object. Neither Socrates nor Sarah Bernhardt exist. They went out of existence. Socrates ceased to exist at some moment in 399 BCE, and Sarah Bernhardt at some moment in 1923. Similarly, your future child does not exist.

Presentism avoids McTaggart's objection to time because only the present is real. His objection was that saying that an event is future, and then saying that it is present, is giving it incompatible, contradictory properties. But future events are not real. Hence, there are neither future events taking on the incompatible present property, nor are there present events taking on the incompatible past determination. Presentists, however, are A-theorists: they hold that time flows. But they deny that future or past times exist. The present is here a little while, and then passes out of existence. The future doesn't exist, but some *as yet nonexistent* event that we "see" in the future—e.g., Pauline will serve Bananas Foster after dinner—comes into being, becomes real, is present for a while, and then passes out of existence.

Initially, as already noted, presentism seems like the view typical of our ordinary thinking. We are in the now, and that's all there is. The ancient city of Troy no longer exists. That was in the past. It stopped existing, perhaps sometime in the thirteenth century BCE. Of course the only things there are, are just the things in the now—present things. What could be more obvious?

Presentism faces a number of questions, and here we consider two of them. A paragraph back, you and I both thought about Socrates. And here's a very simple straightforward sentence about Socrates: Socrates lived in Athens. We easily understand the meaning of the sentence. But now ask the presentist how we are to understand this proposition. (This debate is typically discussed using the term *proposition*.) Or: what is this proposition about? The presentist seems to be committed to saying that it is about nothing at all! Socrates doesn't exist! Then how is a proposition that's about nothing make sense? It certainly seems as though the proposition is about Socrates, not nothing. Nor can the presentist say something like Socrates existed in the past and lived in Athens.

Neither Socrates nor the past exists. There is only the present. Presentism may be our commonsense conception of time. But it seems at odds with our commonsense understanding of some straightforward propositions.[21]

A related question arises from our concept of causation. The hurtling baseball causes the window to break. Moments before, a well-timed swing of the bat caused the baseball to hurtle in the direction of the window. One event causes another only if both events must exist. A statement of the form "X is the cause of Y" must be false if X does not exist.

Different presentist theorists suggest different ways of responding to these objections.[22] Thus, for example, it has been suggested that when Socrates ceases to exist, all those propositions referring to Socrates also cease to exist. This invites further questions, however, about the nature of propositions. Are propositions the sort of thing that come into and go out of existence? More troubling perhaps is the thought that Socrates ceasing to exist somehow brings about the demise of many propositions. How does it do this? And why?

A further suggestion, offered by Ned Markosian, is that we might distinguish between the propositional content and the linguistic meaning of the proposition "Socrates lived in Athens."[23] *Strictly speaking*, there is no content to this proposition. It expresses no features of the world. Yet we make use of that proposition in a range of contexts in order to convey a linguistic meaning. Propositions make sense even when they don't connect to real objects. Consider the proposition "There's a unicorn in my back garden." It isn't about a unicorn. Still it might be wondered whether this is the solution to the problem or bringing the problem back under a different name.

Markosian recognizes the challenge of the causation objection. In his view, it is a special but important case of the problem of explaining or accounting for apparent relations between nonexistent objects and existent objects. Markosian suggests that there is a sufficient temporal overlap between cause and effect. If there is at least a partial temporal coincidence—that is, a time when both cause and effect exist—then the causation problem seems resolved.

In that case, a chain of causes is most likely needed to explain many of our causal claims. Consider the assassination of Archduke Ferdinand as a cause of World War I. The assassination took place on June 28, 1914, but the war did not begin until early August of that year. An obvious way to think

---

21   St. Augustine raised a similar objection: 1949; see also Zimmerman 2008, p. 212.

22   See also Savitt 2017.

23   Markosian 2004.

about this involves a causal chain filling in this gap: the assassination caused other events, which caused still other events, ... which caused the beginning of the war. But can this solve the problem? Remember that events (on the view we're considering) are instantaneous: they don't have a duration. So unless two events are simultaneous, they don't overlap; so they can't form a chain of overlapping incidents connecting the assassination and the war. Well, suppose that we conceive of the links in this chain as objects with duration. Then they can overlap, but still the assassination itself did not exist when the war started.

Time Travel

You may know the stories. A high school student travels back in time, only to find that he must make sure his parents, then only high school students, fall in love, else he and his siblings will cease to exist. A cybernetic organism travels back in time on different occasions, first to terminate, later to protect from another terminator. A futuristic mafia illegally sends those people it wants to be rid of thirty years back where a mafia assassin awaits them.

Time travel is the stuff of science fiction. But there are genuine philosophical and empirical issues to consider. So let's begin at the beginning: is time travel logically possible?

The Logical Possibility of Time Travel

The philosopher David Lewis focused on the issue in his "The Paradoxes of Time Travel."[24] Lewis distinguished between *personal time* and *external time*. The former is the time relative to our imagined traveler, or, as Lewis describes it, the time on the traveler's wristwatch (or in the early twenty-first century, on the traveler's iPhone). The traveler gauges the duration of the travel according to his or her way of gauging time. External time is intended by Lewis to correspond to some objective time measurable by some standard independent of the traveler.

We know from physics that the closer to the speed of light one travels, the slower is one's time. Send Pauline off in a space ship traveling near the speed of light. To her, the trip might take a year, according to her personal time; by some external standard, say an earth calendar, her trip has lasted some three centuries. Thus, we might designate personal time relative to a

---

24   Lewis 1976.

frame of reference identified by the speed of the traveler. And external time would then be the time according to the frame of reference of some observer or group of observers on earth.

Ordinary experience finds external time coinciding with personal time. Julia's travel into the future of tomorrow coincides exactly with the travel to tomorrow of Jack and Andie and a few billion other people. Here we have our first bit of time travel—we travel into the future all the time. (Here we will use these expressions without worrying about A- or B-series orderings.) This unproblematic "time travel" is not, however, the stuff of science fiction. The problem arises for immediate travel into a more distant future.

Traveling into the past both piques our imaginations and raises familiar questions. The broadest or most general challenge to time travel is that of logical possibility. Is there anything self-contradictory about time travel to the past? Although some have presented interesting arguments against the logical possibility of time travel, others have offered responses that suggest that time travel is not self-contradictory or logically impossible.

Grandfathers and Changing the Past

The most noted challenge to the possibility of time travel into the past is the **Grandfather paradox**. Imagine traveling into the past. You meet your grandfather. What happens if you "terminate" your maternal grandfather, say when he is still a child? Well, your mother would not be born. Consequently, there would be no you. Indeed, you would never have existed. If you never existed, then there is no you to travel to the past and terminate grandpa. And this is a logical contradiction: it is logically impossible that you both exist and never existed.

There is a way to see time travel into the past as logically consistent. That is, there is a way to understand why it is *not logically possible for you to kill your grandfather*. A principle, cited in various contexts, is the fixity of the past. That is, past events cannot be altered in any way. More colloquially, "what's done is done." If on your thirteenth birthday your only birthday present was socks, there is no way to change that. If you forget your anniversary, there is no way to "erase" and remember in time. Once it happens, it cannot "un-happen." Indeed, the concept of changing the past is itself self-contradictory and hence logically impossible. But if you can't change the past, you can't kill grandpa. Since you are traveling back in time, clearly you exist. And the principle of the fixity of the past entails that you can't not exist. Killing your grandfather, however, has the consequence that you never existed. Given the fixity of the past, you cannot have these contradictory properties, having existed and never having existed.

Adrian Bardon explicitly frames the issue by thinking of time travel, given the truth of the B-theorist's view of static time. Consider the B-series ordering of events. In the block universe, then, all past events timelessly exist. Or, as he notes, "The past BE just the way it BE, and there is no changing it."[25] You can thus travel to the past. But you cannot change it. So, time travel is consistent with B-series ordering of time.

Travelers Timelessly a Part of History

Consider an example of how this might work. Imagine that you travel back in time to early morning on December 7, 1941, in Honolulu. You cannot change anything that happened. But you are timelessly part of the events of that morning. You are part of that event, no less than the sailors or pilots or civilians. The morning's events occurred *with you there.*

This explains how you can be part of the past without changing the past. Imagine that "once in Honolulu" you brush aside some leaves underneath a tree so that you can sit down. Aren't you changing the past then? No. Once again your brushing aside the leaves is part of that morning's events. Those leaves are *timelessly*—in the B-ordering—brushed aside. They weren't once undisturbed throughout the morning and also brushed aside. You don't change the past; you are unalterably part of that past.

Backwards Causation and Causal Loops

Our usual conception of causation is that causes precede their effects. (Or at least, a cause is coincident with its effect, e.g., the sofa cushion compressing occurs *as* I sit down.) Consequently, we think that the *causal arrow* is one way, from earlier to later. Backwards causation—an earlier effect brought about by a later cause—is thus apparently ruled out by the usual conception. Yet once we acknowledge the possibility of time travel to the past, backwards causation is no longer ruled out. Imagine that the day after you first read these lines, I (somehow) travel to Honolulu and on the early morning of December 7, 1941, I brush aside leaves. I came into existence *later* than the brushing of the leaves.

---

25   Bardon 2013, p. 130.

But I am nonetheless the cause of the leaves being moved. *After* brings about *before*. Like other aspects of our world, the possible features of the world are sometimes puzzling.

The conceptual connection between backwards causation and the *reversibility* or the *symmetry* of time begins to come into focus here. (It is arguable whether these issues are purely metaphysical or empirical issues.[26] In this context to call them "empirical" is to say that we should look to some science for the final answer to the question. Here we treat them as metaphysical issues.) If we accept the B theorist's block universe view, then there is no reason to think that the direction of time is from earlier to later. All times exist equally. If this is correct, then there is no reason to see the essential nature of time as a sequence of moments, directed from 1941 to 2016. There is thus no *ontological* priority of an event that we identify as being earlier than some other event. Although our ordinary conversations might do so, we shouldn't assume that those conversations reflect the nature of reality. Given this picture of the reversibility or symmetry of time, *backwards* causation may be infrequent, but it is metaphysically possible.

---

26   See Lowe 2003, p. 332.

An odd consequence of time travel and backwards causation is the possibility of causal loops. Let us think of causal loops as two events, causally connected, but we cannot say which is cause and which is effect. Perhaps a little more precisely, an event brings about (at least partially) a second event. But the second event is then at least one of the causes of the first event. For example, suppose that Deirdre enters her time machine, which she constructed, travels back in time to give the time machine blueprint to her earlier self. Earlier Deirdre then studies this blueprint. As "later Deirdre" she has mastered the blueprint sufficiently to construct the time machine, climb inside and take the blueprint to Earlier Deirdre. Who will then study the blueprint... Question: where is the origin of the blueprint? Earlier Deirdre gets the blueprint from Later Deirdre, but Later Deirdre gets it from Earlier Deirdre who gets it...? There is no origin in this loop, no original source of the information. As E.J. Lowe remarks, this is an information loop: there is no origin of the information. Or consider a variation of an episode of the BBC science fiction series, *Dr. Who*. Imagine Danny in the twenty-first century, hearing Beethoven's Fifth Symphony. Danny writes down the score for the piece and travels back to the nineteenth century. He gives it to Ludwig for his birthday, telling Ludwig, "It's your idea; publish it under your name." Which Ludwig does. Where is the origin of the symphony?

If causal loops were somehow logically contradictory, that would count against the logical possibility of time travel. Now there is no denying the oddness of causal or informational loops. But there is no apparent logical contradiction in the concept. Thus, it's logically possible that some causal loop might occur as a result of time travel. Odd, to be sure.

We have already looked at the logical puzzles about time travel involved with changing the past. Do these make time travel logically impossible? Ways of trying to circumvent these paradoxes (sometimes seen in science-fiction stories) is that a time-traveler is prohibited from, or incapable of, making any changes when visiting the past. Another story has travelers trying to keep changes to the absolute minimum, but, of course, even the brushing away of a leaf can have consequences; when travelers arrive back in their own day, they sometimes find things completely different from when they left, as causal consequences of the tiny past alterations they could not avoid making during their visit. But what about the grandfather paradox? David Lewis's position on the matter is that a time traveler *could* kill her own grandfather—there's no particular weird physical constraint or logical impossibility of this happening—but, as we know from the premises of the story, she *didn't*. Only ordinary ways in which something intended doesn't actually happen are required—maybe her gun jams, or she loses his address.[27]

Is time travel against the laws (of nature)?

As stimulating as the thought of time travel is, there remains one huge question. Could it *actually* happen? Could someone travel to the past? Is that a *physically possible* event? While there is no consensus on the matter, there are those who hold that it is empirically possible.[28] If some physicists are to be believed, however, the physical possibility of time travel is a possibility only in the distant future, and for human beings that are greatly technically superior to us.

The conditions for time travel appear to require huge masses and huge amounts of energy. Very large masses, contemporary physics tells us, distort space. Under the right conditions, "wormholes" could be created, which in principle might allow travel to the past. Imagine a time-traveling astronaut. Danny could travel through a wormhole ("located" in the right place) to Alpha Centauri, and then return to earth in a spaceship traveling at 99.5% the speed of light. Danny's return to earth would be a few months before he left. All he need do is "wait patiently" and he could shake hands with his past self as that "past Danny" is getting ready to leave![29]

An equally complicated and intriguing mechanism for travel to one's past is suggested by J. Richard Gott, a professor of astrophysics, in his book, *Time Travel in Einstein's Universe*.[30] Gott points to "cosmic strings," incredibly thin, infinitely long, and hugely massive strings, composed of a matter different from our protons and electrons, which are predicted by some theories. Such strings would distort space around them. Gott suggests that were there two infinitely long cosmic strings, roughly parallel to each other, and planets on either side, a time traveler from one planet could visit the other along a particular path, and return in time to greet his "earlier" self.

Gott's explanation is much more detailed than this, covering several pages. Perhaps this description is sufficient to illustrate that given certain facts about our universe, time travel to the past is possible. Yet as Gott cautions, "... don't

---

27   Lewis, 1976, p. 150; for a "fun" survey of the paradox, see also webpage by Peter Christofuro 2019.

28   Bardon 2013, p. 133.

29   Gott 2001, p. 123.

30   Gott 2001.

call your travel agent just yet." Nor should we expect that anyone will be building a time machine in their garage. Rather, time machines are "at best projects for civilizations of the future."[31]

You Can't Go that Way

Popular imagination and science fiction frequently conceive time travel as sitting down in a time machine and, by some unexplained mechanism, traveling backward in time. There is at least one restriction, however: you can't go back the way you came. Imagine that the time machine remains stationary throughout the travel. Now imagine Andie and Alyssa sitting down in the machine's seats. Within moments of their beginning their trip, they would bump into their prior selves! If their trip begins at 11:11 pm, at 11:12 *external time*, they would encounter their earlier selves. But the same space cannot be occupied by two different objects. And we have two sets of two different objects vying for the same space. So at the very least, time travel *to the past* requires some other "route" than the one taken from the past to the start of the travel.

This difficulty reappears in slightly different form for travel to the future. In the 1960 movie *The Time Machine*, the character H.G. Wells, played by Rod Taylor, uses his time machine to travel into the distant future. As this time machine is also stationary, the trip can proceed into the future on condition that the machine encounter no future objects where it (the machine) is located. Thus, if 150 years into the future, aficionados of H.G. Wells had erected a large statue *in the same place* as the time machine, this would have placed a limit on the travel path.

Although there are quite serious *natural* constraints on time travel to the past, nonetheless it appears physically possible; and while time travel is logically possible, it opens up possibilities that challenge the imagination. Huge masses, energy, spacetime conditions would need to conspire together to make time travel to the past possible.

The metaphysics and the science of time both emphasize the unusual nature of time. Perhaps St. Augustine was more prescient than he knew when he remarked that he knew very well what time was ... until you asked him.

---

31   *Ibid.*, p.129.

Key Concepts

- block universe
- four-dimensionalism
- A-series
- B-series
- eternalism
- presentism
- Grandfather paradox

Reading Questions

1. Explain the central difference between the block universe and the growing block universe. Which of these do you think yields a better account of time? Why?

2. Explain the A-series and B-series notions of time. How are they important for McTaggart's argument?

3. McTaggart assumes that without change time is unreal. Do you agree with this assumption? Why?

4. Who do you think has a better view of the "change" nature of events, McTaggart or Russell?

5. Is presentism our commonsense view of time? Explain. What do you think of Markosian's defense of presentism?

6. After having read the chapter, what is your view of the relation between what scientists tell us about time and what philosophers tell us about time? Should we look first to philosophers' theories about the metaphysics of time? Or should we let what scientists tell us about time and let them guide our metaphysics? Explain.

For Further Reading

The central text in discussions about time remains McTaggart 1908, reprised in McTaggart 1927, available in its entirety online. An extremely useful and accessible book on the various issues discussed in the text along with several others is Bardon 2013. The book includes accounts of time by both philosophers and scientists prior to the twentieth century, and of course several chapters address issues raised since the theory of relativity emerged.

Excellent surveys of the issues are in E.J. Lowe 2002, Chap. 17, and Loux 2006, Chap. 7. Already noted is *Real Time* by D.H. Mellor, a contemporary B-theorist as noted in the text. W.H. Newton-Smith's *The Structure of Time* is more challenging in several places, and considers in great detail the mathematical or topological structure of time.

Many of the central essays in recent work, including McTaggart's, are collected in Robin Le Poidevin and Murray MacBreath, eds., *The Philosophy of Time*. Another useful collection of about thirty essays is Heather Dyke and Adrian Bardon, eds., *A Companion to the Philosophy of Time*.

L. Nathan Oaklander's *The Ontology of Time* covers a broad range of issues and is a defense of the modern B-theory. Dean Zimmerman's defense of the A-theory is a version of presentism in "The Privileged Present: Defending an A-theory of Time" 2008 and is a very helpful survey of the relevant issues and defense of presentism.

Steve Savitt considers time and the passing of time in relation to modern physics and the notions of being and becoming in Savitt 2017.

Carlo Rovelli 2018 and Lee Smolin 2014 are two prominent physicists (especially with respect to loop quantum gravity) who hold opposing views of the nature of time. Rovelli argues that our sense of the flow of time is a result of our limited perspective. Smolin attempts to defend our commonsense view of the flow of time.

The scientist and popular science book writer, Paul Davies, wrote *About Time: Einstein's Unfinished Revolution* 1996, a pleasant and instructive book on both scientific and metaphysical issues about time, including black holes, quantum time, and imaginary time. Like Smart, one of whose essays Davies cites approvingly, and Mellor, Davies is a B-theorist who subscribes to the block universe.

In addition to J. Richard Gott's *Time Travel in Einstein's Universe: The Physical Possibilities of Travel Through Time*, Robin Le Poidevin's *Travels in Four Dimensions: Enigmas of Space and Time* 2005 covers many issues related to the nature of time and considers the Grandfather Paradox in Chapter 10. Peter Christofuro 2019 can be found at Time Travel & the Grandfather Paradox Explained (astronomytrek.com).

CHAPTER TEN

GOD

Nature and Existence

PERHAPS IT'S PUZZLING TO FIND A CHAPTER ON WHETHER OR NOT GOD exists, and, if so, what God is, in a brief tour of metaphysics. God is not your ordinary "thing," of course. One of the tasks of metaphysics, though, is to tell us what *kinds* of things exist—so the question of the existence of God is a part of what metaphysics considers. And the traditional monotheistic notion of God has played a special role in the history of metaphysics. It is not only theists that had occasion to discuss the nature and existence of God; various philosophers, both theistic and atheistic, have thought that some concept of God has structured our thinking about the nature and make-up of the world. We begin by explaining a few of the attributes usually ascribed to God. Then, we will look at versions of the three main arguments for God's existence: the design argument, the cosmological argument, and the ontological argument. Lastly, we look at an argument that claims to show that the existence of God, as he is normally characterized, is logically incompatible with the existence of evil in the world.

Divine Attributes

God is perfect. That is the heart of the traditional monotheistic notion of God, especially of a *personal* God, that is, a divine being that has, to some extent, the same kind of characteristics, in the same way, as ordinary persons do (as opposed to being wholly indescribable, or wholly abstract). We will be exploring five divine attributes in more depth. They are *omnipresence, omniscience, omnipotence, eternality*, and *immutability*.

Omnipresence

Omnipresence is being present everywhere, but this requires clarification. Most philosophers and theologians have not been panentheists. *Panentheism* is the view that God is *in* or *interpenetrates* all that there is, including finite creatures or objects—or, more properly, the view that all is in God. Two influential American panentheists were the essayist Ralph Waldo Emerson (1803–82) and the twentieth-century philosopher of religion Charles Hartshorne.[1]

In *The Divine Attributes*, Joshua Hoffman and Gary Rosenkrantz note that omnipresence can mean literally being at every location. But of course, God is generally understood as a spiritual, not a material or a spatial being. God's omnipresence is not like being located everywhere in the same way that a puppy is located in the living room. So, Hoffman and Rosenkrantz conclude that this ordinary sense of omnipresence is not the sense in which it is a divine attribute.[2] In this they agree with a number of other philosophers and theologians. St. Thomas Aquinas influentially explained omnipresence analogically; that is, he thought of divine omnipresence as describing the extent of God's knowledge and power. God is everywhere in the sense that nothing is *outside* of God's control or his knowledge. An "earth-bound" analogy might serve: laws of nature govern and "control" everything in the physical world; nothing escapes natural law. In that sense, natural law is everywhere present. God is omnipresent then, but in a similar metaphorical, nonphysical sense.[3] Similarly God's knowledge also is *as though* he were present at all places—which leads us to our next attribute.[4]

---

1   See Hartshorne 1967 and 1976; Dombrowski 2013.
2   Hoffman and Rosenkrantz 2002.
3   Swinburne 1977; Hoffman and Rosenkrantz 2002.
4   See Swinburne 1977, p. 104.

Omniscience

God is **omniscient**: God knows everything there is to know. That God's knowledge extends to all truths may seem a truism, but it is more difficult to understand what this actually means, since "knowing all" is no doubt different in kind from ordinary human knowing. Aquinas again interpreted this analogically. Much of human knowledge is based on reasons. Yet God's knowledge is not mediated; rather it is direct and immediate. God doesn't make inferences, draw conclusions based on premises or reasons; much less did he acquire any knowledge by being told by some other being. Nor does God's knowledge depend on some sensory process, as much of human knowledge does. (Though, interestingly, Isaac Newton described space as God's "sensorium"—the sum of perception.) Thus, God's knowledge never requires an intermediary, whether that of some sensory state or some testimony or some inference. All things—all truths—are immediately present to God.

Much, perhaps all, of our knowing depends on or is *through* concepts. God's knowledge, however, is often described as *intuitive* knowledge. His knowledge is not dependent on concepts the way human knowledge is. Thus, the *content* of God's knowledge is perhaps difficult to describe. Yet, as omniscient, as all-knowing, the content of God's knowledge takes in all that there is to know.

Omnipotence

God's unlimited power is of course one of the central divine attributes; God's **omnipotence** is that he can do anything or is all powerful. Yet many theologians and philosophers have recognized a "limitation" on God's power. They suggest that God can't do the logically impossible; to the statement "God can do anything," they add the caveat "so long as that act is logically possible." But why? Wouldn't a genuinely all-powerful being be able to do *anything at all*? Most believers accept that God can defy the laws of nature—that's presumably what miracles are about. So, why not the laws of logic?

When we say "Sam can play the piano," we know what action we are saying he is able to do. Similarly, "God can make a mountain out of pure gold" ascribes a substantive ability that we understand, even though it takes a bit of imagination. Now imagine that someone insists that God can make a triangle with four sides, or an uncle who has no siblings, or a blue thing that's not colored, or a tree that's not a tree. Are we sure that there are things here for God to do?

The logically impossible is the self-contradictory. So if someone asks for a four-sided triangle, we want to say "*There's no such thing*," since a triangle with four sides contradicts its own nature. A triangle, to be a triangle, can't have four sides. Asking me to draw a triangle with four sides is asking me to draw... nothing. There is nothing that could correspond to this description. Unlike the phrase "gold mountain," which we all understand the meaning of, the phrase "triangle with four sides" names *nothing*. It is thus no limitation on divine power to say that God can't do the logically impossible.

Can God make a rock heavier than he can lift? Of course we should not imagine God as a super Hercules, wrapping his divine arms around a big rock, picking it up and hurling it into Hudson Bay. Still the question seems to involve a bit of a dilemma.

Suppose God makes a big rock, but can't lift it. Then there is something that God can't do—lift the rock. On the other hand, suppose every rock that God can make is a rock he can lift. Again, we stumble across something God apparently can't do—make a rock too heavy for even him to lift. God's power thus seems limited.

Perhaps this is another example of asking whether God can bring about the logically impossible. But some suggest that this example shows that the concept of omnipotence makes no sense; the concept of omnipotence is itself self-contradictory. Hoffman and Rosenkrantz suggest seeing the notion of omnipotence as a comparative notion: God is maximally powerful. No being is nor could be more powerful than God.[5]

Could God do something evil? Could God will a particular bad or evil circumstance to occur? The question immediately draws our attention to another of God's attributes—God's goodness, or *omnibenevolence*—and the issue of how an all-powerful and all-good God could permit the evil that we seem to see in the world. We explore a special version of this question in the last section of the chapter.

Aquinas suggests that God cannot do anything that violates his own nature. Perhaps you are familiar with some of the lyrics from "I've Gotta Be Me":

> I've gotta be me, I've gotta be me
> What else can I be but what I am

---

5   Hoffman and Rosenkrantz 2002, p. 167; similarly, see Clack and Clack 1988, pp. 66–69; for another view, see Swinburne 1977, pp. 153–58.

While this popular musical number hints at various philosophical questions about identity, it also points to something important about the divine nature. God's "character" is no accident. It's not that God just happens to be an "omni-nifty" guy. Quite the contrary. God's attributes are *necessary*; these attributes are part of what it is *to be* God. To put this another way, these attributes are essential to God's nature. Thus, God essentially wills the good.

Aquinas suggests, then, that is it no limitation on divine power to say that God is limited by his own essence.[6] To be able to will or perform some evil act is to be able to engage in an act that signals some sort of defect. God's inability to do evil is simply a result of possessing no defects. Hence, not "being able to do" evil is no limitation on God's omnipotence.

Brahman and Ātman

For many Westerners, Brahmanism is perhaps the more familiar philosophy of India. This view comes down to us through the Vedas, the Upanisads, and the oft-mentioned *Bhagavad Gītā*. These are the sacred hymns, texts, and scriptures of Hinduism.

While Hinduism is often associated with polytheism—especially Brahman, Vishnu, and Shiva—there is a form of Hinduism that might be seen as monotheistic.

In this view, the one ultimate reality is Brahman. All of creation is ultimately traceable back to Brahman, who is the ultimate creative force. (In some views, Brahman is properly thought of as an ultimate entity, not a person.) Indeed, early Vedic hymns characterize Brahman as *food*, a unique combination of matter and energy. In the monotheistic view, all Hindu gods are ultimately traceable to Brahman.

A particularly important manifestation of Brahman is Ātman, the ultimate consciousness, the (true) Self, or "controller." Each of us experiences our own particular egos, but we make a mistake if we think that this individual empirical ego is ultimately real. In fact, individual egos are but particular manifestations of Ātman. It is Ātman that is real. The *Upanisads* are particularly concerned with the nature of Ātman.

---

6   See Swinburne 1977, pp. 158–59.

And *moksa*, or liberation from the cycle of suffering, occurs when we attain the knowledge that not only are our egos manifestations of Ātman, but that Ātman and Brahman are in fact one—a unity which is suggested by the metaphor of two birds in one tree in the *Upanishads*. This knowledge can be attained in different ways, including by rigorous yoga practices, but also by study and reflection on the Hindu scriptures.

Eternal

Unlike all humans, God isn't here for a time and then—alas—gone. **Eternality** is one of the essential divine attributes; God wouldn't be God without it. There are, however, two very different interpretations of this attribute. The fundamental difference is whether God is *in* time or *outside of* time. If God is a temporal being, then he extends infinitely back in time and infinitely forward. God has a past, present, and future, and is thus described as *everlasting*. With the latter interpretation, God is atemporal or *timeless*. God is outside of time, and all moments in time are present to him at once.

By way of comparison, think of the number line, extending infinitely back and forward from zero. Let this line represent, not numbers, but moments in time. As a temporal being, God exists through all the moments of the "time line." The atemporal comparison is a bit trickier. God is not "in" the time line, but outside of it. Yet the entire line—every moment in time—is before him. Of course, it is easy to lapse into a description of a timeless God that makes use of temporal terms, e.g., saying that the entire time line is *always* present to him.

There is a significant drawback to the atemporal view. God acts; God creates; God speaks to some individuals; God intervenes through miracles. All these acts are *events*, God doing something. And events seem to be essentially temporal. Put a little differently, if God is to act *in time*, to intervene in temporal affairs, then it would appear that God, too, must be temporal or in time. Aquinas responds to this worry by noting that if God's decisions were made from eternity, there is no need to see God acting in time. The worry about acting *in time* arises because we think of God as "stepping" in at various points in time. But this is not the nature of God's decisions, in Aquinas' view. Still, critics of the timeless view might wonder how a "timeless intention" could nonetheless be manifested in time.

Immutable and Impassable

Does God change? Aquinas argued that since a perfect being is already perfect, there's no room for change.[7] For a supremely perfect being, supreme in power, knowledge, and goodness, remaining perfect requires staying as it is: no changes. Hence, God is often held to be *impassable*; he is held not to be susceptible to "mental changes." But is that right?

Three related concepts are important here. **Immutabilty** is the idea that there is no changing in any way whatsoever. Often attributed to the influence of Greek philosophy and Plato especially, this view is held by Augustine, Boethius (840–?), and Aquinas, who link immutability to timelessness; change occurs in time, so a God who is outside of time must be unchanging. A weaker notion than this is available, **incorruptibility**: a being is incorruptible if there can be no changes to that being's character. Finally, there is the notion of **impassability**, or the idea that a being cannot be a subject of emotions or feelings.

Various reasons suggest that God in fact changes—is not immutable or impassable—yet remains incorruptible. God may change attitude or opinion, or even be the subject at one time of one feeling or emotion and still another emotion at some other time. However, God remains incorruptible since his character—his essential goodness—does not change.

Various theologians and philosophers point to textual evidence in the Old and New Testaments, which seems to indicate that God is subject to various feelings: anger, compassion, and sorrow among them. Similarly various passages suggest a God open to persuasion or a change in intent. The most famous perhaps is Abraham "negotiating" with God over the fate of Sodom and Gomorrah, securing successive promises to spare the cities if a handful of good people are found. Similarly, various passages note that God *relents* because of suffering or that he is *concerned* about their distress. And books have been written about Job's "argument" with God over Job's misfortunes, followed by God's apparently defiant, "Who is this that darkeneth counsel by words without knowledge? Gird up now thy loins like a man; for I will demand of thee, and thou answerest me" (Job 38: 3–4).

Some think such passages are not simply metaphors or literary devices. While God remains incorruptible, some claim God can *increase* in value;

---

7   Aquinas 2008, Pt. I, Q. 9, Art. 1.

he does so through the activities of and his interaction with his creatures.[8] Others suggest that God's identifying with our suffering is a necessary component of understanding God's goodness in light of the terrible evil that befalls so many.[9] To some, an impassable being appears "lifeless" or "inhuman" or—worse—"impersonal."

An immutable view of the divine nature is coherent, however. But we leave the matter here. We will look at one additional attribute, *omnibenevolence*, later. But first we turn to three arguments for the existence of God.

Three Arguments

Arguments for the existence of God touch on a number of philosophical and theological issues, such as whether belief in a divine being is rational and what is the extent of what we can know about God. This brief survey leaves aside not only those issues, but also a number of other arguments for God's existence. These three, however, play a significant role in thinking about whether God exists.

The Design Argument

We begin with a version of the **design argument** (also known as the teleological argument), which holds that there is sufficient evidence of purpose or design in even brute and unfeeling nature to lead us to the conclusion that a designer—God—exists. *Telos* is a Greek word meaning "purpose" or "goal." Teleology is linked to design: if something is designed, then it is directed toward an end, some aim that it is designed to serve. Often enough, complexity or coordinated functioning of many components signal design or purpose—a given set of things working together because they were made to achieve some end. Some have found such "signals" of design in nature. As early as the seventeenth century, defenders of the existence of God found this sort of evidence in the complexity of parts of organisms.

At the heart of the teleological argument lies the thought that if we observe *design* or *purpose* in nature, then we require a very special explanation of that design. The empirical or *a posteriori* nature of the argument is then evident, since it is observation that leads us to recognize design or purpose

---

8   Hartshorne 1984, pp. 6–10; Viney 1985, pp. 36 ff.
9   Marilyn McCord Adams 1999.

in nature. The observation of this apparent purpose serves as the basis for inferring God's existence.

The structure of the argument is fairly simple: observations of nature provide good evidence of design. Some things occur or are found together—say, a pile of rocks and branches at the bottom of a steep slope—because of happenstance or an accidental convergence of factors; parts of the slope gave way after a heavy rainfall. But, in other cases—say, for example, the existence of DNA—there is reason to suspect more than just coincidence. We find parts working together to achieve an apparent goal. Such coordination seems to imply design, which of course implies the existence of a *designer*.

Perhaps the most famous version of this argument is by William Paley (1743–1805). At the beginning of his 1802 book, he encapsulates the spirit of his argument:

> In crossing a heath, suppose I pitched my foot against a stone, and were asked how the stone came to be there, I might possibly answer, that, for anything I knew to the contrary, it had lain there forever: nor would it perhaps be very easy to show the absurdity of this answer. But suppose I had found a *watch* upon the ground, and it should be inquired how the watch happened to be in that place; I should hardly think of the answer I had before given, that for anything I knew, the watch might have always been there. Yet why should not this answer serve for the watch as well as for the stone; why is it not as admissible in the second case as in the first? For this reason and for no other ... when we come to inspect the watch, we perceive—what we could not discover in the stone—that its several parts are framed and put together for a *purpose*.... There must have existed, at some time, and at some place or other, an artificer or artificers, who formed [it] for the purpose which we find it actually to answer; who comprehended its construction, and designed its use.... Every indication of contrivance, every manifestation of design, which existed in the watch, exists in the works of nature; with the difference, on the side of nature, of being greater or more, and that in a degree which exceeds all computation.[10]

10　Paley 2006, p. 7; second emphasis added.

Paley continues throughout the book to trace the evidences of design in the natural order. And the evidence of design or purpose in nature is the coordinated functioning we find, just as the coordinated functioning of the parts of the watch evidence design or purpose. In the case of the watch, we reasonably infer a designer ... and *maker*. Similarly, we are reasonably entitled to infer the existence of a designer and *maker* of nature—and by extension, the whole of the universe.

We are then, Paley holds, entitled to infer the existence of a "universe maker," that is, a creator. Of course, such an argument will say nothing about whether such a being possesses all perfections, whether such a being is omni-benevolent or perfectly just, or omniscient or omnipotent. In other words, the argument cannot prove the existence of a supreme being and creator. But as the last line of the passage above indicates, given the degree of complexity of design in nature, the creator of that complexity has to be pretty smart and powerful! Thus, the conclusion of the design argument is that nature gives us good reason to believe that there is a sufficiently powerful intelligence that made or created the universe. If this proof were compelling, such a conclusion would indeed be remarkable.

One of the more serious objections, heard especially recently, is perhaps the most obvious: Does the existence in nature of complicated coordinated systems warrant the inference to a powerful intelligence? Put another way, is Paley's the only explanation? Couldn't there be some purely non-intelligent explanation of this apparent design? Couldn't all this be explained by a "watch-maker" without purpose ... by a *blind watchmaker*?

> Paley's argument is made with passionate sincerity and is informed by the best biological scholarship of [Paley's] day, but it is wrong, gloriously and utterly wrong. The analogy ... between watch and living organism is false. All appearances to the contrary, the only watchmaker in nature is the blind force of physics, albeit deployed in a very special way.... Natural selection, the blind unconscious, automatic process which Darwin discovered, and which we now know is the explanation for the existence and apparently purposeful form of all life, has not purpose in mind.... It does not plan for the future. It has no vision, no foresight, no sight at all.... If it can be said to play the role of watchmaker in nature, it is the *blind* watchmaker.[11]

---

11   Dawkins 1986, p. 5.

The evolutionary biologist Richard Dawkins thus challenges the idea that design requires *intention*. In Dawkins's view, appeal to natural selection provides all the conceptual resources necessary to explain the "apparently purposeful form of all life." It should be noted that Dawkins agrees with Paley about one important matter. Dawkins suggests that prior to 1859 it would have been unreasonable to be an atheist. He thinks that the complexity of life—the complexity of the world—requires *some* explanation, and that Paley drew on the best science available at the time. That story, however, was seriously incomplete, and the fuller story dispels the basis for Paley's inference.

The eighteenth-century philosopher David Hume made several objections to the teleological argument. He questioned whether the universe showed features that necessitated a designer: whether it really is orderly and harmonious, and whether it is really complex—compared to what? He pointed out that we know by experience that artifacts—watches and buildings and so on—have designers; but we have no such experience of the designing of the universe— obviously a unique, completely different sort of thing. He mentioned that even if there were evidence the universe was intentionally designed, it wouldn't be evidence that there is a single designer, with the attributes conventionally assigned to God.[12]

Criticisms of the design argument need not deny the *function* of certain organs or chemicals or proteins. Ribonucleic acid, RNA, for example, serves several roles or functions in living organisms. And thus there is a sense in which, according to some, *purpose* can still be identified in nature. Ernst Mayr, one of the preeminent evolutionary biologists of the twentieth century, explains:

> Where, then, is it legitimate to speak of purpose and purposiveness in nature, and where is it not? To this question we can now give a firm and unambiguous answer. An individual who—to use the language of the computer—has been "programmed" can act purposefully.... [T]hey [organisms] all act purposefully because they have been programmed to do so.[13]

An "internal principle"—the genetic program—sets or fixes the purpose of a wide range of behaviors of individuals in the animal kingdom. Mayr calls this sort of view *teleonomy*. Purpose in nature is the result of law; thus we have

---

12 Hume 1980.
13 Mayr 1988, p. 31.

"law-governed" purpose. Critics thus claim that teleonomy preempts the need to invoke the design argument or a powerful *supra-natural* intelligence as the designer of the natural world. But Mayr claims that science offers an alternative account of what might otherwise appear to be design. This obviates the need for a non-natural explanation of the complexity that so struck Paley, presenting a real obstacle to the design argument.

The Fine-Tuning Argument

The design argument resurfaced in various ways in the late twentieth century, some of which may be familiar to you. But one version in particular is worth mentioning. This version is called the "fine-tuning" argument. The argument notes that if certain physical constants (such as the ratio of the strength of electromagnetism to the strength of gravity) were even slightly different, life would not exist. This, it is argued, cannot be simply the result of happenstance. Hence, there must be a designer. Many also think "fine-tuning" warrants believing in multiple universes; if there were many universes, many inhospitable and a few hospitable to life, we would of course find ourselves in one of the hospitable ones. To some, this notion of multiple universes shows that the fine-tuning we observe does not require a designer; for others, however, the idea plays a role in some of the arguments *for* a designer. In his 2011 *Where the Conflict Really Lies: Science, Religion, & Naturalism*, Alvin Plantinga devotes a chapter to analyzing the argument. He considers several objections to fine-tuning, including those that claim the fine-tuning argument involves a misinterpretation of the probabilities involved. In the end, he thinks that fine-tuning may offer some support for theism, but it is not compelling. A physicist's perspective and book-length treatment is Victor Stenger's 2011 *The Fallacy of Fine-Tuning: Why the Universe Is Not Designed for Us*. Stenger thinks that current physics and cosmology can explain those instances of apparent fine-tuning, without appealing to design.

The Cosmological Argument

Our second argument takes its cue not from a certain subset of natural things, but from all things, and that they all seem to have this feature in common: they come and go.

A NECESSARY BEING?

Qualia ... and God

Robert M. Adams's contributions to metaphysics, philosophy of religion, and philosophical theology are extensive. He is one of the leading proponents of divine command theory and, among his many essays, "Primitive Thisness and Primitive Identity" (1979) is still frequently cited in the metaphysics of particulars.

Perhaps you recall the notion of qualia from Chapter 6. Qualia are the *what it is like*, the *how it feels* of various kinds of experience. How something tastes, for example, is a qualitative experience; it's the having of a particular quale.

In an intriguing essay, "Flavors, Colors, and God" (1987), Adams suggests a surprising response to the difficulty of explaining why some particular neural event should be correlated with some one color rather than another, or some one taste rather than another. The most reasonable explanation for this connection, Adams suggests, is the existence of God: God correlated particular types of neural activity with particular types of qualia.

It is no surprise that many would resist this conclusion. But it perhaps points to the need for a general explanation addressing the relationship between qualia and the brain.

In the science fiction comedy *Back to the Future*, the main character Marty confronts the possibility that he *might not have existed*. The protagonist accidentally travels back in time to 1955 and finds himself caught up in the high school life of his parents. His presence threatens to keep his parents from falling in love, a possibility that threatens his existence. That he exists at all depends on his parents meeting and falling in love. There was nothing necessary about his existence; in fact, during various points in the movie, the character's existence depends on very slender threads—had circumstances been only slightly different here or there, his "future parents" might not have been his parents at all.

Beings that might not have existed—these are *contingent* beings. Beings that must exist, no ifs, ands, or buts about it: *necessary* beings. Of course, like the time-traveling Marty, you and I, the Grand Canyon, the Milky Way, are contingent beings. Is there a necessary being?

The notion of necessity is important in understanding the divine nature and in proofs for the existence of God. In addition to other divine attributes, theists hold that God differs from other beings or objects in this respect: God's existence is *necessary*. Indeed it's part of God's nature to *necessarily exist*. A contingent thing depends for its existence on other things and events; without them, it wouldn't have existed. They thus tend to come and go. A necessary being *must* exist.

The reason for this particular divine attribute, in the theist view, is easily found. God's nature is such that he possesses all perfections to an infinite degree. And, in addition to, say, omniscience or omnibenevolence, necessary existence is another perfection. Indeed, how could God only *contingently* exist? Could the divine nature be like that?

The **cosmological argument** trades on the notions of contingent and necessary beings; according to this argument, an adequate explanation of the existence of contingent beings requires the existence of a *necessary being*—God. Versions of the argument are traced to Plato, to Aristotle, and to medieval philosophers, such as the Persian philosopher Avicenna (980–1037) and the Jewish philosopher Maimonides (1135–1204). Later, Descartes and Leibniz, as well as Samuel Clarke (1675–1729), the English theologian and philosopher, all offered versions of the cosmological argument. Here we begin with a version offered by Thomas Aquinas as part of what he called the *Five Ways*.

THE FIVE WAYS

In the thirteenth century, St. Thomas Aquinas offered the *Five Ways*, five proofs for the existence of God. There is some disagreement about Aquinas' attitude toward the proofs, and the intended structure of and relationship among the proofs. Some hold, for example, that he was recounting then well-known arguments for the existence of God, arguments that every theologian should know. Some hold that the first three Ways are but different presentations of one argument; others consider that the first two make up a single argument, but hold that the Third Way is a distinct argument.[14] All of the proofs, however, are *a posteriori*: they reason from *observed* effects to the nature of the ultimate cause of those effects.

Whatever the final verdict on Aquinas' intent in presenting the proofs, there is wide agreement that the first three are instances (or, an instance) of the cosmological argument. Here is one translation of the Third Way:

---

14   Davies 1982, p. 39.

Our experience certainly includes things capable of existing but apparently unnecessary [contingent], since they come and go, coming to birth or dying. But if it is unnecessary for a thing to exist, it did not exist once upon a time, and yet everything cannot be like this, for if everything is unnecessary, there was once nothing. But if such were the case, there would now be nothing, because a nonexistent can only be brought into existence by something already existing. So that if ever there was nothing, not a thing could be brought into existence, and there would be nothing now, which contradicts the facts. And so not everything can be an unnecessary kind of being: there must exist some being that necessarily exists. But a thing that necessarily exists may or may not have this necessity from something else. But just as we must begin somewhere in a succession of causes, the case is the same with any succession of things that necessarily exist and receive this necessity from others. Hence we are compelled to suppose something that exists necessarily, having this necessity only from itself; in fact, it itself is the cause why other things exist.[15]

According to Aquinas, it is readily apparent that there are contingent beings. We observe them, and as is the nature of contingent beings, they come and go. They come into existence and then drop out of existence. It's obvious such beings aren't *necessary*, otherwise they would always be there. There must be, then, a necessary being, which brings the contingent beings into existence, otherwise there would have been nothing at some point.

Aquinas infers a necessary being as the ultimate *causal* source of contingent beings. It is through the necessary being's causal power that the contingent universe comes to be. And because this being is necessary, we do not need to look to something outside of it to understand why it exists. A necessary being is its own explanation. The point of the Third Way is to prove that such a necessary being exists.

The crux of Aquinas' argument is a striking assumption: If only contingent beings exist, there would have been a time when nothing existed. Had such a time existed—a time when nothing existed—there would be nothing now. And this is based on the principle, which comes to us from the ancient Greek philosophers, that from nothing, nothing comes; in Latin, *ex nihilo, nihil fit.*

---

15   Aquinas 1972, Pt. I, Q. 2, Art. 3, pp. 123–24.

The truth of this assumption, however, is a little less than obvious. Of course, any particular contingent thing will not exist at some time. But how does that fact give us a reason to think that there was a time at which no contingent things existed? There might have been an infinite series stretching backwards of contingent beings. Once we recognize this problem, the Third Way seems uncompelling.

Brian Davies, Thomist scholar and philosopher of religion, suggests that Aquinas no doubt was aware of these sorts of obvious failings in the Five Ways; others are not as sure.[16] Perhaps there is a different way to think about the structure of the argument.

ANOTHER VERSION

In 1948, some centuries after Aquinas wrote the Five Ways, a radio debate took place, broadcast by the BBC.[17] No, this wasn't about politics, or public policy, or cultural norms. It was a debate ... between two philosophers! Great philosophers to be sure—the great British philosopher Bertrand Russell and the philosopher Frederick Copleston, S.J., the author of a venerable multi-volume history of philosophy. At one point in that debate the issue arose of whether the existence of the universe required an explanation. Russell and Copleston took opposite sides, as they had during much of the debate. Russell held that the existence of the universe is just a brute fact—inexplicable. Once one has observed that the universe exists, there is nothing more to be said. Indeed, nothing more can be said. Copleston, on the other hand, held that the existence of something, even the universe, requires explanation. And Copleston invoked a "revised version" of the Third Way argument, suggesting that some necessarily existent "thing" must be invoked to explain how we have all these contingent beings. So consider the following.

First, contingent beings need not have existed. A contingent being comes about *because of* something else. Generally "local explanations" are enough for us. Where did this egg come from? That chicken. So we point to something else to explain the existence of any contingent being. If this "something else" is itself only contingently existing, the same question can arise. Where did that

---

16   Davies 1982 and 1992; Wippel 2006.
17   Transcript in Hick 1964, pp. 167–91.

chicken come from? This is also the story of your ancestors: where did grandma come from? Great grandma. And where did she ... well, you get the idea.

Instead of this "horizontal series"—the linear causal ancestry of any contingent being, e.g., grandparents, great grandparents, great-great grandparents ... —consider the "whole" of contingent being. How does a contingently existent being come into existence? Unlike the series including your great-great-great grandma, we are asking how there came to be any contingent beings *at all*.

The cosmological argument says: contingent beings came from a necessarily existent being. Any other answer—any appeal to more contingent beings—inevitably leaves us with the same question. The only answer—the only *satisfying* explanation—is this necessary being, which is always existing and can't not exist. Here we have the ultimate cause of all contingently existing beings.

Keith Yandell raises the same point about a similar version of the cosmological argument, an argument he formulates in considerable detail. Once the question is raised about why there are any contingently existing creatures, citing more contingently existing beings will not suffice, since that is indeed the point of the question. The options, Yandell notes, are three: refuse to answer; claim that this is an inexplicable fact about the nature of the universe; or appeal to something other than a contingently existing being.[18] Of course the theist is not willing to follow those who, like Russell, want to say that the contingent existence of everything is just a brute fact.

Russell's argument here is that in an endless series of contingent causes and their effects, there is an answer, at every point, in principle, to the question, "Why did X happen?" The answer is, "It was caused by Y." But if we shift the question to "Why did this whole series happen?" Russell claims that this is not a legitimate question. By analogy, he says, the fact that every person has a mother does not imply that there exists one mother for the whole of humanity.

We might spend a moment more on the "endless explanation" option. The theist thinks that tracing the history of contingently existing beings is no explanation at all.[19] Imagine Julia tells Jack that she will explain to him how to solve quadratic equations (e.g., $x^2 + 2x + 1 = 0$). One minor hitch: the explanation *goes on endlessly*. It's easy to see that Jack might think he isn't getting an explanation at all. Similarly, why should anyone be satisfied with

---

18 Yandell 1999, p. 196.
19 Pike 1977.

being given one contingent being after another, only to be finally told, this goes on forever; that's just the way it is?

So the critic, according to the theist, is left with the option of joining Russell, asserting that the existence of the universe is merely a brute, inexplicable fact. The theist then observes that "Why does this series of contingent beings exist at all?" seems like a legitimate question that deserves a real answer. If it is, it seems reasonable to conclude that a necessary being exists.

BUT IS IT REASONABLE?

Brian Davies addresses precisely this issue: Is this form of the cosmological argument reasonable?[20] It might make sense to disagree with Russell about whether or not there is a point to asking how the universe came to be. Davies, however, notes that the cosmological argument might be wildly implausible or even irrational, *even if* it makes sense to ask the question of origin.

Davies first examines whether our notion of cause is applicable in this case. Though his argument is considerably more detailed, Davies claims that our natural inclination is to think that it is reasonable to ask about the cause of all contingent being—and he finds that this is indeed the case.

It becomes harder to defend the reasonability of the cosmological argument when we ask a further question. Is it reasonable to accept that the cause of contingent existence is itself something *not caused*? Or, in other words, is it reasonable to accept that the cause of contingent existence is itself a necessary existent, requiring no explanation of what caused it?

The challenge to the defender of the cosmological argument can be put in this way. We insist on being told the *cause* of various things. We don't accept an infinite series because we think each new item in the series requires an explanation of its cause. But then we invoke this "new" kind of being, and say it causes *other* things... but this one doesn't need a cause! Now, how can defenders of the cosmological argument do this? How do they keep insisting on being told the cause, and then suddenly assert "Aha! here's 'something' that is itself uncaused!"?

Davies suggests that this uncaused cause not be thought of as a *being* like other beings.[21] The necessary cause is of a different order than contingent

---

20   Davies 1982, pp. 42–47.
21   *Ibid.*, pp. 46–47.

argument gave Anselm what he wanted—a "master argument," briefer and more readily accessible.[23] The argument drew an immediate and still discussed critical response from the French monk, Gaunilo. It was otherwise largely ignored for a couple of centuries, but in the thirteenth and fourteenth centuries philosophers and theologians began weighing in on the argument. Aquinas rejected it, as did William of Ockham, though it was defended by John Duns Scotus. Later on, Descartes gave a version in the *Meditations*, and Leibniz later undertook to bolster Descartes's version. Kant's criticism is, along with Gaunilo's, one of the two most known criticisms. Two twentieth-century philosophers, Norman Malcolm and Charles Hartshorne, undertook to refocus the argument. There is no consensus about the argument, and it remains one of the more discussed topics in philosophy. The argument's general outline, drawn from Chapter 2 of the *Proslogion*, is very simple. Perhaps this is part of its continuing lure: its apparent simplicity. Alvin Plantinga remarked that although no one has probably ever been led by the argument to believe in God's existence, there remains the suspicion that no one has yet given a full and convincing refutation of the argument.[24]

Why is it called the *ontological* argument? The argument proceeds by reflecting on God's nature or *essence*, and claiming to derive God's existence from his nature, or, more precisely, from our concept of that nature. This contrasts with both the design and Cosmological arguments. Whereas those arguments are *a posteriori*, proceeding from observed effects to the claimed cause, the ontological argument is *a priori*.

The outline of the argument is strikingly brief. Chapter 2 of the *Proslogion* is barely a page, and the argument occurs in a long paragraph:

> Now we believe that you [God] are something than which nothing greater can be thought. So can it be that no such nature exists, since "The fool has said in his heart, 'There is no God'" (Psalm 14:1) ... So even the fool must admit that something than which nothing greater can be thought exists at least in his understanding, since he understands this when he hears it.... And surely that than which a greater cannot be thought cannot exist only in the understanding. For if it exists only in the understanding, then that than which

---

23 Thomas Williams 1996a, p. xviii.
24 Plantinga 1967, pp. 26–27.

a greater cannot be thought is that than which a greater can be thought. But that is clearly impossible. Therefore, there is no doubt that something than which a greater cannot be thought exists both in the understanding and reality.[25]

The concept of God expressed at the outset is what drives the argument. When we think "God," what are we thinking? God is *perfect*. That's the divine nature—he lacks nothing. So to think of God is to think of the greatest being that could ever be conceived.

Is this idea of God perhaps something unique to Anselm, something "subjective"? Anselm takes himself to be expressing the "common concept" shared by all parties to the debate about God's existence, not some idiosyncratic notion. This is what we mean by "God": you can't think of anything greater because there isn't anything greater. If you can think of something greater, you haven't yet understood the concept of God.

Obviously, this concept exists in the mind—or, as Anselm calls it, the "understanding." Thus, the concept of that which nothing greater can be thought is at the very least *mentally real*. It is real because it exists in the mind.

Anselm now wants to draw his readers' attention to a very important point. A concept can be—and often is—about something existing *outside* the mind. The content (what the concept is about) might only exist *qua* mental item, or it might also exist externally, independent of the mind's conception. A whimsical example. You might have overheard someone say that Santa Claus is real because he's "really" in our hearts and minds. And since there's a real thought of that jolly old elf, Santa Claus is real to that extent. Still, famous newspaper editorials aside, Santa Claus doesn't exist *outside* the mind. A more practical example: think now of an American hundred dollar bill, Ben Franklin's likeness and all. That content is of course *mentally real*; as Anselm says, your concept of the hundred dollar bill exists in the understanding. But you'd feel a bit differently about that content if it existed outside the mind, say, tucked into the pages of this book, wouldn't you? Which is "better," the merely *mentally real* idea of that banknote? Or the referent of that idea existing *external to the understanding*—the money right there in your hand?

Anselm says that if we have a concept of a being greater than which nothing can be thought, that necessarily leads us to the idea that such a being exists

---

25 Anselm 1996, pp. 99–100.

not only in the mind, but outside the mind, as well. Compare these two concepts: (a) greater than which nothing can be thought, and existing *only in the mind*, and (b) greater than which nothing can be thought, and existing *outside the mind, as well.*

Which of these two concepts, Anselm asks, is really the concept of a being greater than which nothing can be thought? Anselm thinks that it is obviously (b). Given (b) then, God exists *externally*, not just in our minds, but also objectively, independently of our minds. Our concept of God leads to the conclusion that God exists *outside the mind*, or else we would have contradicted ourselves: we would not yet have the concept of that greater than which nothing could be thought.

By taking the concept of God, which expresses God's nature, and reflecting on that concept carefully, we find that we are committed to a God that indeed exits. The move from concept to conclusion might be put thus:

1. God is that than which nothing greater can be thought.
2. This entity, than which nothing greater can be thought, exists (at least) in the understanding.
3. Either that which nothing greater can be thought exists (a) only in the understanding, or (b) also outside the mind.
4. It is greater to exist outside the mind than to exist only in the mind.
5. So, if God is that than which nothing greater can be thought, then God must be thought as existing outside as well as in the understanding.
6. So, God exists.

GAUNILO: A PERFECT ISLAND

The monk Gaunilo thought he had diagnosed what was wrong with this argument. Given this line of reasoning, *the existence of the perfect anything can be proved!* The perfect apple pie, the perfect golfer, even the perfect island, an island "with an indescribable abundance of all sorts of riches and delights":

> Suppose someone tells me all this. The story is easily told and involves no difficulty, and so I understand it. But if this person went on to draw a conclusion, and say, "You cannot any longer doubt that this island, more excellent than all the others on earth, truly exists somewhere in reality. For you do not doubt that this island exists

in your understanding, and since it is more excellent to exist not merely in the understanding, but also in reality, this island must also exist in reality."[26]

The island example, says Gaunilo, demonstrates that there is something faulty about Anselm's reasoning. If "existence in reality" could be proved from the existence of the concept of the greatest X that can be conceived, then we would have to be committed to the existence of all sorts of perfect things. But this result is clearly a mistake. So, something is wrong with Anselm's argument.

Put the matter this way: which is better: something that exists or something that doesn't? That doesn't make sense: we aren't comparing two things, which differ only in properties. There's only one thing—the one that exists! This argument, it seems, gets off on the wrong foot from the word go by talking about two kinds of existence. Something that we only imagine doesn't exist, period.

Many agree with Gaunilo: you can't derive existence from a concept or a definition. Once you start with concepts, you're stuck with concepts. You

---

26   Thomas Williams 1996b, pp. 124–25.

need some further premise or claim to connect the concept (or the mental content) with a really existing object.

This objection suffers from a misunderstanding, Anselm claims. He notes that there is a difference between the concept of a *contingently* existing thing and a thing than which nothing greater can be thought. No island, perfect or otherwise, is "that than which nothing greater can be thought." To put this another way, Gaunilo thinks of the perfect one of a given *type*. But the argument is about the perfect type of thing *period*. There is nothing contradictory about the concept of a perfect island that doesn't exist. There is something contradictory about the concept of that than which greater cannot be thought, which still might not exist![27] Gaunilo's mistake is to think that the concept of any isle—"blessed," perfect, or otherwise—is analogous to the concept of an unsurpassable being.

KANT: EXISTENCE ISN'T A PROPERTY

Although Gaunilo's objection is still recounted almost a millennium later, undoubtedly it is Immanuel Kant's objection in his *Critique of Pure Reason* that is now the most widely endorsed objection. Simply, Kant held that existence is not a property, a claim which is sometimes cast as "existence is not a perfection." Kant claimed that nothing was added to the concept of something if we say that it exists. "By whatever and by however many predicates [property] we may think a thing—even if we completely determine it—we do not make the least addition to the thing when we further declare that this thing *is*."[28] If Sam tells Sara about a chair he saw at the department store—blue, a recliner, cotton fabric—he conveys to Sara the properties of the chair. She thus acquires a concept of the chair. Were Sam then to say, "Oh, yeah, and it exists," Kant claims Sam would add nothing to Sara's concept of the chair. Some think Kant's point is reflected in modern symbolic logic, which indeed treats existence differently from other properties. (Modern predicate logic employs an "existential quantifier" *there exists*; its "grammatical position" is different from the "grammatical position" of symbols for properties.)

Aside from modern logic, is there a good reason not to think that existence is not a predicate? Some do claim that existence is not like other properties.

---

27   Anselm 1996, pp. 132–34.
28   Kant 1965, p. 505.

And they might offer two kinds of reasons. First, some think that we assume existence when we explain the concept of some object, or "predicate" some characteristic of the object. Deirdre says that Julia is athletic; she's presupposing Julia exists. If attributing some property to an object already presupposes the object exists, then why "add in" that it exists? But William Rowe—who describes himself as a "friendly atheist" and has helped shape the current debates in philosophy of religion—thinks that this does not seem terribly convincing. We frequently ascribe properties or "predicates" to nonexistent objects. It seems perfectly legitimate to say that the Mad Hatter is having tea, even though the existence of the Hatter is not assumed.[29]

The second sort of reason stems from the function of our descriptions—we ascribe properties or characteristics to pick out the *type* of thing and the particular *individual*. Saying that the object exists serves neither of these functions. Again, Sam tells Sara the *kind* of thing—a chair—and which *one*. Describing it as existing apparently contributes nothing to this concept.

A defender of the ontological argument thinks this is not quite right. There are occasions when existence *adds* something. We learn something new about the concept of a car that drives itself when we are told, "Oh, yeah ... they've made some. It's not just a 'concept car' any longer." Again we can note Rowe's remark that "there is some question ... whether anyone has succeeded in giving a really conclusive argument for the view that existence is not a predicate."[30]

A NEW INTERPRETATION: HARTSHORNE AND MALCOLM

Two twentieth-century philosophers hold that the real version of the ontological argument occurs in Chapter 3 of the *Proslogion*. The theologian and philosopher Charles Hartshorne (1897–2000), who gave the first "modal version" of the argument (a proof that uses a system of modal logic), and philosopher Norman Malcolm (1911–90) both held that the core distinction in the argument is between that which can be conceived as contingently existing and that which can *only* be conceived as *necessarily* existing. Anselm's second sentence of Chapter 3 is direct: "For it is possible to think that something

---

29   Rowe 2000, p. 36.
30   *Ibid.*

exists that cannot be thought not to exist, and such a being is greater than one that can be thought not to exist."[31]

Malcolm held that while existence is not a perfection, *necessary existence* is a perfection.[32] He holds that the proof in Chapter 3 argues that God's existence is either impossible or necessary. Since the concept of God is not self-contradictory, God's existence is not impossible. Thus, God's existence is necessary. Hartshorne's modal logic version makes a similar point and is valid.[33]

Here is a slightly different, more informal version of the Chap. 3 argument, drawing on both Malcolm and Hartshorne. It relies crucially on what Hartshorne calls the "True Anselmian Principle," namely that which can only be thought as *necessarily existing* is greater than that which can be thought as *merely contingently existing*.

First, remember that God is that than which nothing greater can be thought. Suppose, then, someone, call him GK, accepts this notion of God but also claims this gives us no good reason to think God exists.

What happens if we or GK suppose God does not exist? What are we imagining? We are apparently imagining a being that might not exist, or that might exist at one time but not another. Hence, this being's existence depends on circumstance or something else.

Once we have arrived here, however, it looks like we have imagined only a contingently existing being. Does this sort of *contingently existing being* sound like a being than which nothing greater can be thought? Anselm, Hartshorne, and Malcolm suspect that even our imagined GK can think of something greater—a being who doesn't exist only contingently, but exists necessarily!

We are now at the heart of Anselm's Chapter 3 argument. When we conceive of a being greater than which nothing can be thought, we have two alternatives. Either we conceive of a being whose existence is contingent, or we conceive of a being whose existence is necessary. And by the "principle" that necessary existence is greater than contingent existence, it appears that we must conclude that God necessarily exists.[34]

Rowe has doubts about granting that a being greater than which nothing can be thought is indeed a possible being. If we grant that, we are in effect granting that God actually exists, or as he remarks, we are ceding a premise

---

31   Anselm 1996, p. 100.
32   Malcolm 1960, p. 46.
33   Hartshorne 1962, 1967.
34   Hartshorne 1965, pp. 85–108; Malcolm 1960, pp. 47–50.

"which is virtually equivalent to the conclusion that is to be proved."[35] Perhaps Anselm would not be dismayed by this criticism. Given the nature of the being under discussion, there is indeed a close connection between possibility and necessary existence. The ontological argument leaves us, then, not quite where we started, but with a question still to be resolved.

God and the Existence of Evil: Incompatible?

In 1755, an earthquake in Lisbon, Portugal, killed somewhere between 10,000 and 100,000 people. Four years later, Voltaire famously satirized one type of attempted reconciliation of such evil with an all-good and powerful God in his novella *Candide*. Candide, the story's protagonist, begins with a naïve and superficially optimistic belief, taught to him by a philosopher, that we live in "the best of all possible worlds." Gradually he becomes disillusioned when he is confronted by the extent of suffering in the real world. We might wonder about the possibility of a supremely good and powerful God given earthquakes and other *natural evils*, and also given *moral evils*—the Holocaust, horrifyingly and brutal abuses and murders of innocent victims, adult, child, and infant.

Theology and philosophy of religion treat this set of issues under the general heading of the "problem of evil." How are we to reconcile such tragedies with the existence of God—more specifically, a supremely powerful and benevolent God? The problem is now thought of as two distinct but related problems: the *logical* problem of evil and the *evidential* problem of evil. Both problems challenge the rationality of theistic belief. These arguments suggest that believing in a God, conceived as an omnipotent, omniscient, all-good being, is incompatible with an incontrovertible fact: evil exists. Either one must reject the existence of evil, it seems, or reject the notion of the existence of God as he is classically conceived.

The Logical Problem of Evil

J.L. Mackie's 1955 "Evil and Omnipotence" was the impetus for much contemporary discussion of the logical problem of evil. Mackie held that two propositions were *logically inconsistent*: that evil exists *and* that God is all-good, all-powerful, and all-knowing. The two propositions can't be true at the same time. Since the existence of evil seems undeniable, then logic

---

35 Rowe 2000, p. 41.

would appear to dictate giving up the other proposition, namely, that there is an all-good, omniscient, omnipotent God.[36] It is easy enough to supply the "missing steps" and make explicit the incompatibility. So far we have the following two propositions:

(1) God exists, and is omniscient, omnipotent, and all-good.
(2) Evil exists.

An all-good or omnibenevolent being would of course not permit evil, if he had the ability. So, let us add an additional step.

(3) An omnibenevolent being would not permit evil.

Just as an omnibenevolent being would not permit evil, an omnipotent being would have the power to eliminate suffering. And if such a being were omniscient, no instances of evil would go unnoticed. Thus, we have two more steps:

(4) An omnipotent being could prevent the occurrence of evil.
(5) An omniscient being would know of any instances of evil.

To put it somewhat starkly, God would have both "motive and opportunity." God would want to preclude evil—his omnibenevolence at work. And no possible evil could escape God's ability to keep it from ever occurring—his omniscience and omnipotence at work. Thus, we are led to this: if the God of the ontological argument exists—*no evil exists*.

Clearly this cannot be right. It seems to be an undeniable truth that there is evil in the world (though a few philosophers and theologians have disputed this). And we cannot have it both ways: the existence of an omni-perfect God is logically inconsistent with the existence of evil. Logical consistency requires us to give up something. Since the fact of the *real existence of evil* seems inescapable, Mackie claims the theist faces the unhappy option of giving up proposition (1), in the argument above.

Alvin Plantinga provided a particular type of *theodicy*, that is, an explanation that reconciles an all-powerful and all-good God with the existence of evil.

---

36 *Ibid.*, pp. 92–97; Adams and Adams 1990, pp. 1–3.

Plantinga's detailed and rigorous defense centers on free will.[37] He argues that it is logically possible that God could not have created genuinely free creatures while preventing the existence of evil. Human beings possessing genuine free will—making decisions, choosing between options—according to Plantinga, opens up the possibility that evil will also exist.

But could not an omnipotent God create free beings while also preventing evil? God's omnipotence, as we saw in the first section of the chapter, extends only to that which is logically possible. Plantinga argues that a world in which creatures freely choose to do the good must include the existence of bad choices, some of which cause suffering, sometimes great suffering. Free creatures choosing to do good things make a world more valuable than an "evil-less" world in which there is no free will. Further, Plantinga maintains that it may be logically impossible to have a world in which there is both freedom and complete absence of evil. Consider this example: a small child chasing a ball runs into the road and is badly injured; the resulting suffering for the child and his family is enormous. In what sort of world would this sort of thing be prevented by God? Maybe God would prevent small children from playing ball, or briefly take over the control of cars when tragedy is imminent. Either way, we would be controlled by such a God in this sort of case and in countless others, ways that limited our freedom to make our own decisions. Most, including critics of the theistic position, now concede that the "free will theodicy" satisfactorily answers Mackie's logical problem—that is, it shows that it's *logically possible* that a benevolent God and *apparent* evils co-exist—that is, given the possibility that these "evils" are only apparent and are necessary for the greater good.

The Evidential Problem of Evil

Still, many critics of the idea of a perfect God suspect that a more serious version of the problem of evil remains: the *evidential problem of evil*.[38] William Rowe's account of the evidential problem is the center of recent discussion. Rowe does not claim that *any* evil is incompatible with God's existence. Rather, he claims that there is *too much* intense suffering. Surely the omni-perfect God could have prevented *at least some*: must the fawn suffer for hours or days after

---

37   Plantinga 1990.

38   E.g., Rowe 1995.

being badly burned in the forest fire? Couldn't such a God have prevented at least a million of the Holocaust deaths?[39] Rowe's version of the argument is elegantly succinct:

1. There exist instances of intense suffering which an omnipotent, omniscient being could have prevented without thereby losing some greater good or permitting some evil equally bad or worse.
2. An omniscient, wholly good being would prevent the occurrence of any intense suffering it could, unless it could not do so without thereby losing some greater good or permitting some evil equally bad or worse.
3. [So] There does not exist an omnipotent, omniscient, wholly good being.[40]

The force of this argument is readily apparent. *Some* of the horrible suffering that we read about or see or experience must be unnecessary. Consider the Lisbon earthquake. Had God moved the earthquake to a sparsely populated area of the earth, or reduced its force a bit, or eliminated it altogether, a tremendous amount of very serious suffering would have been prevented. Plantinga's point is that it is *logically possible* that all that suffering was necessary for a greater good, and that even a little less suffering wouldn't have done the job. Critics agree that it's logically possible, but wonder whether there's good reason to think that *all suffering* is really necessary for the existence of free will. Suppose we just concentrate on *unnecessary* evils. There appear to be plenty of examples of this. And if there is such unnecessary evil, then an all-powerful, all-good God does not exist. We will touch on three common theistic responses that are worth considering. All these present perspectives for seeing apparent evil as necessary.

God Knows Best

Creatures' relationship to God is like that of child to parent. Children often do not know, indeed, cannot even understand the "why" of their parents' behavior. Yet this doesn't necessarily mean the parents aren't good or that they aren't extremely powerful relative to their children. Similarly, God's creatures

---

39   E.g., Taliaferro 1998, Chap. 9.
40 · Rowe 1979; Adams and Adams 1990, pp. 127–28.

might not understand the *reason for* the suffering we witness. Our inability to discern God's purpose or to see justification for the suffering that occurs reflects human limitations. It just might be that the suffering we notice is, after all, necessary, but we don't see how it is. It need not reflect God's lack of power or goodness. We cannot then conclude that God is not both omnibenevolent and omnipotent.[41] But consider this analogy. A small child sometimes cannot understand how his parents could be benevolent when they take him to the dentist or deny him another cookie. But that means that the child, of course, doesn't understand what real benevolence is. If that is like our position with regard to God, then we don't understand what real benevolence is either, and, lacking that concept, our talk is something like nonsense when we attribute "benevolence" to God.

Soul-Making

In his *Evil and the God of Love*, John Hick offered another sort of view on why suffering might actually be good for us: it serves for "soul-making."[42] Also relying on the parent-child metaphor, Hick emphasized our moral development. In Hick's view, suffering is essential to that development and thus essential to the relationship between creature and Creator. Especially important, in this view, is the role that suffering plays in the process of creatures coming to see and accept God's love. So, for example, every bit of the massive amount of suffering caused by the Lisbon earthquake was effective and essential for humanity's moral development. Still some suspect that every bit of the suffering is necessary for our moral development.

God's Participation in Suffering

Marilyn McCord Adams (1943–2017) emphasized a Christian resolution of the evidential problem.[43] She emphasized the *passability* of God—his emotional nature. God participates in the suffering of created beings by becoming one of them. The incarnation—Jesus, as a person of the Trinity, becoming a human being—is the bond between Creator and creature in which God both experiences the suffering of created beings and honors that suffering,

---

41   Wykstra 1984.
42   Hick 1978.
43   Marilyn McCord Adams 1999.

according to Adams. She also claimed that her view provides a present justification for intense suffering: a person can find meaning or justification in suffering through seeing God's own experience of that suffering. So this means—again—that suffering is actually a good thing, and God is benevolent in creating or allowing it. This understanding of "benevolence" might seem suspect, however. We perhaps understand parents whose benevolence extends to letting their children "learn from their mistakes" and the suffering of both child and parent that might go along with such learning. Parent and child perhaps become closer. But do we really think it's reasonable if a mother lets her child go through extreme and continued suffering because the mother also suffers and such mutual suffering will draw them closer? Might we not insist instead that more reasonable persons intervene and protect the child from such "bonding"? Whether one finds, or *should* find, satisfactory these or any of the other many responses to the evidential problem of evil need not be settled now. It suffices to note that the evidential problem of evil continues to draw the attention of both theist and atheist. In doing so it perhaps draws attention, as critic and proponent alike have noted, to the ultimate nature of the human condition.

Key Concepts

- omnipresence
- omniscient
- omnipotence
- eternality
- immutability
- incorruptibility
- impassability
- design argument
- cosmological argument
- ontological argument

Reading Questions

1. Explain how theists defend the claim that God is omnipotent. Do you think it is a limitation on God's power to not be able to "do" the logically impossible? Do you think it is a limitation if God can't do something evil? Explain.

2. What are the two ways of understanding God's eternality? Which of these two do you think is the better interpretation? Why?

3. Explain the *Proslogion* Chapter 2 version of the ontological argument? Do you think Anselm succeeds in responding to Gaunilo? Why or why not?

4. How would you explain the difference between the Hartshorne/Malcolm interpretation of the ontological argument and the Chapter 2 version? Do you think Hartshorne and Malcolm give us a better version of the ontological argument? Why or why not?

5. What is the logical problem of evil? The evidential problem?

6. How would you assess Plantinga's response to the logical problem of evil? Which of the three responses to the evidential problem seems most promising? Why?

For Further Reading

Most surveys of the philosophy of religion include sections or chapters on divine attributes. Clack and Clack 1998, Brian Davies 1982, and Charles Taliaferro 1998 are all very helpful. Joshua Hoffman and Gary Rosenkrantz 2002 is a book-length consideration of the relevant issues. Richard Swinburne 1977 is still a classic work, which analyzes various interpretations as well as presenting Swinburne's own view. Chapter 8 explores the question of whether God is free.

Again, standard introductions to the philosophy of religion cover the arguments for the existence of God, e.g., Rowe 2000. David Hume 1980 includes his critique of the design argument, as well as his reflections on the problem of evil. Keith Yandell 1999 engages in a very detailed analysis of the Five Ways, especially the Cosmological argument and the ontological argument. Alvin Plantinga 1968 includes several important essays on the ontological argument. Charles Hartshorne 1965 is his evaluation of historical views of the ontological argument together with a presentation of his own view. Donald Viney 1985 is a helpful account of Hartshorne's work.

Marilyn McCord Adams and Robert M. Adams 1990 is an excellent collection of essays on the problem of evil, which includes Alvin Plantinga 1990. Nelson Pike 1958, although ostensibly a commentary on another essay, is also helpful in understanding the traditional problem of evil. Again, philosophy of religion introductions typically explain and analyze the problem of evil; William Rowe 2000 includes a balanced, excellent presentation of the difficulty. Thomas Senor 1995 includes several essays on the rationality of faith, some of which address specific issues related to the problem of evil. Marilyn McCord Adams 1999 offers a unique perspective and approach to the problem of evil. Taliaferro 1998 has a very nice survey of the problem of evil, including extensive quotations from original sources.

Zimmer 1951, Pt. III, Chap. III is an exploration of Brahmanism, with extensive quotations from the Hindu Scriptures. Michael Molloy 1999, now in its eighth edition, includes an extensive chapter on Hinduism, and is intended for students and lay audiences. It is replete with photographs that Molloy took during his travels through the many historical sites of the world's religions. Carl Olson's 2007 is also a wide-ranging and accessible exposition of Hinduism.

CHAPTER ELEVEN

WHY IS THERE SOMETHING RATHER THAN NOTHING?

WILLIAM JAMES CALLED IT THE FIRST QUESTION AND "THE DARKEST in all philosophy."[1] *Why is there something rather than nothing?* James was decidedly pessimistic about our ability to answer it. Yet the question continues to intrigue philosopher and physicist, theologian and student. Cosmological questions can easily lead from science to philosophy and back.

Setting the Stage

Why questions ask for an explanation. An explanation that tells us *why* there is anything—any *world*—at all, or more specifically, why there is this world rather than nothing, would seem to be telling us something very basic or ultimate. Finding such an explanation, however, is more than a little daunting.

---

1   James 1911, p. 38.

Asking for an explanation of why there is something rather than nothing differs from asking "what caused this to be?" about every particular object we encounter. Gottfried Leibniz, for example, noted that we must turn from being natural scientists (his term), asking about the beginning of particular objects, to asking a metaphysical question, "Why is there something rather than nothing?" Leibniz held that reason demands that there be a sufficient reason for the existence of any fact, even of a "fact" like the existence of the world taken as a single totality. This **Principle of Sufficient Reason**—the principle that "each thing that exists has a sufficient reason why it exists"[2]—is itself controversial. Still it is worth noting that many—but not everyone—thinks that there is some explanation that could be given, were all the facts known.

The idea of a sufficient reason invites thinking about the rather different ways one might approach the question of existence. We might suspect, along with James, that we can provide no answer to the question "Why is there something....?" James thought that answering this question was beyond our cognitive ability. He called this question "the darkest in all philosophy"[3] and believed that it was so deep that human thought would never be able to answer it. Another reason, however, that there might be no answer is that the question is like "What time is it right now on the Sun?"—a bit of nonsense. "Why is there ...?" questions, after all, are appropriate for an object within a spatio-temporal setting, when there is something different from that object to explain it. But that question makes no sense when asked about *everything*.

Suppose, however, one thinks that an answer can be given. This broad category—being able to give an answer—can then be separated into two broad categories: the necessary and the contingent. That is, one category of answer to the question provides a version of the answer "It must be this way" or "It's necessary that there is something rather than nothing." The contrary of this is that "It's purely contingent" or "It just happened." We will see later that some describe this as a "brute fact."

The *world*, as we will use this term, comprises all objects, along with their characteristics and relations to other objects; this includes the space and time in which these objects are located, and any additional dimensions that may exist. (Some physicists and cosmologists speculate there may be ten dimensions.) In addition, using "world" in this way includes not only our solar system and

---

2   Michael Della Rocca 2012, p. 139.
3   Russell 1959, p. 46.

our Milky Way Galaxy, but all others as well. The *world* is everything that is, including that which lies outside the observable universe.

But philosophers and cosmologists speak of other, merely possible but not real worlds. One of these worlds (perhaps) is the *null* or empty world. The *multiverse* refers to all of these worlds combined. In referring to the multiverse, we are referring to worlds *in addition to this one*. Some might be smaller, some larger; some with only slight variations in physical laws and magnitudes, some hugely different. These are entirely distinct. At the very least, there would seem to be a countably infinite number of them.

"Why is there something rather than nothing?" can now be interpreted in two ways (at least!). First, it might be understood as, "Out of all the possible worlds, why is *this* world a world in which there is something instead of nothing?" Thus, the question asks why is ours a non-empty world, a world with something in it, as opposed to the empty world.

There is a second way to understand the question: In all the worlds in the multiverse, why is *this particular world* real, rather than any other world, whether one of the infinite merely possible worlds or the empty world? Why is our world like this? Isn't it at least possible that our world with different laws and objects might have existed? Current estimates are that there are 10^{80} basic particles in the observable universe, and we learned at an early age that the speed of light is 186,000 miles per second. Surely there might have been fewer particles or the world might have been finite rather than infinite, as it is currently thought. Some answers or explanations intend to provide answers only to the former—why is there anything at all—while some approaches intend to explain not only this question, but also why there is *this particular world*.[4]

Necessary or Contingent?

As noted above, the first type of explanation invokes or adverts to the necessity of something rather than nothing. This approach in fact branches. One branch is that of what we might call a traditional answer. The traditional approach appeals to the existence of a necessary being, and that being is, in turn, causally responsible for the existence of the contingently existent objects in the world. Of course, this necessary being in the Western tradition and in religions such as Islam, Judaism, and Christianity is thought of as *God*.

---

4   See Derek Parfit 1998.

In some Hindu traditions Brahman necessarily exists.[5] A necessarily existing being could not have failed to exist. So, there could *not* have been nothing. Of course, the hard part of such an approach is showing that there is such a necessarily existing being. And in a moment, we will look at one argument that attempts to show that the obvious existence of *some thing*—you, me, this clock on the table, the Grand Canyon, bits of gold, electrons, Cleveland, or the moons of Jupiter—commits us to the existence of a necessarily existing being.

Another appeal to necessity seeks to show that there are "un-godly" objects, which still exist necessarily, namely abstract objects. Again, we will see interesting answers offered.

Could It Be Just a Brute Fact? Or a Confused Question?

Before looking more closely at the necessitarian approaches to the question, consider one type of alternative response. In Book I of his *Physics*, Aristotle implies (but does not state explicitly) that the world had no beginning. Aristotle claims that matter—or any object or state of the world—could have only come from some precedent matter. There is no beginning to this chain of matter. Trace this chain as far back as you please; pick any object or group of objects—some matter will *necessarily* have preceded it. This *a priori* argument, drawn from the Aristotelian understanding of the concept of matter, leads to the conclusion that *necessarily*, given that there are objects—alternatively, that there is matter—there *could not have been nothing*.

Once again, however, we are drawn to see that there are two different options before us. An Aristotelian notion of matter gives rise to a type of *necessity* response. Thinking about the "stuff" in the world can also lead to a second, very different option that there is no explanation for this *contingent* but endless series of stuff, extending back "beginninglessly" in beginningless time. Why is there something rather than nothing? There just is something; there is no explanation, much less any deep metaphysical explanation.

Let's call this second option the "brute fact" answer. It holds that *the fact that* there is something rather than nothing admits of no explanation. And it admits of no explanation because there isn't any reason why there is something rather than nothing. Not theology, not science, not philosophy can discover the reason, since there is no reason to be discovered. When Fr. Frederick Copleston

---

5   See C.J. Bartley 2013, Chaps. 1 and 4; J.N. Mohanty 2000, Chap. 5.

asked *inter alia* during their "famous" debate, "Why is there something rather than nothing?" Bertrand Russell demurred, responding that there is no answer to that question; there just is something—and that's a brute fact.

"Brute facts" might be thought of as the starting point, the basic or the primitive. Upon reaching a brute fact, we've reached something primitive, something basic—and the end of explanation-giving. There is, for example, an explanation of the motion of the tides and the elliptical orbits of the planets in our solar system. We learn from Isaac Newton that the universal attractive force—gravity—is at the heart of the explanation. We learn further from him that the attractive force between any two bodies is inversely proportional to the square of the distance between them. But that there is this attractive pull, that there is gravity is a brute fact: there is no answer. Why is it inversely proportional to the distance between two bodies? Newton warns us not to "hypothesize" about it.

It might take a certain mindset to accept some feature or state of the world as a brute fact. Counting something as a brute fact or "just obvious" may preclude legitimate explanation or discovery. Einstein's Special Theory of Relativity (1903) provides an explanation of gravity. Refusing to count one of Euclid's axioms as self-evident eventually led to the discovery of non-Euclidean geometry. One mustn't grant brute-fact status too easily. When Copleston insists that there must be an explanation for the fact of something existing, despite Russell's calm acceptance, he is insisting that we can find another explanation. Yet Russell was unmoved. He thought there was no further explanation to be offered. Perhaps any "theory of the world" must take something as basic and inexplicable. The hard part of course is identifying those features of the world that admit of no deeper explanation, whether scientific or philosophical.

Others have argued that the question itself is confused, that is, we are asking a type of question that simply doesn't apply to that "domain," much like asking "what time is it on the Sun?" This criticism holds roughly that it makes sense to answer of any particular object or group of objects why they exist. But it is a conceptual confusion to ask of the whole, of the world or the multiverse, why it exists.[6] Here again, as with the "brute fact" option, we may have reached a fundamental difference in outlook about the types of legitimate "why questions" and explanations.

---

6   See, for example, Stephen Maitzen 2013.

It Can't Be Nothing vs. Subtraction

Suppose we follow Copleston's suggestion and look for some explanation that something exists. We have already seen one line of thought deriving from Aristotle: it's impossible for there to be nothing. Aristotle's view depends on his concepts of matter (and cause). More recently, a different argument arrives at a similar conclusion.

There's Nothing to Our Concept of Nothing

Initially it seems as though we have a grasp of the concept of nothing; not all agree, however. If there is no content to the concept, then there must be something. Bede Rundle holds that we cannot *conceive* of nothing.[7] Since nothing is explicitly inconceivable, it is not sensible to ask why there is something rather than nothing. Initially it seems to us there are two options—something and nothing. But, according to Rundle, a little reflection tells us that there is no second option. There can only be something; thus, something is inevitable.

Why does Rundle think that there is no content to our concept? A short answer is that we are always "cheating." He "suspect[s] that our attempts at conceiving total non-existence are irredeemably partial."[8] We might start by taking away the objects, by "subtraction," as though we were taking out the objects in the room one by one. But an empty room is not nothing. Nor is an empty space, no matter how big that space is. Indeed, a popular account of the Big Bang holds that there was literally nothing—certainly no things, but also no space and no time—prior to the primeval explosion. Yet we have no way of conceiving this complete absence. Rundle argues that our grammar—the way we talk about such things—may deceive us into thinking there is some content to our concept of nothing. As he notes, the proposition that there might have been nothing is not a truth about anywhere, or about the way things might have been. Indeed, that proposition does not describe "anything at all."

Rundle suggests that the notion that there might have been nothing at all is shown to be incoherent because a particular fact would still exist—there is nothing. We cannot, he urges, get away from the existence of this fact. Thus, an apparently empty world still contains something: this fact.[9]

---

7   Rundle 2004, pp. 108–17.

8   *Ibid.*, p. 110.

9   *Ibid.*, p. 112.

We think that "nothing" refers, yet this is a mistake. Notice, for example, our apparent difficulty in thinking about *what it is like* prior to the Big Bang. In Rundle's view, it's not that it's difficult. It's impossible! Rundle goes on to argue that there has to be a material world, although this materialism should not be identified with physicalism or the naturalism held by many today, including philosophers and scientists. But we need not pursue that here. Rather, consider a sketch of an argument that illustrates that there might have been nothing.

Subtraction Argument: A Possibility of Nothing

Rundle suggests that we never quite succeed in thinking about nothing, even if we imagine taking objects away, one by one. The **subtraction argument** suggests that we can give sense to **metaphysical nihilism**—that there might have been nothing at all—by doing just this.

The critic of Rundle might argue that Rundle is asking for something that cannot be provided: we can't describe nothing. Indeed, Rundle offers just this sort of retort on behalf of his critic. Rundle, however, argues that we are mistaken if we think we are talking about *how things might have been.* Existing and not existing occur within a way of thinking, a framework which presupposes something.[10] The critic, however, may insist that of course we cannot *describe* nothing. But that does not show the logical incoherence of nothing existing. Rundle is not without a line of response, however. He is not arguing that we are unable to describe the attributes of *nothing.* Rather he is claiming that our way of thinking is such that we can't have a concept of nothing. We are always conceiving of *something.* We always cheat a little, imagining, say, some giant empty vessel.

One further perhaps speculative account of the concept of nothing might be offered. Concepts about objects, even theoretical objects (such as quarks or possible worlds) are *discriminatory.* To have a concept of electron seems to involve being able to say when we have one and when we don't. (This is not to rule out "vague" concepts, but vagueness is not the issue here.) This much should be acceptable to both Rundle and critic. But, the critic might ask, don't we have a reasonably clear idea of when there is nothing and when there isn't? Indeed, it might seem unfair to require someone to explain what this nothing is like—precisely because nothing is not like any*thing,* whether that thing be an object, a mind, a space, or some tenth dimension. Thus, the advocate of

---

10   Rundle, *op. cit.*, p. 113.

the coherence of the concept of nothing might insist that this is enough to rebut Rundle.[11]

This dispute is not easy to resolve. It might turn on what we expect of a concept, or more precisely, a concept of nothing. Somewhat analogously, we are sometimes presented with a picture of our universe endlessly expanding. Being told that there is *nothing* outside our universe might signal that we have a genuine concept of nothing, or, Rundle might claim, that we have reached the limits of coherence. Or it might turn on some deeper intuition about metaphysics. There is, however, a different path to the idea that there *must* be something.

Necessitarianism: It *Must* Exist

Suppose that our concept of nothing signals a genuine alternative to something existing. That is, for the moment set aside those, such as Rundle, who think that "nothing" (in this metaphysical context) fails to describe a contrast to "something exists." There is nonetheless a type of argument to show that *it is necessary that something exists*. Alternatively, it's not possible that nothing would have existed. This view is sometimes called **necessitarianism**.

A necessary being is a being that cannot fail to exist. Consequently, this type of being neither begins nor ceases to exist. Our experience, however, is with contingent beings. Whether animal or artifact, quark or quasar, plant or planet—even our universe: one and all came into being. And will "someday" cease to exist. One and all are contingent. Each has some cause or set of causes. Geologic structures like the Sierra Nevada or the Great Lakes or the Grand Canyon came about as the result of some long, complicated chain of causes. Our universe too, according to some, had a cause, albeit a very different kind of cause—a sort of random bubbling of a quantum field.[12] Contingent beings come and go; not so a necessary being—if there is such a being.

Two points can be drawn from this. If a necessary being exists, we would have an answer to why there is something rather than nothing. Because there is a necessary being, nothing was never an alternative. This differs from a view such as Rundle's. Rundle thinks there is no real contrast to something. But someone who points to a necessary being can very well accept that there

---

11   See Gonzalo Rodriguez-Pereyra 2013, pp. 197–214, for further discussion of the subtraction argument.

12   See, for example, Lawrence Krauss 2013 and Alex Vilenkin 2007, esp. Part I.

is some content to "nothing," while still holding that the possibility of there being nothing is necessarily excluded.

A second point is that an argument for the existence of a necessary being is not an argument about the Big Bang or about the physical origins of the universe. It is different in kind from the theories proposed by physicists and cosmologists such as Lawrence Krauss and Alex Vilenkin. Theirs are theoretical hypotheses or arguments, certainly. The theoretical background of such hypotheses is our best empirical theories and the relevant data that can be brought to bear. An argument for a necessary being, of course, exceeds the theoretical reach of scientific cosmology. Many deny the existence of something outside the reaches of science. That isn't quite the issue here. The point is that an argument for a necessary being is not your typical empirical or scientific argument.

Arguments for the existence of a necessary being are of two types: ontological or beginning from observation. The ontological argument for the existence of God—one of the two most famous arguments in philosophy—begins by looking at the nature or essence of this being, and concludes that God necessarily exists (see Chap. 10). The second type of argument begins with an observation of some fact about our world and proceeds to ask, "How is it possible that this fact could obtain?" Both types of argument differ from the arguments we find in contemporary scientific cosmology. Sooner or later, in both types of argument, we take a distinctly metaphysical turn.

Within this view, we can identify three different approaches. The first argues that our world is a *Spinozistic* world. Once we understand the nature of this world, we see that this particular world had to exist; it could not be otherwise than it is. This of course is a very strong claim. A related argument attempts to show that the existence of this world leads to the conclusion that there is a necessarily existent being, a being that is in some way responsible for the existence of the world. The third argument holds that there are necessary existents, perhaps not beings or objects in the way we normally think of such things. Yet we can identify these existents, and more importantly, argue that they exist necessarily. That is, it is not possible that they should not have existed. Let's consider each of these in turn.

Ours Is a Spinozistic World

The seventeenth-century Rationalist philosopher Benedict de Spinoza argued that once we properly understand the concept of substance, we will see that the existence of this world is necessary. This is a considerably stronger claim than the simple "some world (or other) must exist." (Indeed, in the last part of his principal work, *Ethics*, Spinoza argues that our rational recognition of the nature of our world and its necessary manifestations will lead to a "taming" of the passions and bring us closer to a happy life.)

Starting with the concept or definition of substance proves important for arriving at a "Spinozistic world." We may think of most objects as independent from one another, that is, each object is not dependent on any other object. We can presumably think about particular individual objects without reference to other objects. To keep the Spinozistic flavor, call such an object *substance*. But now ask what it is to be such a substance, that is, independent in both reality and thought. This Potpourri Press coffee cup sitting before me does not qualify as such a substance. Initially it might seem that I can have a conception of the cup independent of anything else: cylindrical in shape, an image of cardinals flying near a pine tree on the side, porcelain. Consider then its coming into being; its existing at all depends on a group of workers some twenty-five years ago. And its continued existence depends on my not knocking it over or the table it sits on not collapsing. Of course, the cup is part of a much more extensive causal network that we need not trace. Rather the thought is that as we think about what it is to be completely independent, to not depend on anything else, we can be led to the conclusion that only the "Whole" is independent in this way. That is, only the "Whole" is causally independent of any other substance. Spinoza called this "Whole" *God*. Equivalently, God is *Nature* or *Substance*. And if God or Nature is genuinely independent, then it cannot have been brought into existence by something else. So, it must have always existed, since no contingent being can bring itself into existence. This cup, that pup, this table, Cleveland—one and all had a beginning, dependent on something else. They are thus contingent; they might not have existed. But God—the Whole, Nature, or Substance—is not like this. Nothing brought Nature, God, (genuine) Substance into being. Hence, it is not contingent. And it necessarily exists. There is no beginning to Substance, and there is no end.

(There are similarities between Spinoza's argument and the classical versions of the ontological argument presented in Chap. 10. But there are important differences. For example, in Spinoza's view there is nothing over and above Substance. That is, there isn't creator and created. There is only the one Substance, conceived in different ways.)

It is important to be clear about the claim of this argument. Our universe, everything in it, all of its characteristics and features, is one indivisible, necessarily existing whole. Oh, we might think about supposedly "individual" objects: Andie might think about that girl, or a paleontologist might think about some fossil, or you might wonder about your car keys. But such thoughts merely reflect our ignorance of the true character of Nature. These thoughts are but partial grasps of Nature or Substance; we are mistaken about the nature of these "individuals." This idea is not unique to western metaphysics. Some versions of Hinduism, for example, hold that the objects of ordinary experience—including our individual egos or minds—are merely apparent. They hide or mask the "real Reality."[13]

Clearly there are steps in this argument that should be queried. Among these is the thought that there is any such truly independent substance. This is in fact one notion of substance, one that various thinkers before Spinoza took seriously.[14] While the notion of individual substance has not disappeared from philosophy (as we saw in Chap. 5), perhaps we should content ourselves with a notion of *contingent* individual substances.[15] In a moment we will see a different type of necessitarian response to the supposition that there are only contingent beings. Still, this Spinozist frame offers a way of thinking about how to resist the idea that there might have been nothing.

Before leaving the Spinozistic world, it is worth pointing out how we could arrive at the idea that it must be *this* world that exists. In addition to this notion of the whole or a completely independent being, a new idea, that of Nature, must be introduced. This Nature has no parts: it is indivisible. If it had parts, it could come apart. But then Nature would not be genuinely independent, since it depends on its parts "cooperating" and sticking together. If Substance has parts, then it certainly appears that there is something more basic than Substance. Once one decides that Substance has no parts, the thought that Substance never could change is not far. How could it? There are no external forces to make it change; Substance is all there is! Neither can it "rearrange" itself, since there is nothing to rearrange. Yet the possibility of "rearranging" is precisely what is needed in order to imagine an alternative arrangement of Nature.

---

13 Mohanty 2000, Chap. 5.
14 See, for example, Harry A. Wolfson 1934, esp. Chap. III.
15 See, for example, Loux 2006 and Macdonald 2005.

Accepting the idea of substance as the independently existing Whole thus leads to the idea that Nature—our world—cannot be different from how it is. Spinoza himself was happy to draw this conclusion. In Part I of his *Ethics*, he is explicit, noting that "Nothing in the universe is contingent ..." and "Things could not have been brought into being by God in any manner or in any order different from that which has in fact obtained."[16] Following a Spinozistic thought leads not only to a necessarily existing world, but to a fully deterministic world. Understandably many resist this conclusion; indeed they resist the underlying assumptions of the Spinozistic world, holding that this is too high a price to pay for an answer to the question "Why is there something rather than nothing?" The consequence of a Spinozistic view is that the universe *must be*; it is logically and metaphysically impossible for there to have been nothing.

God's Necessary Existence

An alternative, and perhaps more familiar, conception to Spinoza's God is the concept of God associated with three monotheistic religions: Judaism, Christianity, and Islam. This conception of God holds that God is not the whole universe, but is the creator or the cause of the universe. God is thus distinct from creation. Yet, according to some, when we stop to think about this creation, we are led to the conclusion that there must be something—God—that must exist. Chapter 10 considers two arguments for God's existence; here we look briefly at the **first cause argument**, for the claim that there must be an eternal first cause "outside" the chain of particular causes that we observe in the universe.

St. Thomas Aquinas, the thirteenth-century philosopher and theologian, is the most important philosopher of the medieval period. Indeed his influence is still significant. The interest here is his argument for the existence of a "first cause." A first cause, by its nature, must exist. Hence, if the argument is successful, there is a clear answer to the question, "Why is there something rather than nothing"—namely, that there is a first cause that always exists.

In the previous chapter, we talked about several of Aquinas' five arguments for God's existence, known as "the Five Ways."[17] Now we consider the second of these: the first cause argument. This argument focuses on one particular

16   Spinoza 1955, Part I, propositions XXIX and XXXIII.
17   Thomas Aquinas 1972, Part I, Quest 2, Art. 3.

notion of cause, that of efficient cause. The efficient cause is the "bringing about" of the effect, the energy or doing that results in the effect. Lightning is the efficient cause of thunder. Freezing and thawing water is the efficient cause of this pothole. It is the carpenter's activity that makes or brings about the cabinet, or it is Michelangelo's activity, his doing, that brings about the *Pietà*. The computer on which I'm writing this chapter has an efficient cause, in a factory. And so do you: our ordinary notion is that you're here because of your parents. They—your parents—jointly were the efficient cause that "brought you about."

The first cause argument begins with an empirical observation. Everything that we encounter has an efficient cause. Everything has something that brings it into existence. We can trace back, in part, the sequence or chain of "intermediate causes," as Aquinas calls them. Thus, your genealogy provides part of the chain of intermediate causes for you. Now, however, a general question arises: Does the chain of intermediate causes extend back to infinity? Does it have no beginning? Or for every intermediate cause is there still another intermediate cause, in a never-terminating chain?

The burden of the argument is to show that this chain must terminate in a first cause; it cannot go on forever. Two thoughts seem to guide Aquinas' argument. First, he claims that nothing is the efficient cause of itself. Something must exist if there is to be the efficient cause of anything. Then no object could be the efficient cause of itself, since it would have to exist ... prior to its existing! Clearly this cannot be. This suggests that there must be a first cause. Yet this is too hasty.

It might look, then, as though there is an equally compelling argument that there is no first cause, only an infinitely extending series of intermediate causes. This option must be rejected, in Aquinas' view. He seemingly held that if there is no first cause, then we can't make sense of the chain of intermediate causes. We can see why he thinks this. Suppose that an efficient cause is the energy or force in an event that gets the effect, the resulting object "going." We need to then ask, Aquinas seems to hold, where did this energy, this "bringing into being" force, originate? If there is no origin, there is no intermediate cause. And thus there is no present object. But that, Aquinas held, is clearly false. The present object is here; we observe it. So, there must be some source for its coming into being.

Here is a slightly different way to view this phase of the argument. We might see Aquinas as holding that such an infinitely extending series fails to be explanatory. Our ordinary explanations have a finite number of steps. Thus, to explain a chirping noise, we point to the fact that the battery in the smoke alarm had run down. That settles it. But an explanation that never comes to an end would not only be unsatisfying; we might suspect that was no explanation at all. Aquinas believes something similar about infinite explanations.

Asking in general "How did this get here?" is met only with an invitation to ask the same question again. Well, it got here because of this other thing. And now we want to ask about this other thing: How did *it* get here? To extend infinitely this series is not to give any answer, Aquinas thought. Indeed it can easily leave us pondering or wondering what sense there is to "How did this get here?" That is, we understand the question only if we get as an answer something of a different order, some cause that doesn't belong to this chain of intermediate causes.

Aquinas thinks something like this. He's willing to grant for the sake of argument that the series of causes extends back endlessly. But he thinks we must look "vertically" to see what it is that sustains or upholds such a series—that is, not look for a cause of the first event, but rather for a cause of the whole series of events, past, present, and future. This sustaining cause cannot be of the same "order" or type. (Aquinas would thus reject the cosmological speculation that the universe in some sense is its own "mother."[18]) Brian Davies remarks that Aquinas was not concerned with merely the chronological series of causes. Rather, using the analogy of a statue continuing to stand only so long as its support remains, Davies tells us that Aquinas' interest lies in the nature of this support. Hence, the endless regress of chronological and finite causes never gets us to this question: What underlies or supports the series?[19] A related account of the argument is offered by John Wippel: nothing can be its own efficient cause.[20] Thus, we will have to look outside this series to see the "first cause."

Aquinas thus held there must be a first cause, more precisely, an *uncaused cause*, which he identified as God. There are significant worries of course about the identification and nature of this uncaused cause, but our concern here is different. The *essence* of an uncaused cause is that it is not brought into being by something else. And if it is not brought into being, then it always exists.

Two further points are worth making. While Aquinas might have found an infinite series non-explanatory, someone else might consider it simply a brute inexplicable fact. Russell, as noted earlier, seems to have been content with just

---

18   J. Richard Gott 2001.

19   Davies 2006, p. 27.

20   Wippel 2006, p. 58.

such an infinite chain. We might then have come upon two fundamentally different metaphysical starting points, each pointing in a different direction.

A second point. Aquinas does not explicitly identify the first cause as a necessary being in this version of the argument. In the Third Way (see Chap. 10), he claims that there is a necessary being, that it is the essence or nature of such a being to exist, always and forever. Simply pointing out that there is a first cause, however, does not automatically require that there must be something. The appeal to a first cause explains why there *is* something, but not that there *must* be something. (Elsewhere Aquinas takes up this issue in the context of efficient causality.[21])

Abstract Objects: Necessary Beings

There is another type of necessitarianism. If abstract objects exist, they necessarily exist. Or so it is widely held. When we think of objects, we typically think of *concrete* objects. Concrete objects are spatial-temporal objects, and hence, the sort of thing susceptible of being studied by some science or other. (Interesting questions arise but can be set aside for "holes," fields of force, clouds, and the like.[22]) If there are abstract objects, and they necessarily exist, then we would have an answer to our question. Universals are one type or kind of abstract object (see Chap. 4).

But why do abstract objects exist necessarily? Why are they necessary existents? In his recent work, Trenton Merricks, for example, argues that propositions—as abstract objects—necessarily exist.[23] But not everyone agrees. Some theists hold that at least some abstract objects exist only contingently. William Lane Craig, who has written about many metaphysical issues related to God's existence, argues that God creates the abstract object "the earth's equator" upon creation of the world.[24] But why think that any abstract objects, e.g., numbers and universals, exist necessarily, if they exist at all?

One line of thought might be something like the following. Numbers are sometimes considered as sets, but they are also thought of by some as universals.[25] Fortunately, that issue need not be settled here. Yet numbers are abstract

---

21 John Wippel 2006, pp. 59–60.

22 For discussion of these, see E.J. Lowe 1998, Chap. 2.

23 Merricks 2015, Part 1, esp. pp. 18ff.

24 Craig 2004, Chap. 5.

25 Lowe 1998, pp. 220–27.

objects. At a very early age, I was taught that I could demolish all the instances of the *numeral* two (an inscription of some sort that "referred to" the number), but I would not for all my effort have done anything to alter the *number* two.

This is simply to reinforce the idea that numbers are not physical (spatio-temporal) objects, but abstract objects. Now imagine any world you want, whether it be this world or some other possible world, where some complete alternative way of things might have been. It seems as though it makes sense to ask about the *number* of things in that world. And it further seems that for that question to make sense, we must be referring to or designating numbers. Indeed, there doesn't seem to be any feature of numbers that restrict them to only the actual world or only some possible worlds. The science writer and physicist

Brian Greene also holds that math is in every world in the multiverse.[26] He and others think that mathematical structures can and do embody all aspects of the universe. As he enigmatically remarks, "Reality is how math feels."[27]

Stephen Yablo offers a more sophisticated (and somewhat technical version) of this sort of argument. Numbers necessarily exist because they enable us to "encode" various *necessary* arithmetical and mathematical truths.[28] Perhaps this argument can be extended to include other types of abstract objects, such as universals. Thus, universals, such as red or self-discipline, enable us to encode conceptual or metaphysical truths. In any world it is true that "red is a color" or "self-discipline is a virtue." And if this is right, then universals exist necessarily.

But now we have a sketch of an argument for numbers (and perhaps other abstract objects) *existing necessarily*. To exist necessarily is to exist in all possible worlds. And for it to make sense to ask within any possible world, "How many....?" numbers must exist in that possible world. Hence, numbers exist in every possible world. So, numbers necessarily exist—and if this is right, there must be something rather than nothing. And numbers are not the only thing that necessarily exists: universals (e.g., *redness*) also do, and there are a lot of these.

Axiarchism: It Exists because It Should

The *value* of existence is not often considered when asking why there is something rather than nothing. But Canadian philosopher John Leslie has been arguing for more than four decades that the universe exists—and must exist—because *it's good that it exists*. Leslie calls this view axiarchism.

A brief sketch of the argument will have to suffice here. Although it misses much nuance and interesting detail, the highlights are worth seeing. Leslie urges us to take seriously that ethical requirements are "out there," independently of us. And it is as a "creative result" of this ethical requirement that the world exists. Leslie doesn't think that this is a matter of deducing the world's existence. Rather, the connection is a "matter of fact."[29] He claims that this is the inexplicable brute fact of his view: the ethical requirement is creatively sufficient for the world to exist. Moreover, it is *necessarily* creatively sufficient.

---

26 Greene 2011, p. 341.
27 Greene 2011, p. 344.
28 Yablo 2002.
29 Leslie 1979, pp. 286 ff.

Leslie realizes that someone might be unmoved by this idea that a world must exist because of an objective ethical requirement. He does offer a rationale, but again, not a deduction. Value matters, according to Leslie. And there is an ethical requirement that value exist. Leslie claims existing because of value provides a better and more direct reason for the existence of something. He compares it to claiming a world exists because of "massive objects."[30] Instead of thinking about massive objects, we might instead borrow some notion from current cosmological theories, such as that of activity in a quantum field. Leslie's point seems to be there is something that holds more directly between *value ought to exist* and *the world exists* than between *quantum fields produce random perturbations* and *the world exists*. He holds, apparently, that we need to know something else to draw an inference in the latter case, whereas there is a direct or intrinsic relation in the former.

But how does this explain that the world must exist? Leslie's view is reminiscent of Spinozism. In his view, however, God is part of the world.[31] Still it is the universe—the Whole—that is self-justifying and hence self-necessitating. "That a thing's constitution justifies or makes ethically necessary the thing's existence means that the thing is self-justifying—or self-necessitating."[32] And, according to Leslie, this leads to the conclusion that the world always has existed and must exist. It cannot fail to exist.[33]

Two features of Leslie's argument are immediately open to question. His view is similar to various Platonist views (or interpretations of Plato): that there are independently existing *normative* standards. For Leslie, these objectively existing standards are *essentially* creative. Others have held and hold similar views.[34] As with all such views, the question arises whether or not there are indeed independently existing standards. One might also be puzzled that Leslie does not claim to provide a deductive argument for his view. Thus, in a sense, the burden of "proof" rests on the coherence of the constellation of concepts Leslie assembles and their explanatory power. Assessing that explanatory power requires also assessing other answers to the question of why there is something rather than nothing. Indeed, one might think there are simpler answers than "essentially creative standards." One of these "simpler" answers was offered by Robert Nozick.

---

30   *Ibid.*, p. 292.
31   See, for example, p. 296.
32   *Ibid.*
33   See also Leslie 2001.
34   See, for example, the section on Alfred North Whitehead, Chap. 5.

You're Not That Special:
The Multiverse and Contingency

Robert Nozick (1938–2002) argued that we should abandon the idea that there is something special about any one kind or type of universe. This *inegalitarian* view leads us to ask questions to which we can give no answer. Instead, Nozick claimed, we should adopt an *egalitarian* view. But this has an interesting consequence: every universe exists. All universes—or the multiverse—exist. And thus we have an answer to this question: Why does this universe exist? Answer: Because they all do!

Nozick identifies inegalitarian theories as those that assert the existence of one or more brute or inexplicable forces or states. He cites Newton's inertial laws as an example, but others might be identified as well. Leslie's universe, from the previous section, is of course an inegalitarian universe. More important, Nozick holds that the question, "Why is there something rather than nothing?" is "posed against the background of an assumed inegalitarian theory."[35]

But what is the inegalitarian background theory? Nozick claims that it is the "theory" that holds that nothingness is the *natural* state. There is some intuitive sense to this. Asking "How in the world did this get in here?" presumes that "it" shouldn't be here. This is not "its" *natural* place. And Nozick thinks that something like that is going on with our "Why is there something rather than nothing?" We can see the analogy perhaps by asking the question this way: "How (in the world) did this get (in) here?"

Nozick wanted to "defang" the force of this question.[36] But how to do so? Become an egalitarian about universes. That is, Nozick urges that there is no reason that one universe—including the "nothing" universe—is more probable than any other. Of course, there will be only one empty universe, and a lot of worlds with something or other in it. So "Why is there something?" is met with a metaphysical shrug: "What did you expect?"[37] A little more precisely, it is exactly what you would expect a random mechanism to produce. If I have a hundred bags, 99 of which with a turkey sandwich and only one with no sandwich at all, it's highly probable that I will get a turkey sandwich.

---

35 Nozick 1981, p. 122.

36 Greene 2011.

37 Nozick 1981, p. 127. Sydney Morgenbesser was as widely known for his philosophical quips as for his philosophy. His response to the something/nothing question: "And if there were nothing? You'd still be complaining."

It might be wondered, however, why Nozick thinks there's 99 turkey sandwich universes and only one empty one. Isn't it just the possibility of something contrasted with the possibility of nothing? "Thoroughgoing egalitarianism," as Nozick calls it, makes no distinction between existing and not existing. In Nozick's view, *all possibilities independently exist*. Imagine a world in which Danny wears a hat, and now imagine one in which he wears a hat and a carnation in his lapel. According to Nozick, once you accept egalitarianism, you've accepted the principle of fecundity: all possibilities equally obtain. Moreover, "There is nothing—that is one of the separate possibilities that is realized."[38] Of course, a consequence of this is that both something *and nothing* are realized. It is perhaps a bit odd to say that "nothing exists." Yet the nothing world and our world do not differ in ontological status, in Nozick's view. Perhaps a countably infinite number of somethings and but one nothing exists. Given this, Nozick claims, there is simply nothing surprising about something existing. Indeed, it is not surprising that we are here!

We arrive at yet another worry: why prefer the egalitarian view? Here we simplify Nozick's apparent line of argument. Nozick claims there are no brute facts in a thoroughgoing egalitarianism. If there is no reason to prefer either of these two views, then it's just a brute fact that one is the metaphysical frame of the world. But egalitarianism precludes brute facts. Thus, in a sense, egalitarianism gets the better of inegalitarianism.[39] Nozick's argument is more technical than this. But perhaps this suffices to illustrate his aim of showing that egalitarianism offers a way out of the metaphysical corner.

We should not be surprised, then, that there is something rather than nothing, since it is much more likely that there is something than nothing. There is after all only one way to be nothing. But there are an infinite number of possible scenarios—possible worlds—that have something.[40]

Perhaps this provides some reason to think that there is something rather nothing.[41] E.J. Lowe objects, however, that he is not as sanguine about our ability to determine that all possible worlds are equally likely. Someone might plausibly hold that the *simplest* world is the most likely to occur. And the simplest world is the "nothing world."[42]

---

38   *Ibid.*, p. 130.

39   *Ibid.*

40   Peter van Inwagen offers a similar argument; see van Inwagen and E.J. Lowe 1996.

41   But see van Inwagen and Lowe 1996.

42   See also John Leslie 2013, p.130, where he asserts that a chaotic world is equally likely.

The equiprobable view might still be counted as an advance: we have some hold on an explanation as to why there is something (even if not this world) rather than nothing. On the other hand, one might hold that when asking the question, it's the existence of *this* world that requires explanation. In asking why is there anything at all, perhaps what we really want is an answer to this question: Doesn't there need to be some reason why it's this one and not some other "something world"?

Key Concepts

- Principle of Sufficient Reason
- subtraction argument
- metaphysical nihilism
- first cause argument
- necessitarianism

Reading Questions

1. Russell holds that the existence of contingent beings is a metaphysically brute fact. Explain what he means by this.
2. Why does Rundle think the idea that there might have been nothing is not conceivable? Is the subtraction argument an adequate response to this? That is, does the subtraction argument provide a sense to "nothing might have existed"?
3. Explain why it is held that abstract objects might explain why there is something rather than nothing. Be sure to include a brief explanation of why it might be thought that abstract objects exist necessarily.
4. It is sometimes suggested that Aquinas illicitly assumes that everything needs an explanation of its cause except God. Does this undermine Aquinas' argument? How might he respond?
5. Briefly explain why Nozick thinks that it's likely that something exists. Why does he think we should adopt an egalitarian view?
6. Write a brief essay in which you explain whether you think cosmological theories—scientific theories—about the beginning of the universe are sufficient to answer the question, "Why is there something rather than nothing?"

For Further Reading

John Leslie and Robert Lawrence Kuhn, eds. 2013 and Tyrone Goldschmidt, ed. 2013 are two excellent collections of essays on the topic. Already noted in the text, Gonzalo Rodriguez-Pereyra's essay, included in Goldshmidt, is an interesting "updating" and defense of the subtraction argument. In addition to the works cited in the text, John Leslie has several works that bear on this topic, including his 2001 and 2007. Leslie 2001 is a work in *philosophical cosmology*. And the 2007 contains an intriguing chapter titled "Platonic Creation." Derek Parfit 1998 is a very readable overview of the range of positions and types of answers. In addition, Timothy O'Connor 2008 approaches the question by considering the nature of explanation, and thus argues that once we do so, we are led to the existence of a necessary being. Roy Sorenson 2020 explores alternative ways to understand nothing. Some of these ways have a different focus than does this chapter, but many of the sections are directly relevant.

GLOSSARY

a posteriori   knowledge that depends on our sense experience. (Chapter 2)

a priori   knowledge that we can have independent of sense experience. (Chapter 2)

actual entities   the basic units of reality, according to Whitehead. Actual entities are individual, but they are not static elements of reality; rather, they are always becoming. (Chapter 5)

actualism   (a term coined by Robert Adams) the view that only actual things exist, with our world the only actual world and the only actual objects those in our world. Possible worlds are actual, but they are abstract objects, not concrete. (Chapter 2)

agent causation   a view of causation held by some libertarians. Agent causation differs from event causation and is a causal power that each self has. Actions are thus caused, but caused by the self. (Chapter 8)

A-series   the view of time as dynamic, as passing. A time changes, passing from future to present to past. (Chapter 9)

behaviorism   the view that the best explanation of behavior is to be found in environmental causes (stimuli) and subsequently conditioned behavioral responses; mental terms disappear, or are understood in terms of their physical reduction to behavior stimuli and responses. (Chapter 6)

Being (Heideggerian view) that which gives the things of our everyday world their being; the "presence-ing" of things. (Chapter 5)

belief a type of mental state that has a particular content or represents the world as being some way or other; see also content and representational states. (Introduction)

bivalence principle every declarative sentence (in a disputed class) is determinately either true or false; Dummett takes it to be characteristic of realism. (Chapter 3)

block universe the universe viewed as four-dimensional, in which all times are equally present. (Chapter 9)

body criterion the view that a person's identity and persistence over time is determined by sameness of body, or sameness of some part of the body, such as the brain. (Chapter 7)

B-series the view of time in which it does not flow; different times do not change from future to past, but are instead statically and permanently ordered as "before" and "after." (Chapter 9)

bundle theory the view that objects are nothing more than collections, or "co-locations" of qualities. (Chapter 5)

coherence theory of truth holds that a belief is true if and only if it belongs to a set of beliefs that is coherent, a set which is an organized or systematic whole; some coherence theorists hold that our beliefs have this "organized whole" character because reality is that way. (Chapter 1)

compatibilism the view that there is a sense of the notion of free will that is compatible with determinism; thus moral responsibility or accountability is also compatible with determinism. (Chapter 8)

concepts concepts classify or pick out or designate types of objects and types of properties. (Introduction)

conceptualism the view that universals are to be identified as those concepts, located in the mind, standing for many individuals. (Chapter 4)

content mental content; the "aboutness" of mental states such as beliefs and desires, which represent the world as being a certain way. (Introduction)

correspondence theory of truth A sentence (or belief or proposition) is true if and only if the sentence (or belief or proposition) corresponds to the facts. (Chapter 1)

cosmological argument an argument for God's existence that argues that an adequate explanation of the existence of contingent beings must include the existence of a necessarily existing being, specifically God. (Chapter 10)

counterparts in Lewis realism the being in another possible world that is most similar to an object in this, our world. (Chapter 2)

deflationism holds that there is no special property or nature of truth for a theory of truth to reveal. Identifying some belief or sentence as "true" is either redundant or a mere linguistic convenience. (Chapter 2)

design argument the complexity and goal-orientation of parts of nature are sufficient evidence for an intelligent creator—God. (Chapter 10)

determinism the view that every event is the necessary outcome of physical laws and prior circumstances or events; more traditionally, the view that every event has a cause. (Chapter 10)

disquotationalism a type of deflationism; the view that the logico-linguistic function of the predicate "is true" is merely to remove the quotation marks from the named sentence in T-sentences. (Chapter 2)

dualism the view that the mental is something different in nature from the physical; a complete physical account of the world inevitably leaves something out, the mental. The two main types are substance dualism and property dualism. (Introduction, Main discussion: Chapter 6)

eliminative materialism the view that some significant class of mental phenomena do not exist; in particular, eliminativists typically claim that states like belief and desire—the basic elements of folk psychology—don't exist. (Chapter 6)

eternal objects Whitehead's term for universals. (Chapter 9)

eternalism the view that all times (including future and past) equally exist. (Chapter 9)

eternality a divine attribute; interpreted in two different ways: that God is in time, and extending infinitely backward and forward; or outside of time, that is, timeless. (Chapter 10)

experience argument for free will an argument for the existence of free will that appeals to our experiencing ourselves as choosing or deciding which actions to perform. (Chapter 8)

fallibilism theories of justification that hold that further evidence—or the acquisition of further beliefs—can always override one's present justification. (Chapter 1)

fatalism the view that every event that occurs is metaphysically necessary and would have happened no matter what preceded it; often distinguished from determinism. (Chapter 8)

first cause argument an argument for God that operates as follows: Every natural object has a cause. An infinite regress back in time is unintelligible, so there must have been a supernatural first cause—God. (Chapter 11)

fission objection an objection to theories of personal identity: a person is imagined dividing into two equivalent beings. (Chapter 7)

four-dimensionalism the view that a whole object is found only in the whole of the time that it extends or occurs or in the whole of its temporal stages; at any particular time only a single temporal part or stage of the object exists. (Chapter 9)

Frankfurt examples examples of which Harry Frankfurt's were the first, all intended to show that a person could be responsible for an action even if that person could not have done otherwise. (Chapter 8)

free will that a person could have done otherwise, given the same course of events till that choice; the view that on at least some occasions, a person's future is open. (Chapter 8)

functionalism the view that the nature of the mental is seen in its function, what leads to or causes it, what it's connected to, and what happens as a result. (Chapter 6)

global realism The position about (at least) the ordinary things that appear around us, that they exist, more or less as they appear. (Chapter 3)

Grandfather Paradox if time travel were possible, then you could travel into the past and kill your grandfather when he was still an infant; thus you would never have existed. But who then killed that man? (Chapter 9)

hylomorphism the view, from Aristotle, that all things, including persons, are a unity of form and matter. (Chapter 7)

idealism the view that the world, or the objects in the world, depend on our beliefs. Typically contrasted with realism. (Introduction. Main discussion: Chapter 3)

immutability the idea that there is no changing in any way whatsoever. (Chapter 10)

impassability the idea that a being cannot be a subject of emotions or feelings. (Chapter 10)

incompatibilism the view that determinism and free will are incompatible; the consequence argument supports incompatibilism. (Chapter 8)

incorruptibility a being is incorruptible if there can be no changes to that being's character. (Chapter 10)

individual identity the qualities or personality that constitute the nature of the individual, which may change over time. (Chapter 7)

individuation question the question of what makes a person this person rather than some other. (Chapter 7)

instantiation every red thing is said to instantiate the universal *redness*. The red things are instances, or instantiations, of the universal. The linguistic analogy: red objects can be said to instantiate the predicate *red*. (Chapter 4)

instrumentalism (in science) the view that the "objects" referred to in scientific theories need not be supposed to exist; their justification is only that they are useful parts of a theory that works. (Chapter 3)

internal realism holds that the concepts of truth and reference have their application only within a language or theory; truth and reference are always *relative* to a conceptual scheme or theory; Putnam contrasts it with *metaphysical realism*. (Chapter 3)

local realism realism about the entities talked about in some particular area or discipline: e.g., about numbers, or the entities in quantum physics. (Chapter 3)

logically possible a proposition is logically possible if it is not self-contradictory. (Introduction)

memory criterion a person's identity is determined by conscious memories. (Chapter 7)

mereology the study of the ways parts relate to their wholes. (Chapter 5)

metalanguage the language of a sentence talking about a possibly different language, or part of it. (Chapter 2)

metaphysical nihilism the view that there might have been nothing in existence. (Chapter 11)

metaphysics a principal discipline in philosophy that, in its most general form, asks about what kinds of things there are in the world, about their nature, and about the structure or relationship among these things. (Introduction)

minimalism as Paul Horwich presents it, the view that "is true" names a property, but it is a "minimal" property; saying that a sentence is true is to say that it has the property of being in the list of all true sentences. (Chapter 2)

modal fictionalism the anti-realistic view of modal sentences that treats our talk about possible worlds in the same way as we treat talk about fictional characters, entities, places. (Chapter 2)

modal realism the view that possible worlds are concrete worlds like our actual world. No less real, no less *concrete*, many inhabited with "counterparts" of you and me, "actual" is relative to a world, but they are completely inaccessible to us. (Chapter 2)

moderate realism moderate realism is the view that our kind concepts refer to universals, but universals exist only in the objects; sometimes called immanent realism. (Chapter 4)

monism only one type of thing exists: physical objects with their physical properties, according to physical monists. (Introduction)

necessary a proposition is necessary if its truth value cannot be otherwise—if it is true in all possible worlds. (Introduction)

necessary and sufficient conditions A is a necessary condition of B if and only if B cannot occur without the occurrence of A; A is a sufficient condition of B if and only if whenever A occurs, B also occurs. (Introduction)

necessitarianism the view that appeal to necessarily existing things is admissible. (Chapter 11)

nominalism the view that universals do not exist; only particular things or particular occurrences of properties exist. (Chapter 4)

numerical identity *A* and *B* are numerically identical when *A* is *B*—that is, when '*A*' and '*B*' are different names for the same thing. Distinguished from qualitative identity. (Chapter 7)

object language in a sentence about a (part of) a language, that language is called the object language. (Chapter 2)

omnipotence a divine attribute, namely that God's power is unlimited. Many hold that this is understood as God's power to do anything that is logically possible. (Chapter 10)

omnipresence a divine attribute, namely that God is everywhere. As understood by many theorists God is everywhere because his knowledge and power are everywhere present. (Chapter 10)

omniscience a divine attribute, namely that God knows everything there is to know. (Chapter 10)

ontological argument an argument for God's existence, which proceeds by reflecting on God's nature or essence, and claiming to derive God's existence from our concept of that nature. (Chapter 10)

ontological relativity the view that to understand a language requires that one understand it relative to some background language or theory. (Chapter 3)

particulars objects or individuals; particulars cannot be instantiated. (Chapter 4)

persistence question (personal identity) the question of what makes a person the same person over time. (Chapter 7)

personhood identity those characteristics that make something, whether human being, animal, robot, or extra-terrestrial creature, a *person*. (Chapter 7)

physicalism the view that everything is ultimately physical; only physical things and properties exist. (Introduction. Main discussion: Chapter 6)

possible proposition a proposition that is true in at least one possible world. (Chapter 2)

possible world is a maximally complete set of true or false possible propositions or is described by one of these maximally complete sets. (Chapter 2)

pragmatic theory of truth a belief is true if it provisionally reconciles new experience with old, as a further step in the ongoing process of inquiry, and proves useful to the believer cognitively and practically. (Chapter 1)

presentism the view that the only time that exists is the present instant. Future times do not exist yet, and past times have ceased existing. (Chapter 9)

Principle of Sufficient Reason the principle that each thing that exists has a sufficient reason why it exists. (Chapter 11)

property dualism the view that there is only one kind of substance—the physical— but distinctly mental properties emerge from particular physical arrangements or structures. (Chapter 6)

proposition what is expressed or "meant" by a sentence; different sentences or sentences in different languages might express the same proposition. (Introduction)

qualia the qualitative aspects of the mental or the felt quality; sometimes "raw feels." (Chapter 6)

qualitative identity when two or more objects have all the same qualities or properties. (Chapter 7)

realism the idea that some area or domain of objects or kinds of thing exist independently of our beliefs or representations. (Introduction. Main discussion: Chapter 3)

realism (about universals) holds that universals are a special kind of object, which exist separately from the many occurrences or instances. (Chapter 4)

redundancy theory holds that there is no genuine content to the predicate "is true." Simply asserting some proposition and saying of that proposition that it "is true" are interchangeable, and adding "is true" to the assertion is redundant. (Chapter 2)

representational states mental states that have contents and represent the world as having certain characteristics or being a certain way. (Introduction)

resemblance nominalism the view that we classify or group certain objects together because they resemble each other. (Chapter 4)

responsibility argument for free will an argument for the existence of free will that asserts that since we are sometimes morally responsible for our actions, and free will is a necessary condition of responsibility, so free will must exist. (Chapter 8)

satisfaction (of a sentence). A sentence with a blank is satisfied by insertion of one (or more) names of objects in the blank that make the sentence true. (Chapter 2)

scientific realism the view that scientific theories contain terms that refer to or designate entities and their properties and relations, and these exist and are independent of our representations of them. (Chapter 3)

semantic conception of truth truth is essentially tied to a language, and relies on the technical distinction between object language and metalanguage, along with the technical notion of satisfaction to explain true sentences. (Chapter 2)

Special Composition Question an important question motivating the metaphysics of particulars. What does it take for a collection of non-overlapping material objects to form an object? (Chapter 5)

states of affairs a circumstance or situation, either possible or actual; actual states of affairs are said to "obtain"; for Austin a statement is true if the picked-out state of affairs obtains. (Chapter 1)

strict nominalism the view that it is an unanalyzable basic metaphysical fact that there are only individuals, which we describe using certain predicates but there is no need to explain why we use the same predicate to describe different objects. (Chapter 4)

substance dualism the view that there are two distinct kinds of substances in the world: bodies, or the physical, and minds, or the mental. (Chapter 6)

substance-attribute view primary substances are our familiar individuals, and these individuals possess attributes or properties; some properties are essential to the individual, and some are accidental or inessential. (Chapter 5)

substratum that which supports or holds together the various properties of an object. (Chapter 5)

subtraction argument the argument that we can make sense of the idea of nothing by subtracting ideas of each existing thing, one by one. (Chapter 11)

Third Man Argument an objection to the existence of universals, which holds that the attribute agreement argument for universals leads to an infinite regress of universals. (Chapter 4)

token identity theory a view of the mental that holds that every occurrence of a mental state, event, or process is identical with some physical state, event, or process; functionalists usually accept this view. (Chapter 6)

tropes a trope is the particular occurrence of a property in an individual; trope nominalism is the view that each occurrence of a property is particular and individual; no two property occurrences are of the same type or class. (Chapter 4)

type identity theory the view that every type of mental state, event or process is nothing more than some type or pattern of brain activity. (Chapter 6)

universal that which can be instantiated by many objects or particulars at the same time; a universal can be shared by any number of particulars at the same time and can be predicated of or attributed to many things. (Chapter 4)

verification the determination of the truth or falsity of a sentence. The verificationist theory of meaning says that understanding a sentence consists of recognizing its verification procedures. Dummett sometimes calls this "justificationist semantics." (Chapter 3)

BIBLIOGRAPHY

Abelard, Peter. 1969. "On Universals." In J.F. Wippel and A.B. Wolter, eds. and trans. *Medieval Philosophy: From St. Augustine to Nicholas of Cusa*. New York: Free P. Reprinted in Schoedinger, Andrew B., ed. 1992. *The Problem of Universals*. Atlantic Highlands, NJ: Humanities.

Adams, Marilyn McCord. 1967. "Is the Existence of God a 'Hard Fact'?" *Philosophical Review*, 76(4), 492–503.

Adams, Marilyn McCord. 1999. *Horrendous Evils and the Goodness of God*. Ithaca, NY: Cornell UP.

Adams, Marilyn McCord, and Robert Merrihew Adams, eds. 1990. *The Problem of Evil*. New York: Oxford UP.

Adams, Robert Merrihew. 1974. "Theories of Actuality." *Noûs*, 8, 211–23. Reprinted in Loux, Michael J., ed. 1979. *The Possible and the Actual: Readings in the Metaphysics of Modality*. Ithaca, NY: Cornell UP. All page references are to this latter volume.

Adams, Robert Merrihew. 1979. "Primitive Thisness and Primitive Identity." *Journal of Philosophy*, 76(1), 5–26.

Adams, Robert Merrihew. 1981. "Actualism and Thisness," *Synthèse*, 49, 3–41.

Anscombe, G.E.M. 2001. *An Introduction to Wittgenstein's Tractatus*, 4th ed. South Bend, IN: St. Augustine P.

Anselm. 1996. *Monologion and Proslogion*. Thomas Williams, ed. and trans. Indianapolis, IN: Hackett.

Antony, Louise. 1993. "Quine as Feminist: The Radical Import of Naturalized Epistemology." In Louise Antony and Charlotte Witt, eds., *A Mind of One's Own: Feminist Essays on Reason and Objectivity*, pp. 110–53. Boulder, CO: Westview.

Aquinas, Thomas. 1953. *Introduction to the Metaphysics of St. Thomas Aquinas*. James F. Anderson, ed. and trans. South Bend, IN: Regenery/Gateway.

Aquinas, Thomas. 1972. *An Aquinas Reader*. Mary Clark, ed. and trans. Garden City, NY: Image Books.

Aquinas, Thomas. 2008. "Whether God Is Altogether Immutable?" *The Summa Theologica of St. Thomas Aquinas*. http://www.newadvent.org/summa/

Aquinas, Thomas. n.d. "Commentary on the First Epistle to the Corinthians." Fabian Larcher, trans. http://www.dhspriory.org/thomas/SS1Cor.htm

Aristotle. 1941a. *Categories*. E.M. Edghill, trans. In Richard McKeon, ed., *The Basic Works of Aristotle*, pp. 7–39. New York: Random House.

Aristotle. 1941b. *De Anima*. J.A. Smith, trans. In Richard McKeon, ed., *The Basic Works of Aristotle*, pp. 533–603. New York: Random House.

Aristotle. 1941c. *De Interpretatione*. E.M. Edghill, trans. In Richard McKeon, ed., *The Basic Works of Aristotle*, pp. 38–61. New York: Random House.

Aristotle. 1941d. *Metaphysics*. W.D. Ross, trans. In Richard McKeon, ed., *The Basic Works of Aristotle*, pp. 681–926. New York: Random House.

Aristotle. 1941e. *Physics*. W.D. Ross, trans. In Richard McKeon, ed., *The Basic Works of Aristotle*, pp. 213–394. New York: Random House.

Armstrong, D.M. 1978. *Universals and Scientific Realism*. 2 vols. Cambridge: Cambridge UP.

Armstrong, D.M. 1989. *Universals: An Opinionated Introduction*. Boulder, CO: Westview.

Audi, Robert. 1988. *Belief, Justification, and Knowledge*. Belmont, CA: Wadsworth.

Audi, Robert. 1993. *The Structure of Justification*. New York: Cambridge UP.

Audi, Robert, ed. 1995. *The Cambridge Dictionary of Philosophy*. Cambridge: Cambridge UP.

Audi, Robert. 1998. *Epistemology: A Contemporary Introduction to the Theory of Knowledge*. Abingdon, UK: Routledge.

Augustine, Saint. 1949. *The Confessions of Saint Augustine*. Edward B. Pusey, trans. New York: Random House.

Augustine. 1993. *On the Free Choice of the Will*. Thomas Williams, trans. Indianapolis, IN: Hackett.

Aune, Bruce. 2001. "Universals and Predication." In Richard M. Gale, ed., *The Blackwell Guide to Metaphysics*, pp. 131–50. Oxford: Blackwell.

Aurelius, Marcus. 2006. *Meditations*. Martin Hammond, trans. New York: Penguin.

Austin, J.L. 1950a. "Truth." *Proceedings of the Aristotelian Society*, 24, 111–28. Reprinted in Austin, *Philosophical Papers*, pp. 117–33.

Austin, J.L. 1950b. "Unfair to Facts." *Proceedings of the Aristotelian Society, 24.* Reprinted in Austin, *Philosophical Papers*, pp. 154–74.

Austin, J.L. 1990. *Philosophical Papers*, 3rd ed. J.O. Urmson and G.J. Warnock, eds. Oxford: Clarendon P.

Baker, Lynne Rudder. 2000. *Persons and Their Bodies: The Constitution View.* Cambridge: Cambridge UP.

Balaguer, Mark. 2014. *Free Will.* Cambridge, MA: MIT P.

Ball, Philip. 2018. *Beyond Weird: Why Everything You Thought You Knew About Quantum Physics Is Different.* London: The Bodley Head.

Bambrough, Renford. 1960. "Universals and Family Resemblance." *Proceedings of the Aristotelian Society, 61,* 207–22. Reprinted in Schoedinger, *The Problem of Universals*, pp. 266–79.

Bardon, Adrian. 2013. *A Brief History of the Philosophy of Time.* Cambridge: Cambridge UP.

Bardon, Adrian, and Heather Dyke, eds. 2013. *A Companion to the Philosophy of Time.* Hoboken NJ: Wiley-Blackwell.

Bartley, C.J. 2013. *The Theology of Ramanajua.* Abingdon, UK: Routledge.

Baylis, C.A. 1951. "Universals, Communicable Knowledge, and Metaphysics." *Journal of Philosophy, 48*(21), 636–44.

Berkeley, George. 1965. *A Treatise Concerning the Principles of Human Knowledge.* Indianapolis, IN: Bobbs-Merrill.

Blanshard, Brand. 1939. *The Nature of Thought.* Vol. 2. London: George Allen and Unwin.

Blanshard, Brand. 1961. "The Case for Determinism." In Sidney Hook, ed., *Freedom and Determinism in the Modern World*, pp. 19–30. New York: New York UP. Reprinted in Campbell, Neil, ed. 2003. *Freedom, Determinism, and Responsibility: Readings in Metaphysics,* pp. 7–15. Upper Saddle River, NJ: Prentice-Hall.

Block, Ned. 1978. "Troubles with Functionalism." In Wade Savage, ed., *Perception and Cognition: Issues in the Foundations of Psychology*, pp. 261–325. Minneapolis: U of Minnesota P.

Borst, C.V., ed. 1970. *The Mind/Brain Identity Theory.* New York: St. Martin's.

Bradley, F.H. 1893. *Appearance and Reality: A Metaphysical Essay.* London: Swan Sonnenschein and New York: Macmillan.

Bradley, F.H. 1909/1914. "On Truth and Coherence." *Mind, 18,* 329–42. Reprinted in *Essays on Truth and Reality*, pp. 202–18. Oxford: Clarendon. Page references are to *Essays*.

Buchler, Justus, ed. 1955. *Philosophical Writings of Peirce.* New York: Dover.

Burger, Ronna. 1984. *Phaedo: A Platonic Labyrinth.* New Haven, CT: Yale UP.

Burgess, Alexis G., and John P. Burgess. 2011. *Truth.* Princeton, NJ: Princeton UP.

Burgess, John P. 1999. "Which Modal Logic Is the Right One?" *Notre Dame Journal of Symbolic Logic, 40,* 81–93.

Burton, Neel. 2012. "The Vanishing Self." In "Hide and Seek," *Psychology Today.* http://www.psychologytoday.com/blog/hide-and-seek/201205/the-vanishing-self

Campbell, Keith. 1984. *Body and Mind*. Notre Dame, IN: Notre Dame UP. Originally published by Anchor, 1970.

Campbell, Keith. 1991. *Abstract Particulars*. Oxford: Blackwell.

Campbell, Neil, ed. 2003. *Mental Causation and the Metaphysics of Mind: A Reader*. Peterborough, ON: Broadview P.

Candlish, Stewart. 1989. "The Truth About F. H. Bradley." *Mind*, 98(391), 331–48.

Carroll, John, and Ned Markosian. 2010. *An Introduction to Metaphysics*. Cambridge: Cambridge UP.

Carter, Rita. 2010. *Mapping the Mind*. Berkeley, CA: U of California P.

Cashmore, Anthony. 2010. "The Lucretian Swerve: The Biological Basis of Human Behavior and the Criminal Justice System." *Proceedings of the National Academy of Sciences of the United States of America*, 7(10), 4499–4504.

Casullo, Albert. 1988. "A Fourth Version of the Bundle Theory." *Philosophical Studies*, 54(1), 125–39.

Chakravartty, Anjan. 2017 (Summer). "Scientific Realism." In Edward N. Zalta, ed., *Stanford Encyclopedia of Philosophy*. https://plato.stanford.edu/archives/sum2017/entries/scientific-realism/

Chalmers, David. 1996. *The Conscious Mind*. New York: Oxford UP.

Cherniss, Harold. 1936. "The Philosophical Economy of Plato's Theory of Ideas." *The American Journal of Philology*, 57(4), 445–56.

Cherniss, H.F. 1965. "The Relation of the 'Timaeus' to Plato's Later Dialogues." In R.E. Allen, ed., *Studies in Plato's Metaphysics*, pp. 339–78. London: Routledge and Kegan Paul.

Chisholm, Roderick. 1964. "Human Freedom and the Self." The Lindley Lecture, U of Kansas, pp. 3–14. Reprinted in Watson, Gary, ed. 1982. *Free Will*, pp. 24–35. New York: Oxford UP.

Chisholm, Roderick. 1967. "Identity through Possible Worlds: Some Questions." *Noûs*, 1, 1–8. Reprinted in Loux, ed., *The Possible and the Actual*, pp. 80–87.

Chisholm, Roderick. 1976. *Person and Object*. LaSalle, IL: Open Court.

Christofuro, Peter. 2019. "Time Travel & the Grandfather Paradox Explained (astronomytrek.com)." https://www.astronomytrek.com/grandfather-paradox-explained/

Churchland, Patricia. 1986. *Neurophilosophy: Toward a Unified Science of the Mind/Brain*. Cambridge, MA: MIT P.

Churchland, Paul M. 1981. "Eliminative Materialism and the Propositional Attitudes." *Journal of Philosophy*, 78, 67–90.

Churchland, Paul M. 1988. *Matter and Consciousness*, rev. ed. Cambridge, MA: MIT P.

Churchland, Paul M. 1996. *The Engine of Reason, The Seat of the Soul: A Philosophical Journey into the Brain*. Cambridge, MA: MIT P.

Churchland, Paul M. 2013. *Matter and Consciousness*, 3rd ed. Cambridge, MA: MIT P.

Clack, Beverly, and Brian Clack. 1998. *Philosophy of Religion: A Critical Introduction*. Cambridge: Polity P.

Copleston, Frederick C., S.J. 1946. *A History of Western Philosophy*, Vol 1. Garden City, NY: Doubleday.

Copleston, Frederick C., S.J. 1974. *A History of Medieval Philosophy*. New York: Harper & Row.

Corcoran, Kevin, ed. 2001. *Soul, Body, and Survival: Essays on the Metaphysics of Human Persons*. Ithaca, NY: Cornell UP.

Craig, William Lane. 2004. *Creation out of Nothing: A Biblical, Philosophical, and Scientific Exploration*. With Paul Copan. Grand Rapids, MI: Baker Bookhouse.

Cross, Richard. 2014 (Summer). "Medieval Theories of Haecceity." In Edward N. Zalta, ed., *Stanford Encyclopedia of Philosophy*. http://plato.stanford.edu/archives/sum2014/entries/medieval-haecceity/

Crumley, Jack S., II. 2006. *A Brief Introduction to the Philosophy of Mind*. Lanham, MD: Rowman and Littlefield.

Crumley, Jack S., II. 2009. *An Introduction to Epistemology*, 2nd ed. Peterborough, ON: Broadview P.

Crumley, Jack S., II. 2016. *An Introduction to Philosophy: Knowledge and Reality*. Peterborough, ON: Broadview P.

Crumley, Jack. *Ms.* "The Third Man: A Reconsideration of the Role of Non-identity."

Damasio, Antonio. 2000. *The Feeling of What Happens: Body and Emotion in the Making of Consciousness*. New York: Mariner Books.

Dancy, Jonathan. 1985. *Introduction to Contemporary Epistemology*. Oxford and Cambridge, MA: Blackwell.

Dauer, Francis. 1974. "In Defense of the Coherence Theory of Truth." *Journal of Philosophy*, *71*, 791–911.

Davidson, Donald. 1967. "Truth and Meaning." *Synthèse*, 304–23.

Davidson, Donald. 1986. "A Coherence Theory of Truth and Knowledge." In Ernest Lepore, ed., *Truth and Interpretation: Perspectives on the Philosophy of Donald Davidson*, pp. 307–19. Oxford: Blackwell.

Davidson, Donald. 1990. "The Structure and Content of Truth" (The Dewey Lectures 1989), *Journal of Philosophy*, *87*, 279–328.

Davidson, Donald. 1996. "The Folly of Trying to Define Truth." *Journal of Philosophy*, *93*, 263–78. Reprinted in Lynch, Michael P., ed. 2001. *On the Nature of Truth: Classical and Contemporary Perspectives*. Cambridge, MA: Bradford. Page reference are to this latter volume.

Davies, Brian. 1982. *An Introduction to the Philosophy of Religion*. New York: Oxford UP.

Davies, Brian. 1992. *The Thought of Thomas Aquinas*. Oxford: Clarendon.

Davies, Brian, ed. 2006. *Aquinas's Summa Theologiae: Critical Essays*. Lanham, MD: Rowman and Littlefield.

Davies, Paul. 1996. *About Time: Einstein's Unfinished Revolution*. New York: Simon and Schuster.

Dawkins, Richard. 1986. *The Blind Watchmaker: Why the Evidence of Evolution Reveals a Universe Without Design*. New York: Norton.

Della Rocca, Michael. 2012. "Violations of the Principle of Sufficient Reason (in Leibniz and Spinoza)." In Fabrice Correia and Benjamin Schneider, eds., *Metaphysical Grounding: Understanding the Structure of Reality*, pp. 139–64. Cambridge: Cambridge UP.

Dennett, Daniel. 1978. *Brainstorms: Philosophical Essays on Mind and Psychology.* Cambridge, MA: MIT P.

Dennett, Daniel. 1984. *Elbow Room.* Cambridge, MA: MIT P.

Dennett, Daniel. 1991. *Consciousness Explained.* Boston: Little, Brown.

Devitt, Michael. 1989. "Against Direct Reference." *Midwest Studies in Philosophy, 14*(1), 206–40.

Devitt, Michael. 1991. *Realism and Truth.* New York: Blackwell.

Devitt, Michael. 2005/2006. "Scientific Realism." In Frank Jackson and Michael Smith, eds., *The Oxford Handbook of Contemporary Philosophy,* pp. 767–91. Oxford: Oxford UP. Reprinted in Patrick Greenough and Michael P. Lynch, eds. 2006. *Truth and Realism,* pp. 100–24. Oxford: Oxford UP. Page references are to this volume.

Devitt, Michael, and Kim Sterelny. 1987. *Language and Reality: An Introduction to the Philosophy of Language.* New York: Basil Blackwell, 1987.

Dewey, John. 1930. *The Quest for Certainty: A Study of the Relation of Knowledge and Action.* London: George Allen & Unwin.

Dewey, John. 1938. *Logic: The Theory of Inquiry.* New York: Holt.

Divers, John. 2002. *Possible Worlds.* New York: Routledge.

Dombrowski, Dan. 2013 (Spring). "Charles Hartshorne." In Edward N. Zalta, ed., *Stanford Encyclopedia of Philosophy.* http://plato.stanford.edu/archives/spr2013/entries/hartshorne/

Donagan, Alan. 1963. "Universals and Metaphysical Realism." *Monist, 47*(2). Reprinted in Loux, ed., *Universals and Particulars.*

Dowden, Bradley. n.d. *Liar Paradox.* Internet Encyclopedia of Philosophy. https://www.iep.utm.edu/par-liar/#SH1b

Dreifus, Claudia. 2002. "Taking a Clinical Look at Human Emotions: A Conversation with Joseph LeDoux." *The New York Times,* October 8.

Ducasse, C.J. 1960. "In Defense of Dualism." In Sidney Hook, ed., *Dimensions of Mind,* pp. 85–90. New York: New York UP.

Dummett, Michael. 1963. "Realism." Reprinted in Dummett, *Truth and Other Enigmas,* pp. 145–65.

Dummett, Michael. 1969. "The Reality of the Past." *Proceedings of the Aristotelian Society.* Reprinted in Dummet, *Truth and Other Enigmas,* pp. 358–74. Page references are to this volume.

Dummett, Michael. 1976/1993. "What Is a Theory of Meaning II." In Dummett 1993. *Seas of Language.* Oxford: Oxford UP, pp. 34–93. Page references are to this volume. Original publication, in Gareth Evans and John McDowell (eds.). 1976. *Truth and Meaning: Essays in Semantics.* Oxford: Clarendon.

Dummett, Michael. 1978. *Truth and Other Enigmas.* Cambridge, MA: Harvard UP.

Dummett, Michael. 1993. "What Do I Know When I Know a Language?" In Dummett 1993, *Seas of Language,* pp. 94–105. Oxford: Oxford UP.

Dummett, Michael. 2006. *Thought and Reality.* Oxford: Oxford UP.

Dummett, Michael. 2013. *Truth and the Past.* Akeel Bilgrami, ed. New York: Columbia UP.

Dunham, Jeremy, Iain Hamilton Grant, and Sean Watson. 2011. *Idealism: The History of a Philosophy.* Montreal and Kingston: McGill-Queen's UP.

Eagle, Antony. 2014. "Chance versus Randomness." In Edward N. Zalta, ed., *Stanford Encyclopedia of Philosophy*. http://plato.stanford.edu/archives/spr2014/entries/chance-randomness/

Eames, S. Morris. 1977. *Pragmatic Naturalism*. Carbondale, IL: Southern Illinois UP.

Edelman, Gerald. 1992. *Brilliant Air, Brilliant Fire: On the Matter of the Mind*. New York: Basic Books.

Edwards, Douglas. 2014. *Properties*. Cambridge, UK: Polity P.

Edwards, Jonathan. 1835. *Freedom of the Will*. In Edward Hickman, ed., *The Works of Jonathan Edwards*. New York: D. Appleton.

Ekstrom, Laura. 2000. *Free Will: A Philosophical Study*. Boulder, CO: Westview.

Emerson, Ralph Waldo. 1987. *The Essays of Ralph Waldo Emerson (Collected Works of Ralph Waldo Emerson)*. Alfred R. Ferguson, Jean Ferguson Carr, and Alfred Kazin, eds. Cambridge, MA: Belknap.

Falk, Dan. 2016. "A Debate over the Physics of Time." *Quanta Magazine*, July 19. https://www.quantamagazine.org/a-debate-over-the-physics-of-time-20160719/

Feynman, Richard. 2015. *The Quotable Feynman*. Princeton: Princeton UP.

Field, Hartry. 1972. "Tarski's Theory of Truth." *Journal of Philosophy* 69(13), 347.

Field, Hartry. 1978. "Mental Representation." *Erkenntnis*, 13(July), 9–61.

Fischer, John Martin, ed. 1989. *God, Foreknowledge, and Freedom*. Stanford, CA: Stanford UP.

Fischer, John Martin. 1995. *The Metaphysics of Free Will: An Essay on Control*. Malden, MA: Blackwell.

Fish, William. 2010. *Philosophy of Perception: A Contemporary Introduction*. Abingdon, UK: Routledge.

Flanagan, Owen. 1992. *Consciousness Reconsidered*. Cambridge, MA: MIT P.

Fodor, Jerry A. 1975. *The Language of Thought*. Cambridge, MA: Harvard UP.

Fodor, Jerry A. 1981. "The Mind-Body Problem: A Guide to the Current Debate." *Scientific American*, 244, 114–25.

Fodor, Jerry. 1987. *Psychosemantics: The Problem of Meaning in the Philosophy of Mind*. Cambridge, MA: MIT P.

Forbes, Graeme. 1985. *The Metaphysics of Modality*. New York: Oxford UP.

Foster, John. 1991. *The Immaterial Self: A Defence of the Cartesian Dualist Conception of the Mind*. New York: Routledge.

Frankfurt, Harry. 1969. "Alternate Possibilities and Moral Responsibility." *Journal of Philosophy*, 66, 829–39.

Frankfurt, Harry G. 1971. "Freedom of the Will and the Concept of a Person." *Journal of Philosophy*, 68(1), 5–20.

Frede, Michael. 2011. *A Free Will: Origins of the Notion in Ancient Thought*. Berkeley and Los Angeles: U of California P.

French, Peter A., Theodore E. Uehling, Jr., and Howard K. Wettstein, eds. 1988. *Midwest Studies in Philosophy Vol XII: Realism and Anti-Realism*. Minneapolis: U of Minnesota P.

Fung, Yu-lan. 1962. *A History of Chinese Philosophy*. Princeton, NJ: Princeton UP.

Geroch, Robert. 1978. *General Relativity from A to B*. U of Chicago P.

Gibson, Roger, and Robert B. Barrett, eds. 1990. *Perspectives on Quine*. Hoboken, NJ: Blackwell.

Gilson, Etienne. 1940. *The Spirit of Medieval Philosophy*. New York: Charles Scribner's Sons.

Gilson, Etienne. 1960. *Heloise and Abelard*. Ann Arbor, MI: U of Michigan P.

Godwin, Dwayne, and Jorge Cham. 2013. "Split-Brain Patients Reveal Brain's Flexibility." *Scientific American Mind, 24*(1), 5.

Goldschmidt, Tyrone Goldschmidt, ed. 2013. *The Puzzle of Existence: Why Is There Something Rather Than Nothing?* London: Routledge.

Gott, J. Richard. 2001. *Time Travel in Einstein's Universe: The Physical Possibilities of Travel through Time*. Chicago: U of Chicago P.

Gracia, Jorge J.E. 1992. "The Transcendentals in the Middle Ages: An Introduction." *Topoi, 11*(2), 113–20.

Greene, Brian. 2011. *The Hidden Reality: Parallel Universes and the Deep Laws of the Cosmos*. New York: Knopf.

Greenough, Patrick, and Michael P. Lynch, eds. 2006. *Truth and Realism*. Oxford: Clarendon.

Griswold, Charles, ed. 1988. *Platonic Writings, Platonic Readings*. New York: Routledge.

Gupta, Anil. 1993. "Minimalism." *Philosophical Perspectives, 7*, 359–69.

Haack, Susan. 1977. "Pragmatism and Ontology: Peirce and James." *Revue Internationale de Philosophie, 31*(121/122), 377–400.

Haack, Susan. 1990. "Rebuilding the Ship while Sailing on the Water." In Robert Barret and Roger Gibson, eds. 1990. *Perspectives on Quine*. New York: Blackwell, pp. 111–28.

Hale, Bob. 1997. "Realism and Its Oppositions." In Bob Hale and Crispin Wright, eds., *A Companion to the Philosophy of Language*, pp. 271–308. Oxford: Blackwell.

Hale, Bob, and Crispin Wright. 1997. "Putnam's Model-Theoretic Argument." In Bob Hale and Crispin Wright, eds., *A Companion to the Philosophy of Language*, pp. 427–57. Oxford: Blackwell.

Harding, Sandra. 1993. "Rethinking Standpoint Epistemology: What Is 'Strong Objectivity'?" In Linda Alcoff and Elizabeth Potter, eds., *Feminist Epistemologies*. New York: Routledge.

Harman, Gilbert. 1999. *Reasoning, Meaning and Mind*. Oxford: Clarendon.

Hartshorne, Charles S. 1965. *Anselm's Discovery: A Reexamination of the Ontological Argument for God's Existence*. LaSalle, IL: Open Court.

Hartshorne, Charles S. 1967. *A Natural Theology for Our Time*. LaSalle, IL: Open Court.

Hartshorne, Charles S. 1976. *Aquinas to Whitehead*. Milwaukee, WI: Marquette UP.

Hartshorne, Charles S. 1984. *Omnipotence and Other Theological Mistakes*. Albany, NY: SUNY P.

Hasker, William. 1989. *God, Time and Knowledge*. Ithaca, NY: Cornell UP.

Hawthorne, John, and Andrew Cortens. 1995. "Towards Ontological Nihilism." *Philosophical Studies, 79*(2), 143–65.

Heidegger, Martin. 1962. *Being and Time*. John Mcquarrie and Edward Robinson, trans. London: SCM P.

Heidegger, Martin. 1965. "The Essence of Truth." R.F.C. Hull and Alan Crick, trans. In *Existence and Being*, pp. 292–325.

Heidegger, Martin. 1976. *What Is Called Thinking?* J. Glenn Gray, trans. New York: Harper & Row.

Heidegger, Martin. 1977. "The Question Concerning Technology." In William Lovitt, trans, *The Question Concerning Technology and Other Essays*, pp. 3–35. New York: Harper Torchbooks.

Heil, John. 1998. *Philosophy of Mind*. New York: Routledge.

Heil, John. 2004. *Philosophy of Mind: A Guide and Anthology*. New York: Oxford.

Heller, Mark. 1999. "The Proper Role for Contextualism in an Anti-Luck Epistemology." *Philosophical Perspectives, 13*, 115–29.

Hetherington, Stephen, ed. 2012. *Epistemology: The Key Thinkers*. London: Bloomsbury Academic.

Hick, John, ed. 1964. *The Existence of God*. New York: Macmillan.

Hick, John. 1978. *Evil and the God of Love*, rev. ed. New York: Harper and Row.

Hoffman, Joshua, and Gary Rosenkrantz. 1984. "Hard and Soft Facts." *Philosophical Review, 93*, 419–34.

Hoffman, Joshua, and Gary Rosenkrantz. 1997. *Substance: Its Nature and Existence*. London: Routledge.

Hoffman, Joshua, and Gary Rosenkrantz. 2002. *The Divine Attributes*. Oxford: Blackwell.

Horwich, Paul. 1990. "Asymmetries in Time." *Noûs, 24*(5), 804–06.

Horwich, Paul. 2001. "A Defense of Minimalism." *Synthèse, 126*(1), 149–65.

Hughes, G.E., and M.J. Cresswell. 1996. *A New Introduction to Modal Logic*. London: Routledge.

Hume, David. 1975. *An Enquiry Concerning Human Understanding*, 3rd ed. L.A. Selby-Bigge, ed., rev. P.H. Nidditch. Oxford: Clarendon.

Hume, David. 1980. *Dialogues Concerning Natural Religion*. Richard Popkin, ed. Indianapolis, IN: Hackett.

Irvine, Andrew David. 2013 (Winter). "Alfred North Whitehead." In Edward N. Zalta, ed., *Stanford Encyclopedia of Philosophy*. http://plato.stanford.edu/archives/win2013/entries/whitehead/

Irwin, Terence. 1989. *A History of Western Philosophy: 1 Classical Thought*. New York: Oxford UP.

Jackson, Frank. 1982. "Epiphenomenal Qualia." *Philosophical Quarterly, 32*, 127–36.

Jacquette, Dale. 1994. *Philosophy of Mind*. Upper Saddle River, NJ: Prentice-Hall.

James, William. 1904/1963. "Humanism and Truth." *Mind, 13*, 457–75.

James, William. 1906–07/1963. *Pragmatism and Other Essays*. Joseph Blau, ed. New York: Washington Square P.

James, William. 1911. *Some Problems of Philosophy: A Beginning of an Introduction to Philosophy*. London: Longmans, Green, and Co.

James, William. 1951a. "The Continuity of Experience." In Max. H. Fisch, ed., *Classic American Philosophers*, pp. 160–64. New York: Appleton-Century-Crofts.

James, William. 1951b. "Does 'Consciousness' Exist?" In Max. H. Fisch, ed., *Classic American Philosophers*, pp. 148–60. New York: Appleton-Century-Crofts.

James, William. 1956. "The Dilemma of Determinism." In *The Will to Believe and Other Essays*, pp. 145–83. New York: Dover.

James, William. 1978. "The Dilemma of Determinism." In John J. McDermott, ed., *The Writings of William James: A Comprehensive Edition*, pp. 146–84. Chicago: U of Chicago P.

Joachim, Harold H. 1906. *The Nature of Thought: An Essay*. Oxford: Clarendon.

Jones, W.T. 1969a. *A History of Western Philosophy: The Classical Mind*, 2nd ed. New York: Harcourt, Brace and World.

Jones, W.T. 1969b. *A History of Western Philosophy: The Medieval Mind*, 2nd ed. New York: Harcourt, Brace and World.

Kaku, Michio. 2005. *Parallel Worlds: A Journey through Creation, Higher Dimensions and the Future of the Cosmos*. New York: Random House.

Kaku, Michio. 2011. "Why Physics Ends the Free Will Debate." *Big Think*, April 12. http://bigthink.com/videos/why-physics-ends-the-free-will-debate

Kane, Robert. 1998. *The Significance of Free Will*. New York: Oxford UP.

Kane, Robert. 2002. "Free Will: New Directions for an Ancient Problem." In Robert Kane, ed., *Free Will*. 2002. Oxford: Blackwell, pp. 222–48.

Kane, Robert. 2006. *A Contemporary Introduction to Free Will*. New York: Oxford UP.

Kane, Robert, ed. 2011. *The Oxford Handbook of Free Will*, 2nd ed. New York: Oxford UP.

Kant, Immanuel. 1965. *Critique of Pure Reason*. Norman Kemp Smith, trans. New York: St. Martin's.

Kim, Jaegwon. 2010. *The Philosophy of Mind*, 3rd ed. Boulder, CO: Westview.

Kirkham, Robert L. 1995. *Theories of Truth: A Critical Introduction*. Cambridge, MA: MIT P.

Koppelberg, Dirk. 1998. "Foundationalism and Coherentism Reconsidered." *Erkenntnis 49*(3), 255–83.

Korman, Daniel Z. 2015. *Objects: Nothing Out of the Ordinary*. Oxford: Oxford UP.

Kosso, Peter. 1998. *Appearance and Reality: An Introduction to the Philosophy of Physics*. New York: Oxford UP.

Krauss, Lawrence M. 1995. *The Physics of Star Trek*. New York: Harper.

Krauss, Lawrence. 2013. *A Universe from Nothing*. New York: Atria Books.

Kripke, Saul. 1980. *Naming and Necessity*. Cambridge, MA: Harvard UP.

Lahey, Stephen E. 1998. "William Ockham and Trope Nominalism." *Franciscan Studies, 55*, 105–20.

Laplace, Pierre-Simon. 1995. *Philosophical Essay on Probabilities*. A.J. Dale, trans. New York: Springer Verlag.

Laudan, Larry. 1986. *Science and Values: The Aims of Science and Their Role in Scientific Debate*. Berkeley and Los Angeles: U of California P.

Le Morvan, Pierre. 2004. "Ramsey on Truth and Belief." *British Journal for the History of Philosophy, 12*, 705–18.

Le Poidevin, Robin. 2003. *Travels in Four Dimensions: The Enigmas of Space and Time.* Oxford: Oxford UP.

Le Poidevin, Robin, and Murray MacBeath, eds. 1992. *The Philosophy of Time.* Oxford: Oxford UP.

LeDoux, Joseph. 2002. *Synaptic Self: How Our Brains Become Who We Are.* New York: Viking.

Leftow, Brian. 2001. "Souls Dipped in Dust." In Kevin Corcoran, ed., *Soul, Body, and Survival: Essays on the Metaphysics of Human Persons,* pp. 120–38. Ithaca, NY: Cornell UP.

Lehrer, Keith. 1990. *Theory of Knowledge.* Boulder, CO: Westview.

Leibniz, G. 1979. *Monadology.* In P.P. Weiner, ed., *Leibniz Selections,* pp. 533–51. New York: Scribner's.

Leslie, John. 1979. *Value and Existence.* Oxford: Basil Blackwell.

Leslie, John. 2001. *Infinite Minds: A Philosophical Cosmology.* Oxford: Clarendon.

Leslie, John. 2007. *Immortality Defended.* Cambridge: Wiley-Blackwell.

Leslie, John. 2013. "A Proof of God's Reality." In Tyrone Goldschmidt, ed., *The Puzzle of Existence: Why Is There Something Rather Than Nothing?,* pp. 128–43. New York: Routledge.

Leslie, John, and Robert Lawrence Kuhn, eds. 2013. *The Mystery of Existence: Why Is There Anything at All?* Malden, MA: Wiley-Blackwell.

Lewis, David. 1973. *Counterfactuals.* Cambridge, MA: Harvard UP.

Lewis, David. 1976. "Survival and Identity." In Amelie Oksenberg Rorty, ed., *The Identities of Persons,* pp. 17–40. Berkeley, CA: U of California P.

Lewis, David. 1986. *On the Plurality of Worlds.* Oxford: Basil Blackwell.

Libet, Benjamin. 2004. *Mind Time: The Temporal Factor in Consciousness.* Cambridge, MA: Harvard UP.

Lloyd, Seth. 2012. "A Turing Test for Free Will." *Philosophical Transactions of the Royal Society, 370,* 3597–3610.

Loar, Brian. 1980. "Ramsey's Theory of Belief and Truth." In D.H. Mellor, ed., *Prospects for Pragmatism,* pp. 49–69. Cambridge: Cambridge UP.

Locke, John. 1975. *An Essay Concerning Human Understanding.* Peter H. Nidditch, ed. Oxford: Clarendon.

Loux, Michael J. 1970. *Universals and Particulars: Readings in Ontology.* Garden City, NY: Anchor Doubleday.

Loux, Michael J., ed. 1979. *The Possible and the Actual: Readings in the Metaphysics of Modality.* Ithaca, NY: Cornell UP.

Loux, Michael, J. 2006. *Metaphysics: A Contemporary Introduction,* 3rd ed. New York: Routledge.

Loux, Michael J., and Thomas M. Crisp, eds. 2017. *Metaphysics: A Contemporary Introduction.* New York: Routledge.

Lovitt, William, and Harriet Brundage Lovitt. 1995. *Modern Technology in the Heideggerian Perspective.* Lewiston, NY: Edwin Mellen.

Lowe, E.J. 1998. *The Possibility of Metaphysics.* Oxford: Oxford UP.

Lowe, E.J. 2002. *A Survey of Metaphysics.* New York: Oxford UP.

Lowe, E.J. 2005. *Locke*. New York: Routledge.

Lowe, E.J. 2006. "Non-Cartesian Substance Dualism and the Problem of Mental Causation." *Erkenntnis, 65,* 1–23.

Lowe, Victor. 1962. *Understanding Whitehead*. Baltimore: Johns Hopkins UP.

Luther, Martin. 1957. *The Bondage of the Will*. J.I. Packer and O.R. Johnston, trans. Westwood, NJ: Fleming H. Revell.

Lycan, William. 1987. *Consciousness*. Cambridge, MA: MIT P.

Lycan, William. 1990. "What Is the 'Subjectivity' of the Mental?" *Philosophical Perspectives, 4,* 229–38.

Lycan, William, and Jesse Prinz, eds. 2008. *Mind and Cognition: An Anthology*, 3rd ed. Oxford: Wiley-Blackwell.

Lynch, Michael P., ed. 2001. *On the Nature of Truth: Classical and Contemporary Perspectives*. Cambridge, MA: Bradford.

Lynch, Michael P. 2009. *Truth as One and Many*. Oxford: Oxford UP.

Lyons, Daniel. 1998. "Immortality at Last." *Forbes*. http://www.forbes.com/ global/1998/1130/0118098a.html

Macdonald, Cynthia. 2005. *Varieties of Things: Foundations of Contemporary Metaphysics*. Oxford: Wiley-Blackwell.

Maitzen, Stephen. 2013. "Questioning the Question." In Tyrone Goldschmidt, *The Puzzle of Existence: Why Is There Something Rather Than Nothing?*, pp. 252–71. London: Routledge.

Malachowski, Alan. 2002. *Richard Rorty*. New York: Routledge.

Malcolm, Norman. 1960. "Anselm's Ontological Arguments." *Philosophical Review, 69*(1), 41–62.

Marenbon, John. 1997. *The Philosophy of Peter Abelard*. Cambridge: Cambridge UP.

Markosian, Ned. 1999. "A Compatibilist Theory of Agent Causation." *Pacific Philosophical Quarterly, 80*(3), 257–77.

Markosian, Ned. 2004. "A Defense of Presentism." *Oxford Studies in Metaphysics, 1,* 47–82.

Marsden, George. 2003. *Jonathan Edwards: A Life*. New Haven, CT: Yale UP.

Martinich, A.D., and Avrum Stroll. 2007. *Much Ado about Nonexistence: Fiction and Reference*. Lanham, MD: Rowman and Littlefield.

Matsumoto, Masakazu. 2009. "Why Does Water Expand When It Cools?" *Physical Review Letters, 103,* 017801.

Mayr, Ernst. 1988. *Toward a New Philosophy of Biology: Observations of an Evolutionist*. Cambridge, MA: Harvard UP.

McGinn, Colin. 2015. *Philosophy of Language: The Classics Explained*. Cambridge, MA: MIT P.

McTaggart, John M.E. 1908. "The Unreality of Time." *Mind, 17,* 467–74. Reprinted in Le Poidevin, Robin, and Murray MacBeath, eds. 1992. *The Philosophy of Time*, pp. 23–34. Oxford: Oxford UP.

McTaggart, John M.E. 1927. *The Nature of Existence Volume II*. Cambridge: Cambridge UP.

Meinwald, Constance C. 1992. "Good-Bye to the Third Man." In Richard Kraut, ed., *The Cambridge Companion to Plato*, pp. 365–96. Cambridge: Cambridge UP.

Meinwald, Constance. 2011. "Reason v. Literature in Plato's Republic: Does the Dialogue Rule Itself Out?" *Ancient Philosophy*, *31*(1), 25–45.

Mele, Alfred R. 2014. *Free: Why Science Hasn't Disproved Free Will*. New York: Oxford UP.

Melia, Joseph. 2008. "Ersatz Possible Worlds." In Theodore Sider, John Hawthorne, Dean Zimmerman, eds., *Contemporary Debates in Metaphysics*, pp. 136–47. Oxford: Blackwell.

Mellor, D.H. 1981. *Real Time*. Cambridge: Cambridge UP.

Merleau-Ponty, Maurice. 1962. *The Phenomenology of Perception*. New York: Routledge.

Merricks, Trenton. 2001. "How to Live Forever without Saving Your Soul: Physicalism and Immortality." In Kevin Corcoran, ed., *Soul, Body, and Survival: Essays on the Metaphysics of Human Persons,* pp. 183–200. Ithaca, NY: Cornell UP.

Merricks, Trenton. 2003. *Objects and Persons*. Oxford: Oxford UP.

Merricks, Trenton. 2007. *Truth and Ontology*. Oxford: Oxford UP.

Merricks, Trenton. 2015. *Propositions*. Oxford: Oxford UP.

Mesle, C. Robert. 2008. *Process-Relational Philosophy: An Introduction to Alfred North Whitehead*. West Conshohocken, PA: Templeton Foundation P.

Meyers, Robert G. 1989. "The Roots of Pragmatism: Madden on James and Peirce." *Transactions of the Charles S. Peirce Society*, *25*, 85–121.

Miller, Mitchell H. 1986. *Plato's Parmenides: The Conversion of the Soul*. Princeton, NJ; University Park, PA: Pennsylvania State UP.

Mohanty, J.N. 2000. *Classical Indian Philosophy*. Lanham, MD: Rowman and Littlefield.

Molloy, Michael. 1999. *Experiencing the World's Religions*. Mountain View, CA: Mayfield.

Montague, Richard. 1974. *Formal Philosophy: Selected Papers of Richard Montague*. New Haven: Yale UP.

Moyer, Melinda Wenner. 2013. "Brain Implant Could Enhance Our Senses." http://www.scientificamerican.com/article/brain-implant-could-enhance-our-senses/

Nagel, Thomas. 1974. "What Is It Like to Be a Bat?" *Philosophical Review*, *83*(4), 435–50. Reprinted in Thomas Nagel. 1979. *Mortal Questions,* pp. 165–80. Cambridge: Cambridge UP; and in Jack Crumley, ed. 1999. *Problems in Mind: Readings in Contemporary Philosophy of Mind*. Mountain View, CA: Mayfield; and http://organizations.utep.edu/portals/1475/nagel_bat.pdf

Nagel, Thomas. 1989. *The View from Nowhere*. Oxford: Oxford UP.

Nammour, Jamil. 1973. "Resemblances and Universals." *Mind, 82*(328), 516–24. Reprinted in Schoedinger, ed., 1991. *The Problem of Universals*. London, Humanities P, pp. 346–53.

NASA. 2001. "Visible Earth." https://visibleearth.nasa.gov/

NeuroscienceNews.com. 2018. "How the Brain Experiences Time." August 29. https://neurosciencenews.com/time-perception-9771/

Newberg, Andrew, Eugene D'Aquili, and Vince Rause. 2001. *Why God Won't Go Away: Brain Science and the Biology of Belief*. New York: Ballantine Books.

Newton-Smith, W. 1980. *The Structure of Time*. Abington-on-Thames, UK: Routledge & Kegan Paul.

Nolan, Daniel. 2016 (Spring). "Modal Fictionalism: A Persisting Problem for Fictionalism about Possible Worlds." In Edward N. Zalta, ed., *Stanford Encyclopedia of Philosophy*. https://plato.stanford.edu/archives/spr2016/entries/fictionalism-modal/supplement1.html

Noonan, Harold. 2003. *Personal Identity*, 2nd ed. New York: Routledge.

Nozick, Robert. 1981. *Philosophical Explanations*. Cambridge, MA: Belknap P.

Oaklander, L. Nathan. 2004. *The Ontology of Time*. New York: Prometheus Books.

Oaklander, L. Nathan. 2011. "McTaggart's Paradox and Crisp's Presentism." *Philosophia*, 38(2), 229–41.

Ockham, William of. 1974. *Summa Logicae, Part I*. In Michael J. Loux, trans., *Ockham's Theory of Terms*. Notre Dame, IN: Notre Dame UP.

O'Connor, Timothy. 1995. "Agent Causation." In Timothy O'Connor, ed., *Agents, Causes, and Events: Essays on Indeterminism and Free Will*, pp. 173–200. New York: Oxford UP.

O'Connor, Timothy. 2001. "Causality, Mind and Free Will." In Kevin Corcoran, ed., *Soul, Body, and Survival: Essays on the Metaphysics of Human Persons*, pp. 44–58. Ithaca, NY: Cornell UP.

O'Connor, Timothy. 2002. *Persons and Causes: The Metaphysics of Free Will*. New York: Oxford UP.

O'Connor, Timothy. 2014 (Fall). "Free Will." In Edward N. Zalta, ed., *Stanford Encyclopedia of Philosophy*. http://plato.stanford.edu/archives/fall2014/entries/freewill/

Olson, Carl. 2007. *The Many Colors of Hinduism: A Thematic-Historical Introduction*. New Brunswick, NJ: Rutgers UP.

Olson, Eric T. 1999. *The Human Animal: Personal Identity without Psychology*. New York: Oxford UP.

Paley, William. 2006. *Natural Theology*. New York: Oxford UP.

Parent, Ted. 2018. "Modal Metaphysics." *The Internet Encyclopedia of Philosophy*. https://www.iep.utm.edu/, October 13.

Parfit, Derek. 1986. *Reasons and Persons*. New York: Oxford UP.

Parfit, Derek. 1998. "Why Anything? Why This?" *London Review of Books*, 20, pp. 24–27.

Peirce, C.S. 1955. *Philosophical Writings of Peirce*. Justus Buchler, ed. New York, NY: Dover.

Pereboom, Derk. 2014. *Free Will, Agency and Meaning in Life*. New York: Oxford UP.

Perry, John, ed. 1975. *Personal Identity*. Berkeley, CA: U of California P.

Perry, John. 1976. "The Importance of Being Identical." In Amelie Oksenberg Rory, ed., *The Identities of Persons*, pp. 67–90. Berkeley, CA: U of California P.

Perry, John. 1977. *A Dialogue on Personal Identity on Immortality*. Indianapolis, IN: Hackett.

Philipse, Herman. 1998. *Heidegger's Philosophy of Being*. Princeton, NJ: Princeton UP.

Pike, Nelson. 1958. "God and Evil: A Reconsideration." *Ethics*, 68(2), 116–24.

Pike, Nelson. 1965. "Divine Omniscience and Voluntary Action." *Philosophical Review*, 74(1), 27–46.

Pike, Nelson. 1977. "If There Is No Necessary Being, Nothing Exists." *Noûs, 11*, 417–20.

Place, Ullin T. 1956. "Is Consciousness a Brain Process?" *British Journal of Psychology, 47*, 44–50.

Plantinga, Alvin. 1967. *God and Other Minds: A Study of the Rational Justification of Belief in God*. Ithaca, NY: Cornell UP.

Plantinga, Alvin, ed. 1968. *The Ontological Argument*. London: Macmillan.

Plantinga, Alvin. 1976. "Actualism and Possible Worlds." *Theoria, 42*, 139–60. Reprinted in Loux, ed., *The Actual and the Possible*.

Plantinga, Alvin. 1986. "On Ockham's Way Out." *Faith and Philosophy, 3*, 235–69.

Plantinga, Alvin. 1990. "God, Evil and the Metaphysics of Freedom." In Marilyn McCord Adams and Robert Merrihew Adams, eds., *The Problem of Evil*, pp. 83–109. New York: Oxford UP.

Plantinga, Alvin. 2011. *Where the Conflict Really Lies: Science, Religion, & Naturalism*. New York: Oxford UP.

Plato. 1951. *Parmenides*. In Francis M. Cornford, author and trans. *Plato and Parmenides: Parmenides' Way of Truth and Plato's Parmenides*. Atlantic Highlands, NJ: Humanities P.

Plato. 1961a. *Laches*. Benjamin Jowett, trans. In Edith Hamilton and Huntington Cairns, eds., *Plato: The Collected Dialogues*, pp. 123–44. Princeton, NJ: Princeton UP.

Plato. 1961b. *Meno*. W.K.C. Guthrie, trans. In Edith Hamilton and Huntington Cairns, eds., *Plato: The Collected Dialogues*, pp. 353–84. Princeton, NJ: Princeton UP.

Plato. 1961c. *Phaedo*. Hugo Tredennick, trans. In Edith Hamilton and Huntington Cairns, eds., *Plato: The Collected Dialogues*, pp. 40–98. Princeton, NJ: Princeton UP.

Plato. 1961d. *Theaetetus*. F.M. Cornford, trans. In Edith Hamilton and Huntington Cairns, eds., *Plato: The Collected Dialogues*, pp. 845–919. Princeton, NJ: Princeton UP.

Plato. 1974. *Republic*. G.M.A. Grube, trans. Indianapolis, IN: Hackett.

Prior, Arthur N. 1959. "Thank Goodness That's Over." *Philosophy, 34*, 12–17.

Psillos, Stathis. 2000. "The Present State of the Scientific Realism Debate." *British Journal of Philosophy of Science, 51*, 705–28.

Putnam, Hilary. 1967. "Time and Physical Geometry." *Journal of Philosophy, 64*, 240–47.

Putnam, Hilary. 1975. "The Meaning of 'Meaning'." Originally published in Keith Gunderson, ed., 1975, *Minnesota Studies in the Philosophy of Science*, vol. 5. Minneapolis: U of Minnesota P. Reprinted in Putnam, *Mind, Language and Reality*, pp. 215–71. Page references are to this reprint.

Putnam, Hilary. 1978. *Meaning and the Moral Sciences*. London: Routledge and Kegan Paul.

Putnam, Hilary. 1979. "What Is Mathematical Truth." *Mathematics, Matter and Method: Philosophical Papers, Vol. 1*, 2nd ed., pp. 60–78. Cambridge: Cambridge UP.

Putnam, Hilary. 1981a. *Reason, Truth and History*. Cambridge: Cambridge UP.

Putnam, Hilary. 1981b. "Why There Isn't a Ready-Made World." Howison Lecture, University of California, Berkeley. Reprinted in Putnam 1983. *Realism and Reason: Philosophical Papers, Vol. 3*. Cambridge: Cambridge UP, pp. 205–28.

Putnam, Hilary. 1983. *Realism and Reason: Philosophical Papers, Vol. 3*. Cambridge: Cambridge UP.

Putnam, Hilary. 1984. "Is the Causal Structure of the World Itself Something Physical?" In Peter French, et al., *Midwest Studies in Philosophy, IX: Causation and Causal Theories*, pp. 3–16. Minneapolis, MN: U of Minnesota P.

Putnam, Hilary. 1997. "James's Theory of Truth." In Ruth Anna Putnam, ed., *The Cambridge Companion to William James*, pp. 166–85. Oxford: Cambridge UP.

Quine, W.V.O. 1961. *From a Logical Point of View*, 2nd ed. New York: Harper.

Quine, Willard Van Orman. 1969a. "Epistemology Naturalized." In Quine, *Ontological Relativity and Other Essays*. New York: Columbia UP.

Quine, Willard Van Orman. 1969b. "Ontological Relativity." In Quine, *Ontological Relativity and Other Essays*. New York: Columbia UP.

Quine, Willard Van Orman. 1970. *Philosophy of Logic*. Englewood Cliffs, NJ: Prentice-Hall.

Ramsey, Frank P. 1927/1951. "On Facts and Propositions." *Proceedings of the Aristotelian Society, 7*, 153–70. Reprinted in R.B. Braithwaite, ed. 1951. *The Foundations of Mathematics and Other Logical Papers*, pp. 138–59. Oxford: Routledge.

Reid, Thomas. 1975. "Of Mr. Locke's Account of Our Personal Identity." In John Perry, ed., *Personal Identity*, pp. 113–19. Berkeley, CA: U of California P.

Roberts, John Russell. 2007. *A Metaphysics for the Mob: The Philosophy of George Berkeley*. New York: Oxford UP.

Rodriguez-Pereyra, Gonzalo. 2013. "The Subtraction Arguments for Metaphysical Nihilism: Compared and Defended." In Tyron Goldschmidt, ed., *The Puzzle of Existence. Why Is There Something Rather Than Nothing?* New York: Routledge, pp. 197–214.

Rorty, Amelie Oksenberg, ed. 1976. *The Identities of Persons*. Berkeley, CA: U of California P.

Rorty, Richard. 1972. "The World Well Lost." *Journal of Philosophy, 64*, 649–65.

Rorty, Richard. 1976. *Philosophy and the Mirror of Nature*. Princeton, NJ: Princeton UP.

Rorty, Richard. 1982. *Consequences of Pragmatism*. Minneapolis, MN: U of Minnesota P.

Rosen, Gideon, and Cian Dorr. 2002. "Composition as a Fiction." In Richard Gale, ed., *The Blackwell Guide to Metaphysics*. Oxford: Blackwell, pp. 151–74.

Rosen, Stanley. 2008. *Plato's Republic: A Study*. New Haven, CT: Yale UP.

Rosenthal, David M., ed. 1991. *The Nature of Mind*. New York: Oxford UP.

Rosenthal, Sandra, Carl Hausman, and David Anderson, eds. 1999. *Classical American Pragmatism: Its Contemporary Vitality*. Urbana-Champagne, IL: U of Illinois P.

Ross, Andrew, ed. 1996. *Science Wars*. Durham, NC: Duke UP.

Ross, David. 1971. *Aristotle*. London: Methuen.

Roth, Paul. 1978. "Paradox and Indeterminacy." *Journal of Philosophy*, *75*(7), 347–67.

Rovelli, Carlo. 2018. "Physics Needs Philosophy. Philosophy Needs Physics." *Foundations of Physics*, *48*(5), 481–91.

Rowe, William. 1979. "The Problem of Evil and Some Varieties of Theism." *American Philosophical Quarterly*, *16*(4), 335–41. Reprinted in Adams and Adams, eds., *The Problem of Evil*, pp. 126–37.

Rowe, William. 1995. "William Alston on the Problem of Evil." In Thomas Senor, ed., *The Rationality of Belief and the Plurality of Faith*, pp. 71–93. Ithaca, NY: Cornell UP.

Rowe, William. 2000. *Philosophy of Religion: An Introduction*, 3rd ed. Belmont, CA: Wadsworth.

Rundle, Bede. 2004. *Why There Is Something Rather Than Nothing*. Oxford: Clarendon.

Russell, Bertrand. 1912/1959. *The Problems of Philosophy*. New York: Oxford UP.

Russell, Bertrand. 1918–19/1956. "The Philosophy of Logical Atomism." Lectures 1, 2. 1918. *The Monist*, *28*(4), 495–527. Lectures 3, 4. 1919. *The Monist*, *29*(1), 32–63. Lectures 5, 6. 1919. *The Monist*, *29*(2), 190–22. Lectures 7, 8. *The Monist*, *29*(3), 345–80. Reprinted in Robert C. Marsh, ed. 1956. *Logic and Knowledge: Essays 1901–1950*, pp. 177–281. New York: Capricorn Books.

Russell, Bertrand. 1947. *A History of Western Philosophy: And Its Connection with Social and Political Circumstances from Earliest Times to the Present Day*, Chap. 29. London: George Allen and Unwin.

Russell, Bertrand. 1949. *An Inquiry into Meaning and Truth*. London: Allen and Unwin.

Sainsbury, R.M. 2010. *Fiction and Fictionalism*. New York: Routledge.

Sartre, Jean Paul. 1956. *Being and Nothingness*. Hazel E. Barnes, trans. New York: Washington Square P.

Savitt, Steven. 2017. "Closed Time and Local Time: A Reply to Dowe." *Manuscrito*, *40*(1), 197–207.

Schmitt, Frederick F. 1995. *Truth: A Primer*. Boulder, CO: Westview.

Schoedinger, Andrew B., ed. 1992. *The Problem of Universals*. Atlantic Highlands, NJ: Humanities P.

Schutte, Ofelia. 1998. "Latin America." In Alison M. Jaggar and Iris Marion Young, eds., *A Companion to Feminist Philosophy*, pp. 87–95. Oxford: Blackwell.

Schwartz, Joshua. 2016. "Quine and the Problem of Truth." *Journal of the History of Analytic Philosophy*, *4*, 1–25.

Schwarz, Robert. 1986. "I'm Going to Make You a Star." *Midwest Studies in Philosophy*, *11*, 427–39.

Scruton, Roger. 1981/2002. *A Short History of Modern Philosophy*. Abingdon, UK: Routledge.

Searle, John. 1984. *Brains, Minds, and Science*. Cambridge, MA: Harvard UP.

Searle, John. 2005. *Mind: A Brief Introduction*. New York: Oxford UP.

Searle, John. 2007. *Freedom and Neurobiology: Reflections on Free Will, Language, and Political Power*. New York: Columbia UP.

Senor, Thomas, ed. 1995. *The Rationality of Belief and the Plurality of Faith*. Ithaca, NY: Cornell UP.

Sher, Gila. 1996. "Is There a Place for Philosophy in Quine's Theory?" *Journal of Philosophy, 96*, 491–524.

Sherburne, Donald. 1971. *A Key to Understanding Process and Reality*. Bloomington, IN: Indiana UP.

Sherman, Daniel. 2013. *Soul, World, and Idea: An Interpretation of Plato's Republic and Phaedo*. Lanham, MD: Lexington.

Shoemaker, Sydney. 2008. "Persons, Animals, and Identity." *Synthese, 162*(3), 313–24.

Sider, Theodore. 2001. *Four Dimensionalism: An Ontology of Time and Persistence*. Oxford: Oxford UP.

Sider, Theodore. 2006. "Bare Particulars." *Philosophical Perspectives, 20*(1), 387–97.

Skinner, B.F. 1974. *About Behaviorism*. New York: Alfred A. Knopf.

Skinner, B.F. 1990. "Can Psychology Be a Science of the Mind?" *American Psychologist, 45*, 1206–10.

Sluga, Hans, and David Stern, eds. 2017. *A Cambridge Companion to Wittgenstein*, 2nd ed. Cambridge: Cambridge UP.

Smart, J.J.C. 1959. "Sensations and Brain Processes." *Philosophical Review, 68*(2), 141–56.

Smart, J.J.C. 2004 (Fall). "The Identity Theory of Mind." In Edward N. Zalta, ed., *Stanford Encyclopedia of Philosophy*. http://plato.stanford.edu/archives/fall2004/entries/mind-identity/

Smart, J.J.C. 2008. "The Tenseless Theory of Time." In Theodore Sider, John Hawthorne, and Dean W. Zimmerman, eds. 2008. *Contemporary Debates in Metaphysics*. New York: Blackwell, pp. 226–38.

Smith, John E. 1978. *Purpose and Thought: The Meaning of Pragmatism*. New Haven: Yale UP.

Smolin, Lee. 2014. "Time, Laws and the Future of Cosmology." *Physics Today, 67*(3), 38.

Snyder, Michael. 2012. "The American Dream." http://nanobrainimplant.com/2012/08/02/they-really-do-want-to-implant-microchips-into-your-brain/

Sorenson, Roy. 2020. "Nothingness." In Edward N. Zalta, ed. *The Stanford Encyclopedia of Philosophy* (Spring 2020 Edition). https://plato.stanford.edu/archives/spr2020/entries/nothingness/

Spector, Dina. 2013. "Is There a Humane Way to Kill a Lobster?" *Business Insider*. http://www.businessinsider.com/scientist-lobsters-can-feel-pain-2013-1

Spinoza, Benedict. 1955. *Works of Spinoza, Vol. II*. R.H.M. Elwes, trans. New York: Dover.

Sterelny, Kim. 1990. *The Representational Theory of Mind*. Oxford: Blackwell.

Strauss, Leo. 1964. *The City and Man*. Chicago: Rand McNally.

Stump, Eleonore. 2003. *Aquinas*. New York: Routledge.

Suzuki, D.T. 1963. *Outlines of Mahayana Buddhism*. New York: Schocken.

Swinburne, Richard. 1977. *The Coherence of Theism*. Oxford: Clarendon.

Swinburne, Richard. 1986. *The Evolution of the Soul*. Oxford: Clarendon.

Swinburne, Richard. 1994. *The Christian God*. New York: Oxford UP.

Swinburne, Richard. 1997. *The Evolution of the Soul*, rev. ed. New York: Oxford UP.

Taliaferro, Charles. 1998. *Contemporary Philosophy of Religion*. Oxford: Wiley-Blackwell.

Tarski, Alfred. 1944. "The Semantic Conception of Truth." *Philosophy and Phenomenological Research*, 4, 341–76.

Tarski, Alfred. 1956. "The Concept of Truth in Formalized Languages." In Tarski, J.H. Woodger, trans. *Logic, Semantics, Metamathematics*. Oxford: Oxford UP. First published in 1936 as "Der Wahrheitsbegriff in Den Formaliserten Sprachen," *Studia Philosophica, I*, pp. 261–405.

Taylor, A.E. 1949. *Aristotle on His Predecessors: Being the First Book of His Metaphysics*. LaSalle, IL: Open Court.

Taylor, A.E. 1955. *Aristotle*. New York: Dover.

Taylor, Richard. 1992. *Metaphysics*, 4th ed. Upper Saddle River, NJ: Prentice-Hall.

Textor, Mark. 2016 (Winter). "States of Affairs." In Edward N. Zalta, ed., *Stanford Encyclopedia of Philosophy*. https://plato.stanford.edu/archives/win2016/entries/states-of-affairs/

Thagard, Paul. 2007. "Coherence, Truth, and the Development of Scientific Knowledge." *Philosophy of Science*, 74, 28–47.

Thagard, Paul. 2010. *The Brain and the Meaning of Life*. Princeton, NJ: Princeton UP.

Thayer, H.S. 1981. *Meaning and Action: A Critical Examination of Pragmatism*. Cambridge and Indianapolis: Hackett.

Thijssen, Hans. 2013 (Winter). "Condemnation of 1277." In Edward N. Zalta, ed., *Stanford Encyclopedia of Philosophy*. http://plato.stanford.edu/archives/win2013/entries/condemnation/

Thomasson, Amie L. 2003. "Realism and Human Kinds." *Philosophy and Phenomenological Research*, 67, 580–609.

Thomasson, Amie L. 2007. *Ordinary Objects*. Oxford: Oxford UP.

Tollefsen, Deborah. 1999. "Princess Elisabeth and the Problem of Mind-Body Interaction." *Hypatia, 14*(3), 59–77. http://muse.jhu.edu/journals/hypatia/v014/14.3tollefsen.html

Urmson, J.O. 1967[/1956]. *Philosophical Analysis: Its Development between the Two World Wars*. Oxford: Oxford UP.

Van Cleve, James. 1985. "Three Versions of the Bundle Theory." *Philosophical Studies*, 47(1), 95–107.

van Inwagen, Peter. 1986. *An Essay on Free Will*. New York: Oxford UP.

van Inwagen, Peter. 1990. *Material Beings*. Ithaca, NY: Cornell UP.

van Inwagen, Peter, and E.J. Lowe. 1996. "Why Is There Anything at All?" *Proceedings of the Aristotelian Society*, 70, 95–120.

Veatch, Henry B. 1974. *Aristotle: A Contemporary Introduction*. Bloomington, IN: Indiana UP.

Vilenkin, Alex. 2007. *Many Worlds in One: The Search for Other Universes*. New York: Hill and Wang.

Viney, Donald. 1985. *Charles Hartshorne and the Existence of God*. Albany, NY: SUNY P.

Vlastos, Gregory. 1954. "The Third Man Argument in the Parmenides." *Philosophical Review*, 63, 319–49.

Wagoner, Robert E. 1997. *The Meanings of Love*. Westport, CT: Praeger.

Walker, Ralph C.S. 1989. *The Coherence Theory of Truth: Realism, Antirealism, and Idealism*. London and New York: Routledge.

Watson, John. 1930. *Behaviorism*, rev. ed. Chicago: U of Chicago P.

Wegner, Daniel. 2003. *The Illusion of Conscious Will*. Cambridge, MA: MIT P.

Weiss, Bernhard. 2002. *Michael Dummett*. Princeton, NJ: Princeton UP.

Weiss, Paul. 1958. *Modes of Being*. Carbondale, IL: Southern Illinois UP.

Whitehead, Alfred North. 1925. *Science and the Modern World*. London: Macmillan.

Whitehead, Alfred North. 1929. *Process and Reality*. London: Macmillan.

Wiggins, David. 1967. *Identity and Spatio-Temporal Continuity*. Oxford: Blackwell.

Wigner, Eugene. 1960. "The Unreasonable Effectiveness of Mathematics in the Natural Sciences." *Communications in Pure and Applied Mathematics, 13*, 1–14.

Williams, Bernard. 1973. "Personal Identity and Individuation." In *Problems of the Self*, pp. 1–18. Cambridge: Cambridge UP.

Williams, Donald C. 1953. "The Elements of Being, I." *Review of Metaphysics, 7*(1), 3–18.

Williams, Thomas. 1996a. "Introduction." In Thomas Williams, ed. and trans. *Monologion and Proslogion*, pp. xi–xx. Indianapolis, IN: Hackett.

Williams, Thomas, ed. and trans. 1996b. *Monologion and Proslogion*. Indianapolis IN: Hackett.

Wippel, John. 2006. "The Five Ways." In Brian Davies, Leonard Boyle, and John Wippel, eds., *Aquinas's Summa Theologiae*, pp. 45–110. Lanham, MD: Rowman and Littlefield.

Wisnewski, J. Jeremy. 2011. *Heidegger: An Introduction*. Lanham, MD: Rowman and Littlefield.

Wittgenstein, Ludwig. 1922/2007. *Tractatus Logico-Philosophicus*. Frank P. Ramsey and C.K. Ogden, trans. London: Kegan Paul.

Wittgenstein, Ludwig. 1953/1958. *Philosophical Investigations*. G.E.M. Anscombe, trans. Oxford: Basil Blackwell.

Wittgenstein, Ludwig. 1968. *Philosophical Investigations*, 3rd ed. G.E.M. Anscombe, trans. London: Macmillan.

Wittgenstein, Ludwig. 2007[/1922]. *Tractatus Logico-Philosophicus*. Frank P. Ramsey and C.K. Ogden, trans. London: Routledge and Kegan Paul.

Wrenn, Chase. 2015. *Truth*. Malden, MA: Polity P.

Wykstra, Stephen. 1984. "The Humean Obstacle to Evidential Arguments from Suffering: On Avoiding the Evils of 'Appearance'." *International Journal of Religion, 16*, 73–93. Reprinted in Adams and Adams, eds., *The Problem of Evil*, pp. 138–60.

Yablo, Stephen. 2002. "Abstract Objects: A Case Study." In Andrea Clemente Bottani, Massimiliano Carrara, and Pierdaniele Giaretta, eds., *Individuals, Essence & Identity*, 2002. Kluwer.

Yandell, Keith E. 1999. *Philosophy of Religion: A Contemporary Introduction*. New York: Routledge.

Young, James O. 2001. "A Defence of the Coherence Theory of Truth." *Journal of Philosophical Research, 26*, 89–101.

Zimmer, Heinrich. 1951. *Philosophies of India*. Joseph Campbell, ed. Princeton, NJ: Princeton UP.

Zimmerman, Michael E. 1986. *Eclipse of the Self: The Development of Heidegger's Concept of Authenticity*. Athens, OH: Ohio UP.

Zimmerman, Michael E. 1990. *Heidegger's Confrontation with Modernity: Technology, Politics, and Art*. Bloomington, IN: Indiana UP.

Zimmerman, Michael E. 1997. *Contesting Earth's Future: Radical Ecology and Postmodernity*. Berkeley, CA: U of California P.

Zimmerman, Dean. 2008. "The Privileged Present: Defending an 'A-theory' of Time." In *Contemporary Debates in Metaphysics*, 2008. Ted Sider, John Hawthorne, and Dean W. Zimmerman, eds., Malden, MA: Blackwell, pp. 211–25.

INDEX

Note: Page numbers in *italics* denote figures.

From the Publisher

A name never says it all, but the word "Broadview" expresses a good deal of the philosophy behind our company. We are open to a broad range of academic approaches and political viewpoints. We pay attention to the broad impact book publishing and book printing has in the wider world; for some years now we have used 100% recycled paper for most titles. Our publishing program is internationally oriented and broad-ranging. Our individual titles often appeal to a broad readership too; many are of interest as much to general readers as to academics and students.

Founded in 1985, Broadview remains a fully independent company owned by its shareholders—not an imprint or subsidiary of a larger multinational.

For the most accurate information on our books (including information on pricing, editions, and formats) please visit our website at www.broadviewpress.com. Our print books and ebooks are also available for sale on our site.

broadview press
www.broadviewpress.com